("Astrology for All" Series, Vol. IV.)

The
Progressed
Horoscope

. BY

ALAN LEO

A Sequel to *How to Judge a Nativity*
Wherein The Progression of the Horoscope is exhaustively
considered, both in principle and in practice
including also
A Full Delineation of Each and Every Possible Progressed Aspect, with
its Influence on Character and Destiny, the Effect of Transits, etc.

To which is added

"The Art and Practice of Directing," a Complete Treatise on
Primary Directions, by Heinrich Däath

PRICE 10s. 6d. NETT
(In America $3.00)

Published by
L. N. FOWLER & CO., 7, Imperial Arcade, Ludgate Hill, E.C.
MODERN ASTROLOGY Office, West Hampstead, London, N.W.

America:—Frederick Spenceley, 26, Music Hall Building, Boston, U.S.A.
India:—The Theosophist and Book Publishing Office, Adyar, Madras

1906

LONDON
WOMEN'S PRINTING SOCIETY, LIMITED
66 & 68, Whitcomb Street, W.C.

THE PROGRESSED HOROSCOPE.

CONTENTS.

PREFACE.

It is held by many that the main value of Astrologic Law is the knowledge it affords whereby the chief events of any life may be known beforehand, if sufficient care is expended on the necessary calculations and due judgment displayed.

I am not wholly in agreement with this contention; for although I must admit the use of Astrology in foretelling the outcome of certain causes, it is not of vital moment (it seems to me) that we should attach more importance to the events than to the causes which led up to those events.

This consideration, of course, opens up the whole question of Fate *versus* Freewill, and it at once determines the difference between the "exoteric" and the "esoteric" astrologer. The former is a confirmed fatalist, who believes himself forever under the bane of Destiny, with his whole life mapped out before him—a life over which he himself has no control whatever. For him there is no re-embodiment of the soul, no continuity of existence, no real meaning or purpose in life. A cruel or a kind fate, as the case may be, has forced him into existence, and has imposed upon him his present environment, and until he is released therefrom by the same capricious power he must abide by its decree; nor can he alter the terms of his bond by one iota.

The "esoteric" astrologer has no such creed. His faith is based upon the belief that *as a man sows, so he must reap;* his motto is "MAN, KNOW THYSELF"; and he knows that man may become master of his destiny, being himself in essence inseparable from the Divine Ruler of that universe in which he is manifesting. It is from this latter standpoint that all the "directions"* given in this work are made, and all its rules are based upon the idea that "THE STARS CONDITION, THEY DO NOT COMPEL."

No statement is made in this book that has not been verified, any suggestions of a speculative character having been reserved for the appendix. No rules are given that have not been tested by the author, the following prefatory note—

"You will greatly assist our scientific work and enable us to check inaccuracies, if you will inform us, at the end of the period for which these directions have been calculated, of the actual result of your experiences (if any), when the events predicted do not coincide with the directions given."

—having been inserted in all delineations of "directions" sent to clients during the period in which the collection

* This is the technical term for calculations of this nature.

of facts required for the composition of this work was proceeding, and the replies elicited having very materially assisted in its compilation. My best thanks are therefore due to the many correspondents by whose help I have thus profited.

In conclusion, a few words as to the mode of " directing" employed in this work. After seven years' investigation, in 1895 I abandoned all adherence to the various ' systems' and ' methods' of directing advocated by the different schools of exoteric astrology, and commenced to evolve from my own study, based on experience, the best method suited to practical requirements. I gradually found myself adopting a system in which the Progressed Horoscope formed the centre, as it were, from which the successive events of life were determined; and this system I have used in my daily practice for the past nine or ten years, with the most satisfactory results. To some it may be already familiar, to others entirely new; to all it must appeal upon its own merits.

Those who have worked on similar lines will know how to appreciate its value, but to those to whom it is unknown I recommend, before passing it by, at least a trial of its principles; for if not the ideal system of prediction, it will at any rate be found, I think, the most simple and on the whole the most satisfactory that has hitherto been put forward.

I desire to record my grateful acknowledgments both to Mr. H. S. Green for valuable help in supervising the whole of the manuscript and for sundry excellent suggestions, as well as for the whole of Chapters VI. and VIII.; and to Mr. Heinrich Däath for permission to reprint his excellent treatise on *The Art and Practice of Directing*, which originally appeared in the pages of MODERN ASTROLOGY, and which he has revised and in some respects amplified and improved; also to Mr. A. H. Barley for his assistance in the various details of arrangement, and for several suggestions, both in the Appendices and elsewhere.

9, Lyncroft Gardens,   ALAN LEO.
  West Hampstead,
    London, N.W.   October, 1905.

NOTE.—A word of explanation is necessary with regard to the price of this book. It was originally intended, following the plan adopted in the previous works of this series, to issue *The Progressed Horoscope* in two parts at 7/6 each. But it has been found possible to condense the work sufficiently to bring the whole within the present compass, uniform with the edition of *How to Judge a Nativity*, *Parts I. and II.*, in one volume and at the same price, namely 10/6 ($3.00); and since such an arrangement seemed likely to suit the convenience of the largest number of readers, this has been done.

Although the utmost care has been taken in the preparation of this work, proof-reading, etc., it is quite possible that here and there errors may have crept in, and the Author will therefore take it as a personal favour if readers will apprise him of any they may discover.

INTRODUCTION.

As has been said in the preface, the principal use to which astrology is applied by those who fail to realise its true purpose takes the form of searching for future happenings, so that predictions may be made and the future known—to a greater or lesser extent according to the skill of the practitioner.

Now it is quite true that the future may be foreseen more or less in every nativity, yet while some persons will respond to every vibration (whether good or evil) that affects them from without, others will fail to so respond, either from lack of sensitiveness on the one hand, or, on the other, through the exercise of a strong will trained to control the sheaths or vehicles of response.

Roughly speaking, there are three separate classes or types of persons, for each of whom the same directions or predictions will have a different meaning. In the lowest class stand undeveloped and untrained souls, those who are yet young in evolution; in the highest, those who are older and more experienced souls, practising self-control and using reason and reflection both in thought and action. Between these two stands by far the largest class, in which are found the majority of souls at our present stage of evolution, souls who can neither be called 'old' nor 'young,' but who are at that critical stage wherein the will has not yet full power, while on the other hand it is not entirely plastic; there is sufficient receptivity to respond to certain vibrations and not to others. Such souls are strong on some points and weak on others, not having obtained as yet that all-round experience which is the result of age alone. Now the exoteric student of astrology would naturally apply the same rules to all three classes and thus would make great mistakes, failing in his judgment in many cases while meeting with remarkable success in others. A careful study of human nature has convinced my mind that fate applies more to the majority—the middle class above alluded to —than to the few, the more experienced souls; and for the purpose of establishing a better system of "directing" or predicting I shall endeavour to make clear in the following pages the best method to adopt when seeking to forecast the future in each individual nativity.

As I have often pointed out in my works there is to my mind no permanent value in the study of astrology without a belief in the idea of the soul's re-embodiment, and those who reject this idea as illusory or valueless will therefore be wasting their time in endeavouring to follow my reasons in astrological thought. I shall not now repeat what I

have so often explained in connection with this idea, but those who have
studied my previous works will be familiar with my views upon this
subject. Consequently, I will take it for granted that my readers
understand what is meant by Reincarnation, and also *what it is* that
reincarnates.*

Every soul that comes into the physical world brings with it the
web of destiny it has spun in previous lives. Thus, for instance, during
this present life we are spinning the web of the next from the fabric-
matter into which are woven those various colours and patterns which
correspond to, and hence are the natural outcome of, our *thoughts* and
desires. We are either weak, or strong ; that is, we are either swayed by
outer circumstances and moulded by environment, or, we compel our
surroundings and conditions to be moulded by ourselves, from within.
The middle course is to be neither wholly the one nor wholly the other,
but to oscillate between the two, sometimes drifting and floating
with the general tide of humanity, in the main careless, indifferent and
slothful, yet sometimes pulling ourselves together and for the time being
dominating and moulding our conditions and circumstances.

The weak-willed are constantly being affected by all desires and
forces outside of themselves, and these forces being too strong for their
inherent will to overcome they eventually succumb to what is called
fate, responding blindly to the major portion of the planetary influences.
The strong-willed on the other hand refuse to be dominated by externals,
and sooner or later they realise that within themselves there is a power
which is superior to matter in any shape or form.

In the former class Desire is paramount, while in the latter class it
is being gradually brought under control and transmuted into Will.

Attraction and repulsion are the two great forces ever at work in
the world of form. Like and dislike, love and hatred, ambition and
sloth, are some of the " pairs of opposites " which dominate more or less
all souls until the permanent higher Self is realised, and duality is finally
conquered.

It is my task in these pages to deal with the subject of the progressed
horoscope in a manner never before attempted ; and in the hints which
the earnest student will discover therefrom he will find the warrant for
my repeated assertion that there is an esoteric as well as an exoteric
aspect of astrology.

*All horoscopes are progressive and contain innumerable possibilities for future
development*. Even the very sign under which the native is born holds
concealed within it characteristics that cannot be fully expressed during
one earth life, and at any time surprises may await those who have
never penetrated deeply enough into their own natures.

The Central Point of every horoscope may be thought of as
representing the nucleus of the *Spiritual Energy*, or Ego, the rays from that
centre gradually either gaining power over, or becoming submerged by,
(according to the Ego's growth and development), the various qualities of
Matter represented by the Signs of the Zodiac and the Planets. The chief

---

* (See *Reincarnation*, T.P.S., 161, New Bond Street, W., price 1s., or the series of
articles on " Reincarnation " in MODERN ASTROLOGY, Vols. XIII., XIV.)

attractive force is in the Ascendant, which is always the first to unfold, as it represents the type of brain and denotes its general character. In conjunction with this will come the Moon, special ruler over the brain cells, infantile stage and the home environment. Then gradually will unfold the Planets and their Aspects; and finally the Sun, as the tendency to self-reliance, self-control and independence more or less slowly asserts itself.

During the first four years of life every child comes under the influence of the Moon as it affects the expanding brain, and during this time almost exclusively reflects its surroundings—the parental influences and the domestic environment. From four to seven the ascendant gradually affects the child, and from about the seventh year onwards the life begins to definitely unfold and express itself through the influence of the horoscope generally.

In some cases the whole life may be occupied in identifying the consciousness with only one minute portion of the horoscope; in others, every spoke of the Wheel of Destiny will be grasped, so to speak, and the planetary vibrations rapidly absorbed; these two extremes marking the difference between a young soul and an older one.

All souls are not of the same age, all did not start upon their long pilgrimage from the divine centre at the same time. Yet all are in essence one, and identical in spirit, though each is coloured differently according to the special planetary ray it was born under and its position in its chain of evolution.

"Each man's life the outcome of his former living is." The horoscope of any man is the outcome of his thoughts, desires and motives in previous lives. These have materialised into a web or garment, as it were, in which the soul is clothed; and this constitutes his "karma," fate, or Destiny.

All are reaping that which has been sown, none have other than that which they themselves have chosen. All may improve, and change existing conditions according to the strength of their will. It is the *will* behind every horoscope that makes it progressive; and this will is either God's will, moving for good, or man's personal will, moving to (apparent) evil. Hence every horoscope must be in some sense progressive, whether moved by providence or by man's blind folly.

In the following pages an attempt will be made to deal with the metaphysical aspect of astrology, and the scientific laws governing human destiny will be fully explained from a practical and common-sense standpoint, in order that the predictive aspect of the science may be rightly understood, and so made useful and helpful to all who have felt the need of this interpretation of the Riddle of Existence.

For it is the glorious mission of Modern Astrology to teach and prove man's Freewill, within limits self-set by God's limitless Divine Will.

[*The reader is recommended to make a brief study of the Table of Contents, which will enable him to find with ease any portion of the book to which he may wish to refer later on.*]

x

HOROSCOPE OF THE AUTHOR.

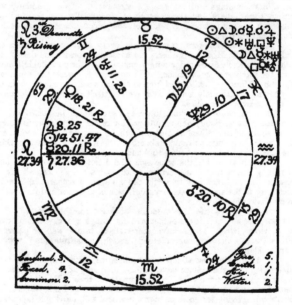

Declinations.

| ☉ 16°23′ N | ♆ 1°37′ S | ♄ 13°34′ N | ♂ 28 6 S |
| ☽ 10 42 N | ♅ 22 6 N | ♃ 18 41 N | ♀ 15 23 N |

☿ 10°9′ N

⊕ ♈ 28°1′   ☊ ♒ 1°11′   ☋ ♌ 1°11′

THE NATIVITY OF THE EDITOR OF "MODERN ASTROLOGY."
(Born 7/8/'60, 5.49 a.m., Westminster.)

THE PROGRESSED HOROSCOPE.

CHAPTER I.

HEREDITY, ENVIRONMENT, CHARACTER.

SOME men pass through eventful lives, others merely drift through theirs, leading a tame, prosaic existence consisting chiefly of routine. It is in fact not uncommon to find one in a family who leads a roving and wandering life, while the remainder spend their days in ease and comfort, free from all care or anxiety—the rover meanwhile passing through a period of suffering, starvation, or shipwreck, perchance, accompanied by hair-breadth escapes from peril.

Why are lives so strangely different? Are some *fated* to be born rich and happy, others poor and miserable, some possessing sound wit and clear intellect, while others are fools or idiots? Or is life merely a matter of chance, a kind of ' fortuitous concourse of influences ' ?

Astrology gives the only clear and definite answer to these questions, as well as to many more, for it is the language (so to speak) of those who govern all things and bring them to a wise and perfect end.

Heredity—Environment—Character. These are the three great factors in human destiny, a right understanding of which makes clear the problem of fate and the way to escape from its bondage.

Heredity is the first fetter which binds the feet of all born into physical existence. We cannot choose our parents, and we find, as soon as we become conscious of the fact, that we have either good or bad parents, rich or poor, healthy or diseased, while we are moreover heirs to various moral conditions which either accord or disaccord with our character as the case may be. Thousands are

I

to-day living wrecks, solely through hereditary conditions over which they apparently had no control at the moment of birth, while thousands on the other hand are blessed with healthy and in every way satisfactory hereditary conditions, kind parents, and easy circumstances. Therefore the problem is to discover the *justness* of such a state of things ; our task is not merely to find out the " How " of life but the " Why ? "

Our various environments, so far as the majority are concerned, are in the main as we find them at birth, altering in some cases for better or worse as life advances. We have no choice over our early environments, they are prepared for us—or we for them. Thousands are moulded and shaped by their surrounding conditions, and environment thus becomes their destiny ; but thousands also alter and shape their own environment and are not ruled by it. Is it their ' fate ' to do either the one or the other, or have they control over it all in the pre-natal and post-natal as well as in the *ante-natal* state ?

Character is different in all beings. Some are born " bad characters," and no amount of moral or mental training can alter or improve them ; they apparently go from bad to worse, cursed from birth by bad heredity and wretched environment, everything conducing to draw out the very worst and the most evil part of their natures. What explanation do we obtain from our moral and religious teachers with regard to these characters ? Is it that a pure soul is placed in an impure vessel in sordid and unholy conditions at birth, or is the soul impure though placed in clean and healthy surroundings at birth, as in the case of the mentally brilliant yet morally deformed ? And if so, why is one soul pure and another impure ?

Astrology throws light upon all these vexed questions. In its scientific aspect it points to the stars (planets) as the cause for the events of life which take their rise from human birth, while in its metaphysical aspect it leads to a knowledge of the cause behind the stars.

The three factors before spoken of, Heredity, Environment and Character exercise their influence as follows :

Heredity supplies the vessel,—pure or impure according to past causes in previous lives—by an affinity of physical particles, like attracting like.

Environment gives conditions in which expression may be made of the latent qualities inherent in the soul, and it harmonises with the actual needs and requirements of the soul in order that the latter may obtain its freedom from the fate of other previous lives by paying off the debts it has incurred and by developing those traits of character for the lack of which the continued evolution of the soul, at the point then reached, would be delayed.

Character is that inherent quality of the soul which it brings with it as an asset, and is the "root of merit" through which it is either susceptible and conformable to its environment, or rises above and dominates, alters or changes it.

In this sense Character becomes Destiny, and this will be the subject of our next chapter.

CHAPTER II.

CHARACTER IS DESTINY.

At first sight it does not seem possible that Character can wholly account for Destiny, in the sense in which this word is often used of a life's career, yet upon careful reflection it is found to be indeed true that Character *is* Destiny. All who have studied or been interested in the growth of young children must have noticed certain traits of character not wholly accounted for by heredity or environment, while in some instances many members of the same family, even where all were distinguished, have been notorious for their great difference in character.

As a factor in the making of Destiny, Character plays the most prominent and important part. Every person we meet in life is endowed with a *character*, strong or weak, good or evil, pronounced or indifferent ; and we are all of us affected consciously or unconsciously, by the character of everyone with whom we come into contact. Bad characters will corrupt weaker ones, and good characters will raise the standard for others. Character *will* make itself manifest, and it will either control, modify or stir into greater activity passing events ; in fact, on close investigation " character " is found to be at the root of every difference that we remark between one human being and another.

A strong character will rise above an environment that is not congenial, while a weak one will succumb to its influence and absorb its conditions, thus proving that within every character there is a *will*—a will which may be either weak, or strong, according to development. Habits that bind are persistent modes of the manifestation of character, these modes being chosen wisely or unwisely as the case may be.

All who study human nature are aware of the complex nature of character. Human beings manifest themselves through (*a*) temperament, (*b*) feelings and emotions, and (*c*) mental expressions ; also (*d*) through phases of thought. These different modes of manifestation of the nature are expressed through the horoscope by (*a*) the Ascendant, (*b*) the Moon, (*c*) the Sun and Planets, and (*d*) " Directions " respectively.

Thus, the Physical Body is of a certain "temperament," and character is in the main dependent upon the temperament through which it is to manifest. A man possessing the *Vital* temperament will not fit comfortably into a hard environment, for he will love and desire ease: through this temperament the feelings and the emotions will affect destiny. Those of the *Mental* temperament will live in the mind, and will be affected by mental conditions more than by physical. On the other hand the *Motive* temperament inclines towards power, organisation and force. Thus each temperament will affect surroundings and environment according to the strength of the character or will that is behind.

Again, if human nature be studied from a higher standpoint than that of the physical alone, we are told by those who are truly clairvoyant that man is surrounded by a magnetic field, termed the "aura," which is coloured by his thoughts, feelings and emotions ; and we learn further that each man is always surrounded by his own aura and that he brings it with him on his entry into each earth-life. Now the child that is newly born is the vehicle or body which this aura surrounds, and when the Ego behind can gain full possession of the body, it makes it answer to the vibrations inherent in it, and this we call Character. But the Ego may not have a mind and body able to express all its latent character. Indeed we rarely if ever see all of the character manifesting through any one body, unless it be through the body of a "Master," or perfect soul.

Hence it will be seen that Character is a very complex and difficult thing to understand, and that is why destiny is not an easy matter to interpret. But the one fact that it is necessary always to bear in mind is, that all living creatures are identical in spirit and in *essence*, though they differ in *manifestation*, according to the matter in which they are clothed and their attitude towards it.

Matter is fated to assume shape and form, yet the life within that form is destined to control it sooner or later.

CHAPTER III.

WHY DIRECTIONS SOMETIMES FAIL

IF all "directions" came to pass exactly as delineated and all predictions were actually verified by *definite events*, it would be an exceedingly strong argument in favour of absolute fatalism, and the fact that directions sometimes 'fail' is evidence for the Freedom of Will, no matter how limited the scope of that freedom may be.

The undeveloped Ego will always be liable to act in response to outside influences, and will be moulded and shaped in mind and feeling according to the circumstances and the surroundings in which he is placed.

A developing Ego, whose mind is less fettered and restrained by external conditions, will not always act in precisely the same manner during repeated experiences, and there will be some exercise of the freedom of choice in certain directions which will tend to break up former habits, and to alter the attitude towards recurring events.

The developed man who has learned by experience the control of his emotions and thoughts will not only maintain an attitude of calmness and serenity when passing through events, (which are merely the result of thoughts and desires set in motion while he was yet in the undeveloped or developing stages), but will also seek to turn those events to a useful purpose in furthering his spiritual unfolding.

Thus we have three classes of human beings for all of whom the same set of interpretations of directions will not answer; and if the same fixed rules are applied to each one some are bound to fail. For instance, a man who is taking his personality in hand and making strong efforts to overcome anger and jealousy, or greed and covetousness, will not act so impulsively as those who *do not know* that they are jealous or greedy; and hence in the case of the developed man evil predictions resulting from any severe affliction to ♂ or ♄ will not prove so unfortunate as anticipated. This is why it is so very important that the Progressed Horoscope should *always* be judged in conjunction with the Nativity, and the fact never lost sight of that " CHARACTER IS DESTINY."

Some " directions" will fail in normal cases from the apparent lack of opportunity, want of ability, indifference, or need of ambition which are a part of the native's character or karma, as shown in the nativity. Therefore a study of that branch of Natal Astrology known as " directions" is never complete until the full possibilities and the deficiencies or shortcomings of the nativity itself are thoroughly understood.

The young spendthrift whose nativity is given at the end of *How to Judge a Nativity, Part II.*, was born under the influence of Mars square Jupiter, Jupiter ruling his third house (mind and intellect) and placed in the ninth house (the wider and broader or " higher " mind), while Mars ruled his second house (money), his ruler, Venus, being moreover in opposition to the cusp of the latter. He was fated to be extravagant and seemed to have no control over his spendthrift habits, and yet he was by nature mean and quite careless as regards those whom he impoverished by his reckless mode of life (Sun square Saturn, angular). This native had some remarkable opportunities to study occultism, but he confessed that he had not the ability to concentrate his thoughts for more than a second on any single subject (Mercury square Uranus). Directions in his case never failed accurately to denote the events through which he would pass. A lawsuit was predicted for him several years before the litigation began, and he could apparently have prevented it, but he let matters run their course, and lost through his legal troubles over £30,000.

The most fateful horoscopes are those in which the majority of planets are in the Common or Mutable signs, and those where Saturn afflicts the luminaries. Jupiter afflicted by Mars, or the Sun by Uranus are fateful nativities, as in the case of P. B. Shelley.*

Apart from cases where a strong will and knowledge are causing the evil influence of adverse aspects to be modified, ' Directions' will sometimes fail owing to the student interpreting positions and aspects erroneously—which of course will be due to his own faulty judgment ; but in the majority of cases that will come before him, at least three-quarters of the predictions, if carefully thought out, should prove correct, especially if the *nativity* is fully understood.

Students of "Directions" must be prepared for the possibility of

* *How to Judge a Nativity, Part II.*, p. 187.

meeting with a few saints and yogis, and also some sinless persons who are on this planet for some special purpose; but he should beware of the individual who claims to be so mighty and strong that he has risen above all planetary influence.   There are a few groups of persons in London and the principal cities of the world who laugh at the idea of their being in any way affected by horoscopes, fixed or progressive, and who glibly deny the interference of angels or archangels in their destiny.   Experience has satisfied the Author that no man does or can live up to all the vibrations expressed in his nativity, and those who deny the influence of the heavens upon them deny the existence of a supreme ruler and his protecting care over the whole of humanity.   To live up to one's horoscope means to be a perfect man, and but a very little reflection is needed to perceive the truth of this statement.   None save the Masters have so entirely purified their astral bodies as to live above the influence of the Signs of the Zodiac, even,—to say nothing of the planetary influence operating upon those signs—and therefore to assert one's immunity from all the vibrations of the planets is merely to make a display of ignorance. It may be granted that people who make such statements are above the *astrologer's interpretation* of those influences.   But the man who is born, say, under the influence of Mars, and who maintains that he is not a martial man, is simply a self-sufficient person who will not give the subject a moment's study.   The Author has met many such people and has found the study of their horoscopes repay him better than the attempt to convince them, while the way in which they respond year by year to the influence of the progressive horoscope is sufficient refutation of their claims.

Nevertheless, the student should be careful not to predict precise events until he has had a great deal of practice, and he should beware of colouring certain aspects by his own peculiar experience, bias or prejudice.   In other words he should, like a scientist, take into account the " personal equation."   He will find his interpretation of " Directions " sometimes fail through his not having allowed for his own mental colouring, or through his want of experience upon a certain line.

It will be seen from the foregoing that a certain allowance must be made for the failure of " Directions," through the student's inevitably limited knowledge, since none save an Adept can really get into touch with the inner motives and internal " root of merit " within the individual.   As the result of a long and very wide experience the Author is convinced that considerably more than half the civilised world respond to " Directions " as ordinarily interpreted, and in his current practice over ninety per cent. of the " Directions" supplied each year prove satisfactory to clients. However, as of the judgments on Nativities very nearly *ninety-nine* per cent. have been pronounced correct, the deficit, representing those clients who were not satisfied, is certainly evidence that " Directions" sometimes ' fail.'

Failure will sometimes arise through not attaching sufficient importance to the Houses ruled by the planets forming the various aspects, and great care will always be necessary to distinguish between the influence of the Progressed Horoscope and that of the Nativity. Preference should always be given to the rulers of the *natal* houses, and too much stress should never be laid upon the houses governing the progressed horoscope, for very few have so far advanced as to overcome the radical tendencies entirely, though here and there such a person may be found, in which case he will respond readily to the progressed horoscope. It will therefore be seen that much depends upon the judgment of the student as to whether he will be successful in ascertaining how the operating influences will act upon the native. More lies in the *interpretation* of these influences than many students imagine, and it is always best to make general predictions only, until the intuition is sufficiently active to form correct conclusions. Otherwise, failure must inevitably occur until he has had a very considerable amount of experience.

CHAPTER IV.

FATE AND FREE-WILL.

MAN is a spirit, or to speak more correctly a SOUL, with a body. His "spirit" is free, immortal, undying and permanent, but his soul is imprisoned in the "matter," or bodies, through which it manifests on the lower planes. Matter is ever-changing, impermanent, limited and circumscribed, hence matter is *fated* while the spirit is *free*. Between motive and act, the spirit and the body (or "matter"), man's soul is at some times bound, at others free—never wholly free, nor wholly bound, but linked to both states of existence by subtle bonds and thus ever harnessed to the Circle or "Wheel" of Necessity.

Astrologers who have thought over the problem of Fate and Free-will express their ideas through *symbols*, which serve as stepping-stones to the higher and more metaphysical thoughts of *involution* and *evolution*.

Beginning at the commencement of a solar system the "word" or *Logos* is symbolised by a point, (.) representing the first appearance out of the darkness of the Divine Spirit who is about to define and circumscribe His universe, which is thus symbolised by the point within the circle, (⊙). From this symbol all other symbols arise, just as from Him all that is to be must come forth. All that exists within His Universe (which we ordinarily term the solar system) came from Himself, and has no other being apart from Him ; for truly "in Him we live and move and have our being."

He is our fate, our destiny, our only hope and guide; for in essence we are but the 'divine fragments' of His life.

In the solar system are moving planets, archangels, angels, and hosts of other living creatures besides ourselves and those we see on the earth: but all move in the One Spirit Life. Each monad* is at one with every other, and all form one indissoluble whole.

* This term, here used in the technical sense adopted by Western students of Eastern philosophy, may be paraphrased as "spiritual individuality" and pertains alike to angels and archangels and to plants and animals, as well as to man, implying the separated fragment of Divine Life which has started on its long pilgrimage through "matter"—this word 'matter' applying not only to the matter of this physical world, but to all the seven planes, physical, astral, mental, etc., of the manifested universe.

Complexities of character arise from the soul's identification with many and various forms of matter. "*The One became many*," and the many were made separate through the sheaths of matter in which each was involved, each sheath of matter belonging to its own plane and being coloured and arranged according to the quality or special nature of that plane.

There are seven of these 'planes,' each of which is presided over by a lord or ruler, and to one or other of those lords or rulers all human beings belong, humanity being divided into seven groups. From each of these Rulers emanates a certain ray or colour, so that each divine monad that we know on earth as 'man' commences his journey with one of these seven primordial rays as a guiding influence and this remains his special 'bent' or 'line of least resistance,' during the whole of his pilgrimage through matter. Throughout ages of evolution connected with many spheres he rises successively through the mineral, vegetable, and animal kingdoms into the human, where, at the *animal-man* stage, he commences to 'turn inwards'—to pass back again, or rather onward and upward again, through the human once more into the Divine.

Throughout the ages both Life and Form have been evolving, consciousness or life gaining more expansion and greater freedom as it gains more and more liberation from the bondage of the grosser forms of matter. At first matter is the stronger and life is apparently the weaker, but slowly and gradually the *life* permeates the *form*, and finally triumphs over it. In this struggle some souls obtain liberation sooner than others. Each is free within certain limits—the limits, in fact, of the matter in which it is encased.

Each portion of man's sevenfold being corresponds to some other portion of the universe. His physical body to the mineral kingdom, over which the planet Saturn ($\hbar$) presides. His psychical counterpart, or envelope through which the life forces play (*etheric double*) to the vegetable kingdom or the Moon ($\mathfrak{D}$). His vitality or life-forces (*prana*) to the Sun ($\odot$). His animal soul or passional nature (*astral body*) to the animal kingdom and the planet Mars ($\mathfrak{z}$). His mind and intelligence (*mental body*) to the human kingdom over which Mercury ($\mathfrak{y}$) presides. His higher self, and the aura which surrounds the monad always (*buddhic body*) to Jupiter ($\mathfrak{z}$). And that divine fragment which is in essence immortal (*atmic vehicle*) to Venus ($\mathfrak{z}$). Man's consciousness may be bound to any one of these divisions of himself, and while he identifies

himself with any particular expression or manifestation of himself
in that direction, so long will he be fated. Ignorance will keep him
bound to the wheel of fate, knowledge will liberate him.

The following article, written by the authro's wife for the pages of
Modern Astrology, will form a fitting conclusion both to this chapter and to
the topic that has hitherto chiefly engaged us—namely, the bearing of
character on "fate" or "destiny"—and after that we shall leave the
discussion of the moral and other problems connected with "directions"
once for all, and proceed forthwith to the scientific and practical portion
of our subject.

Should there be any who are inclined to fancy that too much space
has already been devoted to this aspect of the matter, and who are
impatient to get on to the "predicting," let them be advised to moderate
their impetuosity, for sooner or later sorrowful experience will force them
to recognise the bearing of such considerations upon every astrological
problem that presents itself.

To put the matter in a nutshell: just as character furnishes a clue to
destiny, so does the nativity supply the key to the progressed horoscope.
Hence a thorough knowledge of the nativity will show in which
direction knowledge lies, and where for that particular soul liberation
may be gained.

FATE *versus* INDIVIDUAL EFFORT.

Among the many minds studying Astrology we find two distinct
types: on the one hand the objective or "practical" mind that directs its
attention chiefly towards external appearances and applies its faculties to
a purely utilitarian study of this science; and on the other, the subjective
or philosophical mind coming under the influence of Uranus—(that
truly occult planet),—a type of mind which focuses the attention chiefly
on the metaphysical and spiritual side of a subject, and seeks to understand, when studying national or individual nativities, the problems of
life and the law of causation involved. These two types of mind may
be respectively compared to the third and ninth houses of the horoscope.

The subjective or higher mind is ever concerned with causes rather
than their manifestations, with the essence of things rather than their
form. This type of mind recognises the presence of law everywhere.
No one, it is true, can study Astrology for any length of time without to

some extent apprehending that the different planetary vibrations producing all events in this physical world must be the emanation of living entities, carrying out in a greater or lesser degree the divine will. But those who think out problems to their conclusion are forced to go one step further, realising that there can be no such thing as " chance," and that every happening is the result of foregone *causes*, acting and reacting upon each other according to certain definite and fixed laws. When this conclusion has been reached, it sometimes happens that a sense of desolation falls down upon the human soul as it realises itself in the grip of a passionless Destiny that can be neither intimidated nor cajoled, finding itself apparently the helpless victim of "blind fate."

There is a beautiful passage in the *Mahabharata* in which the great warrior and hero Bhîshma is depicted lying wounded on the field of battle, and holding his life within his shattered form by his own indomitable will, until he considered the aspect of the heavens suitable to his departure. While in this state, there drew round him young and old, to ask him to teach them, as his wisdom was remarkable. And one among the number asked this memorable question: "Tell us, oh Bhîshma, of two forces which is the stronger, Effort or Fate?" Bhîshma gave it as his opinion that of the two great forces Effort was the greater, and that exertion wedded to knowledge could overcome Fate.

Now Fate is not a single force or energy with which we are born as something complete at birth, in itself a totality, but on the contrary is a constantly changing quantity. Our very nativity changes, unfolds and unrolls, different aspects come into play, different vibrations fall upon us, bringing changes of environment, and changes both of character and consciousness. Hence the value of rightly directed effort—note the qualification, *rightly directed* effort—at every step on life's journey, whereby the one force may often suitably change and transmute the other.

Thus, a person may be born under the complete aspect of the Sun in square to Saturn. But as the planets progress he will in the thirtieth year of life come under the aspect of the Sun in sextile or trine to Saturn. This will considerably modify and reduce the malignancy of the square aspect at birth and will afford an opportunity whereby the habits formerly set in motion and made concrete under the square of Saturn may be broken up : this would be all the more patent if Saturn were the significator at birth, and the horoscope by progress had changed the sign upon the ascendant. Innumerable further instances could be given to show how the horoscope is always being modified by the progress of the planets, and how one aspect may considerably modify another. The person born with the Sun square Saturn at birth, for instance, might have that luminary applying to a trine aspect of Jupiter. Again, the Moon must pass to a favourable aspect with Jupiter several times during her passage round the zodiac, and therefore every person who reaches the age of twenty-eight, by which time the progressed Moon arrives once more at her own radical place, has during his life had several opportunities, indicated by the Moon's various aspects to Jupiter, whether by conjunction, sextile or trine.

Thus each nativity may be compared to a kaleidoscope, every turn causing a new pattern to be formed. What that new pattern is will depend partly upon the angle through which the kaleidoscope is turned, and partly upon the shapes and colours (inherent mental and moral tendencies) of the fragments from which the pattern is composed. Let any one devote a few minutes to the study of this "child's toy," as it is often contemptuously termed, and the meaning of what has been said will be brought home to him in a very striking way. Let him take two kaleidoscopes and turn them both simultaneously, and see what different patterns are formed by the same amount of turning, and he will then understand the better how life holds such different possibilities for two different people. No better illustration of a horoscope and its progression could be given.

Predictions about the future sometimes fail, and yet they work out fairly accurately in the majority of cases. Why is this? Because most people drift along the stream of life, never taking themselves in hand at all—the mind or the emotions entirely ruling them, instead of their being able to some extent to dominate both mind and emotions. Such persons collapse under disaster, or sit tamely down without opposing the force by will and by exertion and effort on their own part. On the other hand, we have cases on record where (for example) a man, though under a train of evil aspects touching his position and circumstances which threatened to completely ruin him, made every exertion and spared no effort, displaying indomitable courage and perseverance, so that what to another would have been a crushing defeat became with him success, for by sustained effort and strength of will he overcame the opposing forces at last and obtained employment of a remunerative kind, even in the teeth of very " bad " aspects.*

It is true that there are some things that we *cannot* avoid. The desires of the past and the thoughts of the past may have been terribly strong, and death may have suddenly cut off the actions resulting from those thoughts and desires. Then, on the reappearance of the man or woman on the physical stage, the event must and will happen, directly opportunity gives the forces previously set going a chance of showing themselves.

It has ever been a problem vexing the minds of students of Astrology as to why certain aspects act in a marked manner in the case of one person, yet do not appear to take effect in the case of another. Let us suppose two men had exactly the same bad aspects in their nativity. The one struggled with all his force and energy to overcome the adverse influences, while the other did nothing whatsoever. Think you the result would be the same in both cases? By no means, for the one making every exertion he possibly could, would be calling forth new force to transmute and change the other, and even if he could not quite wrest victory from defeat would at least be able to avert the full measure of the calamity. If this were not so, we should be forced into a position of blind fatalism, so that if we saw from his nativity that some-one whom we were tending in illness could not possibly recover, we might leave him severely alone, without nurse or provision, saying the person must die and all efforts would be useless.

But that would be a fatal error. It is our duty in such a case to leave no stone unturned to seek to save that life. For it may be that our will and skill employed may supply just the force that will turn the balance. And whether it proves so or not we should have the conscious-ness of duty perfectly rendered. Indeed, the activity of the moment makes all the difference, and we should do all that is possible at a crisis to counteract undesirable influences, remembering that each person's will is a force in the universe. Effort is greater than Fate. Fate is not that rigid, unbending monster that we set up for ourselves, but is capable of being modified—and indeed is changing at every moment.

If we each felt our own inherent divinity strong from within, we should each have more power to act. Let us use well the liberty and

* The horoscope of the individual in question will be found on the last page of *How to Judge a Nativity, Part II.*

freedom we have, and not bind ourselves so much by the shackles of fate. Let us try to understand the law and then work with it. When we have sufficient knowledge to do this we shall be masters of Fate, which will then be our willing servant. We are helpless because we do not know, because we do not understand, that there is One Universal Law working; the LAW OF GOOD, and that to that law we must conform ourselves.

Let us remember that after all it is the attitude of the mind to events that really matters, and not the events themselves. The sea bather who is inexperienced, or too rash, may be overthrown by the surf before he has even fully realised his danger, or on attempting to swim may have his back broken by the inrolling breaker. As for the timid, he will never venture in beyond his knees. But the well-trained swimmer knows how to choose his steps as he wades through the surf, he keeps his eyes ever on the approaching wave, and just as its crest towers over him he plunges boldly into it—and the arching glassy wall that threatened a moment ago to dash him to pieces goes thundering harmlessly behind, whilst he himself emerges freshened and exhilarated by the encounter! So if we meet dangers and difficulties with courage and resolution they will work us little harm, while backed by skill and judgment they may become lifting forces rather than crushing blows. When we see a misfortune coming, let us not lose hope and so allow ourselves to be crushed by it, but let us be strong and make it a help. If we tried to *adapt* ourselves to things and circumstances and people, the strain of life would be much easier to bear. Let us try to understand the laws of life, those unseen laws that guide human evolution. The ignorant man must drift and become the victim of fate, but fate is burnt up by knowledge. Still, it requires strength to act according to law rather than impulse; great strength to forgive and think kindly of an enemy; greater strength to pardon all wrong-doers; greater strength still to control the mind, letting only pure thoughts and pure desires hold sway; greatest strength of all to put the personality on one side and do right at any cost.

If we are to conquer fate in the future we shall all have to become graduates in the science of life, to understand and obey the law of harmony, to burn up all the evil that comes to us, transmuting it into good by sending out vibrations of peace in return. But many of us need strength; rarely can an astrologer tell a person of a misfortune likely to fall upon him because in most cases he could not stand it; it would be too great a shock, and he would live in constant fear. And yet such a person often exclaims, "I wish I knew all my past lives!" Suppose that they *had* that vision, and saw a thunder cloud of past wrong-doing about to discharge its contents on them—why, their present life would know no peace or comfort! No, it is only when the soul has become indifferent to pain and pleasure as it affects the personal self, that the past can become known. For in very truth we meet our present lives better because the past is hidden. All action is the ripened fruit of the past, and if we would control action or fate we must first control desire and thought, which are the seeds of action; for according to the seed we sow so must the reaping be. Hence, as we do not know the past and thus can only dimly gauge the future, it is well to act without the "incubus of fate" hanging over us. To judge with our best mind, to put forth our best efforts, remembering always that no event can really injure us except when we allow despair and want of hope to crush us. It is *that* that defeats us, and not "fate." There are many sad cases to be read in the daily papers of people who through despair have committed suicide, just at the very moment when help was on its way towards them. Let us ever bear in mind that "Man's extremity is God's opportunity."

For any student of Astrology to say: "Oh, I have this bad aspect in my nativity!" or, "My horoscope is such a very unlucky one, and therefore I cannot help myself," is to deliberately fall under the wheels of the chariot of Fate, instead of electing to be oneself the charioteer. There is a certain law known to occultists which shows that the horoscope of birth only represents us *as we were*, not as *we are* to-day. We are all in advance of our nativities, for the past overlaps the present; and it is the soul's inner attitude, its present thoughts and aspirations which *really* matter, as these determine its future nativity.

When shall we rightly understand and apply the great truth that "morality is science applied to conduct," and that its laws are based on fundamental principles in nature? When we do this we shall be ruling our stars in very truth, for as we become harmonious we cannot vibrate with an inharmonious nativity. A generous soul cannot be born with a mean horoscope, and *vice versâ*, for this earth plane is the field of action of spiritual forces, and this wonderful play of life in action that we call

B

stellar influences ever works towards the development and unfoldment of consciousness.

Let co-operation with these spiritual forces be our aim. Life is given us " to do the will of God," says a writer. But it is more than that, it is—*to become it!* When we apply our science to conduct and are giants in morality we shall then be Masters of Destiny, and Fate will be our servant.

CHAPTER V.

THE AUTHOR'S SYSTEM.

EVERY horoscope is progressive. This is no speculative hypothesis but an actual matter of fact. For even if a soul born into the world resolutely refused to make progress on its own account, the progress of nature would inevitably carry it beyond the stage into which it was born; infantile complaints, enforced changes of mood on the part of the parents, new environment, altering conditions and fresh faces would all do their silent work of affecting the matter in which that soul was imprisoned.

Hence no soul can continue in exactly the same state. Changes in climate and temperature, the growth of the body, interchange of physical and other particles with other human beings, all these must and do influence, modify and affect the soul, *whether the mind is conscious of it or not*.

At birth, the planets impress their especial modes of vibration upon the ether and the matter which is drawn around the incoming Ego. Each day, month, and year after birth these natal centres are being unceasingly modified and affected, both by the progressive motions of the planets and luminaries and also by the daily transits and aspects of fresh planetary influences over and to the places marked at birth.

What is it, then, that is marked at birth?

A child is born, and at the first breath which is independently taken it starts upon a cycle that is *its own*. The first inrush of Prana, or positive breath, contains the Solar breath. If the Sun at birth is throwing its rays in a benefic or adverse aspect to a powerful planet, the Prana is charged with this planet's influence. At the first inhalation there is also a Lunar breath charged with the Lunar influences. Into every pore of the skin, into every atom of the body, there is an indrawing of the electric and magnetic atmosphere upon which the influences of all the planets impinge. Upon each degree of the Zodiac as it rises upon the horizon with the turning of the earth on its axis—which degree acts as a talisman *throughout the life* of each form born at that moment into the world—all other rising and setting or planetary motions and lunar cycles have their effects, either modifying or accentuating its own inherent nature, and thus extracting or suppressing its own essential qualities. This degree, the Ascendant, is thus the keystone of the whole nativity, for in it are synthesised the whole of the multifarious elements of the natal chart, *of which there is no exact duplicate for ages afterwards*. Thus the nativity is truly called the 'radix,' the Root, out of which each Progressive Horoscope springs as do the leaves upon the branches of a tree.

These considerations have been put as emphatically as possible—for it is impossible to overrate their importance. It is not too much to say that they constitute the foundation of the whole subject of "directing" (as it is usually termed), and the student will do well before going further to recapitulate what has been said. For if he once firmly impresses upon himself the principles here enunciated he will not make the mistake that so many do, of expecting from "Directions" that which is not promised by the Nativity. A great teacher has said "Men do not gather grapes of thorns, nor figs of thistles," and this truth is just as applicable to the study of horoscopes as in other departments of life. Let it be said once more, the nativity is the Root from which all future manifesting must spring, and according as it is a vine, a fig tree, a bramble stock or a furze stem, so must we expect grapes or figs or prickles.

Let us think of the world as a living entity floating in space amidst other planets and around the Sun, the atmosphere around the earth extending for some considerable distance but enclosed in a shell through which the rays of the Sun penetrate. The solid earth may be thought of as the yolk and the atmosphere as the white of an egg, while the shell of the latter will represent the etheric garment which confines the atmosphere to the earth. Within this shell we find (1) *The Atmosphere* in its various forms of density, each sphere interpenetrating the others, and consisting of air and ether, and (2) *The Earth*, consisting of land and seas, the two together supplying the four ancient 'elements,' Fire, Earth, Air and Water (or etheric, solid, gaseous and liquid matter respectively) and corresponding to the first four signs of the zodiac, *Aries, Taurus, Gemini, Cancer*. Outside of the earth's sphere there are other planets revolving, each having a special vibration or influence of its own, and affecting the earth and the other planets each in its own peculiar manner.

The solar system is one Great Family, composed of ☉, ☿, ♀, ⊕, ♂, ♃, ♄, ♅, ♆, and ☽, each possessing the same essence or spirit as its centre but a different colouring and mode of influence according to the arrangement of the matter composing its body and atmosphere. Observation and close study have enabled astrologers not only to distinguish a great difference in the nature of each planet's influence but also to understand the essential nature of these differences. Thus ♄ is proved by experience to have a cold, binding and restricting influence, ♂ on the contrary a hot, expansive and explosive influence. Again, ♃ is a warm, temperate and harmonising planet, ♀ a brightening, cheerful and loving influence, while ☿ comes between these four, and acts as a receiver for each in turn, absorbing and reproducing the influence in a more or less modified condition, it being found to affect the mind more directly than any of the planets.

All these varying influences have been fully described in the previous books of this series, but it is imperative that we should be fully conversant with the nature of each planet in its *radical* influence before we attempt to study its effect in *directions*. For, as has been hinted before, unless the student is capable of judging the nativity with tolerable accuracy, it will be quite hopeless for him to attempt to determine the nature of the " directions " arising therefrom.

THE SUN AND HIS INFLUENCE IN " DIRECTIONS."

The Sun is the ruler of the Will and Motive or Moral power, that which is summed up as the Individuality, the solar rays being coloured and modified according to the sign through which they were passing at birth. This Individuality is either *permanent* in its expression of the mind, or unstable and *changeable*, according to the stage of the native's progress in evolution. It is modified by the planets aspecting the Sun, in the same manner that the feelings and emotions are modified by the planetary positions and aspects affecting the Moon.

The pure Individuality of *all* human beings is represented by the Sun apart from the sign through which any one soul receives its rays during any separated earth-life. For the Sun is the true Ego, the immortal and undying part of all life and consciousness, a proof, when realised, that we are all one in essence though manifesting differently. The solar rays come direct from the Sun, but the Moon borrows its light from the Sun, having no light of her own, and therefore in this sense the Sun is giver of *all* life and consciousness. Both light and heat, and similarly both intellect and feeling, all have their primal source in the Sun, whose rays—whether physical, astral, or mental—the Moon and Planets receive and break up or modify according to their nature and rate of vibration.

The Sun may be considered as the life of the mind, the highest centre man can reach while he is human, and is that which may be conveniently considered the Individuality in each human being. There is but One Mind, the Universal Mind, which is the Wisdom of God. Man receives as much of that mind as he can absorb or express through his mind, body and desire nature, being limited in his expression on the physical plane by the law of *Karma*.

The passage of the Sun [*mind*] through each of the signs [*desire*] colours the Universal Mind according to the particular nature of that sign and so man uses (or abuses) his mental powers according to his degree of ignorance or enlightenment—in other words, according to his desire nature, whether it be pure or impure. The following classification will explain this :—

☉ *in* ♈	*Use*	Patriotism, heroism, love of truth, intellectual keenness.
	Abuse	Selfish ambition, exaggeration, deceit, indecision.
♉	*Use*	Stability of purpose, sympathy, obedience, firmness.
	Abuse	Obstinacy, stubbornness, dogmatism, pride.
♊	*Use*	Wise thought, pure intellect, perfection of details.
	Abuse	Diffusiveness, lack of purpose, fickle-mindedness.
♋	*Use*	Tenacity of mind, keen memory, firm will, kind thoughts.
	Abuse	Wavering, changeable mind, innate love of the sensational.
♌	*Use*	Harmonious mind, loving thought, pure emotions.
	Abuse	Sensual thoughts, love of display, arrogance and pride.
♍	*Use*	Discriminative mind, keen analysis, the higher criticism.
	Abuse	Hyper-critical, carping and selfish mind, self-deception.
♎	*Use*	Balanced intellect, clear vision, pure love, compassion.
	Abuse	Separative mind, unfair comparison, isolation.
♏	*Use*	Keen judgments, profound intellect, mystical mind.
	Abuse	Unbelieving, cynical and sarcastic intellect, and a cruel nature.
♐	*Use*	Religious intelligence, prophetic speech, wide sympathy.
	Abuse	Rebellious mind, shallow intellect, unreliability, effusiveness.
♑	*Use*	Profound reason, noble conditions, love of service.
	Abuse	Selfish ambitions, self-interest, and low servility.
♒	*Use*	Wide understanding of human nature, devotional mind.
	Abuse	Indifferent, proud intellect, dogmatism in religious matters.
♓	*Use*	A philanthropic and hospitable mind, profound sympathies.
	Abuse	Over-pliable mind, and indolent vagueness of intention.

THE MOON AND HER INFLUENCE IN "DIRECTIONS."

The Moon is a symbol of the instinctual consciousness in each individual and represents the lower mind as the Personality, with all its sensations, feelings, and emotions. She is ever changing, fluctuating, and altering the moods of those who come more or less under her influence.

The position of the Moon at birth will denote the nature of the native's personal feelings and his power to respond to external vibrations —either from the planet or planets in aspect to her, or the vibrations of the quality of the sign in which she was placed at that time. The influence of Mars to the Moon will expand the feelings and intensify the response to sensation, sensation chiefly of the physical and psychic order. The influence of Saturn on the other hand will contract, restrain and chill or subdue the feelings and emotions; Jupiter will temperately expand and harmonise the feelings, raising them to a high level of morality and pure sentiment. Venus will make the feelings pleasurable, cheerful, refined and joyous. Mercury will raise the feelings and emotions and blend them with the intellect, either for good or evil according to the nativity. Uranus and Neptune will also affect the Moon according to the condition of the nativity; but as the average man is only slightly affected by these two planets, little must be expected from them in most cases, except in the case of severe affliction by either, which will produce calamity, disagreements or losses.

The Moon in the signs of the zodiac will tinge the soul or personality according to the nature of the sign it is in, and the aspects of the planets will increase the sensuousness, or purity, of the emotions according to the nature of the aspect and the planet concerned. The sign occupied by the Moon will modify or accentuate the aspects according to the quality of the sign, as follows :—

☽ in ♈ { Feelings joyous, enthusiastic, impulsive, though controlled by mind and intellect; very responsive, and easily affected by external conditions.

♉ { Feelings reserved in their expression, bound by pride or dignity and restricted by conventional habits or fear of consequences, rather than by the inner will. The mind is somewhat resentful, jealous and very concentrated, but sensuous and considerably though silently affected by others.

♊ { Feelings refined but fickle, changeable and dualistic, much affected by circumstances and by temporary aspects.

♋ { Placid, retentive and sensitive, extremely fond of sensation however, pure or otherwise, according to the aspects in operation.

☽ in
♌
{ Keen emotions; fondness for pleasure; poetical or musical inclinations. Refined ideals but strong feelings.

♍
{ Critical in feeling; discriminative over sensations. Emotions controlled, desiring either purity or ample return for any expression of feeling, according to state of advancement.

♎
{ Refined emotions, artistic feelings; temperate in sensation or expression.

♏
{ Keen feelings well hidden; strong impulses to sensation, but good control unless very depraved. Curious regarding emotions, proud and secretive.

♐
{ Enthusiastic feelings; fond of expressing emotion or religious sentiments; affectionate and impulsive.

♑
{ Chaste feelings; devotional tendencies. Or, selfish emotions; social ambitions, and great tenacity and concentration as regards the feelings.

♒
{ Humane feelings, faithful and constant emotions; pure sensations; artistic and refined in expression. Some erratic tendencies.

♓
{ Sensitive and receptive feelings; kind and humane in expression; easily affected by surroundings.

The Moon affects the fancy, the speech and the expressive side of the nature generally whenever sensation or personal feeling is concerned. She is therefore very easily modified by the influence of any of the other planets, graduating from coarse and vulgar sensations through feelings sensuous, sympathetic and refined, to the purest emotions and the loftiest moral expression of the soul. This may be imaged by the Moon waxing and waning, by her changes and motions from New Moon to Full, when she receives most light from the Sun. But in all cases she should be studied as the Personality, or that fleeting, transient part of the nature which is impermanent, changeable, and inconstant. She is therefore the representative of the native during the one physical earth-life, in which experience is being gathered and garnered for permanent expression through the mind or Individuality.

THE PROGRESSIVE ANGLES.

The Mid-heaven and the Ascendant and their opposite points, technically known as the "angles" of a horoscope, are fixed points of the celestial sphere, and their zodiacal position is decided by the moment of birth; it is therefore essential that the exact moment of birth be accurately ascertained, by a proper rectification of the horoscope, if necessary.

(See *Astrology for All, Part II.*, chapter VIII.; also the article on "Rectification" in MODERN ASTROLOGY, Vol. II., New Series.)

These points are really the points of intersection with the zodiac of the meridional and horizontal circles respectively ; they serve to mark off the space around the earth in the plane of the birthplace at the given time ; they decide the nature of the Houses in each nativity, and also, what is scarcely less important, the exact positions of the Planets as regards these Houses.

Each day after birth represents one whole year of life. During that time, the M.C. (as the midheaven is called) has progressed about one degree. The astronomical reason for this is clearly explained in *Astrology for All*, *Part II.*, page 8.

Hence in any given number of years, the M.C. will have advanced about an equal number of degrees, and this advanced M.C. is what is meant by the term ' Progressed Midheaven ' or ' prog. M.C.'

At the same time, the Ascendant will also have similarly advanced, *but not always quite at the same rate,* as a reference to a " Table of Houses " for the place of birth will show. This advanced ascendant is then the ' Progressed Ascendant.'

In a subsequent chapter the method of calculating this will be explained in a way that admits of no difficulty being encountered.

CHAPTER VI.

THE PROGRESSION OF THE HOROSCOPE.

THE movement of the signs and planets away from the places they occupied in the horoscope of birth is due to two factors; first, to the rotation of the earth on its axis, whereby all the heavenly bodies appear to rise, culminate, and set ; and second, to the revolution of the various bodies in their orbits, the Moon round the earth, and the earth and planets round the Sun.

Upon these two movements are based the two chief systems of directing followed at the present day, the so-called Primary and Secondary systems.

I. *Progression by Axial Rotation.*

This system is so fully described in Section D. of this book that very little need be said of it here. In order to understand how the earth's rotation forms directions, it is necessary to grasp clearly the distinction between zodiacal and mundane position. If the horoscope of the Princess of Wales (p. 28) is taken by way of illustration, it will be seen that the *zodiacal* position of the Moon is 8°♓23′ and that its *mundane* position is about the middle of the ascendant. Similarly the *zodiacal* position of Neptune is 14°♈21′ and its *mundane* position about a quarter of the house space below the cusp of the second house. The effect of the earth's axial rotation upon any heavenly body in the horoscope is to separate zodiacal position from mundane position. In the present instance, the Moon's zodiacal place gradually rises ; and when 8°♓23′ is exactly on the cusp of the ascendant, the direction " asc. ☌ ☽ zod." will be formed. At the same time, Neptune will be passing out of the second house into the first ; and when 14°♈21′ occupies the same mundane position (about the middle of the ascendant) as that which was occupied at birth by 8°♓23′, the direction "☽ ☌ ♆ zod." will be formed. Both these are conjunctions, but aspects are similarly formed. For instance, when the Moon's place has risen above the ascendant, it will enter the twelfth house ; and when 8° ♓ 23′ has arrived at the mundane position which was occupied at birth by 14°♑21′, the direction " ☽ □ ♆ zod." will be formed.

In this system, the so-called ' mundane' directions differ from the preceding in being based upon mundane aspects instead of upon zodiacal aspects. For instance, the zodiacal square of Neptune, as we have just seen, is 14°♑21′, but its mundane square is a point the same proportional distance below the cusp of the eleventh house as Neptune was at birth below the cusp of the second. When the Moon reaches this point, the *mundane* direction ☽ □ ♆ will be formed.

The rules for working this system are so framed as to show how many degrees of Right Ascension pass across the meridian while a given direction is being formed ; and these are then converted into years and months by means of the " measure of time," which is about one degree for each year of life.

II. *Progression by Orbital Revolution.*

The revolutions of the earth, moon, and planets in their orbits bring about great changes in the positions of the various heavenly bodies; they take up new places in the signs and houses, and form new aspects among themselves. These changes are tabulated in order, are classified, and then interpreted according to the rules given further on. The measure of time in this system is one day. That is to say, the changes among the heavenly bodies during the first day of life symbolise the events that will occur during the first year of life ; the second day, the second year ; and so on.

The Princess of Wales was born on May 26th, 1867, 11.59 p.m., at Kensington Palace.

If a new map of the heavens be calculated for one complete day later, May 27th, 11.59 p.m., it will form what is called a "Progressed Horoscope" corresponding to the date when the Princess was one year of age, on May 26th, 1868.

A map for ten complete days after birth will form a Progressed Horoscope for ten years of age.

A map for twenty-six complete days after birth, will form a Progressed Horoscope for twenty-six years of age. This will be

HOROSCOPE OF BIRTH.

Princess of Wales, born 26th May, 1867, 11.59 p.m. 50°30′ N. Lat., 51″ W. Long.

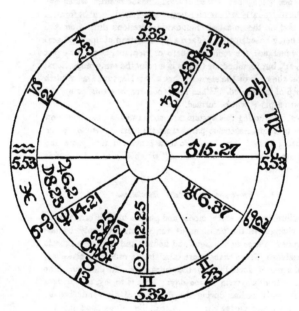

Planet.	Latitude.	Declination.	Right Asc.	Mer. Dist.	Semi-arc
	° ′	° ′	° ′	° ′	°
Asc.	—	18 S 49	—	—	—
M.C.	—	21 S 14	243 37	—	—
☉	—	21 N 11	63 17	0 20	60 50
☽	1 N 2	7 S 28	339 40	83 58	99 29
☿	0 S 12	19 N 50	57 12	6 27	63 2
♀	1 S 49	10 N 57	31 40	31 49	73 56
♂	1 N 32	17 N 41	138 23	105 14	113 38
♃	0 S 57	10 S 12	338 10	85 27	103 4
♄	2 N 25	15 S 21	227 56	15 41	69 50
♅	0 N 19	23 N 27	97 13	33 36	56 41
♆	1 S 33	4 N 14	13 49	49 50	84 40

calculated for June 21st, 1867, at 11.59 p.m.; and will measure to May
26th, 1893. This was the nearest birthday to the date of the Princess's

Princess of Wales.   Progressed Horoscope, twenty-six years of age.   21st June, 1867, 11.59 p.m.

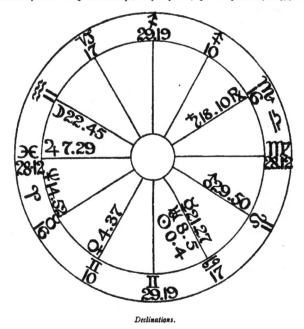

Declinations.

	°	′		°	′		°	′
0 Asc.	43		23 ♉	30		14 ♄	59	
23 M.C.	27		19 ♀	52		23 ♅	31	
23 ☉	27		12 ♂	37		4 ♆	25	
11 ☽	53		9 ♃	45				

marriage (July 6th, 1893). This map is given here, and it shows at a glance the changes that have taken place in the houses, signs, and planets.

In calculating this map, as well as the horoscope of birth, the recorded birth time, 11.59 p.m., is assumed to be Greenwich Mean Time; and as the birth place was about 51 seconds in time West, the true local mean time of birth would be 11hrs. 5min. 9secs., for which latter time, therefore, must the *houses* of horoscope be computed.

A comparison of the two horoscopes will show that the ascendant has progressed to the end of Pisces (the Prince's ascendant is the beginning of Aries) and the cusps of the other houses have altered proportionately.

The method of tabulating directions from two such maps as these will be explained in Chapter VII., but in the meantime it may be mentioned that in this case the following are the chief directions significant of marriage,

$$\odot p. \ast \delta p. \qquad \odot r. \delta ♀ p.$$

The letter p. after a planet refers to the progressed horoscope; the letter r., the radical horoscope (that of birth). These two directions therefore signify that the progressed Sun is in sextile to the progressed Mars; and that the progressed Venus has advanced to the conjunction of the radical Sun. These are both very characteristic of such an event as marriage.

A comparison of the two horoscopes will show that the mid-heaven and the Sun both advance, roughly speaking, about one degree per annum; the rate of advance of the ascendant depends upon whether a sign of long or short ascension is rising. But the fact that there should be any advance at all of the angles of the horoscope at the end of each complete day is extremely important; for it shows that although the primary method of progression by axial rotation can be nominally separated from the secondary method of progression by orbital revolution, in reality the two go on together, are perfectly co-ordinated, and the second includes and necessitates the first.

As we have seen, if a progressed horoscope be drawn for each successive day of life, the mid-heaven is found to have advanced about one degree in each map. At this rate, at the end of 365 days, the cusps of the houses will have performed one complete rotation, and the signs will be found again as they were at birth. The complete rotation which takes place once every day, also takes place once every year; the day is, as it were, spread out over the year, and made to measure the year. All the directions that are included in the primary system, without a single exception, are also involved in the secondary system. The separation of the two systems is only a matter of convenience, because different methods of calculation have to be followed; but there is no such separation in nature; they are two halves of one whole.

TABLE OF ROTATIONS.

Diurnal.		Annual.	
Time	M.C.	Date	M.C.
Birth	6° ♐	Birth	6° ♐
2 hours	3° ♑	1 month	4° ♑
4 "	2° ♒	2 "	1° ♒
6 "	2° ♓	3 "	2° ♓
8 "	4° ♈	4 "	5° ♈
10 "	6° ♉	5 "	7° ♉
12 "	6° ♊	6 "	7° ♊
14 "	4° ♋	7 "	4° ♋
16 "	2° ♌	8 "	3° ♌
18 "	2° ♍	9 "	4° ♍
20 "	5° ♎	10 "	5° ♎
22 "	7° ♏	11 "	7° ♏

This table illustrates the rotation of the day, and compares it with that of the year. Starting with the Princess of Wales's horoscope, the mid-heaven of which is 6° ♐, it shows that two hours after birth the mid-heaven has advanced one sign; four hours after, two signs; and so on, until it describes a complete circle in twenty-four hours. Starting again from birth, if a new horoscope be drawn one calendar month afterwards, at the same hour and minute as at birth, the mid-heaven will be found to have advanced one sign; two months after birth, two signs; and so on, until this also describes a complete circle in twelve months. The circle of the day is thus prolonged over the year, and any given two hours of the day may be shown to correspond to a month of the year. The other houses of the horoscope of course follow the motion of the mid-heaven, as may be seen by reference to a Table of Houses for London; but for the sake of brevity only the mid-heaven is shown here.

These two rotations go on together. Starting from the moment of birth, the meridian describes one complete circle, and returns to its radical position at the same hour and minute the next day, *plus* its advance of about one degree. During the second day of life a second rotation occurs, and the meridian has advanced another degree at end of it. On each day, therefore, there is the diurnal rotation, which given in the first half of the table, and the increase of one degree, the day's proper proportion of the annual rotation, given in the second half of the table.

In calculating progressed horoscopes, the student must not forget that, between any consecutive two of them, one complete diurnal rotation has taken place, during which all those combinations of positions which constitute primary directions have been formed and dissolved. This diurnal rotation between the progressed horoscope for one birthday and that for the next, corresponds, of course, to the intervening year of life, at the rate of two hours to the month. The months when malefics or their radical places are angular in this diurnal rotation are unfortunate ; and it has been shown that the ascendant calculated in this way is sometimes the same as the actual rising sign at the moment of some important occurrence. For cases bearing upon the moment of death, treated in this way, see *Modern Astrology*, Vol. II. (New Series), p. 311.

If the question be asked why these changes among the heavenly bodies should correspond to the events of life, we find ourselves compelled to assume that it is because similar changes are taking place within the man himself. At birth, the subtle forces operating in man's body, and constituting his characteristics and powers physically expressed, answer exactly to the positions of signs and planets ; and Natal Astrology is simply an interpretation of the latter in terms of the former, of planets and signs in terms of character and fate. After birth, changes at once begin to take place within the man, answering to similar changes occurring outside him in the heavens. We are apparently driven to the conclusion that those sets of changes which, in the universe, the macrocosm, take place in a day, in man, the microcosm, are spread out over a year. So that when such a direction as the conjunction of the Sun with Venus takes place (as in the Princess's horoscope) twenty-six days after birth, the similar subtle changes within the living human being are not completed until twenty-six years of age ; and this is why the direction measures to the event.

If we examine the experiences through which a man passes, we find that they are divisible into two classes ; events originating within himself, due to changes of character or conduct, good or bad, over which he has, or ought to have, control ; and events forced upon him by his environment, and over which he has no control. As an illustration of occurrences belonging to the first of these classes, we may take trouble caused by some expression of ill-temper on his part, or pleasure resulting from some manifestation of affection or benevolence. As an illustration of the second class, there are such events as sudden death in a railway accident, or the inheritance of a title by the eldest son of a peer ; for over these he has no control. Of late years there has been a growing tendency to interpret the horoscope, both radical and progressed, in terms of character and its modifications. This is as it should be ; for, as the world at large very well knows, most of our troubles are more or less our own fault ; that is to say, they belong mainly to the first of the two classes just mentioned. Events that belong solely to the second class are comparatively few ; and there cannot be much doubt that Astrology in the past has been far too fatalistic, far too much inclined to regard all events foreshadowed in the horoscope as if they were a necessary and unavoidable fate. The Great Architect of the Universe can bring events to pass through a man's own actions as well as through those occurrences which he cannot control.

It is easy to see how those subtle changes within a man's own being, to which reference has previously been made, can produce changes of mood, temper, disposition, character ; how one change may conduce to irritability, another to displays of affection, a third to despondency, and so on ; and how corresponding events may result from these. The second class of events, those that cannot be averted, necessitate our belief in the intervention of those superhuman controllers of man's destiny who are appointed to carry out the divine will and purpose in evolution. The suggestion has been made that possibly the two systems of directing, the primary and secondary, may correspond to the two classes of events ; the former to the inevitable occurrences and the latter to those resulting from modifications of character and mood. But this is at present only con-jecture—though it indicates a profitable time of research for enthusiastic students.

Readers interested in the points here raised will find some interest-ing suggestions in Appendices II. and V. at the end of this book, in the former of which is given an easy way of determining the principal " primary " directions for any year.

CHAPTER VII.

An Example of the Calculation of a Progressed Horoscope, from the Nativity of the Editor of "Modern Astrology."

It will no doubt assist the reader if an example is given of the manner of calculating the Progressed Horoscope: and it will perhaps be well also to show how the aspects should be computed and set down in a systematic manner, so that important ones do not get overlooked, as might otherwise happen.

We will take by way of illustration the nativity of the Editor of *Modern Astrology*, which is given on the page facing Chapter I., and the simplest and quickest method of going to work will be described; the one, in short, which requires the least amount of calculation.

We will suppose that we require the Progressed Horoscope for the year 1907. We will not introduce the expression "47th year of life," because one is apt to get muddled between the two years, that in which a man is in (say) his "47th year" and the year following, when he is "47 years old": the method given avoids that difficulty.

We proceed thus, counting by tens to avoid any "slips":—

Birth	5.49 *a.m.*	7/8/'60	corresponds to the year commencing August 7th,			1850
then	,,	,, 17/8/'60	,,	,,	,,	1870
and	,,	,, 27/8/'60	,,	,,	,,	1880
,,	,,	,, 6/9/'60	,,	,,	,,	1890
,,	,,	,, 16/9/'60	,,	,,	,,	1900
,,	,,	,, 22/9/'60	,,	,,	,,	1906

The date last given is the one we want, since it furnishes the P.H. for the year required, 1906-7.

The Progressed Horoscope is therefore to be calculated for 5.49 a.m., (which may be taken as the true local time, since the birthplace,

Westminster, is less than 30 seconds W. of Greenwich), 22/9/'60, just as one would calculate an ordinary horoscope : thus,

	h.	m.	s.
Sidereal Time at Noon, G.M.T., 21/9/'60	12	2	20
Add time elapsed (12h. om. + 5h. 49m.)	17	49	0
Correction from mean to sidereal time, 17h.		2	48
„ „ „ „ 49m.			8
	29	54	16
Less circle of 24 hours	24	0	0
Gives S.T. for Progressed Horoscope	5	54	16

The cusps of the houses are therefore duly inserted in the map in accordance with this Sidereal Time.

IMPORTANT NOTE.

At this point it becomes possible to introduce a modification which means a great saving of labour where many maps have to be calculated, and which need lead to no confusion or mistake if reasonable care is exercised.

In order to avoid any possible misunderstanding let us explain all in detail. In the given map,

5.49 a.m. 22/9/'60 measures to the year commencing August 8th, 1906
and 5.49 a.m. 23/9/'60   „   „   „   „   August 8th, 1907
consequently if the planets' places were calculated for any time between these two dates, say 5.49 *p.m.*, 22/9/'60, they would represent the progressed places of those planets on a date *between* August 7th, 1906, and August 7th, 1907 ; namely, in this instance, February 7th, 1907.

All this is quite obvious, or if not, a moment's thought will make it clear. In the same way, therefore, if this process is reversed, the planets' places could be ascertained so as to correspond to any date desired— January 1st, 1907, for instance. But the most useful application that can be made of this principle is, to utilise the position of the planets just as they are given in the Ephemeris, *i.e.*, for mean noon, Greenwich time (G.M.T.) on any date.

For, to take the horoscope we are dealing with, if 5.49 a.m. measures to August 7th, and twenty-four hours is, as has been shown, equivalent to one year (2hrs.=1 month: 4 mins.=1 day), it is clear that *noon* will measure to three months and two days later, *i.e.*, November 9th. Hence, if we take the planets' places as given in the Ephemeris for noon on September 22nd, 1860, we shall have their "progressed positions' corresponding to November 9th, 1906, which is quite near enough to the commencement of 1907 for our purpose. For the sake of distinction we will call this date of the year corresponding to noon on the day on which the P.H. falls due (November 9th in this case) the "limiting date."

It can easily be seen what a saving of time this means—when calculating the progressed maps for a family of people, for instance—for instead of making any calculations whatsoever, as regards the planets, one has only to copy out the degrees and minutes exactly as they are given in the Ephemeris.

Clearly, of course, if the given time of birth in this case had been *p.m.*, noon would have measured to 3 months and 2 days *before* August 7th, namely, May 5th. Similarly any other time can be adjusted to noon by considering the progressed horoscope to date from the equivalent portion of the year, instead of from the birthday, as it otherwise would.

N.B. (1) It is important to avoid the error of computing the *houses* for noon; as has been shown in the calculation given above, they must be reckoned for the actual time at birth, *a.m.* or *p.m.* as the case may be, on the given day—which latter, by the way, has by some been called The Progressed Birthday, a very convenient term. (2) Another important thing is to understand clearly that such a horoscope is a "makeshift," a convenience, and not a true astronomical figure. In order to avoid any confusion, it is advisable to write the letters P.A.N. (*planets at noon*) boldly in the centre of the figure: otherwise all sorts of mistakes might be made, especially if the map were shown to anyone without explanation. (3) Further, if one desires to include the Part of Fortune, that *must* be properly calculated for the correct time, though the moon's place itself may be given its noon position in the map. (4) As can easily be seen, the *true* Progressed Ascendant at the date given, November 9th, would be about 11' more than is here shown, namely ♍ 29.10; similarly, the true progressed M.C. should be ♊ 28.52; but it is scarcely necessary to trouble about such precision of detail in ordinary cases. (5) *In the case of Foreign Horoscopes, the student must be careful to calculate his "limiting date," as we have called it, by the difference between—not the given Local or Standard time of birth, but—the equivalent G.M.T. of birth and (Greenwich) Noon of the day under consideration. Neglect of this precaution in the case of American horoscopes, for instance, would throw calculations out three months or more.*

The two maps can now be compared.

PROGRESSED HOROSCOPE FOR 1907.

Dating from November 9th, 1906, to November 9th, 1907.

(Houses calculated for 5.49 a.m., Planets for 0.0 p.m., 22/9/'60 : London.)

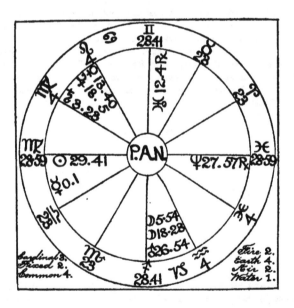

NOTE.—The two positions given for the Moon indicate its progressed position for 9/11/'06 and 9/11/'07 respectively.

1. The first thing to look at is the *angles* of the new figure, to see if either of these has arrived at the conjunction or aspect of any radical planet: if so, this forms a "Primary" direction, and is of great importance; this matter has been touched on in Appendix II. In the present case, we find the progressed Descendant coincident with the radical Neptune; we also find the progressed Ascendant coincident with the progressed Sun.

These aspects, which are quite *sui generis*, may be tabulated thus

Asc. p. ☌ ☉p.; 8 ♆r.

2. The next thing to do is to compare the declinations. They need only be expressed to the nearest degree, and it is unnecessary to add N. or S. Parallels of declination should not be considered unless within one degree of completion. They remain in force for a period of several years, serving as a "balance in hand," so to speak, buoying up other aspects that may be in force meanwhile. It is well to consider them as a class quite apart from "aspects" properly so called, since they are measured in another plane, virtually perpendicular to the Zodiac.

DECLINATIONS.

	Radical.	*Progressed.*
	°	°
☽	11	25—24—23
☉	16	0
☿	10	1
♀	15	15
♂	28	25
♃	19	16
♄	14	12
♅	22	22
♆	2	2

Here we see that the Moon is moving to the parallel of Uranus (*r.* and *p.*), that Jupiter has moved to the parallel of the radical Sun, and Mercury to that of Neptune: these we state thus

☽ p. P. ♅ r., p.   ♃ p. P. ☉ r.   ☿ p. P. ♆ r., p.

3. The next thing is to determine the aspects proper. To do this systematically, the best way is to set down in parallel columns the radical and progressed positions both of the planets and also the *angles*.

A	B	C	D	E	F	G
(+15)		Radical.		Progressed		(±15)
13	28	♌	Asc.	♍	29	14
1	16	♉	M.C.	♊	29	14
5	20	♌ .... ☿ .... ♎			0	15
3	18	♋ .... ♀ .... ♌			14	29
0—30	15	♌ ....☉ .... ♎			0	15
5	20	♑ .... ♂ .... ♑			27	12
23	8	♌ .... ♃ .... ♌			18	3
13	28	♌ .... ♄ .... ♍			3	18
26	11	♊ .... ♅ .... ♊			12	27
14	29	♓ .... ♆ .... ♓			28	13
0—30	15	♈ .... ☽ .... ♑			6	21
				Dec.	7	22
				Jan.	8	23
				Feb.	9	24
	NOTE.—The Moon's mo-			Mar.	10	25
	tion being about twelve			Apr.	11	26
	times that of the planets,			May	12	27
	it is necessary to set down			June	13	28
	the position for each			July	14	29
	month.			Aug.	15	30—0
				Sept.	16	1
				Oct.	17	2
				Nov.	18	3

The making out of a table like this occupies but a very few minutes, and requires absolutely no calculation. The nearest degree is set down, the zodiacal symbols being placed as shown for the sake of clearness. The columns headed "(±15)" are formed by adding or subtracting fifteen to the adjacent number; thus, in the first column, 28—15=13; 16—15=1; 8+15=23, and so on. The Moon's position is given separately at the foot, and will be considered later.

The use of this table is as follows:—The figures in all the columns represent those which alone can indicate any complete aspect. If therefore on taking the planets in order, the figures given on the right are also found in either of the left-hand columns, there is a possibility of those two being in aspect. This *possibility* can thus be seen at a glance and calls for no reckoning, while a moment's thought will show whether or no they really are in aspect or not.*

We first find the aspects of progressed planets and cusps to radical, and next the aspects of the progressed among themselves.

For instance, in column F " Asc. p. " is seen to be 29. A glance to the left shows us ♅ 29 in column B; and a further glance, that these are ♓ and ♍ respectively. Accordingly we write down, "Asc. p. ☍ ♅ r., ◻ M.C. p." We find no other 29 in either of the left-hand columns; but there is a 28 — twice over — and so we write down Asc. p., ⚺ Asc. r., ♄ r.

Next we take the M.C. p., 29: in the other column we see ♄ 28; and we write down M.C. p. ⚹ ♄ r.

Again, we find ☿ o (15) and, on the left, ☉ 15 (o): this suggests, and a glance confirms it, that ☿ p. is ∠ ☉ r.

And so we proceed, taking the planets in order one after the other, and referring the progressed planets first to the radical, and afterwards to the remaining progressed planets.

This plan may seem tedious in description, but it is very simple in actual use. In reckoning up the aspects, the simplest plan is to take the numbers given in columns F and G against the planet whose progressed position is being considered. Cast the eye first down column B, and if either of the numbers appears, a possible aspect to a *radical* planet or angle is indicated, which if confirmed on examination is entered on this list : next, the same process is repeated with column F, which will show in the same way any aspect to a *progressed* planet or angle. A few minutes' practice will render this both rapid and easy.

Remember this : figures occurring both in columns B and F indicate ⚺, ⚹, ◻, △, ⚼ or ☍ : figures occurring both in columns B and G (or A and F) indicate only ∠, ⚻, or no aspect at all.

---

* For only 15°, 75°, and 105°, of spaces which are *not* aspects, can be so shown : all others, therefore, *must be aspects of some kind*, those between either of the outer columns and an inner column being either semi-square or sesquiquadrate aspects.

We thus become possessed of two lists for each series, Solar, Mutual and Lunar.

SOLAR.

P. to R.	*P. to P.*
☉ ∠ ☉	☉ ☌ ☿
☿ ∠ ☉	☉ ☌ Asc.

MUTUAL.

☿ ⊡ M.C.	☿ □ M.C.
♀ ☌ ☉	♀ ∠ M.C., ∠ Asc.
♀ ⊡ ♆	♀ ⊡ ♆
♂ ⊼ ♄, Asc.	(♂ △ Asc., ⊼ M.C.)
♄ ∠ ☿	♂ ⊡ ♅
	♂ ⚹ ♆
♅ ⊼ ♄, Asc.	♅ ☍ Asc., □ M.C.

LUNAR.

☽ ⊡ ☿,	Oct., 1906		
☽ ⊼ ♃,	Jan., 1907		
☽ ⊡ ♅,	Apr. „	⊼ ♅, May, 1907	
☽ ⊡ ♄,	June „	⊼ ♀, July „	
☽ ⊼ ☉,	Aug. „		
☽ △ M.C.,	Sep. „		
☽ ☍ ♀,	Nov. „	⊼ ♃, Nov. „	

As to the lunar Aspects, since the Moon moves in a year (day) twelve or thirteen degrees, it is advisable to set out each degree passed through during that time, and also the $\pm$ 15 degrees corresponding thereto, remembering that each after the first will fall due about a month later, so that the last in the list, if it should prove to be in aspect to any planet, would not come into operation till about October, 1907. This has been clearly shewn in the example list just given.

No doubt a little practice will enable the student who is quick at figures to dispense with the trouble of making out a table in the manner here given. But it has this great recommendation, that it ensures that no aspect shall be overlooked; and semi-squares and sesquiquadrates are especially likely to be missed—except of course by those who are very experienced. Should there be any doubt, the student can refer to the table of aspects given on p. 48.

When all the aspects are set out in this way, the list looks somewhat formidable at a first glance, but a very little judgment will enable one to select the most important ones. For instance, ☉ ∠ ☉, ♀ ☌

⊙, ♂ ⚺ ♄, *radical :* and ⊙ ♂ ☿ and Asc.,* ♂ △ Asc. and ✱ ♆, *progressed :*
are the most significant in the present case. (Asc. ♊ ♆ and ⊙ ♊ ♆r. and
p. are within orbs but are actually past at the period for which this map
is calculated.)

It now only remains to look out the meanings of each individual
aspect as given in the latter part of the book, and the work is done.

In Section B. of this book the Solar, Lunar and Mutual aspects
are severally given in the order of the planets from Mercury to Neptune,
the aspects following in rotation thus,

P. ♂ ⚺ ∠ ✱   □   △   ⬠   ⚻ (150°) ☍ .

The meaning of each one may be looked up in turn, and then an
endeavour made to synthesise the whole, so as to form some idea of the
" net result," so to speak, of a series of very various influences.

It should of course never be forgotten that the fundamental aspects
are ♂ □ ☍ △ ✱, and that the others are all subsidiary to them.

---

* This, however, does not become *exact* during the year.

CHAPTER VIII.

Subdivisions of Signs.

There are many methods of subdividing and classifying both the zodiac as a whole and also each separate sign. The reader will be familiar with the division into pairs of houses, each pair ruled by one planet; into the three qualities, rájasic (cardinal), támasic (fixed), and sáttvic (common or mutable); into the four elements, fire, earth, air, water; and into the six male or positive and six female or negative signs.

TABLE OF TRIPLICITIES AND QUALITIES.

		Cardinal.			Fixed.			Mutable.
Triplicity.	Sign.	Nature.	Sign.	Nature.		Sign.	Nature
FIRE	+ ♈	Impulsive	♌	Organising		♐	Inspirational
WATER	− ♋	Tenacious	♏	Solidifying		♓	Relaxative
AIR	+ ♎	Uniting	♒	Concentrative		♊	Diffusive
EARTH	− ♑	Retentive	♉	Decisive		♍	Analytical
PERIOD		Short duration		Long duration			Medium duration

There are even more methods of subdividing each of the signs; but for the purposes of the present work, the only two that need detain us are the " decanates " and the " dwadashámshas."

TABLE OF DECANATES.

	First.	Second.	Third.
Sign.	1°-10°	10°-20°	20°-30°
♈	♈	♌	♐
♉	♉	♍	♑
♊	♊	♎	♒
♋	♋	♏	♓
♌	♌	♐	♈
♍	♍	♑	♉
♎	♎	♒	♊
♏	♏	♓	♋
♐	♐	♈	♌
♑	♑	♉	♍
♒	♒	♊	♎
♓	♓	♋	♏

In the classification by decanates, each sign is divided into three equal parts containing ten degrees each. In any sign, the first decanate is of the nature of the sign itself; the second contains an undercurrent of influence from the next sign of the same triplicity, counting in the order of the signs; and the third contains a similar influence from the third sign of the same triplicity. This will be made clear by the table.

Thus the first decanate of Aries is purely Aries; the second is Aries with a sub-influence of Leo; and the third is Aries with a sub-influence of Sagittarius. It must not be forgotten, however, that in each case the influence of the sign as a whole comes first in importance; and that the influence of the subdivision only modifies that of the sign slightly without altering its inherent nature.

(It may be mentioned that these influences are real and actual in their natures, quite as much so as those of the signs. A case is recorded in which the elder of two twins was picked out from a photograph solely from a knowledge of the two decanates, ♍-♑ and ♍-♉, under which the children had been born.)

TABLE OF DWADASHÁMSHAS.*

(First Decanate.)				(Second Decanate.)				(Third Decanate.)			
i.	ii.	iii.	iv.	v.	vi.	vii.	viii.	ix.	x.	xi.	xii.
0°	2¼°	5°	7½°	10°	12½°	15°	17½°	20°	22½°	25°	27½°
2¼°	5°	7½°	10°	12½°	15°	17½°	20°	22½°	25°	27½°	30°

Sign.

Sign.	i.	ii.	iii.	iv.	v.	vi.	vii.	viii.	ix.	x.	xi.	xii.
♈	♉	♊	♋	♌	♍	♎	♏	♐	♑	♒	♓	♈
♉	♊	♋	♌	♍	♎	♏	♐	♑	♒	♓	♈	♉
♊	♋	♌	♍	♎	♏	♐	♑	♒	♓	♈	♉	♊
♋	♌	♍	♎	♏	♐	♑	♒	♓	♈	♉	♊	♋
♌	♍	♎	♏	♐	♑	♒	♓	♈	♉	♊	♋	♌
♍	♎	♏	♐	♑	♒	♓	♈	♉	♊	♋	♌	♍
♎	♏	♐	♑	♒	♓	♈	♉	♊	♋	♌	♍	♎
♏	♐	♑	♒	♓	♈	♉	♊	♋	♌	♍	♎	♏
♐	♑	♒	♓	♈	♉	♊	♋	♌	♍	♎	♏	♐
♑	♒	♓	♈	♉	♊	♋	♌	♍	♎	♏	♐	♑
♒	♓	♈	♉	♊	♋	♌	♍	♎	♏	♐	♑	♒
♓	♈	♉	♊	♋	♌	♍	♎	♏	♐	♑	♒	♓

In the classification by dwadashámshas, each sign is divided into twelve equal parts of 2¼°. This is a Hindu method of subdivision, and more than one way of applying it has been indicated by the various schools; but the one we have hitherto found to give the best results is that employed in the accompanying table.

* "Sesqui-alterate" would be the equivalent *Latin-derived* word, corresponding to "decanate."

It is a well-known principle in occultism, that each part of a whole reflects the whole within itself. Thus, each one of the seven cosmic planes reflects the whole cosmos within itself, and so becomes divisible into seven subplanes. When this principle is applied to the zodiac, we have each of the twelve signs reflecting the whole twelve within itself, and so giving rise to the dwadashâmshas.

As with the decanates so here; it must not be forgotten that, no matter into how many parts a sign may be divided, the influence of the sign is predominant everywhere, and the influence of the part is subordinate to that of the sign. On the other hand, it is also true that each part, when considered alone, is a whole in itself. Thus each sign, although only a twelfth part of the zodiac, is complete and perfect in itself; and so is each decanate and each dwadashâmsha, when considered apart from all the rest. It would not be correct, for instance, to assume that the influence of the first dwadashâmsha of Aries is composed of the influence of the first degree of Aries plus that of the second degree plus that of the first half of the third degree. It is quite true that it covers this extent of longitude; but nevertheless, each dwadashâmsha, when considered in itself, is an indivisible whole, uniform throughout.

The manner in which the decanate modifies the influence of the rising sign in the horoscope of birth has been given in *How to Judge a Nativity, Part I.*, Chapter VI.; and the modifying influence of decanates upon the progressed ascendant is given in Chapter IX. of the present work. The reader who is familiar with these two chapters will be able to estimate for himself the modifications that will be introduced by the successive dwadashâmshas through which the ascendant progresses by direction after birth; and it will, therefore, not be necessary to tabulate them in detail. One or two illustrations may be given, however, to make the method clear.

Let us suppose that, in any horoscope, the ascendant has progressed so as to be just entering the first dwadashâmsha of Aries. This is an ♈-♉ influence. While passing through this division, the energy and impulse of Aries will be directed towards pleasure, enjoyment, holiday-making, etc. (♀ ruling), and some financial matter will arise for settlement, whether favourable or the reverse will depend upon the prevailing directions.

When the ascendant enters the second dwadashâmsha of Aries, which is ♈-♊, intellectual matters, or affairs bearing upon books, writings, education and brethren, will be to the fore, and many short journeys will be taken.

While passing through the third dwadashâmsha, ♈-♋, home and the household will occupy the attention; sometimes a move will be made, or a house acquired for the first time; the affairs of the mother may come forward in the life, or a journey by water be undertaken; and if the directions are bad, sorrow may result from any of these causes.

The occult teaching is that our whole solar system, visible and invisible, forms the body of one great Being, its creator and sustainer. His consciousness and vitality permeate it everywhere, so that all smaller modes of energy and consciousness within the system are only modifications of His own, appropriated and altered by the various classes of lesser beings through whom it flows. The twelve signs of the zodiac are twelve modes of this life and consciousness transmitted through twelve different classes of beings, each class a mighty host in itself; and to one or other of those classes every human being belongs spiritually.

Concerning the subdivisions of these signs, we have as yet little positive information from occultists; but the probability is that analogy holds good. We may look upon decanates, dwadashâmshas, and such other subdivisions as are really existent in nature (in contradistinction from those that are only mathematical abstractions) as representing classes of beings subordinate in nature and powers to those belonging to the sign as a whole, but each one as truly living and conscious an entity as is man himself, and each with a definite part to play and work to do within the system. This helps to explain the apparent anomaly that some of these subdivisions of signs are represented by other signs not in sympathy with the one in which they fall; for instance, the sign Aries contains the Taurus, Cancer, Libra and Pisces dwadashâmshas; and Mars, the lord of Aries, is not well placed in any of these. Here we have groups of energies, modes of consciousness, called forth under various circumstances and exercising various powers, not really antagonistic to those pertaining to the main sign, Aries, under which they are classified. The work of the beings representing the subdivisions is in furtherance of that of the greater beings who represent the signs, although differing in detail; just as the work of a private soldier is different from that of his colonel, and both of these from that of the Commander-in-Chief.

It is also highly probable that the influence of subdivisions is not exerted uniformly. It seems likely that one planet when passing through a sign, may tend to call out the influence of one particular kind of sub-division, and another planet that of another. By this it is meant not merely that Mars, for instance, is strong in an Aries subdivision and Venus in a Taurus one; but rather that one planet tends to subdivide a sign by, say, three, another planet by seven, and another by twelve. Thus, when the planet signifying three is rising, the influence of deca-nates will be far more noticeable than at another time; and when the one which signifies twelve rises, the dwadashâmshas will be the most potent.

Some such variation as this must certainly exist; for, as the student will discover from personal experience, while the signs are unmistakable in their natures, the subdivisions do not seem to be of uniform importance in all horoscopes.

TABLE OF ASPECTS

SHOWING THE VARIOUS DEGREES IN ASPECT TO ANY GIVEN DEGREE.

Degree and Sign	30° ⚹	45° ∠	60° ✶	90° □	120° △	135° ⚼	150° ⚻	180° ☍
♈	♓ ♉	♉ ♒ ♊ ♓	♊ ♒	♋ ♑	♌ ♐	♌ ♏ ♍ ♐	♍ ♏	♎
♉	♈ ♊	♊ ♓ ♋ ♈	♋ ♒	♋ ♓	♍ ♑	♍ ♐ ♎ ♑	♎ ♐	♏
♊	♉ ♋	♋ ♈ ♌ ♉	♌ ♈	♍ ♓	♎ ♒	♎ ♑ ♏ ♈	♏ ♑	♐
♋	♊ ♌	♌ ♉ ♍ ♊	♍ ♉	♎ ♈	♏ ♓	♐ ♈ ♑ ♈	♑ ♈	♑
♌	♋ ♍	♍ ♊ ♎ ♋	♎ ♊	♏ ♉	♐ ♈	♐ ♒ ♑ ♉	♑ ♊	♒
♍	♌ ♏	♏ ♌ ♐ ♍	♐ ♌	♑ ♋	♒ ♊	♒ ♉ ♓ ♊	♓ ♉	♈
♎	♍ ♐	♐ ♍ ♑ ♎	♑ ♍	♒ ♌	♓ ♋	♓ ♊ ♈ ♋	♈ ♊	♉
♏	♎ ♑	♑ ♎ ♒ ♏	♒ ♎	♓ ♍	♈ ♌	♈ ♋ ♉ ♌	♉ ♋	♊
♐	♏ ♒	♒ ♏ ♓ ♐	♓ ♏	♈ ♎	♉ ♍	♉ ♌ ♊ ♍	♊ ♌	♋
♑	♐ ♓	♓ ♐ ♈ ♑	♈ ♐	♉ ♏	♊ ♎	♊ ♍ ♋ ♎	♋ ♍	♌
♒	♑ ♈	♈ ♑ ♉ ♒	♉ ♑	♊ ♐	♋ ♏	♋ ♎ ♌ ♏	♌ ♎	♍

o	o	o	o	o	o	o	o	o
1	1	16	.	1	1	1	16	.	1	1
2	2	17	.	2	2	2	17	.	2	2
3	3	18	.	3	3	3	18	.	3	3
4	4	19	.	4	4	4	19	.	4	4
5	5	20	.	5	5	5	20	.	5	5
6	6	21	.	6	6	6	21	.	6	6
7	7	22	.	7	7	7	22	.	7	7
8	8	23	.	8	8	8	23	.	8	8
9	9	24	.	9	9	9	24	.	9	9
10	10	25	.	10	10	10	25	.	10	10
11	11	26	.	11	11	11	26	.	11	11
12	12	27	.	12	12	12	27	.	12	12
13	13	28	.	13	13	13	28	.	13	13
14	14	29	.	14	14	14	29	.	14	14
15	15	30	.	15	15	15	30	.	15	15
16	16	.	1	16	16	16	.	1	16	16
17	17	.	2	17	17	17	.	2	17	17
18	18	.	3	18	18	18	.	3	18	18
19	19	.	4	19	19	19	.	4	19	19
20	20	.	5	20	20	20	.	5	20	20
21	21	.	6	21	21	21	.	6	21	21
22	22	.	7	22	22	22	.	7	22	22
23	23	.	8	23	23	23	.	8	23	23
24	24	.	9	24	24	24	.	9	24	24
25	25	.	10	25	25	25	.	10	25	25
26	26	.	11	26	26	26	.	11	26	26
27	27	.	12	27	27	27	.	12	27	27
28	28	.	13	28	28	28	.	13	28	28
29	29	.	14	29	29	29	.	14	29	29
30	30	.	15	30	30	30	.	15	30	30

EXAMPLE.—Suppose the degree we are concerned with is ♌20°, the ⚹ is ♒20° or ♍20°, the ✶ is ♊20° or ♎20°, and similarly with the others; the ∠ will be ♋5° or ♎5°, and the □ ♏5° or ♈5°. In the same way, also, the aspects to any other degree may be seen at a glance.

Section B.

CHAPTER IX.

THE PROGRESSED ASCENDANT.

As has been explained in a previous chapter the horoscope progresses, at the rate of about one degree per year, until in course of time a new sign comes to the ascendant—thereby to a certain extent transferring the rulership of the Progressed Horoscope to its own ruling planet, though the influence of the original ruler of the nativity remains paramount throughout life. Thus if Gemini ascends at birth, Mercury is the ruling planet during the whole life; but when the progressed ascendant becomes Cancer, then the Moon begins to exercise a powerful influence over the temperament, though the Mercurial characteristics will still reign supreme over the disposition as a whole.

There is yet another consideration, and that is the sub-influence of each decanate. The nature of these has been described in Chapter VIII. of the last section, and their general influence on character and fortune as they progressively control the ascendant will form the contents of the present chapter.

As regards the planetary rulership of the Progressed Ascendant, it should be borne in mind that the ruler of the sign itself will during the period of the said sign's ascendancy have the main influence over the life, but it will have as assistant and coadjutor the planet ruling the decanate rising. For instance—if the first decanate of Aries is rising (♈-♈), the influence will be wholly Martial; if the second decanate (♈-♌), chiefly Martial, but partly Solar; if the third (♈-♐), chiefly Martial, but partly Jupiterian; and so on with the others.

To sum up. At any given moment in the native's life the most prominent zodiacal influences affecting him will be those having control over the following factors, in the order given, the first having the widest

D

and most general and the last the most restricted and limited yet particular influence.

FUNDAMENTAL INFLUENCES.

(A) SIGN   on the cusp of the Ascendant at Birth and its ruler*
(B) DECANATE   „   „   „   „   „
(C) Dwadashamsha   „   „   „   „   „
  (D)Degree   „   „   „   „   „

SUPERIMPOSED INFLUENCES.

(a) SIGN   on cusp of Ascendant of "Progressed Horoscope" and its ruler†
(b) DECANATE   „   „   „   „   „   „
(c) Dwadashamsha   „   „   „   „   „   „
(d) Degree   „   „   „   „   „   „

In considering these in their relation to each other, *a b c* and *d* may figuratively speaking be regarded as " growing grain," in the " husks " of *A B C D*. For simplicity's sake, the influences of *C, D, c, d,* may be altogether neglected for the present.

IMPORTANT NOTE.—The delineation given of the first decanate of each Sign will apply in a general sense to *the whole Sign;* the first decanate initiates the life impulse given by the sign, the two subsequent decanates modify and refine it.

THE PROGRESSED ASCENDANT.—ARIES.

♈—♈   The ascendant of the horoscope having progressed to the
 ♂-♂   first decanate of Aries, all matters relating to the head, and also all "first house " affairs, will now be prominent in the native's life. He will want to lead and be at the head of things, and will in all probability meet with some recognition in the sphere in which he moves He will be more aspiring and ambitious, will desire progress, and will wish to reform existing conditions.   He will be actively inclined towards intellectual pursuits, and will be very anxious to learn and gain all the knowledge and information he can.   This decanate of Aries rising indicates that he is becoming more progressive, also that he is ready to take a keener and deeper interest in life.   He will now have abundant opportunities for progress, but he has arrived at that stage wherein the

* Called the Radical Ascendant and Radical Ruler.
† Called the Progressed Ascendant and Progressed Ruler.

progress will be rather of an intellectual and mental than a purely physical nature. The influence of the planet Mars will come prominently into his life, giving him much mental energy with considerable enthusiasm.

♈—♌ If the native could accomplish all that this indicates, and take ♂·☉ advantage of all the opportunities that this progressed ascendant brings, he would join head and heart, and thus quickly accomplish the mission of life; which is the turning of Thought into Wisdom. While this decanate is passing over his ascendant, he will have heart experiences, and will probably have his emotions called out to the full; for it will bring feeling prominently into the life, and will awaken something of the deeper side of his sympathies. It will bring the rejuvenating principle to the fore, causing new life and the advent of fresh experiences. For it is the influence of summer that follows spring, and denotes a period when some of the ambitions may be realised, and when by merit and power he may rise to a higher and better state of things. It will bring a little more of the speculative element, also more enterprise and a loftier spirit, in fact, there is every prospect of gaining many advantages and making much progress while under the influence of this progressed ascendant.

♈—♐ This denotes the probability of some travel, and will very ♂·♃ likely bring an opportunity of going abroad, or of taking some very long journeys. This progressed ascendant brings a somewhat philosophical and religious frame of mind, and marks the advent of loftier views; and it will probably awaken in the native a desire to investigate some of the deeper problems and inner mysteries relating to consciousness and the future: at least, this *should* be the state of his mind, if he has progressed with his horoscope. To those who are as yet unawakened it will cause a more rebellious spirit and a tendency to go against established law and order; but even this will have its good side, for it will tend to stir up the nature to action until a realisation of true law and order comes as the result of the mental activities. If at this time the " directions "* are very evil there will be danger of legal troubles if any dispute or contention should arise; but otherwise this progressed ascendant gives promise of a more fortunate period commencing.

* See footnote, Chapter X., p. 68.

TAURUS.

♉ — ♉   The influence of this sign coming into the life will bring a
♀ - ♀   firmer, more determined tendency into the nature. The native
will be much more practical in his aims and methods, and at the same
time somewhat disposed to be dogmatic in his opinions. He will be
more interested in money-matters and financial affairs will come more
prominently into his life at this time, so that if he engages his mind in
such matters he will now bring increased perseverance and sound method
to bear on his natural activity, resulting in increased prosperity. The
general tendency will be to awaken in the native a spirit of greater
obedience; that is, if he is *really* progressing: but if not, then a far more
obstinate and stubborn nature will be manifested. To cultivate this
obedient spirit he should endeavour to bring out the true attribute of
this sign, which is a silent, persistent, calm recognition of the power of
the internal will within, which can command because there is latent the
power to obey. This may be realised by any one who will dwell upon
the saying of the Teacher, "Whosoever will be chief among you, let
him be your servant."

♉ — ♍   This will bring a more discriminative and critical frame of
♀ - ☿   mind, and cause the native to be not only intuitive but intellect-
ually perceptive as well. It will bring more practical ability either for
business or profession, special work or general industries, and he will
moreover have experiences in connection with sickness and nursing, or
with regard to health matters. He will probably take an enquiring
interest in the laws of hygiene, or become interested in food reform, or
the general welfare of the physical body. The nervous system will
undergo some change, matters wherein the mind will be more active
than heretofore will now engage the attention, and if he can respond to
the new conditions of this decanate it will benefit him in many ways.
If he wishes to investigate occult and mystical things he has now a
good opportunity to do so, for this decanate of Taurus will enable him
to study the psychic side of things from an intellectual standpoint. But
the best attribute of this progressed ascendant is the solid and practical
yet discriminative tendency which it gives, together with the ability to
criticise and analyse all things—including *oneself*.

♉ — ♑   This will awaken some ambition, and stimulate the plodding
♀ - ♄   tendency of Taurus into a more persevering, thrifty, prudent

and industrious expression. The native will now have opportunities to hold more responsible positions in life, and to rise into a higher state wherein some recognition and honour will be acquired. All matters relating to profession or general pursuits in life will now come to the fore ; and if the "root of merit" is well established he may rise to a very high position, or at all events to a much higher sphere in life than that into which he was born. To those who are really progressive this decanate brings a much more steady and thoughtful frame of mind, and a desire for chastity, purity and the acquisition of the physical virtues It marks the commencement of these latter, as described by the blending of the earthy signs, denoting the first step from the mundane and material order of things to the higher and more subjective condition. This is attained by raising the thought atmosphere to a higher standard through a more purified form of physical life, so that the higher and finer vibrations may be felt; and this is frequently brought about by the occult sense of clairaudience, which is sometimes awakened through latent musical ability.

GEMINI.

♊ — ♊   This will bring the native into an entirely new set of conditions,
☿ · ☿   either physical or mental. He will now aspire more eagerly after mental attainments, the mind inclining more in the direction of study and intellectual pursuits than formerly ; and in all directions where knowledge can be obtained he will find either the brain-mind or the sub-conscious mind attracted. He will either travel now more than formerly or have great inclination thereto, or otherwise make many short journeys or excursions, even if it be but taking more walking exercise than usual, the desire for movement being more keenly alive than formerly. More-over he will either come more into contact with relatives or kindred and be more closely concerned in their affairs, or in some way or other they will interest themselves more in his. Correspondence and writing of all kinds will enter more into the daily life, and as he comes more under the influence of this decanate he will find literary work more interesting and of more importance. To those who are making much progress this influence will bring a far greater motive force, and a more intense desire for intellectual advancement and mental improvement. This decanate will bring an enhanced sense of refinement and an accession of thoughtfulness : it is the most positive (physically) of the three decanates.

♊—♎   This will introduce a more peaceful and evenly balanced period,
♉·♀   and probably bring more pleasure and quiet than formerly.
Someone will come into the native's sphere who will influence him for
life, and the two careers will now run on similar lines; so that, each
working in the same groove with the other, much of the responsibility of
life will be shared, and the native's pathway will thus be smoothed to a
considerable extent.   This union with another life is a marked feature of
the decanate; for there has now been reached a stage in evolution when
the active bustle and turmoil of life is to be put on one side for a time.
To those who are making great progress this brings an opportunity to
develop or to cultivate the higher sense of clairvoyance, or clear vision;
to those, however, who are not ready to advance into the more subjective
planes it will bring clearer perception, and awaken a deeper appreciation
of comparisons, allowing them to see both sides of every question in a
far clearer light than hitherto.   Even should no external progress appear
to be made, the advent of this decanate upon the ascendant will bring an
internal progress that will manifest later.

♊—♒   This will bring a new cycle into active expression, for to the
♉·♄   intellectual perception acquired under the sign Gemini a more
fixed and concentrative mentality will be added, giving the native more
power to concentrate his thoughts than formerly and to apply his mind
to deeper studies.   He will now make some new friends, and their
friendship will be very helpful and beneficial.   He will also be brought
into touch with groups of persons and with associations, either of a
scientific or occult order.   This progressed ascendant offers some splendid
opportunities for the growth of a more stable mind, and develops a
peculiar ability to judge human nature from an impersonal and unpre-
judiced standpoint; but only those who are really progressive can
abstract all its virtues, for it gives a keener interest in the highest of all
opportunities—the opportunity to enter into the purely human side of
the nature and to abstract the mind from that side of the nature wherein
the lower or personal mind has a stronger voice than the higher or
subjective.   To the ordinary person, however, it merely brings new
acquaintances and increased social intercourse with others.

CANCER.

♋—♋   This new sign ascending will bring into the life a keener interest
☽·☽   in all domestic and home affairs.   It will open up a softer side

of the nature so that it will become receptive and sensitive, more keenly alive in fact to feelings and sensations, and the general psychic (or internal) conditions of the environment and surroundings. The native will find himself feeling vibrations that he was not conscious of before, and a new world will open up within him—of which he may or may not be physically conscious, according to the progress he has made in evolution. To those who can fully respond to this progressed ascendant a psychic centre will awaken, and a greater interest will be taken in all occult and mystical things. But with the ordinary individual, carried blindly along by the tide of evolution, the sensational side of the nature merely will be touched, and the feelings will thus have opportunities to expand; either through personal attachments, or through ties and engagements of one kind or another which will draw out the personal feeling and so evolve sensitiveness. To all it will bring a firmer grip on life, and give that persistence and tenacity which bring keener experiences to the personality.

♋—♏   This progressed ascendant brings the native to a critical stage
☽·♂   in his evolution; and as the influence of each decanate extends over a period of about ten years, he will feel the effects of its influence more or less during the whole of that time. It will bring deaths into the family circle, and sorrow through the feelings and emotions; it also marks a critical stage for the personality, giving liability to infection and to come into contact with some very disagreeable conditions. It will accentuate the passional side of the nature, giving subtler and keener feelings than have hitherto been experienced. To those who are progressing, and advancing their individual growth, it will cause a far deeper interest to be taken in occult and mystical matters, with an ardent desire to understand the mystic side of nature. To the ordinary slowly developing person it will bring more curiosity, a greater love of secrecy, and some secret transactions which will be related to the feeling and emotional side of the nature. To all it will bring an acquisition of dignity, with some danger of jealousy and pride. It will stir up all that is latent in the feeling side of the character and cause the native to undergo some striking experiences.

♋—♓   This will bring an opportunity to ultimately close the account
☽·♃   of the sign Cancer. The effect of this influence upon the life may be unmanifested in its external physical expression, for it is more likely to be felt internally and psychically than outwardly. The native

will become very receptive and far more negative than usual under its influence, so that he will receive vibrations from without to such an extent as to make him painfully sensitive to his environment and general surroundings. He will thus be able to feel the conditions of others and to sense them in a peculiar way, so that he will find himself more than usually hospitable, kind and sympathetic. It will bring some connection with hospitals or institutions into the life, probably for the first time, perhaps some temporary confinement, either through ill-health or other unavoidable causes. To the very progressive this gives the opportunity to taste of that universal love which is free from personal taint; but only to the very advanced comes this touch of the "universal solvent." To the ordinary slowly progressing individual it awakens a fuller sympathy, and brings the feelings to a stage wherein that deeper emotion is experienced which is rather silent than inclined to seek expression.

LEO.

♌ — ♌   An entirely new set of experiences will now commence. The
☉ - ☉   native will have his heart awakened, and the feeling side of the nature will be turned from personal attachment into individual feeling and emotion. He will expand his sentiments and make positive and vital his sympathies, according to his growth in evolution. To the truly progressive, love-ties and heart-emotions will be purified in the fire that ever burns in the heart, and the love-nature will be indrawn until it radiates like the Sun, free and powerful, and illuminative to all. To the ordinary individual it means an excess of vitality, a greater love of pleasure, and to the undeveloped profligacy, or an excess of feeling which may run back into sensation. It will give a keen appreciation of the drama, and some ability to imitate and mimic, the mirthful and cheerful side of the nature being now increased; but to all it will give an opportunity to be more magnanimous and generous, to act kindly, and to be more noble and high-spirited than previously. It will give strength and independence, good health and much better prospects; for the ambitions will be laudable, and ever for the higher development of character and general welfare.

♌ — ♐   This is a fortunate and a more progressive portion of the sign,
☉ - ♃   and it gives many opportunities to expand the Leo characteristics. It will bring a far more philosophical and religious frame of

mind, and cause the native to have more respect for law and order, bringing out the internal harmony of Leo through a philosophical attitude of mind. He will probably take a long journey or travel, and will also come into touch with some phase of higher thought and take some interest in those things that relate to the subjective world. To those who are undeveloped this progressed ascendant will bring a gambling spirit, and a desire to follow speculative or risky ventures. To those able to take advantage of it in the proper manner it means a fortune by speculation ; but the whole of the " directions" must be fortunate to bring about this result. To the fully progressive this decanate will awaken the power to prophesy, or to give vent to very prophetic utterances. While under this influence, the native will have some remarkably vivid dreams and should note them, for they will have some special meaning. It will be a period when the higher mind will act and the intuitions be keener than usual.

♌—♈   This will temper the outgoing energies of Leo and bring more

☉-♂   reason and mind development to balance the feeling and emotional side of the sign. There is, however, some danger of going to extremes while under the rule of this progressed ascendant, for it gives a liability to impulse and to some rash and hasty actions. The native will be more assertive and positive than usual and inclined to become enterprising and very energetic. It will accentuate the activities and cause him to view life from a more progressive and ambitious standpoint. To those who are very progressive it will bring much more of the pioneer spirit and a great desire to lead, and will, if opportunity affords, increase patriotism and enthusiasm : with the ordinary person it will develop more intellect, so that there will be an effort to blend heart with head. But very few can realise the highest standard of this progressed ascendant, which is—*Truth*, and the courage of conviction, enabling one to carry out principles through all obstacles and difficulties. The native will have plenty of force and a great deal of courage, and should under favourable directions profit in many ways through the influence of this decanate ; more especially by his own power and assertiveness, which in its highest aspect should be Will and Self-control.

VIRGO.

♍—♍   This will bring a much more practical and critical frame of mind,

♍-♍   which will ultimately make the native more discriminative and thoughtful than he has hitherto been. It is not a fortunate decanate so far as worldly progress goes, for he may have to keep quiet and work without much apparent result; but it has its lessons to teach, chief of which is discrimination, out of which wisdom is to evolve. Therefore the experience he will gain will be of benefit, and if looked at in this light "the end will justify the means "; for he will be liable to make mistakes under its influence, especially with regard to inferiors in business or those who are of a lower social standing. While under this progressed ascendant he will have an illness or at least will not enjoy his usual health, but will be subject to nervous troubles, especially if he worries or gives way to anxiety. It may bring him somewhat into touch with psychic matters and awaken an interest in the occult, but nothing very vivid or marked will be noticed; except it be the realisation that ability needs opportunity, and that environment is sometimes to be reckoned with, no matter how strong the Ego.

♍—♑   This will awaken the native's ambitions and cause him to be
♉ - ♄   more persevering and anxious to rise in life and gain some recognition; and he will obtain some honour, or have some responsibility placed upon him. It denotes a period in which he will have opportunities to rise in life, or to gain advantages through perseverance and anxious endeavour. He will gain diplomacy and tact either through business pursuits, work and employment, or through daily contact with others. To those who are very progressive it brings the opportunity to serve, and through service to gain honourable success: to those so placed it will bring wealth, honours, and some public recognition. A great improvement in the affairs of life is often brought about through personal merit; but to the majority it means very little, simply the opportunity to gain advancement with some promotion, and a certain amount of success in achievement: to all, however, it brings a more steady and enduring time, when stability of character and persevering tendencies improve the general conditions.

♍—♉   This will soften the critical and somewhat selfish side of Virgo
♉ - ♀   and bring a more intuitive and receptive tendency into the life. The native will now find his financial prospects improve and he will have opportunities to bring monetary affairs into a better condition than formerly, according to his ability to use the influence. He will find him⁻ self more obstinate or self-willed or stubborn and firm, but may turn this into determination and strength of purpose. To those who are very pro-

gress ve it will bring that true obedience which gives all the sympathetic qualities combined with an eager mentality; for it is an attempt to combine Venus and Mercury, that is love and intellect, so that by this obedience service of the highest kind may be the result. The most successful are those who work for the sake of work, without the motive of self at the back of the effort; but this is a very high ideal. For those who are making ordinary progress it will bring better conditions and an improvement in financial affairs.

LIBRA.

♎—♎ This will bring an entire change into the environment and
♀·♀ cause the native to have a much easier and more even period. This progressed ascendant will bring out his faculty of comparison and enable him to take a more balanced and just view of life; in fact he will tend to regard life far more from the standpoint of justice than hitherto. This means that a critical period has commenced, in which he will be weighed in the balance, all things tending to come to a point at which a new departure is to be made; and much will depend upon his decision during the ten years or so in which it rules over the ascendant. The influence of another will now become very marked, and partners will play a very prominent part in the native's career. To the very progressive individual this change of sign will bring the opportunity to develop clairvoyance or clear vision, and denotes a period wherein the animal side of the nature is sacrificed for the purely human. To the ordinary person it shows the arrival at a point of equilibrium, and a balancing-up of minor accounts preparatory to a new departure upon the ocean of life.

♎—♒ This is a very favourable ascendant, especially for those who
♀·♄ can rise to that point where response may be made to the highest vibration that it produces. It will give the native a much firmer and more stable frame of mind and cause him to become social, independent, and free; for it awakens and liberates a more social and artistic condition, hitherto more or less latent. He will now make some lasting and faithful friendships, and also form attachments that will be very helpful and beneficial to him. His mentality will become more refined, and inclined towards the more metaphysical and subjective types of study; and if he can abstract the inner virtue of this decanate he will find it leading him to the study of higher thought and occult or

mystical subjects. To the very progressive it brings associations with groups of persons, societies and public gatherings, and awakens the truly humanitarian side of the nature. The native will be able to study and comprehend character and human nature with ease if he develops the best side of this influence. He will be pure-minded, have potent desires, and make much progress in purity of thought and refinement of expression during the time that this decanate occupies the progressed ascendant.

♎—♊   This will awaken the mental side of the sign Libra and cause
♀-☿   the native to take a keener interest in all intellectual pursuits. He will be fond of reading and learning, and should now make much progress in all intellectual pursuits. This influence, moreover, will either bring some travelling or changes, or a great desire to travel and take journeys. It will bring kindred, relatives, or their affairs more prominently into the life, and some connection between the native and his relatives is sure to occupy his attention. The chief influence, however, of this progressed ascendant will be felt upon the mind, which will become more active, so that he will develop and gain success through writing, correspondence and literary affairs: indeed, he will be able to make the most use of this influence by turning his attention to literature or general mental improvement. It brings a greater attention to details into the life, and greater gain is shown throughout the smaller affairs of life than through large concerns.

SCORPIO.

♏—♏   This is a very pronounced and decided influence, and its effect
♂-♂   upon the native's life will be to awaken the latent possibilities of his nature. He will be more determined, and will become very firm in his decisions, and may through fixity of purpose carry his ambitions to a successful issue; but there is a dangerous side to this progression of the horoscope. For with the feeling of firmness that will accompany it he will gain some knowledge of his own inherent power, and this will arouse any pride or dignity that may be latent in the nature. He will also experience feelings of jealousy, and will be inclined to sarcastic and caustic utterances when vexed or offended, for the gentler side of the nature will be overlaid by this apparently coarser vibration; but it is the awakening of the real potency of the nature that will give rise to this change. If this manifestation does not occur then it will be a sign that

he has not yet come under its influence. To the very progressive it will bring a strong occult tendency, and awaken a love of the mystical and mysterious side of things. The native will be more than usually secretive, and will experience in the decade that lies before him more than he has done for many years past.

♏—♓ This will bring many unique experiences; it marks a somewhat
♂·♃ critical period, when danger threatens. Some great sorrow will come into the native's life during the ten years over which this progressed ascendant rules. He should be very guarded in all his actions, for there is some trouble indicated by this influence; his health also is likely to suffer and he may have some connection with hospitals or kindred institutions while it operates. It denotes some kind of confinement, either concerning the native himself or others. The very progressive individual is much drawn to the occult in some form or other at this time, becoming either mediumistic or else in some other way very receptive to psychic influences. The native should be very temperate now and onward, and live as discreetly as he can, for he will pass through many temptations while this decanate is upon the ascendant. He will come into contact with persons who are passing through much trouble, and in general will see the sad side of life in many forms. He should live as purely as he possibly can, and should also be on guard against treachery and enemies; especially females, who are not well disposed towards him.

♏—♋ This will bring some domestic experiences of a rather sad and
♂·☽ sorrowful nature. It will bring deaths into the family circle and cause domestic changes of a troublesome type. It will incline the native to be sarcastic, and will cause him to be exceedingly receptive to psychic influences of all kinds; it is not a good period that it heralds, and will bring many very strange experiences into the life while it lasts. To those who are making great progress it will bring a very strong leaning towards the occult, and a love of all things mystical. To those who are in any way receptive to its vibrations it will cause romantic and peculiar attachments, though nothing very favourable will come out of them. It seems to indicate changes that are enforced rather than sought. It denotes a peculiar psychic and weird period when happenings of an unusual character are almost sure to eventuate. If the directions are evil it will be a very trying time, when affairs will tend to go wrong more or less; therefore the whole time should be one of care and caution.

SAGITTARIUS.

♐ — ♐   This will bring some improvement into the native's general
♃ - ♃   affairs, and tends to awaken a more favourable vibration. He
will now take a more philosophical view of life, and will tend to look
upon all things from a more hopeful and independent standpoint. He
will probably take a long journey, or may even have some foreign travel
while under this progressed ascendant. He will investigate higher
thought, and, if he will allow it to do so, the higher mind will influence
him more than the lower. To those who are still living more in the
material and physical side of their nature than the mental, it will give a
deep interest in sports of all kinds, outdoor exercise, walking, driving,
boating, etc.; but to all who are under its influence it will bring greater
hope of success, and an increased love of freedom and independence.
To those who are still unawakened it will bring a very rebellious spirit and
a disregard for established law and order, with a tendency to be careless
and indifferent. But in its highest expression it will cause the native to
have a greater respect for true law and order, and to seek to know
something of religious truths.

♐ — ♈   This will bring a somewhat independent and impulsive attitude
♃ - ♂   of mind, so that the native will now incline to act rashly and
without sufficient forethought; and if he is not careful he will suffer
through carelessness or lack of caution: he will be assertive and
inclined to act from self-will, displaying too much forcefulness. He will,
however, do much to push himself forward and will take the lead in
whatever he attempts; in fact he will not be satisfied now unless he is
at the head of things, and if the current directions are good he will
improve his general conditions by his own inherent force and energy.
He will now be very liable to go to extremes and act in a manner that
may cause him regret later on; therefore he should endeavour to avoid
impulse and to act as discreetly and cautiously as possible. The mind
and intellect of the native will be keen and bright, but he will not have
sufficient self-control to avoid danger, and he is therefore liable to
accidents.

♐ — ♌   This will bring some impulsive attachments and cause the
♃ - ☉   native to express emotion rather too impetuously. He should
be guarded in his dealings with others, especially where the feelings are

concerned, avoiding extremes, or excesses, and refraining from too much demonstration. This progressed ascendant is not good for those who are tempted to speculate, since it brings some tendency to gambling or unwise venturesomeness. If however the directions are *very good*, then much gain by speculation, or better still through judicious investment or enterprise, is denoted. In those who are very progressive the intuition of the heart will be awakened, and a philosophical and prophetic spirit will be the result of this influence. It will be accompanied by many remarkable dreams, some of which will come true; also by a keen desire to make improvement in general affairs. To those who are naturally cautious and careful it will bring good fortune and success; but only when rashness and carelessness are avoided.

CAPRICORN.

♑—♑ This will bring a more ambitious and withal diplomatic attitude
♄·♄ of mind, and if progressive enough to respond to this new vibration the native will gain advancement in life and rise to a higher position than that held at birth. He will become much more industrious and persevering and with endurance and tact may now make great headway; though it too often happens that those under this progressed ascendant have not the inherent ability to take full advantage of its influence. To the very progressive it is a grand opportunity to gain recognition and to obtain a footing which will make the whole of the future; for it means eventually independence and position to those who have the ability to rise through their own merit. To the advanced, it brings a love of service to others; to the ordinary individual, industry, thrift, economy, prudence and chastity. It will benefit the native according to the directions operating, but it is an influence that only the progressive can truly appreciate.

♑—♉ This will bring some acquisitiveness into the desire-nature, and
♄·♀ it will cause the native to acquire wealth according to his ability to make the most of the directions operating. He will now become more persistent and plodding, working on toward the desired goal quietly and cautiously, yet with determination. He will have a fixed ambition to rise and to make progress, and should therefore gain many financial advantages. To those who are advanced it will give increased intuition, both regarding material and spiritual things; but it

is chiefly an influence that brings about a very practical and "common-sense" attitude with regard to all things. It is a very good progressed ascendant for those who are naturally thrifty and painstaking, but is apt to be somewhat indifferent to the ordinary person. By those who would progress with this new influence the "sterner virtues" should be studied and practised. The greatest success will come to those who can live purely, and also to those who are not so obstinate as to stand in their own light; for firmness and determination are obtained under the influence of this decanate.

♑︎—♍︎   This will make the native very practical and adaptable in his
   ♄ - ♉   ambitions, causing the latter, however, to be tempered by a discriminative and critical frame of mind. He will be in danger, consequently, of being somewhat selfish under this progressed ascendant, and should therefore be careful not to allow his activities to carry him to extremes. A great deal will depend upon the directions in force as to how this influence will operate: it will in any case assist him in arranging his affairs so that by a wise and careful judgment he may see clearly the best course of action in any difficulty. It is a decidedly favourable influence for those who are naturally tactful and painstaking, but there will be a tendency for the health to fail if there is too much worry or anxiety while this progressed ascendant operates. It will cause the native to be very practical and to use common-sense methods in all his actions: he will not, however, meet with all the success he may desire, for it is not a very "lucky" period, being a time for *sowing* rather than for *reaping*.

AQUARIUS.

♒︎—♒︎   This will bring a new cycle into the native's life; it marks the
   ♄ - ♄   beginning of a period when he will take more refined and humane views generally, and will endeavour to look at all things from a higher mental standpoint. He will have fresh experiences in connection with friends and acquaintances, and some new friendships will be formed that will play a very important part in his life history. He will now join groups of persons or associations of some kind, and will form attachments that will be idealistic in nature or of a mental character rather than in any way emotional or sensual. The directions operating will affect him mentally, and he will be very much inclined towards all

things that are in the nature of reform, will begin to have humanitarian views, and will be drawn to "higher thought" subjects. He will now develop a faculty for reading character and judging human nature, and will be deeply interested in all occult studies, possessing the ability and having the opportunity to investigate those things which are connected with aspirations and hopes that are mental or spiritual rather than physical and material. The above description applies chiefly to the more adaptable and progressed types of humanity. The very ordinary person will be only slightly affected by the mental influence and will respond merely to the tendency towards fixation, becoming pronounced in his views and tenacious of his rights and privileges, inclined to acquire or deal in land and property. In any case, however, the native will now meet with persons who will become his friends whether for good or ill; and hence he cannot be too careful with regard to the acquaintances whom he cultivates while under this influence.

♒—♉ This will cause the native to take a deeper interest in all
♄-♉ intellectual pursuits. He will become very refined, and will develop literary tastes, and, if he has the natural ability, he will now write or engage in correspondence—in fact, exercise the mind in many ways, to his great advantage. He will find friends amongst kindred or relatives who will help him, and attachments now formed are likely to be of a very refined and advanced type. He will, moreover, take some journeys while under this influence, probably in the interests of some society or brotherhood. He will find his mind now becoming much more active, and will live in the mental side of his nature much more than the physical, so that the good aspects to Mercury under these directions will be accentuated. To those who are very advanced, this progressed ascendant will bring a desire to express their principles in detail, and to systematise plans for the benefit of the many.

♒—♎ This will cause the native to form some attachment, to have
♄-♀ the life of another linked with his own for some years to come. He will find a more balanced and equalised state of mind coming to him under this new influence, will become very refined mentally, and will have social experiences that will be more to his liking than formerly. To the very advanced this brings the opportunity to open up the higher sense of clairvoyance, or clear vision, and brings that state of 'balance' which is aimed at by all who desire to make true progress. It will develop a very keen sense of justice, so that the native will act con-

B

scientiously and honourably in all dealings with others. It will give him also the faculty of comparison, and the power to see both sides of a question equally. This progressed ascendant will help the native to take full advantage of all the good aspects operating during the period in which it is in force.

PISCES.

♓—♓ This will bring some trouble; the native will be over-
♃-♃ anxious and inclined to worry. For it will bring him into a more gloomy, brooding, and melancholic side of his nature, and thus make him liable to give way to depression and despondency; this tendency must be combated by a firm will. He will now have many experiences that will be far from pleasant, and will come in contact with persons whose influence will not be beneficial. To those who are progressive it will bring a keen love of animals, or dumb life, causing also an awakening of the deeper sympathies, with a desire to help all who suffer; and in any case the native will now begin to be more hospitably inclined, with a far wider sympathy for others than formerly. It is not in any sense a fortunate period (unless at birth Jupiter was very well aspected and the Sun between the fourth and seventh houses), and if the directions are not good it will bring sorrow and some confinement, which will be imposed upon the native by circumstances. If the directions are good its effect will not be so evil, but a hampering or restrictive influence of some kind there is sure to be.

♓—♋ This will make the native more than usually sensitive, and very
♃-☽ sympathetic. He will now experience some domestic troubles and will feel very keenly home affairs, which will affect the life greatly. Under this progressed ascendant he will form some romantic attachment, yet will tenaciously hold on to any engagement that he may have previously entered into. He will experience many strange events affecting the emotional side of the nature; for the personal feelings will be very keen, and may in fact tend to become hyper-sensitive. It is not a good period on the whole, but some advantages may be gained in connection with psychic affairs. The native will be rather too mediumistic or receptive to the influence of others, the effects of which he will feel very keenly; hence he should endeavour to create a more independent spirit and cultivate more self-reliance. For he will certainly need it when the directions are evil,

♓—♏ This will tend to bring deaths and sorrows into the native's life:
♃-♂ he will be rather anxious, inclined to worry and fret, and to be
too easily affected if affairs "go wrong." There will be a danger of his
becoming somewhat jealous and resentful, and he should therefore
endeavour to keep the lower nature well under control. This period will
prove a rather trying time all round, and he should do all he can to avoid
giving way to any of the evil tendencies that the directions may indicate,
for the emotional and passional nature will be re-awakened. It will be a
good period, however, for psychic development but only if the mind is not
too much absorbed in material things; for unless good directions are
operating it is apt to cause the native to be too easily influenced by others,
and hence as easily affected by degraded and impure conditions and
surroundings as by the highest and most spiritual psychic influences.
He should do all he can to awaken the self-controlled and dignified side
of this decanate, so as to strengthen the sign Pisces, which is always
more or less *weak*, being a sign to which humanity as a whole is unable
as yet properly to respond.

CHAPTER X.

SOLAR ASPECTS.

THE SOLAR ASPECTS are those formed by the Sun to the Moon and planets.

The SUN is as it were the 'short hand' of a clock marking the *hour*, the time when the " directions "* are due.   The MOON is the ' long hand' pointing to the *minute*, the time when the influence will operate.   It may happen that a solar aspect is in a sense anticipated, by the Moon forming a similar aspect some months prior to the actual formation of the solar aspect; or it may on the other hand be delayed until the lunar aspects coincide some months after the solar aspect is formed.   Solar aspects operate during a period of three years or more.   One year when the solar aspect is becoming complete, a year when complete, and another year as the influence passes off.   It may be in force for several years, as is the case when the Sun passes from a radical aspect to any planet towards an aspect of the same planet's progressed place.   In this way such a position as ☉ ☌ ♂, for instance, may extend over a period of a decade or more in its general influence, though the most acute effect will of course be when the conjunction is exact.

A great deal depends upon the *sign* and *house* occupied by the Sun at birth as to the precise nature (and also the duration) of an event indicated by the solar aspects, but in a general sense they may be said to operate as described in the following pages.   It is of course impossible to enumerate, let alone separately describe, all the possible combinations of sign, house and aspect, but the reader should have little difficulty in making the requisite modifications due to the influence of (1) sign and (2) house, these being successively subordinate to the planetary influences, as has been before explained.

In all the ensuing delineations to avoid circumlocution the pronouns " he," " him," " his," etc., have been used, but it need hardly be said that they are intended to apply equally to both sexes.

---

* This is an awkward word, but it is retained for convenience, and because it is generally familiar in this connection.   Its application in this sense is not obvious at a first glance, but the word is derived from the practice of the mediæval astrologers, who " directed " the Sun (say) along its own arc to the conjunction, sextile, etc., of the meridian (M.C.), or Ascendant.   It is in this way that the word has come to be popularly associated with the events of life signified by progressed aspects, etc.—the ' fruit ' of the horoscopical tree, so to speak.

IMPORTANT PRELIMINARY NOTES.

The Solar influences bring the vital part of the "directions" to what may be termed an epoch in the native's evolution, and changes, the nature of which can be seen from the following pages, come into the life at the time when the Lunar influences are of such a nature as to *focus* the Solar influences and make them active. But apart from the Moon's period of influence these changes are already in a state of activity on other planes, higher than the physical, and they only await a physical link to bring them into objective existence. This has been already commented on in the preceding pages.

Mentally they will affect the native by causing the motive power to work toward the consummation of the influence; but, unless his will is very powerful, he will have to *wait for the time to ripen*, as explained above, till the aspect can take tangible shape in the physical life and its general surroundings. *All Solar aspects last over a period of three years at least.*

When there are no Solar aspects operating, during the period for which the calculations concerning "directions" have been made, the year that lies ahead is not likely to be so important or eventful as would have been the case had the Sun met any aspects during his progress through the horoscope. And no matter how important any other influence may seem it will have far less potency and power to affect the life, for good or ill, than would have been the case had the Sun an aspect to mark the cycle and stamp its primary character upon the life at the stage the native may have reached.

It is, on the other hand, possible to make a finer use of the Lunar aspects, for they will not be hindered or affected so much as if there were Solar influences also at work. Yet the "directions" as a whole will be less definite in their influences and more restricted in their scope.

N.B.—The whole of the ensuing Solar aspects are considered as being formed between the *progressed position* of the Sun and the *radical position* of the planet in question. Thus, suppose ♃ is 27°♋ and ☉15°♋ at birth; when by progressed motion ☉ has arrived at 27°♋, this will be "☉ ☌ ♃" in the sense here used: it will be some 12 year-days after birth, and Jupiter will have moved meanwhile to [say] 1°♌, so that the actual ☌ in the ordinary sense would not be reached until four years later. These readings may nevertheless be taken as applying also to aspects formed by the progressed ☉ to *progressed* planets; with this proviso, that, in the latter case, the native will be affected only so far as he is able to take advantage of every helpful circumstance and is able to build on foundations he has himself laid in the present life. Moreover, these positions should be interpreted in terms of the Progressed Horoscope rather than of the Nativity.

⊙ P. ☽ A very important position, for it denotes beneficial changes and the forming of new attachments which will eventually prove favourable and helpful. Domestic affairs, feelings and affections will be to the fore under this influence, and some general improvement or desirable changes will be produced thereby. It shows the advent of some inner changes, and the conquest of a certain part of the lower nature, which will expand the consciousness and lift the native to a higher level of thought and feeling. This will have also its corresponding effect in the outer world, and bring opportunities to rise higher in life socially, mentally or morally. Some credit or honour will be obtained from this aspect, or rather " position," and as it is generally in operation for a few years, it gives time for all that it indicates to be consummated. N.B.—It is not so favourable in the case of a female.

⊙ ☌ ☽ This is a powerful influence and denotes an entire change in the native's life, producing either advancement and elevation to a much better state of things, or a critical period in which a crisis of affairs is reached, and important changes follow. It is a beneficial position for the luminaries. The Moon, being a conductor of the solar force, brings heat and vitality into the system and quickens all the vital forces; and this is good, if the natal influences are not too poor to allow the solar fire to permeate the whole system, in which case danger is threatened from too much life, feverish tendencies being then the result. In the matter of environment it is good, and a new influence is coming into the life which will materially benefit the native, bringing opportunities for success and gain, more especially where the higher emotions and inner feelings are concerned. N.B.—It is not so favourable in the case of a female.

⊙ ⚹ ☽ This is a rather weak aspect, but as the Sun is the greater light, and the Moon the lesser, the Moon benefits by the illumination. It denotes some personal benefits, also beneficial changes with the probability of better prospects in the immediate future. From a financial standpoint it will benefit the native somewhat, and it gives hope of some advancement, either social or mental. It will make domestic conditions peaceful and harmonious, and generally tends to give opportunities for improvement of surroundings and environment. This will be a good time to push all affairs of the heart, or those matters in which the greatest interest is taken, and use should be made of all good lunar aspects to take action in these matters.

⊙ ∠ ☽ This is an unfavourable aspect which threatens unpleasant, and unfavourable changes that will bring trouble unless care is taken to avoid making changes in either environment or general affairs, except when the ☽ is otherwise very favourably aspected. Especial care should be taken of health, in order to prevent sickness, as ill-health would now tend to be prolonged and not very easily removed. It is an unfortunate period for the native's financial affairs and for social or domestic concerns, and sometimes brings affliction or other causes for sorrow, so that care should be taken of those dependent upon him, or intimately connected with him, whether by family ties or personal attachments. It is a generally unfortunate and unsatisfactory period and especially so for females.

⊙ ✱ ☽ A very fortunate and also generally favourable aspect: all affairs tend to go well, the health is good and the mind hopeful, bright and cheerful. This aspect produces beneficial attachments and some new undertakings, which will affect the domestic or social welfare. The whole period during which this good solar aspect operates will be successful for the native, and his consciousness will expand, new light coming from various sources: in fact the real nature of this aspect is to influence the mind and enable it to see clearly and intuitively, and therefore able to make the most of opportunities. It tends to bring either travel or some entire change of a favourable nature, often bringing satisfactory removals and changes that mean happiness and better conditions. Its influence is towards improvement in every way, physical, mental and moral.

⊙ □ ☽ A very unfortunate and unhappy aspect, for it denotes changes in the physical body which will either produce illness or so debilitate the general health as to bring grave liability thereto. This is one of the most unfavourable aspects, producing sorrow and grief, often bringing death into the family circle, and denoting a very sorrowful time generally. It signifies disappointment, especially in connection with domestic affairs, also disputes with superiors and acquaintances, separations and estrangements. It is, in fact, a very trying and harassing period, when all things tend to go wrong, and nothing appears to go right. Viewed from a higher standpoint this is a *good* vibration, as it quickens the personality and calls out all its strength to battle with the changing fate; for the changes, although apparently disastrous, are for eventual good.

☉ △ ☽ An exceedingly favourable and beneficial aspect, tending to bring general sunshine and happiness into the life. It denotes a period when a fortune may be made either by speculation or investment, this being the time for new enterprises and successful undertakings. The health will be good, the mind very hopeful and buoyant, and the ideas sound. The native's consciousness will expand, so that he will be enabled to see the best course to pursue in the future. This aspect either brings lasting attachments, or unions and agreements which bring another influence into the life which is helpful and fortunate; and hence the native will obtain advancement, social success and recognition in the sphere in which he moves. It is a period of general success, and whenever the lunar aspects are favourable, the native should push all his affairs to the utmost; for much will depend upon his own action and the attitude of his mind at this time.

☉ □ ☽ This is an evil aspect, affecting in some degree health, honour and reputation. It brings an altogether unfortunate period, in which unpleasant changes are threatened, and affairs tend to go wrong, bringing much worry, anxiety and disappointment. The native should look well to his general health, tone up the system and keep the circulation in good order, avoiding all things that are likely to produce sickness and ill-health. He should enter upon no fresh undertakings, and should keep clear of enterprises involving risk, as financial loss and monetary troubles are threatened. This aspect produces a trying period, and either brings deaths into the family circle, causing sorrow and grief in that way, or else affects those to whom the native is attached, thus affecting him indirectly.

☉ ⊼ ☽ *This, although somewhat weak in its influence, is favourable on the whole, for the Moon gains by the influence of any illumination which it receives from the Sun, no matter how slight that may be. It brings some material gain or benefit, but is not good for health; for there is an advent of new life under this influence, and the quickening of the life forces is apt to bring some feverish tendencies until the system has accustomed itself to the new stream of life which is flowing through. Some changes are denoted about this time, according to the position of the Moon, and the other lunar aspects operating. But much will depend upon the *mental attitude* as to the good that can be derived from this aspect.

* This symbol denotes the quincunx or 'inconjunct' aspect of five signs (150°).

⊙ 8 ☽ A very critical position, but in an inner sense a remarkable position for those who are developing psychically. This is the period when a crisis is reached in the native's life and matters long held in abeyance will now come to a climax, this being a culminating influence in every respect. Separations, deaths, disappointments, sorrows and troubles are now threatened him, and enemies will now seek to injure and annoy him. Important changes are made and the native is brought into fresh surroundings; there is every probability of old ties being broken, and the severance of attachments under this opposition. This position affects parents, guardians, partners, friends and all who are bound by social and domestic ties; it awakens painful emotions and stirs up all feelings that are bound up with the personal side of life.

⊙ P., ⚹, ⚺, ✳, △ ☿ * The Sun progressed to any of these aspects signifies an important change of consciousness, a much higher state of mentality being experienced under such influence, which is good for travel, changes, literary work, correspondence, interviews, writings, and in short for all those affairs in which an active mind, diplomatic dealings with others, and adaptation to new and fresh surroundings or undertakings are required. Any connection with solicitors, agents, literary persons, and those who act as intermediaries will now be successful and advantageous. It is, however, rather the influence of *mental* quickening, and is hence the forerunner of greater activities to come in the future rather than the immediate indicator of events; so that it depends for outward effect much more upon the lunar aspects than any other solar influence.

· ⊙ ∠ or □ ☿ † The Sun progressed to these afflictions of Mercury, the mental ruler, denotes troubles of a mental nature and the experience of anxiety, worry, etc., in various ways. The mind will be unsettled, changeable, and prone to make mistakes and to look at things from an unfavourable standpoint. Care is necessary in dealings with agents, messengers, servants, inferiors, or those who transact business for others, such as solicitors, lawyers, and literary persons; caution is advisable with regard to letters, writing, signing papers, and in all correspondence or personal interviews. This influence of the Sun and

---

* It is clear that ⚺, ∠, ✳, □, △, can only apply to the aspect made by ⊙ p. to ☿ r. for ☿ is never more than about 28° distant from the Sun.

† See previous footnote.

Mercury is not wholly bad, but tends away from full realisation, preventing matters coming to fruition.

☉ P. ♀   The Sun in parallel with the planet Venus is a very good position, indicating pleasure, success and prosperity. This very beneficent position is, however, largely dependent upon the corresponding of others in the directions operating, for it extends over rather a long period and has no definite or fixed moment when its influence acts directly, unless the Moon is at the same time forming a favourable aspect to Venus, when it will operate specifically at that time. This may therefore be called an indecisive influence, in which good vibrations abound and are thus helpful in many ways. To take full advantage of this position, financial affairs should be looked after and steps taken to increase monetary benefits, or to extend the social sphere of influence, taking all advantage of the opportunity now afforded for cultivating the feelings and emotions, to make attachments more binding and thus bring about union, or to effect permanent amalgamations for mutual benefit.

☉ ☌ ♀   The Sun in conjunction with the planet Venus gives light and life to all that is signified by this most benefic planet. The native will now come into very close contact with those to whom he will be drawn by sympathy and affection, and his prospects will look brighter and happier than they have done for some time. He will enjoy the blissful feelings of gratified emotions, which will thus be expanded for greater indulgence in pleasure and the pursuit of happiness, all things tending to bring increased ability to live in the better and more hopeful and cheerful side of the nature. The native will come into new and congenial society, will make new friends, and will gain in many ways through others and through his own attitude towards them. It is a very splendid solar influence, especially in regard to the cultivation of the feelings and higher emotions. *This position often denotes Marriage.*

☉ ⚺ ♀   This solar influence is, on the whole, favourable, although the aspect is one of the weakest, and not at all decisive in its character. It is a good time to improve the general financial conditions, and it is also favourable for social and domestic attachments. The native may now profitably invest or seek to gain financially ; for the influence of Venus, although weak, is very responsive to all that makes for happiness and improving conditions. He will form good and profitable connections, and find it easy to get on with others, while the feelings will now tend to be refined and keenly sensitive to any call that may be made upon them by or through others. The fact of the Sun and Venus being in touch is in itself good, but a great deal depends upon the native's own ability to avail himself of the benefits it offers.

☉ ∠ or □ ♀* An unpleasant, and, in many ways, unfavourable influence. It brings many drains upon the purse, a tendency to lose money, coupled with domestic afflictions, and sorrows and disappointments of many kinds. Matters in which the feelings and emotions are involved will suffer, and existing ties will be severed, or the native will lose friends and those to whom he is deeply attached under its influence. It is not a good time for any domestic affairs, and all those who make up the family circle will in some way or other feel the influence of these solar aspects operating. Care is necessary in dealing with those who have a share in the affections, and also with regard to all monetary interests, lest losses of affection or of property, as the case may be, occur under its unfavourable vibration. The mind will not be over-cheerful, nor will any matters related to pleasures, society or entertainments be successfully negotiated.

☉ ⚹ ♀ The native should make the very most of this period in all directions, financially, socially, and also as regards the affections; for he will now be able to improve his financial and social condition according to the capacity within him to respond to the good influence that Venus always brings, for opportunities will come in his way, advancement, recognition and general uplifting being the usual result of this beneficial solar influence. Attachments and relations with others will now produce unions and permanent connections, while all will go well with the native as regards the feelings and emotions, happiness resulting as the outcome of all present engagements and undertakings; it will, therefore, be advisable to make the most of this very good influence, which marks an important stage in evolution.

☉ □ ♀* *See* ☉ ∠ ♀.

☉ △ ♀* A very fortunate influence, denoting financial gain and many benefits, all of which tend to improve social and domestic affairs, so that the native will now enter upon a happy and pleasurable period in which success and prosperity may be looked for. All investments, speculations and enterprises will be prosperous and beneficial and the

* The square or trine aspect can, of course, only be formed between the prog Sun and the rad. Venus, and very rarely even then.

more he seeks to exalt and improve his position the more success will attend his efforts. His affections will have a good issue and all those to whom he becomes in any way attached will help him to realise his hopes and wishes, and happiness will follow all engagements and connections with others. Both socially and mentally his influence will increase and expand, until he has reached the highest point his capacities will allow; for this is an influence which expands the whole of the nature, more especially however the feelings and emotions.

☉ P. ♂   A malefic influence, in which there is every tendency to accidents, inflammatory conditions, and a generally feverish state. While this parallel of the solar orb and Mars operates (which is generally for an extended period overlapping other aspects) it will be necessary to act as discreetly and temperately as possible: a great deal will depend upon the inherent temperament and natural liability to act impulsively and rashly, for all the outgoing energies will now be accentuated. The native should on no account allow this feverish state to cause him to act without thought or premeditation, or it may lead to very difficult and trying conditions, through which he will seriously suffer; for he will feel a desire to be more than usually active, and will be very easily excited or provoked. Much will, however, depend upon the current Lunar Aspects, as to how this solar influence will operate.

☉ ♂ ♂   A very critical and unfavourable position, representing a condition in which the spirit and its counterfeit will be linked together, giving far greater animal heat than is usual. It therefore produces a more feverish state, the native becoming easily excited, much more readily angered than usual; self-assertive and somewhat aggressive; very energetic, active and enterprising, however, and very much inclined to acts of daring, and hence he will need to practise self-restraint lest he should become too adventurous or over-forceful. He will now meet with martial persons of various kinds and their influence upon his life will be to accentuate the feelings, stirring them into greater activity, and making him more hopeful and expectant, perhaps, than is desirable. He should safeguard health and not allow the blood to become over-heated, should make no more changes than are necessary, and be careful to avoid quarrelling with anyone, or it will bring serious trouble. He will incline to be very liberal, indeed extravagant, at this period.

☉ ∠ ♂   This is rather a weak aspect, but slightly good and

favourable for new enterprises, and dealings with those who are
venturesome and of active habits. The native will not gain anything
of a very marked nature from this aspect, but it is good for activities
generally and for all actions requiring courage, force and energy. It
will to some extent awaken any acquisitiveness that he may have latent
within him, and if he at the same time comes under similiar vibrations
from other influences in the nativity he will benefit from this solar aspect
weak though it is. In any case he may extract some good from it, if he
uses discretion in pushing himself and his affairs to the front, without
allowing the forceful side of Mars to over-ride the dignity of the Sun; for
this influence stimulates the positive and progressive attributes of the
Sun, and balances the animal tendencies of Mars, making both more
harmonised.

⊙ ∠ ♂   This is an unfavourable aspect, one to cause a great deal of
petty annoyance and trouble likely to arise from hasty and impulsive
conduct. The native should now avoid disputation of any kind, or any
tendency to excess of feeling, living as calmly and as temperately as
possible. He will find himself liable to monetary losses, to make mistakes
in judgment with regard to personal matters, and also to form acquaintances who will be neither creditable nor beneficial. He will be in danger
of suffering from feverish complaints and his health will suffer through
inflammatory tendencies while this aspect lasts. It is a somewhat weak
solar influence, but at the same time it denotes a liability to sharp and
somewhat acute attacks, which will have effect according to the lunar
aspects, whether good or ill; for it stirs up the heat of the body, and
renders the native mentally active, but of a rather turbulent state of
mind.

⊙ ✳ ♂   This is a very favourable aspect for enterprise, new
ventures, and all matters requiring independence of action, and where
courage and determination are necessary. It increases the vital heat
and brings the native into contact with very positive or martial people,
awakening in him also a desire for activity, adventure, and risk: he will
be very energetic and industrious, ready to enter upon any new scheme
or fresh undertaking, and apt to busy himself in all directions. It will
make the mind alert, and will incline the native to travel, to remove or
make changes or to seek fresh outlets for his restless energies. It is a
good aspect in many ways, causing him to make new friends, to become
attached to others, and to agree with relatives and those who will

become bound up with his life. In fact it shows a very active and progressive period, when the executive faculties are at their highest.

☉ □ ♂ A very evil and unfortunate aspect, fraught with disastrous tendencies. It will be necessary for the native to safeguard his health, to avoid all liability to accidents as far as possible, and to refrain from disputes with others. He will have serious domestic troubles, or estrangements and disappointments, and any undertaking or engagement entered into during this period will end disastrously and sorrowfully. It is not a good time to remove or to make changes, to have connections with others, or to allow the feelings to enter into any affair in which the native may be engaged. He must now look to his honour, and do nothing likely to produce scandal or injure his reputation ; for he will not pass through this period without misfortune. He should therefore act discreetly, avoiding impulse or rashness, and quarrelling with no one. *This is a very critical period, necessitating the exercise of great care.*

☉ △ ♂ This is a very favourable influence, and tends to make this period successful, although nothing very extraordinary can come from Mars alone. While this influence lasts, the native will be courageous, more enterprising, competent, and adventurous than usual. He will come into contact with persons who will stir him up both mentally and physically, and whose influence upon his life will be such as to make it active and bold, generous and free. He will be likely to give way to feeling and to form attachments which will be ardent and eventful while they last, but, as it is not an influence that is permanent in its nature, when the magnetic vibrations it has induced pass off, he will realise that he has only been stirred into activity from outside, as it were, more from excitation of the Desires than the energy of the inner Will. *An eventful period, which will be remembered for years to come.*

☉ ☌ ♂ This is an evil solar influence and tends to cause feverish conditions, liability to accidents, and many troubles which result from impulsiveness, from over-estimating, and from want of sufficient caution and premeditation. The native will have losses and disappointments, and will suffer through separations, disputes and estrangements. He cannot act too temperately, or use too much care to escape the evil effects of this aspect ; for it rarely passes without disturbing the health, setting in motion causes that eventuate in illnesses of an inflammatory or feverish nature, and it often moreover affects relatives or those to whom he is attached. He should not travel while this influence lasts, neither is it wise to invest money or to speculate, nor to have any dealings with others where enterprise or new ventures are concerned. He is liable to be endangered by fire or accidents, and therefore should use care in all his actions, avoiding above all things rashness or impetuosity.

☉ ⚹ ♂ This solar aspect is the quincunx or "inconjunct" (150° apart). It is not always an important aspect, but when the health is not good and the constitution weak it threatens much sickness and feverish tendencies, giving a liability to inflammatory diseases. The native must therefore safeguard his health, and act very discreetly while this solar influence is in force, not giving way to impulse or any rash tendencies ; or he will thereby precipitate the evil of Mars and cause the aspect to act as a conjunction, which in this case would be a malefic influence. If any of the family are ailing it is a critical time for them, and shows danger to those with whom the native is closely associated, or to whom he is in any way attached. In many cases this aspect has been found to be weak, but in others, especially where there has been a tendency to act impulsively, it has been most unfortunate; therefore, temperance and discretion are imperative while it operates ; and extremes of all kinds should be avoided.

☉ ☍ ♂ The period during which this influence operates is always one of danger and grave risk, and it is a very evil aspect in many ways, for it gives great liability to accidents, feverish complaints, and inflammatory diseases; the native's health is seriously threatened, and the utmost care will be necessary to prevent an illness of a severe nature. He will do wisely not to exhibit too much bravery, nor to rush headlong into danger, also to use the greatest discretion in everything he does, taking especial care to safeguard his health, and maintaining as far as possible a calm and steadfast will. This opposition is not wholly bad, for it has a very deep and important meaning in a higher sense, as it signifies a crisis in human evolution in which the animal and the divine in man struggle for supremacy ; and this war between the two sides of the nature, the higher and the lower, will follow the ' line of least resistance ' in each case. Will and Desire will be opposed, one part of the spirit striving against the other ; and if the native cannot consciously realise the struggle, then trouble and difficulty will fall upon him to awaken him to a realisation of his true nature. *To most, if not to all, this will prove to be the most memorable period of the life.*

☉ P. ♃ This influence will spread over a number of years, and whenever the Moon has good aspects to Jupiter, she will stir into activity this very powerful influence, bringing as a result good fortune, good health and social success. The nature of this parallel aspect is such as to bring enduring influences, not specially limited to one month or year, but extending over a number of years; it fact it overlaps, as it were, both previous and subsequent periods to some extent, with an influence more or less beneficial according to the other aspects operating (especially the lunar aspects). The native may now enter upon new undertakings, and arrange for his future welfare in the manner he thinks best, for very little harm can come to him under this very good solar position, which tends to a very successful and prosperous time, during which all things will go well, both socially and financially. [It should be pointed out that ☉ P. ♃ may coincide with ☉ □ ♃, in which case the losses and difficulties indicated by the latter will be met with a cheerful and buoyant spirit.]

☉ ☌ ♃ This is a very fortunate solar position, denoting success, good fortune and much gain, with many social advantages, a favourable issue to all undertakings in hand, financial prosperity, and benefits connected with new undertakings, travel and association with others. The health will be good, and the constitution much stronger than hitherto; but care must be taken to avoid excesses, for the life forces are considerably quickened by this conjunction, and some tendency to indulgence is likely in consequence. The feelings and sympathies will be awakened and the native will form unions, attachments, and ties that will be very beneficial to him in every way. When the lunar aspects are good he will meet with all the success he can desire ; but he must avoid pride and not allow himself to become over-confident, for though success will surely come in the future as a result of this conjunction yet other influences at work must be considered as well, and especially also the radical influences. For this position is much less fortunate to one who has an afflicted Jupiter at birth ; especially if the affliction be from Mars. Nevertheless, the influence in itself is wholly good, and only foolish extravagance or excess can nullify its beneficial nature.

☉ ⚹ ♃ This is not very powerful, but is in a minor sense a good aspect, which will benefit the native according to his power to respond to its influence. It will bring some gain and shows improvement in the general welfare, the advent of new friends, fresh engagements, and social advantages, with every prospect of financial gain and the opportunity to improve the monetary prospects. It is on the whole a good aspect, whereby success and prosperity accrue from any effort or endeavour made by the native, so that it will be a good time for him to push his affairs, and to commence new undertakings. The sympathies and feelings will be called out by others, he will form attachments that will be favourable ; but the best good will come when the lunar aspects are of a like nature, for then this somewhat weak aspect will be strengthened.

☉ ∠ ♃ A weak aspect of a more or less adverse nature, threatening financial losses and some difficulty in getting money as easily as usual. It is not good for health, nor for any social affairs ; in fact care will be necessary in all dealings with others in the social world. This aspect acts chiefly in the direction of hindering and delaying progress, but is very weak in its real power for evil ; still the period is not good, notwithstanding the fact that Jupiter is a benefic planet. Disappointments in dealings with superiors or those with whom the native is associated are probable, and he should take care not to offend, or cause a severance in affection, as the feelings are now likely to suffer, while financial losses may ensue as the result of disagreements between himself and others. It is not a good time to travel nor to have dealings with the clergy, lawyers or religious people, nor to commence any new undertakings ; but rather a time to live quietly and temperately, keeping in the background as much as possible.

☉ ✶ ♃ This denotes a very prosperous and successful time, when all things will go well and when the mind will expand and become hopeful, being able to see clearly the best course to adopt for general improvement and success. Under this good influence, which is one of the best of solar aspects, the native will obtain his desires, his ambitions will be gratified, his social affairs will profit him, and he will gain from friends or relatives, or those with whom he is associated. He will also form honourable and lasting attachments, good and favourable unions or connections with others. Under this influence he will either travel or make important beneficial changes ; while correspondence and writings will bring success, new undertakings will turn out successfully, and the whole period during which this aspect lasts will be beneficial and prosperous. It is in fact a most fortunate time, and will mark an epoch in the career.

☉ □ ♃ This denotes a period unfavourable and subject to much trouble and difficulty, affecting adversely domestic affairs and also social

F

matters in general. The native will suffer losses and trials which will extend over a somewhat protracted period. However, the planet Jupiter is a benefic, and therefore the square aspect, though evil in itself, will have much of its malignancy lessened by this fact. The native must be prepared for financial difficulties, and for many minor troubles, also for losses through others, particularly those that affect the domestic sphere and the social engagements. He will lose someone either by death or separation, and suffer from the actions of others, experiencing sorrow and disappointment. He should not lend money at this time, and he should be on his guard against deception, treachery and hypocrisy. It is an unfortunate time, but may be turned into good, for out of this evil good often comes: it represents the struggle of pride against the spirit, Jacob wrestling with God.

☉ △ ♃ One of the finest and most fortunate of solar influences. It denotes that the native has reached an epoch in his life, for the opportunities that are now before him surpass those he has had in the past or will have in the future, and he should therefore make the most of this favourable time. He may now either invest or speculate to advantage should he so desire, for gain and financial prosperity are shown by this aspect; he will obtain advancement and social successes, and will have the satisfaction of seeing his ambitions gratified; he will form lasting and permanent attachments, and become linked with others to mutual advantage, and all things will go right with him. There is a spiritual as well as a material side to this aspect—which only comes once in a lifetime—and this will enable the native to obtain a deeper insight into religious matters, and also to become more philosophical in his thought and wise in his actions. Thus he may use the aspect for the uplifting and improvement of character, or for worldly gain and advantage, just as he chooses.

☉ ⚼ ♃ This influence is unfavourable, and one likely to bring trouble and loss while it lasts. The native will find his circulation affected and his health not at all favourable about this time; but strict temperance and moderation in all things will do much to counteract this influence, which causes suffering to health through surfeit and excess, the balance of forces in the system undergoing readjustment. It is an ill time to lend money, to invest or to speculate, and care should be taken in every way to avoid monetary losses. Sorrows and disappointments of some kind are certain, for the native will be either estranged or separated from those to whom he has become attached, or whom he has allowed to share in his feelings and emotions. Nevertheless, although an unfavourable aspect it is between benefic planets, and is therefore not so evil as in other cases, but generally speaking such an aspect otherwise would indicate an unfavourable time, and with discordant lunar aspects this period is likely to prove a very trying and difficult one.

☉ ⚹ ♃   This is a rather critical aspect in regard to money affairs, and is likely to bring the native trouble in connection with any speculative enterprises he may be disposed to enter into at this time. He will find himself subjected to considerable strain between two contrasting influences, the desire for expansion and increase—either as regards worldly matters, the emotions, or the religious aspirations—and the internal spiritual or moral nature; and this may lead him into courses he will afterwards regret. In a modified form, this may be taken as somewhat analogous to the square aspect (*q.v.*), but less crucial in its effects, and related rather to the mental or spiritual, than to the physical plane of being. The native should keep a watchful eye on all investments he may be concerned with at this time, and look carefully after his pecuniary interests in every way. Social or religious disputes, also, are likely to occasion him annoyance.

☉ ☍ ♃   This is a very unfortunate position and will bring the native a rather trying time: he is liable to suffer through opposition from others, separations, legal difficulties and very serious disappointments. Either those to whom he has been attached, or with whom his life has been bound up, will now grievously disappoint him, or else he will fall under an illusion and become more bound up in them, only to realise greater trouble later on. He will meet with financial losses, and social disadvantages, probably by disagreeing with those who have been his friends, or perhaps through their own peculiar conduct. It often happens that *apparent* good comes out of this position, (owing to Jupiter being a benefic planet), but the good is only apparent and should be well examined, for it generally brings with it the opposition that the aspect implies. The native should not "stand upon his dignity" too much; should not be too expectant; and should moreover avoid excesses of every kind, or his health will seriously suffer. He should endeavour as far as possible to maintain a just and balanced state of mind, but he will find it a difficult task.

☉ P. ♄   This is a truly evil solar influence, for this vibration lasts

for a long period and is in operation for several years, on and off, until
other influences intervene and counteract its malefic character. It has
the effect of hindering the vital forces of the Sun, and thus often
debilitates the physical system, tending to bring on illnesses of long
duration, and also causing a number of sorrows and trials while it lasts;
it is therefore an unfortunate aspect, and every care should be taken to
keep the body in good order, and to promote a good circulation, so as
not to feel its worst physical effects. While this malefic parallel is in
operation, all affairs tend to go wrong, and disappointment, deaths, and
many trials may be expected. It is therefore especially necessary for
the native to keep the mind hopeful and cheerful by the exercise of the
will, and not to allow the despondency which often accompanies this
influence to overcome him. (All aspects between the Sun and Saturn
are more or less unfavourable owing to the restricting and limiting effect
that ♄ has upon the ☉, and to its action upon the individual nature.)

☉ ♂ ♄   The conjunction of the Sun with the planet Saturn is a
very unfavourable position, denoting a very critical time, in which all
affairs will tend to go wrong, thereby causing the native to become more
than usually suspicious and apprehensive of danger ahead, for though
the will is strengthened by this conjunction, yet on the other hand, it
tends to cramp and warp the mind when the true nature of this position
is unrealised. It is a position that brings responsibility, and a more
anxious period into the life, and if the native can respond to the higher
vibrations of Saturn it need not be at all evil but will prove to be the
very best influence for him to rise by; for it increases the ambition,
giving more personal character and more stability than usual. It is a
position that strengthens the individuality and causes the disposition to
be more steady, persevering and industrious; as a character-producer it
marks an epoch in the life. But it is not a favourable position for those
who in 'forming the crystal' become too narrow and limited; for in
this case the health suffers through poor circulation, resulting in liability
to rheumatism and a danger of taking cold or chill easily. The faculties
of hope and a courageous spirit should be encouraged. Physical exercise
will be beneficial.

☉ ⚹ ♄   The effect of this is almost nil, but it tends somewhat to
solidify and strengthen the current "directions," and shows a tendency
to use more caution and forethought in the affairs; hence it may bring
some slight financial benefits. It will in any case improve the native's

stability, and will induce a more firm and self-reliant attitude, which will be of service if he has realised his latent possibilities. He will come into contact with someone older than himself whose advice will be helpful, while some temporary responsibility may advance his prospects for the future. A great deal will depend upon himself as to how this aspect will operate, for it is a somewhat weak influence, but if he can exercise thrift and seek by diligence to place himself in a permanent position it will prove beneficial. When the lunar aspects are good it gives new opportunities for development.

☉ ∠ ♄   A weak evil aspect, of such nature as to cause hindrances and delays to progress. The native will have to be careful to avoid monetary losses, also to guard against fraud, or financial losses through others. This aspect sometimes heralds a death in the family circle, or amongst friends, or those to whom the native is in some way related. This aspect tends to bring disappointments, and probably owing to the manner in which the native will look upon circumstances, he is apt to stand in his own light and to go against his own personal interests. He should now endeavour to keep his mind as cheerful as possible and not give way to despondency, or allow himself to look upon the dark side of things, for this aspect will tend to make him unfortunate by his attitude towards the affairs of life, being fearful and lacking in sufficient courage to overcome the difficulties that will appear in his way. He should cultivate all the hope he can and assume as cheerful an aspect as possible, or when the Moon forms any adverse aspect to Saturn he will be a pitiable victim of depression and despondency.

☉ ✶ ♄   This is in many respects a very beneficial aspect, as it steadies the mind and makes the character more firm and thoughtful. The native will now have opportunities to assume far greater and more permanent responsibilities than he has previously undertaken. It is a very fortunate influence for those whose " root of merit " is fairly established, for the individual characteristics are strengthened and the moral character rendered more reliable and capable of developing the physical virtues. The native will now meet with persons older than himself, who are truthful, honest and sincere, and they will benefit him and prove to be reliable and permanent friends and helpers. His mind will become steadier, more concentrative and persevering, and he will go deeper into and endeavour to realise more of his inner nature than formerly. Honour and reputation will tend to become established under this powerful solar influence, and he should do all in his power to place himself in a position of trust, or where the future will be secure against change or uncertainty.

☉ □ ♄   This will tend to make the whole of the current directions more or less unfortunate.   The native will have sorrow and grief while its influence is in operation, and there is every probability of someone in the domestic circle passing out of this physical world while it is in force.   He will experience domestic troubles and will find it difficult to keep the mind free from worry and anxiety while the aspect lasts.   He should not make any changes unless they are absolutely necessary, and should be very careful in all dealings with others, especially those older than himself.   It is an evil period, but more so if he despond or allow himself to become depressed, for it will then affect the health and may cause him to suffer from long illnesses of a somewhat protracted nature, as it awakens any latent tendency to rheumatism, and has some tendency to produce chronic disorders.   The native should be careful in all his actions, and in his mental attitude towards others, as he is liable to suffer disappointments and also to be affected by the evil thoughts and wishes of others.   Altogether it is a critical period, and calls for caution, steadfastness and courage.   *A very unfortunate and trying influence.*

☉ △ ♄   This is a good influence, but too much material benefit must never be expected from this aspect, for Saturn is not a very fortunate planet in regard to material things, being the planet of *mind*.   However, it is the best aspect the Sun can have to this planet, and it denotes a period in which all things will solidify and make more permanent conditions, so that the native will assume greater responsibilities than formerly, and he will now rise to an important position in life, and secure for himself a fixed condition whereby both honour and reputation will profit.   He will also come into contact with those whose influence upon his life will have a permanent effect, and by internal strength of character he will mould his future on a much firmer and more solid basis than formerly : he will do well to take up sound investments and improve his financial prospects under this influence.   Saturn is the planet of refinement, chastity and temperance, and by a study of all the virtues which make for purity, industry, patience, and perseverance, much progress may be made.   A great deal will depend upon the native himself of course, and the methods he adopts, as to whether he will come under the most favourable side of this good aspect or not.

☉ ☐ ♄ This will be for the native a somewhat evil time, and it will be well for him to act discreetly and also to safeguard his health. He should avoid taking chill, and be careful to keep the circulation in good order, or he will suffer from colds and general debility. He should be wary not to offend others, especially elders, or superiors in rank. This aspect often produces either a death or separation, and severe disappointment or sorrow, therefore he should watch his feelings and not give way to the depression or melancholia which often follows. The native's attitude towards others, and their effect upon him will not be good, as his magnetism will not be attractive under this influence ; it is in fact an unfortunate period generally, and he must make a courageous stand against the difficulties and worries that now threaten him. His circulation should be kept in good order and his general health up to the highest standard ; and he should cultivate hope and remember that all restraints put upon him may be for a good purpose, although this may not be apparent at the time.

☉ ⚻ ♄ The quincunx or " inconjunct " (150°) aspect of the Sun to Saturn is not a good influence and is more than likely to affect the health, owing to its chilling and debilitating effect. It is a rather weak aspect, however, and may not produce any appreciable effect if the mind can be kept cheerful and free from despondency. It will, however, strengthen the whole character, if the body is able to absorb the united influence of these two forces, the one expansive, and the other contractive ; for by blending the two it is possible to obtain that steadfastness and perseverance which ♄ gives ; but it will be advisable for the native to look well to his own health, and to expect any of those connected with him, the family circle, etc., who are ailing or suffering to be likewise affected ; if the lunar directions indicate it, there is danger of a loss by death under this influence.

☉ ☍ ♄ A very malefic influence. The native will suffer in health, will experience much opposition, and many obstacles will come in his path while it lasts. Disappointments, losses by death, sorrows and trials of all kinds are indicated by this influence, and he cannot act too wisely while it operates, for the mind will tend to despair and will ever look on the dark side of things. Despondency and depression will assail him, and it will require all his care and forethought to keep his head above water while it lasts, for he will have both financial difficulties and many other troubles to endure. There is an occult significance attached to this aspect ; and that is, the combat between the higher and the lower nature, between moral character and selfishness, between generosity and over-carefulness. The best attitude to this adverse opposition will be one of hope and calmness and the inner feeling that " whatever *is*, is best." If the lunar aspects coincide therewith, especially, it will be a very trying time. *A very critical and memorable period.*

☉ P. ♅   This influence will extend over a period of several years, and will manifest a spasmodic influence at certain times, when there are other influences congenial to the Uranian vibration, operating. This influence will act peculiarly upon the native's consciousness, causing him to take a deep interest in occult and metaphysical matters, and so to expand and broaden his views, rendering him original in thought and free from conventional limitations. This influence will render the native either irritable or excitable at times, passing through magnetic changes that have a peculiar influence upon others. He will meet with persons holding what seem strange ideas, and they will affect him mentally, bringing him into a train of thought above the average commonplace level.

☉ ☌ ♅   This marks an epoch in the life in which great changes of consciousness will take place and expansion of mind result therefrom. The native will either pass through a very romantic and adventurous period, or be estranged from friends and have intimate associations with others, associations of a far more mental character and of a more exalted type than such usually are. This influence denotes *changes*, but rather of a mental and subjective than of an objective nature. It is a period when sudden and unexpected events happen, when ties and attachments of a peculiar nature are formed or broken. The native should exercise great care with regard to those who come into his life, as very strange engagements and peculiar episodes occur under this conjunction. This influence only eventuates when the mind is ready to respond to higher vibrations, and when reforms are coming into the life ; it brings experiences that are to awaken the higher part of the nature, and therefore it is necessary to be prepared for changes, and events that will tend to alter the future very considerably. This aspect affects friendships and unions, more, perhaps, than any other influence.

☉ ⚺ ♅   This weak aspect is favourable in a measure for changes, and for the advance of new thought, or the undertaking of any study connected with the occult or with psychic affairs of any kind. The native will meet with friends or acquaintances whose interest in these matters will concern him, or draw his mind into a condition that will enable him to investigate matters relating to higher thought: he will feel more expansive mentally, and much more interested in all metaphysical subjects than formerly. It will probably not affect him directly in any remarkable way, but will make it easier for good aspects to the Moon, etc., to act: he may gain some money unexpectedly or gain benefits from others in a manner not previously thought of. It is good for the mind, more especially for all mental pursuits of an original nature, and if the native is that way inclined his inventiveness will be unusually active: some new undertakings may be entered on, productive of future benefit.

☉ ∠ ♅ This is a somewhat weak but adverse aspect, likely to bring sudden and unexpected changes. It shows an unsettled and somewhat anxious period, and it will be well for anyone under its influence if he can avoid trouble and difficulty while it lasts. The native will incline to be abrupt, and at times irritable, liable to offend others through his own mental attitude towards them. The native's magnetic conditions will not be harmonious, and it will be advisable for him to act discreetly and to do nothing impulsively while this aspect lasts—especially where others are concerned with him in any domestic or social relationship. A great deal depends upon his own attitude at this time; for any exhibition of temper, excitability or nervous irritability will tend to make enemies and cause others to take a sudden dislike to him, and by reaction he will feel resentful of their attitude and inclined to act without careful thought or full control. While this influence lasts the whole period of its operation will be unfavourable.

☉ ✶ ♅ This is likely to bring the native sudden benefits and unexpected gains. His magnetism will increase, so that he will affect others by the magnetic conditions which this solar influence will cause him to generate, and he will probably take some long journey under this influence and gain by travel or changes which will tend to be for his good in some direction which may not at first be apparent. This aspect will greatly benefit the native's mind, and cause him to be inventive, ingenious, and full of original ideas. His mind will expand, becoming interested in the higher thought, and in metaphysical subjects, and he may take some definite step towards embracing occultism or mystical studies. This is a very favourable aspect in many ways, but particularly as regards the mental conditions, and under this influence the native will form new friendships and fresh acquaintances, or join some society or body of persons interested in higher thought, æsthetic culture or original studies. *It is a good time to study astrology.*

☉ □ ♅   This is probably the worst aspect known (except perhaps ♂ □ ♅). Matters will now tend to go suddenly wrong, and unexpected events of an unfavourable nature will occur. The native will meet with sudden and severe disappointments and will have unexpected separations and sharp disagreements to contend with. His mind will become peculiarly irritable, and his health will suffer from strange ailments and peculiar nervous disorders. This is not a good time to make any changes, although change or removal may be necessitated by circumstances, so that the native may be unable to prevent making unfavourable changes: his feelings will be affected, and those intimately related to him will cause him annoyance and worry, and perhaps disgrace. It is quite an evil period: matters of importance should be postponed, and all travel avoided if possible; estrangements and unfortunate discoveries are likely. If the current lunar aspects are evil then a critical period is at hand; otherwise, until other aspects coincide it will not act with full force. *A time of great stress, which will challenge the native's full powers.*

☉ △ ♅   This will bring unexpected and sudden gains and advantages. The native will increase in magnetic power and broaden considerably in mind, taking very advanced views of life, becoming more than usually original, inventive and constructive. He will travel, or make important changes of a favourable nature, or will come into intimate contact with original persons and will take up the study of some metaphysical subject, astrology, or occultism in some form. He may gain suddenly through investments or by speculation, especially through railways or other methods of rapid transit. It is a good time for such as are of a reforming and advanced turn of mind, anxious to improve surrounding conditions; and the native will gain through friends and acquaintances, and will probably also have some romantic or novel experience which will be quite out of the common.

☉ ⚼ ♅   This is an evil aspect, likely to cause sudden and unexpected troubles, affecting the health and tending to upset the nervous system. The native will feel irritable and inclined to become excitable, or very easily provoked, and will either offend others by his

attitude towards them, or strongly and fanatically resent their attitude
towards himself. It is not a good time to travel or make any important
changes, and the native should endeavour to keep always as calm and
self-controlled as possible: he will now be liable to disappointments and
separations between himself and his friends, and he should act as
discreetly as possible, and be guarded in all dealings with strangers, or
those with whom he is accidentally brought into contact, as he is
liable to misrepresentation and slander or at least very harsh criticism.
If the lunar aspects are evil in nature while this solar influence is in
operation, it will be a very bad time; but if they are good then this
solar aspect will not be so severe.

☉ ⚹ ♅ The quincunx or " inconjunct " aspect between Uranus and
the Sun is in general of a similar nature to the semi-sextile, but it is in
the main more separative in its nature and somewhat more drastic in its
operation (though this is chiefly confined to the mental plane, unless
Uranus be badly aspected at birth). It is, moreover, far more likely to
affect the health, if moderation and simplicity of life are not followed.
This is a splendid aspect for the truly regenerate, bringing an expansion
of consciousness that will not pass away. For the densely stolid and
practical person it will have little advantage, and will effect merely a
few minor worries or misunderstandings.

☉ 8 ♅ A very evil influence. All the native's affairs will now tend
to go wrong suddenly, and unexpected events of an astounding nature
will happen during this period : he should avoid travel or making any
changes or removals, if possible. He will meet with strenuous opposition, will suffer through separations and estrangements, and will also be
liable to lose friends and to come into unforeseen conflict with strangers
and to suffer thereby. His magnetic conditions will be inimical to others,
and he will be liable to act suddenly, impulsively, and very rashly while
the aspect operates. He cannot be too careful in all dealings with
others, nor weigh too carefully the consequences of his actions, for he
will be very liable to make mistakes, or to be made to act against his
will by the desires or the hypnotic influence of others. He should avoid
disputes and keep clear of all legal affairs, do nothing to offend others or
to bring himself into unmerited disgrace or ill-repute.   This aspect
marks a very critical stage in the career, and it will not pass without
causing sorrow, anxiety and trouble, from which an expansion of the
consciousness will result. *An extremely significant and important influence,*

likely to throw the native off his balance, unless he summons all his strength to combat it.

[The following are from the pen of a subscriber who has made a special study of the planet Neptune, but they are offered rather as suggestions than descriptions of the influences concerned. Little is actually known of this strange planet, save by individual experience.]

☉ P. ♆   This is the same as the conjunction in its general effect, but operates for a longer period and indicates a general over-hanging influence of the nature described.   It is unlikely to affect any but the most advanced souls to any great extent.

☉ ☌ ♆   This is a deeply mysterious influence and its full effect is scarcely likely to be felt by the majority, at least as regards material matters: much will depend upon the aspects to Neptune at birth, and also on whether this planet is prominent in the nativity in any way; but an extremely remarkable experience of some kind is likely to result from this influence if such should be the case.   A psychic awakening of some sort is sure to take place and according to the stage of unfoldment reached by the soul, this may range from a romantic love episode to poetic or musical inspiration or clairaudience; or, on the other hand, some weird experience connected with the sea or with haunted houses.   In any case the experience is sure to be accompanied with either incarceration or restriction of some kind: at least the renouncal of some long coveted or dearly prized object.   For Neptune is peculiarly connected with the *soul* of things.

☉ ⚹ ♆   The general nature of this influence will approximate to that of the conjunction as to the kind of experience denoted, but it is likely to be still more recondite and obscure.   Employment as a secret service agent would be an appropriate experience under this aspect for one whose nativity denoted such capacities; in a more ordinary horoscope, affairs connected with hospitals, workhouses or mortuaries.

☉ ∠ ♆*   This denotes a period of mysterious misfortunes, which dog the native's footsteps in a peculiar and unprecedented way.   Psychic matters are sure to enter into the life in some way and affect it injuriously, but the aspect, in any case, is a weak one, and unless the planet is heavily afflicted at birth little serious trouble is to be anticipated.

☉ ✳ ♆*   This is probably the most favourable influence of all, denoting (if other aspects are favourable) an idyllic period of blissful contentment.   The musical or poetical faculty will be strongly

* [See also ☌ ♆ above.]

awakened, and a pronounced tendency to mysticism—or refined sensuousness, according to the type of horoscope—will be displayed. In a material sense it denotes a period of surprising "good luck"; but this of course depends on the aspects at birth.

☉ □ ♆* This is the most evil aspect of the Sun to Neptune. If the latter is afflicted at birth the effects are likely to be most serious. An involved state of affairs in every phase of the activities is sure to ensue, and a deep depression of the emotional nature may lead to some rash act. Neurotics and other psychically sensitive persons are the most likely to feel the worst effect of this aspect, which tends to weaken the moral fibre and to ruin the constitution: this only when Neptune is much afflicted at birth.

☉ △ ♆* Other influences being favourable, this aspect inaugurates "halcyon days." Prosperity of the most unusual description—a "boom" to use a slang word—may be looked for, unless the aspects at birth preclude such good fortune. Riches and favours will be showered on the native and his cup will be full to overflowing. This as regards material welfare: to those who are more spiritually inclined this period is one of religious exaltation and great blessing in a spiritual sense, or of extreme creative fecundity in the case of a poet or musician.

☉ ⚼ ♆* This is similar in effect to the semi-square. Delays, disappointments, and tantalising experiences of an unusual kind may be anticipated, and the period is one that is likely to live in the memory as unique in its way, grinding, as it were, "slowly, yet exceeding small."

☉ ⚻ ♆* This, the quincunx or "inconjunct," is similar in its effect to the semi-sextile, but is somewhat longer in duration and more far-reaching in its effects. Its true mission is to effect a purification of the individuality.

☉ ☍ ♆* This is, perhaps, the most tremendous obstacle that the individuality has to cope with; for the soul is here weighed in the balances—and too often 'found wanting.' All the antagonistic forces of the lower nature, or the undeveloped part of man, rise up and seek to swamp him, and powerful indeed must he be if he can breast them. Only the pure can do so, and even they must prepare to see their most cherished schemes totter in apparent confusion to the ground. Failure, however, consists not in failing to maintain, but in ceasing to strive; and for the overcomer the reward is great.

* [See also ☌ ♆ p. 92.]

CHAPTER XI.

LUNAR POSITIONS AND ASPECTS.

THE Moon's aspects to the Sun and planets are always *very important*, for the Moon is the collector of influences and brings them to the stage of fruition; for without the Moon's co-operation the "mutual" and "solar" influences would be vague and uncertain. And therefore the Lunar aspects—apart even from the tendencies which they denote of themselves—act as an outlet or medium through which the Solar and Mutual influences can function. The Moon's passage through the various houses of the Radix and of the Progressed Horoscope indicates, according to the house through which she passes, the nature of the events most likely to affect the native.

In the following pages the influence determined by the house the Moon passes through is described, and also the signification of the various aspects, whether to radical or progressive planets.

In connection with the latter, it is well to take it as a standard rule that the Moon's aspects to *radical* planets are to be interpreted in terms of the Radix, while those to the *progressed* planets are to be rendered in terms of the Progressed Horoscope. Thus suppose Saturn is lord of the radical M.C., but of the ninth house in the progressed horoscope, and that the Moon comes to a bad aspect, first of the radical and next of the progressed Saturn. The first should be regarded as affecting the tenth house matters of the native—his parents or profession, or social status (especially as concerns such fixed matters as family interests, entailed property, etc., etc.), while the latter would show out its influence in ninth house affairs, journeys, philosophical studies, etc., etc., according to the general tenour of the radical and progressed ninth house and the character of each of the two horoscopes as a whole.

IMPORTANT NOTE REGARDING THE
MOON'S ASPECTS.

The Moon's aspects, formed by the progress of the Moon round the horoscope, are only of vital significance when they coincide in nature with the Solar and Mutual aspects. When this is the case during the period for which the " directions " have been calculated, attention should be drawn to the fact by a mark or note, so as to assist the judgment. Otherwise, the lunar aspects are only indications of what *may* or *could* happen under the lunar influences. It is, however, the *correspondence of the Lunar Aspects with the Solar or Mutual influences which makes the years eventful*, for the Moon brings matters to the culminating point and marks the time when the major aspect has reached the stage of fruition, when causes already set in motion on the mental or psychic planes will begin to manifest on the physical or material plane. Lunar aspects, when not coincident with the major aspects, are somewhat uncertain in their operation and may pass by without any appreciable effect, no matter how strong the aspect in itself, and hence at best they are only indications of *probable* events.

The same remark applies, of course, also to the Solar and Mutual Aspects. For instance, the ruler of the radical ascendant having progressed to the conjunction of the ruler of the progressed ascendant means, that the lord of the twelfth house of the progressed horoscope is in conjunction with the lord of its ascendant—a hampering and restrictive influence as far as the progressed horoscope is concerned, but having absolutely no influence upon the radical horoscope, unless it should take place in some degree that is in aspect to a radical planet or house cusp.

In a similar way, the passage of the Moon through the various houses of the horoscope must not be expected to produce events of like importance in all cases. Much for instance will depend on the prominence of the *sign* corresponding to the house in question in the nativity. Thus if Gemini is tenanted by many planets, or if Mercury is afflicted in a 'day' horoscope, the passage of the Moon through the radical or even the progressed third house, is sure to be fruitful of events. Here, as always, the student's own individual judgment must be brought into play, and the map with its aspects, etc., taken as a whole, before conclusions are formed. Indeed, in all true science as in all true art, analysis and synthesis *must* go hand in hand.

As before, the significations given apply primarily to the aspects of the progressed Moon to radical planets, but may also be interpreted in terms of the progressed horoscope in the manner indicated on p. 69.

A. The Lunar Position.

I. The Moon passing through the *First House* of the nativity or the progressed horoscope* will bring all matters connected with the personality to the fore, and much will depend upon the native's own actions and upon his own attitude of mind as to how the "directions" operating will affect him. This position generally tends to break up existing conditions, and consequently sometimes affects the health, in accordance with the strength of the Moon at birth or the solar influences operating in the progressed horoscope. As the Moon going over the cusp of the ascendant nearly always produces *changes*, it will be well for him to note carefully the kind of changes he desires, so as not to make mistakes. In a general sense he may expect the personality to come more to the fore, and all matters connected with the *form* side of existence to engage his attention more than previously; and as the Moon now commences that half of her circle which lies *under the earth*, he must prepare for the change of condition which the Moon's passage over the ascendant nearly always brings, for, as has been stated elsewhere, the lower half of the horoscope (houses I. to VI.) concerns the personality chiefly rather than the individuality.

II. The Moon passing through the *Second House* will bring to the fore all matters connected with finance. There are many advantages to be gained from the Moon's passage through the second house, for any good aspects that the Moon receives during each month will tend to be profitable from a financial standpoint, and those who are able to take advantage of this can nearly always find means to increase their incomes, either through judicious investment or through engaging the mind in general financial affairs to their own benefit. It is a good position for those who have the inspirational faculty, for imaginative and historical authors, etc.

III. The Moon passing through the *Third House* will affect the

---

* What has been said before regarding the distinction to be observed between the radical and the progressed horoscope will also apply here. The native may be regarded as having, in effect, two personalities—the hereditary or root temperament and disposition he was born with, and the modification or outgrowth thereof that he has evolved for himself from the former by the play of his thought and will upon the physical environment he found himself placed in. The former will remain unaffected except by such influences as disturb the radix or *nativity*, the latter will be amenable (more, or less, according to the progressive character of the soul) to every modification of the *progressed horoscope*.

mental conditions, giving great activity in all matters connected with the mind, stimulating to greater thought, and also tending to bring changes. As the lunar orb is below the earth, the native will be liable to brood over his conditions, desiring to alter in some way the environment in which he is placed. And so this progression of the Moon through the third house never fails to give some restlessness, while it also brings one into close contact with relatives, or persons who have some claim upon the native. The objective consciousness will be far more active than the subjective, the mind being more drawn towards objects and externals and by these means stimulated and rendered more inclined to think deeply.

IV. The Moon passing through the *Fourth House* of the nativity will tend to awaken interest in all domestic affairs, causing the native to have his mind concerned about his residence, and may bring changes and removals or at least make him restless and desirous of change. From an occult standpoint the Moon's passage through this house is favourable, as it will precipitate many things that have been held in suspension : there will, moreover, be an occult vein running through the native's consciousness, whether he recognises it as such or not, this being one of the psychic houses in all of which the Moon has some strength, being able to receive all the vibrations that are active in the nativity. It will have a correspondence with the *latter half* of the day, *i.e.*, from sunset to dawn, making this the best portion of the day for him for the time being, and will also bring him into touch with persons who are likely to affect him in the home life. Although the Moon in one sense has not much ' strength ' when passing through the fourth house, still she has a natural sympathetic relation with it, owing to Cancer, the *natural fourth house*, being the sign of the Moon.

V. The Moon passing through the *Fifth House* tends to awaken the emotions in connection with love affairs, children, pleasure generally, and even games of hazard, gambling or business enterprises ; for this house governs everything of a speculative nature. It is a good period to engage in investment or speculation and to seek pleasures generally. In certain respects the fifth house has sympathy with the emotions,* tending to awaken all the feelings of the native to the utmost and allowing him to give vent to them along those lines of least resistance

---

* That is, the *fiery* emotions, or those of the heart, as distinguished from the *watery*, or those of the physical senses.

which are offered when the Moon is passing through this house. When, however, she is receiving evil aspects, care will have to be taken where the feelings are concerned, similarly also in matters of a speculative nature, for financial losses are then probable; but under good aspects the native may invest to advantage, or profitably engage his mind in any speculative venture which prudence may sanction.

VI. The Moon passing through the *Sixth House*, not altogether a fortunate house for the Moon to pass through, as it tends to bring some sickness or indisposition, will therefore be likely to affect the health, which should be well guarded during this period. The native should also be very careful in all dealings with inferiors, as this is one of the "unfortunate" houses of the nativity; although it is true that it gives some psychic tendencies; but this is merely owing to the latent side of the nature being awakened. All afflictions that the Moon receives while passing through this house will be likely to affect the health and cause indisposition, unless careful attention is paid to hygiene, and hence will probably prove to be the commencement of any ill-health that will follow. Therefore, when such afflictions occur, the native should take care to keep the health in good order, so that when the Moon meets any *benefic* aspect to the other planets he may use those vibrations for the purpose of improving his general health; for this house is intimately connected with hygiene, and is just as powerful for benefiting the health as for impairing it, being related to the regulations or adjustment of the physical system generally.

VII. The Moon passing through the seventh, a house that is connected with marriage, unions, partnerships, and association with others, the native is likely to be brought into contact with others who will greatly influence his life; and he may enter into partnerships or unions, to his great advantage, if done while the Moon forms a favourable aspect to any of the other planets which is not itself afflicted. All favourable influences coming from the planets to the Moon while she passes through this house will tend to unify the native with others and to bring him into contact with those whose lives will run parallel with his own; but no ties or attachments—no unions particularly—should be formed when the Moon in her progress through the seventh meets any *affliction* to the other planets. The nature of the aspects the Moon meets should be carefully noted, so that the best time to become united or attached to others may be observed. The natal aspects between the respective rulers of the first and seventh houses, and any affliction thereto, should also be carefully borne in mind and all testimonies duly weighed.

VIII.   The Moon passing through the *Eighth House*, considered the "House of Death," it is probable that deaths may occur in the native's social circle, or deaths will in some way affect him.   In a higher sense, however, the passage of the Moon through this house has a very deep significance, for it awakens interest in occult matters and usually brings some phase of the occult very prominently into the life : hence the native is likely to have some of his inner senses stimulated into greater activity by this lunar position.   But much, of course, will depend upon the aspects that the Moon forms to other planets during her passage through this house, which lasts for sometimes as long as three years or more. The good aspects will bring gain either by will or legacy, and the adverse aspects, sorrow and trouble in connection with losses, especially in relation to the partner's income.   A careful study of the aspects will be necessary before deciding definitely how the Moon's passage will operate.

IX.   The Moon passing through the *Ninth House*, a rather fortunate influence, tends to considerably improve the horoscope as a whole, causing the mind to be interested in all matters connected with either the occult life, or philosophy and religion, and if the native can aspire high enough he will now be able to come into touch with that plane of knowledge wherein all things are known : therefore, by awakening the intellectual side of the nature he will be greatly benefited by the Moon's passage through the house.   Sometimes voyages are indicated when the Moon goes through the ninth house, but of course much will depend upon the aspects, both those in the radical and also those in the progressed horoscope.

X.   The Moon passing through the *Tenth House* will probably bring some responsibility, and it will certainly accentuate the native's sense of justice, bringing out all the moral tendencies; for the tenth house has much to do with elevation to a better position in life, always giving advantages for progress and stimulating the moral side of the nature, making the native endeavour to improve his surroundings and thus making the period a good time for asking favours or raising one's self into a higher phase of efficiency and service.   All matters of a business nature will now come to the fore, and everything connected with work in which he is interested will tend to become more prominent

in the native's life, so that many advantages may be gained while the
Moon is passing through this house. It will also have something to do
with domestic arrangements, affecting the maternal side of the home,
and generally bringing activity into the life according to the aspects,
good or bad, that the Moon may meet.

XI. The Moon passing through the *Eleventh House* will cause all
matters concerned with friendships to be brought prominently to the
fore. The native will either make new friends or acquaintances, or be
closely associated with those whom he considers his friends, and as
this house is also connected with hopes, wishes and desires, his desires
will become much stronger, and the more hope he can cultivate the
more successful will he be during the time the Moon passes through
this house. At the same time, a great deal will depend upon the aspects
formed by the lunar orb, for under adverse aspects care will be
necessary with regard to friends and acquaintances, while under good
aspects help and assistance may come through friends, also much
success in dealing with them. This house is somewhat fortunate for the
Moon, therefore the most should be made of all the opportunities that
come in the native's way as she passes through it.

XII. The Moon passing through the *Twelfth House* will probably
bring sorrows and troubles, for this is considered the most unfortunate
house of the twelve. However, there is a side to this influence that is
worth noting, and that is the occult and psychic tendencies which it
gives, and the ability to come into touch with the deeper part of the
nature; for it brings out all the sympathies, awakens the truly hopeful
tendencies, and does much to stir into activity the deeper emotions
which are latent in the native's character. He will probably have some
experiences of a sorrowful nature which will awaken his feelings, and it
is moreover possible that he may also suffer some treachery from the
hidden enmity of others while the Moon is passing through this house;
but he should remember that nothing can come to him that is not his
own, and therefore if he has made no enemies in the past he need not
fear the Moon's passage through this house: yet if he has committed
any acts which necessitate the working out of the fate attached to them,
then while the Moon goes through this house he will reap the results of
those his former acts. For this is especially the house through which
" Karma," or the fruit of past actions, works out its own destiny—both
the suffering experienced and the wisdom gained thereby.

B. The Lunar Aspects.

☽ P. ☉ An influence tending to awaken and make manifest the solar influence. The native will now find his mind prone to change, somewhat ambitious and aspiring, with the desire behind it to improve his general surroundings and to experience new conditions of a more beneficial nature. This is a position that is mainly dependent upon other aspects to give it character and definite shape, and while it often gives the desire for change it does not always bring the opportunity to carry out that desire. But it has however an effect upon the other lunar aspects, as it strengthens the Moon's aspects to the other portions of the horoscope, and brings individual effort into play either to change or to improve the environment. It often affects those who are indirectly connected with the life, without actually causing any difference in the native's own affairs, affecting others indirectly through himself. In some cases it is a weak influence, in others very powerful, according to the influence and power of the Sun both in the nativity and the progressed horoscope.

☽ ☌ ☉ This position of the luminaries will bring changes, and either social advancement or some success and gratified ambition. It is not always a favourable position for health, changes taking place in the system which bring a liability to feverish complaints, affecting the circulation and the general health according to the normal condition of the constitution, and also the present mode of living, habits, etc. The native will either change his residence, experience some radical change in environment, or undergo internal changes which will have a permanent effect upon his future; for this influence marks a minor cycle in life, bringing new undertakings, fresh responsibilities, and attachments or unions that affect the future according to the opportunities the environment affords and the use that is made of them to gain all the advantages which this important conjunction offers. He may now act with more confidence than usual, and seek to bring about those conditions which his personal needs demand, for if he acts discreetly he will gain his object.

☽ ⚹ ☉ A very weak but nevertheless avourable aspect, tending to make the mind more hopeful and cheerful, and also giving an opportunity for the better influences in the horoscope to operate. It will bring some slight improvement in the native's monetary affairs, and some gain from superiors, paving the way for improvement in the general conditions of his environment. There is here a harmonious blending of the positive and negative forces, which will allow other aspects in the nativity to work freely, so that gain and success will attend effort on the part of the native to improve himself and his prospects in a general and all-round manner. The aspect is not a strong one, nor does it promise much ; but its favourable nature sets in motion the vibration that will allow the other good aspects to be strengthened, and the evil aspects to be minimised. Monetary advantages are indicated.

☽ ∠ ☉   An unfavourable aspect, though weak : generally produces some slight indisposition, which may turn to more severe and evil results ; it is therefore an influence rather of the nature of a warning note than an actual presage of evil. If the native does not live correctly the circulation of the blood will be affected, the system will become clogged and the functions sluggish, causing a feverish state which may either be quickly remedied by proper attention and abstemiousness, or if neglected will lead to more serious complications, according to the attitude of his mind towards the result it produces. He should not allow himself to become excited or over-heated, or enter into any disagreement with another, or disappointment and disfavour will be the result. It is not a good period for monetary affairs, nor for matters connected with pleasure, society, friends or attachments.

☽ ✳ ☉   The chief influence of this aspect is to brighten the mind and give a very hopeful outlook, inspiring confidence and leading the energies into a more enterprising and ambitious channel. Success will attend many of the native's undertakings while this aspect lasts, he will meet with prosperity and will gain from others, while if any short journeys are undertaken, or travel, he will obtain success and benefit from the change. This is a good period in which to make changes, either mental or physical ; also to form new attachments, to make new friends and acquaintances, and to seek for social advancement. The native may obtain favours from others, or will come in contact with those who are mentally and socially his superiors, and benefit through them. This aspect favours all literary work, writing, reading and correspondence ; also general intercourse with persons who are cultured and refined or in good positions in the world. The most should be made of this good influence by exercising the mind as much as possible.

☽ □ ☉   The native may expect to pass through a rather anxious time, for domestic and family affairs are now likely to become disorganised, since this aspect not only threatens his own health, but also the health of others in some manner connected with him, either by relationship or friendly attachment. He must guard his health, for sickness is threatened him if he allows the digestive organs to get upset, or the circulation to be weakened, rendering him subject to some indisposition or other, which will affect him according to his general strength of constitution and physical condition at the time. He will find troubles and difficulties and several anxieties now affecting him. It is not a good time to make changes or removals, neither is it good for travel, nor for entering into any new undertaking. If the other " directions " operating at the time become too severe it will signify a death in the family or social circle, or some rather serious trials. This is one of the critical positions, depending for its actual effect upon the current Solar aspects.

☽ △ ☉   The native will now enter upon a period of success, bringing the satisfactory realisation of many of his ambitions, hopes, and wishes, in accordance with his capacity to answer to the aspect and to his own inner nature. It will bring him opportunities to improve his general conditions and surroundings, and is a good time to invest or to speculate, or to enter upon new enterprises and fresh undertakings. He will have joy and pleasure from his feelings and emotions, will form new and honourable friendships, and will gain through friends and those who are bound up with his general welfare in life. He may ask favours of superiors, enter into fresh enjoyments, and do all to further his interests. This aspect denotes the advent of a pleasurable and fruitful time in which all matters connected with the domestic circle will proceed favourably, and is a good time for health and for the enjoyment of life generally. Much, however, depends upon the native's own power to extract all the good out of the opportunities he will meet with.

☽ ⊡ ☉   Malignant in its nature and likely to cause trouble and anxiety while it operates. Fortunately, although sharp and acute while it lasts, it is an aspect that does not endure for any considerable time, but while it is in operation the health is liable to suffer, and great care should be taken to cure colds and all feverish tendencies. This aspect affects the health through changes in the vital system, altering the circulation and bringing a liability to suffer from ill-health subsequently, if care is not taken to keep the mind calm and free from anxiety. The native will now suffer from disappointments and will either offend those with whom he is intimately related or suffer through them in some peculiar way. It is an adverse aspect for dealing with superiors, or those in higher social standing than himself, and it will be well for him to act discreetly and cautiously.

☽ ⊼ ☉ The Moon in forming this very weak aspect to the Sun's radical position is but indifferently affected thereby; it will, however, operate favourably when the Solar or Mutual aspects are good. The native may take advantage of this influence by safeguarding his health, for it denotes a change in the system; and these changes produced by the luminaries in any aspect may affect the health—according as the general liability is to suffer or not to suffer when the magnetic currents alter. If the digestive organs are normally strong the aspect has little effect in this particular; but when there is any tendency to worry or to become upset by domestic affairs or emotional states, then the health is affected, and this period becomes the forerunner of changes in the system that eventually re-act adversely upon the general well-being.

☽ ☍ ☉ A very critical position, often the culminating point of a train of "directions," and bringing with it unpleasant and trying conditions, in which anxiety, worry and sorrow are experienced. This aspect is essentially separative in its nature, and is therefore liable to produce separations, by death or otherwise, parting of friends, and disappointments, also loss of dignity, or such events as affect honour and social standing. In common with all aspects between the luminaries it produces changes, and tends to break up existing conditions. But although this aspect is malefic in its nature it will not act disastrously unless the solar influences are also evil, in which case ill health, losses, deaths, or domestic troubles are threatened. It will be well not to expect any favourable termination to any dispute with superiors; neither is it a good time for the feelings and emotions, which are now likely to suffer.

☽ P. ☿ This influence is very favourable for mental activities. It will bring changes, new friends, advancement, and intellectual energy, and will extend over a period of several months; it will act chiefly in accordance with the primary (*i.e.*, mutual and solar) directions in force rather than alone; but in itself it is good for the mind, and for general operations in which both thought and industry are required. The native should make the most of this influence, whether for purposes of reading and studying, or for travel, for a link is here formed between the brain mind and the stored-up mental ability. Hence it is a good time to attend lectures, to visit intellectual persons, and to improve the mind generally.

☽ ☌ ☿   This position is very favourable for the Moon, and denotes a time when the mind will be most receptive and very keen and alert. The native will find himself acute and diligent, eager to be busy. This is the time, then, when he may know the power and strength of his mental abilities, for a link is now formed between the brain cells and the true mentality: hence in accordance with the stored-up knowledge within, so may he exhibit consideration, thoughtfulness, and method: the memory should now be very good, and if exercised will serve well in all directions. It is, however, proper to remark that this *may* be just as unfavourable as favourable, according to the Solar or Mutual influences operating in the nativity or the progressed map. To make it favourable, the native should study, and exercise the mind with ideas, and think as freely as he can; above all, he should learn the value of *concentration*, for thought dissipated over a thousand different objects is merely a great energy wasted.

☽ ⚹ ☿   This is a favourable aspect, although not very powerful in its operation. Like all lunar-mercurial aspects it will have the effect of linking up the brain with that portion of the mentality which is always more or less latent. It will bring opportunities to improve the mind by study or reading; and it will awaken an interest in general mind improvement. The native may gain financially through mental activities, since this aspect will stir the mind into a more energetic condition, arousing his curiosity and giving him the ability to improve his monetary prospects either by writing and correspondence, or by agencies and dealings through others. This lunar aspect will tend to bring him into new undertakings, and thus always denotes a more or less busy period: but a great deal will depend upon his own growth and progress as to how far it will affect him beneficially; for it *may* only indicate agility and quickness physically, instead of mental alertness or the two combined.

☽ ∠ ☿   This is not a strong aspect, but its influence is not good and while it operates it will be well for the native to endeavour to avoid disputes, and to abstain from any sort of speech that is not quite accurate or the future result of which he is not fully conscious of. For this aspect brings a liability to be indiscreet both in speech and also in writing, therefore all should be carefully thought out before he commits himself either in speech or writing. This is not a good time for the native to travel or to deal with others, especially those who have any power to draw him out and use what he may say as evidence against him. He should not quarrel with anyone, should be guarded in all dealings with relatives or kindred, but above all things should use care in writing or in speech, sign nothing of importance, and keep his own counsel, trusting to no one while this aspect is operating.

☽ ⚹ ☿ A very favourable influence, which will make this a successful and fortunate period according to the native's own innate ability; moreover, the mind will tend to enlarge and grow under its influence, so that it is a good time to learn and study, and to improve the mind generally. For there is now a most effective link between the objective and subjective consciousness, which will stimulate him into gathering more knowledge, thus enabling him to expand mentally in all directions. It is a very good time to travel, to make changes, and to deal with relatives or kindred. The native may either deal personally with others, or, if more advantage is sought, write and correspond; for he will now be able to express himself clearly and to the purpose, the mind being at its best, bright and clear and capable according to the inherent abilities and acquired mentality. He should make the most of this period, for progress may be rapid under this aspect.

☽ ☐ ☿ This is an evil aspect, for it tends to bring a disturbing element into the surroundings, which may have the effect of upsetting or disarranging domestic affairs. It is not good for any dealings with kindred or relatives, and denotes disputes with them. The native should now use care with regard to all correspondence, for it is an evil time for expressing oneself in any way, and he is therefore likely to be misunderstood, so that misconceptions will arise which will for the time interfere with his peace of mind. He should not travel this month, and should keep himself free from engagements or appointments as far as possible until this aspect has passed, having no dealings with solicitors or agents, and signing no important papers unless compelled to do so. This is the aspect that brings libel or slanderous reports to those who from the positions at birth are liable to attacks from others. It is not good for any literary work, but, fortunately, it does not endure long.

☽ △ ☿ This will give great activity of brain, stimulating all mental energy, and enabling the native to display as much talent as he has latent within him, a strong link being now formed between the brain and the mental powers, allowing him at this time to fittingly express all that is latent within him : and in accordance with the mentality stored within him so will he make this period fortunate and successful. He will display an enquiring mind and diligent mental activity, and if he gives his mind to study will learn much under this influence. It is a good time for writing or correspondence, also for travelling, and to make changes, or to remove if necessary. All literary undertakings and business pursuits will now prosper, and the more the mind is energised and stimulated, the more alert and operative will it become. A great deal depends upon the innate ability to use this period wisely, yet it is a stage where good and useful work may be done, not for the present only, but also for the future.

☽ ☐ ☿   This is not a good aspect, and it is likely to make the mind sarcastic and the tongue inclined to expressions that will not be peaceful or harmonious. The native's relationship with others will not be conducive to a satisfactory understanding, and the less he has to do with others at this time, especially kindred and relatives, the better. He should not travel or enter upon any fresh undertakings, but postpone all affairs that can conveniently wait over, as signings of papers, etc., and dealings with others generally, are not likely to be profitable or satisfactory at this period. He will be liable to suffer from ill repute and from personal attacks whilst this lunar aspect operates, and therefore should do nothing likely to give rise to misunderstanding but deal towards all with whom he may come into communication in an impartial and non-personal way, taking care to offend no one. It is not a good time for writing or for correspondence, and in speech great caution will be necessary.

☽ ⚹ ☿   This is a somewhat unimportant aspect. It will operate in accordance with the native's mental development, for all aspects between the Moon and Mercury denote a link of a more pronounced type than usual between the brain and the mind, and it will therefore give him an opportunity to express himself more readily, and to use whatever latent mental ability he may have in a more direct and decisive way than usual. It will be a good time to plan and arrange, also to correspond, or to undertake literary work of any kind, especially critical reviews, etc.   He will be more expressive, and may make himself better understood than usual. This is a good time to study and learn, and just as the mind is used so will the brain be willing to respond. If the mental abilities are stimulated it will now be a good time for independent thought, with freedom from personal bias.

☽ 8 ☿ This is a very unfavourable influence, for it will tend to make the mind over sharp—too keen and alert, causing the native to over-reach himself in some way, and to overstep the bounds of moderation or discretion. This will either bring him into disrepute, or cause him to quarrel with others and thereby arouse much opposition. He will do well to avoid all correspondence or writing, and leave the signing of important papers until the mind can see clearly, freed from all prejudice or personal bias. This aspect gives a liability to distort things, and to view things in a wrong light, and the native should therefore be careful in all dealings with others, especially agents and " 'cute " people generally. It is not a good time to travel, to make changes, or to remove; in fact it is an ill time for the mind, which is prone to worry and become over anxious, seeing things in a jaundiced way due partly to an overwrought condition, for the nervous energy will be disturbed under this aspect. The native should use great care in all he does at this time.

☽ P. ♀ This is a very favourable position, and likely to benefit the native and bring him good fortune and success while it lasts; and as it is not confined to one month alone it is quite a general aspect for good. It will improve the mind, making it cheerful, bright and mirthful, inclined to pleasure, and to take things in a lighter vein than usual. The native will obtain some social advantage under its influence, and will have dealings with others that will tend to bring about attachments or engagements of a very favourable nature, his feelings and emotions being stirred to respond to any demonstration of affection or display of feeling on the part of others. He should make the most of this period, for it is a good time for all things; and if he uses it for advancing his own interests he will find all things going smoothly and easily with him.

☽ ☌ ♀ This is a very good position, denoting a favourable time for all pleasures, for attachments, engagements and social affairs generally. The feelings and emotions will now be pleasurably excited, and the native will respond to all display of affection readily and with full sympathy, for this will bring friendships, and those attachments which will link him to others and make lasting ties of a very beneficial nature:

it is a good time to seek pleasure, and to make oneself as attractive and pleasing as possible. This position very often brings a marriage, or its equivalent, a partnership or tie that is favourable and good. The native's mind will now be peaceful and happy; he should therefore make the most of his good opportunities, using this harmonious vibration for the refining and purifying of the personality. It is a favourable position for all artistic matters.

☽ ⊼ ♀ Although a weak aspect this is good, and tends to improve the mind by making it more pleasure-loving and peaceful, also more inclined to society and the fellowship of others. It is a good time to form new acquaintances, to make friends, or to form attachments. It is not a sufficiently strong aspect to bring matters to a state of fruition, but it is good for the native to make himself active in regard to feeling, so that his affections may find a safe outlet. This aspect is slightly good also for monetary affairs, and he should improve his financial prospects under its influence. He will find it good for visiting and making friends, and for extending his social circle, also for generally benefiting his domestic affairs. It is only slightly good, being a weak aspect, but much more may be made of it by taking it as an opportunity to be *utilised*.

☽ ∠ ♀ This is not a good influence, though it is in many respects a weak one. It will cause the native some disappointment, or will arrest the flow of feeling and emotion. He will not be able to show or demonstrate all he feels, and will find some delay or hindrance to his affections. It is not a good time to form new attachments or to make friends and acquaintances, and he will do well also to watch expenditure, as he will be liable to some monetary losses. If careful, not allowing sensation or personal feeling to affect him, nothing serious will disturb his affections while this lunar aspect lasts; but it will be just as well, by not looking for more than ordinary sympathy, to avoid having the personal sensitiveness affected while this aspect is in force—rarely longer than one or two months at the outside.

☽ ✶ ♀ This is a very favourable and fortunate lunar aspect, and it will benefit the native in many ways. The mind will be more clear and lucid while it operates, and the feelings and emotions will be stirred, so that he will find an outlet for feeling through the affectional side of his nature, forming attachments or unions that will be very successful, and linking himself to others in a manner that will be highly beneficial and fruitful. He should make the most of this aspect to bring to a satisfactory issue the links that exist between himself and others; for his feelings will be at their best, and the whole of the nature will be filled with pleasant emotion under this aspect. It is a good period for financial success, and the monetary prospects should improve and bring success and gain. The native should do all he can to advance himself socially, mentally, and morally; for it is one of the best lunar aspects and should be used to improve the general conditions.

☽ □ ♀ This is not a favourable aspect, and is one likely to cause some trouble, especially with regard to the feelings and emotions; for the native is likely to suffer disappointment, or to have disagreements with others, which will cause him sorrow and anxiety. His attachments and engagements are likely to go wrong under this aspect, and domestic affairs to be upset and disarranged. This aspect also denotes some monetary difficulties, therefore it is advisable to use care in all financial matters. It is not a good time for social undertakings, and the greatest care will be necessary to keep from fretting, and from unduly feeling the adverse vibrations now operating. If the native allows personal feeling to affect him, he will now be very sensitive and easily wounded. He cannot be too careful in all dealings with the opposite sex, and should not allow himself to form any attachments that are not in accord with his ideals.

☽ △ ♀ This is a remarkably good lunar aspect, and if it coincides with other good directions operating it will mark an epoch in life. The native will now find his feelings and emotions having a very satisfactory outlet, for it will make his attachments and engagements fruitful, and tend to bring all matters concerning the affections to a satisfactory issue. It is a very good time for pleasure, for social success, and for general advancement and prosperity. It is good also for finance and monetary prospects, and will bring gain, pleasure, and profit in many directions. The native will be wise to make the most of this very favourable lunar aspect, and to do all he can to bring about his desires. A great deal will depend upon his environment at this time: he will have the *opportunity*, and it will be for him to respond himself to the opportunity that this influence will bring. In any case it is a good aspect, and will bring good in accordance with the indications shown in the nativity.

☽ ⧠ ♀ Not a very important aspect, but when other influences are evil it denotes a death in the family circle, or some loss which is keenly felt. The native's feelings and emotions will suffer in some way, especially if his affections have not been altogether well placed ; financial matters, moreover, should be watched while this aspect lasts, for there is some liability to losses. Though not a powerful influence it will act adversely if the personal feelings are easily wounded, for there is a tendency to make more of events that relate to attachments and engagements than would otherwise be the case. It is not a good time for domestic affairs and for social concerns. The native should be careful in all dealings with the opposite sex ; also with regard to his expenditure, which is likely to exceed his income, for this is rather a wasteful aspect : in fact, it is one that brings a great deal of anxiety if at the same time other influences are adverse.

$D \times \venus$ This is a very weak aspect, and only likely to affect the native actively if the feelings and emotions have been called out, and he has any attachments or engagements into which some of the personal feelings have been poured. It will slightly benefit him financially or socially ; and if he exerts himself personally during its operation it will benefit him according to his ability to influence others in his favour. It is a good time to visit, and to form new friendships, since acquaintance-ships now made will be likely to prove satisfactory ; moreover domestic affairs will go well while this influence lasts. It is, however, one that will soon pass off, and it is even possible that nothing at all of importance may occur. A great deal will depend upon the native's own attitude towards others at this time.

$D \; \eighthnote \; \venus$ This is very unfavourable and is likely to bring sorrow and disappointment. It may produce a death in the family circle, or in some other way bring grief, for it is an aspect that affects the feelings and emotions, and will tend to produce a rather trying time whilst it operates. The native cannot be too careful with regard to friends and acquaintances, or any attachments or engagements he may have in prospect. It will be an evil time for his financial affairs, and he should guard against monetary losses. All associations with the opposite sex will now require great care, for there is a liability to get into trouble or disgrace through connections with others at this period. If the other directions are operating adversely this will be a very bad time, and great care will be necessary to avoid separations, disappointments, and sorrowful experiences generally.

D P. $\mars$ This is a very evil position while it lasts, and it is likely to last for a longer period than other aspects. During its operation the native should be very guarded in his actions, avoiding all impulse and tendencies to rashness. This is a time in which all disputes and quarrels must be carefully guarded against, and all dealings with others should be marked by discretion and tolerance. It is also a time when there is a liability to accidents and feverish complaints. The mind should be kept calm and the actions temperate, for any of the major (mutual or solar) aspects that may be evil at this time will be liberated by this lunar position. The native will be liable to infectious diseases, to incur debts that will be difficult to pay, and to go to extremes in many ways. All excesses and out-rushings of energy should be checked or tempered, for this extends over a much longer period than other influences, and it always becomes acute when brought into action by the native's rash attitude towards circumstances and general surroundings. Let his watchword now be CAUTION.

☽ ☌ ♂   This is an evil position for the Moon, as it excites and stirs into greater activity any latent desires that the native may have, and causes him to act more from impulse and out-rushing energy than at any other time. To those who are passionate it awakens passion and anger, to those who are uncontrolled it gives opportunity to go to extremes, and it brings, moreover, a danger of accidents, fevers and inflammatory complaints. To all it denotes a time when rash and hasty conduct should be deliberately guarded against. The native should be careful in his dealings with others, also with regard to attachments and friendships; he should also avoid travel as much as possible. Health will not be good under this lunar position, and in all things where personal affairs are concerned it is a period that may be marked in large letters DANGEROUS. If, however, the native has his animal nature under full control he need fear nothing from this position except a little excitement or increase of mental energy.

☽ ⚹ ♂   This is a (weak) good aspect between the Moon and Mars, if any aspect between these two can be called good; but it is only such in the sense that it increases energy and adds fire and tone to the personal character. It will probably bring a little more activity into the life and increase the feeling side of the nature, making the native more expressive or impulsive and inclined to venture where otherwise he would have hesitated. It may give him a little more prospect of financial benefit, but all rash or hasty conduct with regard to monetary

affairs should be guarded against. He should not allow his passions to
get too strong, or the mental energy to be over-stimulated, but should
treat the aspect as a little more force added to the desire-nature which
can be fitly used for those purposes he has at heart, but not for the
personal gratification of any excess of feeling.

☽ ∠ ♂   This is a weak but also an evil aspect, for it brings excitement and an accession of force which it will be difficult to use up as
mental energy alone; hence an over-flow of this force is likely to make
the native hasty and too apt to act from impulse, without stopping to
think of consequences. He should endeavour not to quarrel if he can
possibly avoid it, and act as carefully as he can in all dealings with
others. Any tendency towards rashness on his part will precipitate any
evil that may be indicated as latent in the nativity. This aspect will
make him assertive and very active, but he should beware of excesses,
and act discreetly where passion is concerned : for extremes would be
likely to lead him into difficulties, and trouble would follow any outburst
of feeling which he might give vent to. It is only a weak aspect, and
therefore may pass with but an increase of mental energy and an
addition of impulse ; it is nevertheless not a time to go against the tide.

☽ ✶ ♂   This will bring great activity and increase all mental effort,
making the native very free and liberal, brave generally, and courageous.
If he can avoid going to any extremes he will find that he now has a
great influx of mental energy, bringing him the power to affect his
surroundings and environment by his own personal efforts. It is a good
aspect for travel and changes generally and if he wishes to add fire to his
personal efforts this is the aspect to give all the ' go ' and energy he could
wish for ; yet to many it will only mean adding fuel to the passional side
of the nature, thus firing the passions to a higher pitch than is good,
as it will stimulate them into much greater activity than usual. If the
native would advance by utilising this force to the best advantage, he
should let it work through his ambitions, and rather through the mind
than the senses, thus bringing good health and plenty of enterprise, and
so proving of lasting benefit.

☽ □ ♂   This is an evil aspect and one likely to bring sorrow and
trouble, but this will depend upon the native's own attitude towards his
environment and general surroundings ; for if he does not rein in the
excess of force which it brings it will cause him to act very impulsively
and to give way to hasty and rash tendencies which will re-act upon him

and cause him to suffer. He should take care of his health, for he is liable to inflammatory and feverish complaints under this aspect, and any excitement or tendency to go to extremes would render him liable to accidents or to suffer through violence in various ways. He should not travel if he can avoid it, nor should he sign any papers or documents that have any risk attached to the signing, dealing only with those whom he can safely trust. He should be very careful in all dealings with those of the opposite sex, the influence of whom upon him at this time will be inimical and likely to injure him in some way. It will be an evil time unless the whole of the animal nature has been subdued, for it excite the lower nature and causes it to be difficult to control and manage; but only on account of the increased force which this vibration brings.

☽ △ ♂ This is a good aspect, but only to those who have their animal nature fully under control; for it increases the passional and impulsive side of the nature and tends to develop a great deal of force, which will work either through the mind or the senses, according to the stage of evolution that has been reached. If used as mental energy it will help the native to push his affairs, and the more enterprising and the more ambitious he is, the more will he succeed and make his undertakings prosperous and successful. It is a good time to travel, and to extend operations generally; it is also a good period for planning and arranging all personal matters. It will make the native free, open-handed and liberal minded, and cause him to be courageous, brave, and high-spirited. He may safely go with the tide of energy that is flowing through him, but he must avoid undue excitement and giving way to over-enthusiasm and zeal. If he uses the force wisely, he may be a power for good, but if unwisely it will make him feverishly impulsive, restless, and unduly ardent; for the martial energy which this aspect denotes is a force which needs wise direction in order to make it beneficial.

☽ ☐ ♂ This is not a good aspect, and if the other directions are evil it denotes a period in which some impulsive conduct will lead to results that will cause sorrow. The native should avoid any conflict or dispute with others, or he will regret his attitude; for it may lead to quarrels and acts whose consequences will bring remorse. He should keep his blood pure also, as he is now somewhat liable to feverish or inflammatory complaints. He should not travel, or make any important changes or removals, unless obliged to do so. This is a weak aspect, it is true, but no aspect between the Moon and Mars is good, and therefore he should keep a guard over his tongue and temper, and not allow himself to become irritable or easily excited, and all will then go well.

☽ ⌅ ♂   This is a decidedly weak aspect, and can only harm those who have not yet fully controlled the animal part of their nature, yet it brings some force to the personal character which if used mentally will be beneficial, but if used through the senses will cause the native to give way to passion, and tend to make him rash and hasty ; he will also be liable to over-heated blood, giving rise to feverish or inflammatory complaints.   He should be discreet in all his dealings with others, especially the opposite sex, and form no new attachments under this influence, but deal with all friends and acquaintances cautiously and with deliberation.   It is not a good time to travel or make changes, nor to remove or commence any fresh undertakings.   It will be well to let things go on as smoothly as possible and avoid all excitement or any tendency to over-activity.   This aspect is useful to those who are attempting physical regeneration.

☽ 8 ♂   This position is very evil, denoting a rather critical time, in which health is threatened, making the native liable to feverish and inflammatory conditions and also apt to act more from impulse than from careful thought.   Hence he must avoid all rash and hasty tendencies, and eschew disputes and quarrels ; for the least excitement is liable to arouse all the fire of Mars and act upon the passional side of the nature, rousing it to its fullest expression.   He cannot be too discreet with regard to the opposite sex, and all actions should be carefully thought out beforehand, as the result of any rash conduct will be likely to cause much sorrow and trouble in the future.   Travel, and the making of any changes, should be avoided, and the native will be well advised to keep as quiet as he possibly can, living temperately and with all the senses well under control. He will now meet with obstacles and opposition and find many difficulties before him.   He should not sign papers unless he is sure of the result, and should do all he can to keep the force flowing through him well under control, for he is now liable to discredit and scandal as the result of any intemperate act, and also to accidents arising from haste or precipitancy.

☽ P.♃   This is a very benefic and fortunate position, which will benefit the native for several months while the parallel lasts.   It is an excellent position for social welfare, also for any friendships or attachments that he may have formed ; for it denotes a peaceful and prosperous time when all things tend to go well, and success comes from all quarters.   He will now do well financially, and will have presents or gain under this benefic position. It will be a good time to travel, and to undertake new enterprises generally, as it will increase opportunities both materially and socially. The health will benefit and the mind expand, inclining the native to be generous and liberal, also somewhat philosophical and disposed to turn towards the deeper side of life, thinking of the subjective or inner world, as well as the objective or outer. When other aspects are good this parallel will accentuate all the good that is promised by the nativity, and the native should make the most of this good period and miss none of the opportunities it will bring.

☽ ☌ ♃ This very benefic position will greatly improve all the native's present conditions and affairs. It will benefit him socially and also financially, and it will bring him personal opportunities and advantages which he should make the most of; moreover all attachments and engagements will prosper and succeed while this influence operates, and he will increase and prosper in all directions, either through personal merit or by the help of others, or both. It is a very good time in which to commence new undertakings, also to seek to increase income and enlarge the future prospects.   Under this influence the native will enjoy life and experience pleasures which at other times he cannot fully appreciate. The more he exerts himself and pushes his own affairs, the more good will this vibration bring, therefore whatever desires or ambitions he may have are likely at this time to ripen and bring forth good fruit. It is not a position that lasts for any considerable time, and therefore he should " make hay while the sun shines."

☽ ⚹ ♃ This, although a slight and somewhat weak aspect, will nevertheless benefit the native, for it shows some probability of financial gain, and also success in all his engagements and general undertakings; but it is particularly good for social matters, and it would be well for the native to give his best attention to advantages in this direction, for the help of friends and those who wish him well may now be secured. If of an enterprising and progressive spirit he may add considerably to his material welfare while this influence is operating, but he should not expect much without the aid of his own personal efforts, which should be exercised in the direction that the aspect indicates. Let him do all he can either to add to his income or to promote his general social welfare, while, by taking as philosophical and temperate a view of all things as he possibly can, this aspect (if it does nothing else) will bring a peaceful frame of mind, and thus benefit both the health and the disposition.

☽ ∠ ♃   This is a weak but at the same time unfavourable aspect, which denotes some social troubles or some temporary financial losses. It is not a good time to push monetary affairs or to enter into any new undertakings, to make fresh engagements, or to generally exert oneself for gain; for the results would not be sufficient recompense for the outlay of energy. It is not good for travel or for religious matters, but is a time when it is best to remain quiet and restful. All speculation and investment of money should be postponed, and all social affairs left over until the Moon has passed away from this aspect. The blood should be kept as pure as possible by living temperately, for blood disorders may arise out of this affliction to the Moon: chiefly, however, through surfeit or excess.

☽ ✷ ♃   This is a splendid aspect for good fortune and general prosperity. It will greatly improve the mind and disposition, and the native will be enabled to gain many benefits and advantages during its operation. He will gain socially and financially, and will prosper in all he undertakes at this time. It is a good time to commence any new undertaking, to visit others, to deal with kindred and relatives, and indeed to do anything in his power to advance his prospects, for this aspect improves the health and denotes a good period generally, when all things will tend to go well; and he should therefore make the most of it by bringing all engagements to a successful issue, and by establishing himself under its influence. If the other principal directions are good then this will be a specially fortunate time, but if the other directions are evil, much less benefit should be expected from it: but in any case the native should push his affairs, and go with the stream of good that is flowing, for he will be able under this influence to deal with all the circumstances of his general environment in the most enlightened way.

☽ □ ♃   This is an evil aspect, though as the planet Jupiter is in itself benefic it does not produce such adverse effects as would otherwise be the case. It is not a good time for either financial or social affairs. The native will find a tendency for expenditure to exceed receipts, and all inclinations towards extravagance or undue generosity should be carefully guarded against. It is not a good period to extend friendship or to make new acquaintances, to commence fresh undertakings or push affairs. It will cause the blood to be liable to disorder, and will affect health if there be any excesses or extremes, and the native should therefore be very temperate in his diet and general mode of living, avoiding extremes of all kinds while this aspect lasts. It is not good for domestic affairs, and care should be exercised in all dealings with kindred.   Changes or removals should be avoided if possible and things taken quietly, not allowing the vibration to awake any undue enthusiasm such as may give rise to an over-expansion of the emotional nature.

☽ △ ♃ Other things being equal, this will be one of the best periods of the life, and in accordance with the native's ability to respond to this very favourable aspect, so will his success be assured. It is a splendid time for all financial and social affairs, and promises good fortune in nearly all directions. It is a good period to commence new undertakings and to begin anything for which a successful issue is especially desired. The native may invest money to advantage, or even speculate, and should do all he can to improve his financial conditions. He will be able to gain benefit from attachments and will form new ties or unions under its influence. This aspect often marks an epoch in the life, when things take a distinct turn for the better, but as to the future, a great deal depends upon the innate ability to respond to the opportunities which it brings and to take the fullest advantage of them. There is one side to this aspect which should be known : it gives *spiritual opportunities*, and to those who have awakened, it means an uplifting of the aspirations, bringing a more devotional attitude, and a more sincere spirit, which tends to raise the consciousness towards higher things.

☽ ☐ ♃ This is a rather weak aspect and not likely to affect the native seriously ; but it inclines to extremes, and therefore all tendency to waste or extravagance should be guarded against, for it generally affects financial affairs, bringing a liability to losses and difficulties where money is concerned. He should now see that his health is not adversely affected by the state of the blood, for any tendency to go to extremes or give way to excess will affect the blood and re-act upon the health. He should not borrow or lend money under this aspect, for losses are indicated. If the native lives temperately he will not feel any great inconvenience from this aspect, but if other directions are evil then this will be an unfortunate and harassing time generally. It is not a good time for social matters; hence visiting or dealing with others should be restricted as far as possible, so as to avoid either social friction or having the feelings unduly affected by others while this inharmonious aspect operates.

☽ ⚹ ♃ This is quite a weak and almost unimportant aspect, but some benefit may be derived from it if the most is made of the vibration produced thereby. It is good for financial and social affairs, also for intercourse with others and for entering upon fresh ventures. It may benefit the health, but it will be necessary to live temperately and to avoid any tendency to excess or to extremes of diet. It will greatly improve the whole of the lunar directions, but to get all the possible good out of this aspect it will be well for the native to push his affairs and to busy himself while it operates. The aspect is not very powerful, but it has all the elements of good in it which will lead on to other things, therefore if hope is cultivated, and the better side of the nature stimulated, the future will bring forth fruit from the seed now sown.

☽ ☍ ♃ This position is not a good one in many ways, but a great deal of good may be obtained from it, if the native will act discreetly and use it for his actual needs. It is not a good time for financial matters, but only so because there will be a tendency to go to extremes and to be rather extravagant. Therefore all waste should be stopped, and expenditure reduced as far as possible. It is not good for social affairs, as there is a liability to be too expansive and over-zealous, thus offending others, particularly with regard to religious matters : the native should act, therefore, as temperately as possible while the opposition is in force. It is not a good time for health because there will be a surfeit in the system and the blood is liable to be disordered, less food being moreover required at this time. If all excess is avoided and he lives as temperately and moderately as possible, keeping the blood pure and not over-heated by stimulants or excitants, the native need have nothing to fear. He may gain through this aspect, but it will be gain at others' loss, and not a legitimate gain. Travel should be avoided, and care taken not to bring about separations, which would prove disastrous. It is not a good time for legal affairs.

☽ P. ♄ This parallel aspect will operate for some months, and during the whole period in which it is in operation the native will have a more or less troublesome time ; for it will cause him to experience much worry, due to disappointments and anxieties of various kinds, affairs tending to go wrong in every direction while this parallel operates. He may lose friends under its influence, have monetary or domestic troubles and experience a great number of petty annoyances which may incline him to give way to despondency. It is a position which *steadies*, causing the machinery of life to slow up; for Saturn is the planet of "fate," bringing all things to a climax, and therefore his aspects to the Moon mark a critical stage.   During this period the native should study thrift and be careful in all things, doing nothing that he will be liable to afterwards regret and having as little as possible to do with those who have power to make him suffer.   It is not a good time, and great care in all things will be necessary.

☽ ☌ ♄   This is by no means a good position for the Moon, as it tends to retard the native's progress and to limit his actions, bringing him sorrowful and depressing experiences.   It is no time for him to embark upon new undertakings or to deal with elderly persons or those whose influence is likely to be hard and unsympathetic, for he will be very sensitive and rather inclined to brood and despond, looking upon the dark side of things. It will be well for him to avoid taking chill or cold, as he is now very liable to suffer if the system is allowed to get out of order, owing to the state of the circulation, which will be debilitated; for this is not a good position for health, nor for domestic or social affairs either, and the best course will be to take things in as philosophical a spirit as possible under this dispiriting influence.   It always marks a critical stage in the progressed horoscope, though its effects are never felt to the full until some time after; for it is but the beginning of changes that are to come, affecting both the health and the environment and the general surroundings: therefore, all affairs should be ordered with great care.

☽ ⚹ ♄   A weak aspect, but one that is in many respects favourable, for it steadies and quietens the whole nature, giving opportunities for the exercise of thrift, economy and carefulness where monetary affairs are concerned, and this is likely to benefit the native financially.   It is good for the native in all dealings with elderly persons, and those who have any definite responsibility with regard to his personal life, and it may bring him some slight personal responsibility himself, at all events a period in which he will exercise more thought and prudence in the management of his affairs.   But nothing important need be expected to happen under its influence, and this time should be used rather for reflection, curbing impulse and over-activity, and steadying the inner nature, rather than for any special efforts in the direction of external activities.   It will act as a retentive and restricting influence in a very good sense, so far as the mind and feelings generally are concerned.

☽ ∠ ♄   Not a good aspect, as it tends to bring some worry and anxiety, especially with regard to finance and general affairs.　The native will be somewhat depressed and inclined to despond and look upon the black side of things while this aspect operates, and it will moreover affect his health by running the vitality to a lower point than usual, so that if he takes cold or gets the blood chilled he will suffer, the circulation being depressed.　It should be seen to that the teeth are in good order, and that the digestion is not impaired by worry or over-anxiety ; for there is a liability for things to go wrong, and disappointments will occur while this aspect operates, although it is somewhat weak in its character.　The native should avoid changes and keep himself free from responsibility or from any serious undertakings, as he is not likely to have much success while this influence is in operation ; he should therefore take things quietly, not worrying or fretting, but trying to be as contented as possible, and preserving a philosophic attitude concerning his difficulties, which will prove in the end to be but of a trifling character.

☽ ✳ ♄　A very favourable influence, denoting some gain through either merit or persistence.　It will bring the native responsibility and perhaps advancement, his affairs having now more stability and security than formerly.　His mind will tend to become more serious, thoughtful and sedate under this aspect, and a more persevering, frugal and sober spirit will underlie all his actions.　He will find himself more earnest and sincere under this influence, while its general tone will be soothing and steadying, and he should therefore make the most of the sobering character of Saturn to put all his affairs in good order, allowing the calming and quieting influence it will have upon him to benefit him in matters relating to any business or duties in hand.　Under this lunar direction he will make new and faithful friendships, and will benefit through the help and advice of those who now become his friends ; he will gain in honour and credit under it, and may rise to a higher position in life through its influence.　If he seeks it, he will gain some notable esteem and recognition in the sphere in which he moves.　A great deal will depend upon his own attitude at this time, and also the progress he has made in evolution, as to how much he will gain and benefit by this aspect : for only nature's older children are capable of benefiting under Saturn's influence.

☽ ☐ ♄　This is a very evil lunar direction, and it marks a very critical time in the native's affairs.　He must now be guarded in all his dealings with others, and especially in his domestic affairs.　It will give him some financial troubles and worries, and throughout the whole of the time that it operates there will be a tendency to despond and give way to depression, for he will fret and worry if he is in the least discontented or unhappy in his environment and general surroundings. It is not a good time for removing or making any changes, nor for taking any new ventures in hand. It will affect the native's health according to the state of his constitution, for the circulation and general vitality will not be so good as usual, and any chill or cold that he may take under this aspect will upset the health and cause suffering until the recuperative powers re-assert themselves. It is always a very critical aspect, and marks a period when the greatest care is necessary to keep all affairs from going wrong; it often brings sorrow and grief, deaths and other sad events according to the major influences operating at the same time. In any case it is always an evil period, retarding progress.

☽ △ ♄ This is a very favourable influence, for it brings a sobering and steadying influence into the life at this time, and the native will either gain promotion or undertake some added responsibility, or otherwise become more important in some way under this lunar direction; for it increases the natural stability and brings opportunities for him to settle into a more fixed and harmonious groove in the daily life. He will find himself much more thoughtful and serious than usual, and a strong inclination will be upon him to carry out duty without any hesitation, so that if he is ready for the new vibration he will become persevering, thrifty, careful, prudent and thoroughly trustworthy. He will get on well with elderly persons, and will make new friends and acquaintances, especially among elders, and should gain help and good counsel from friends. His honour and credit will improve, and he will have some recognition in the sphere in which he moves or do something that will advance his interests, making sure and steady progress towards a better state of affairs. He should now do all he can to obtain a permanent post or to arrange his affairs on a substantial foundation.

☽ ⚼ ♄ This is not a good aspect, for Saturn will act as a disturbing element and tend to bring disappointments and sorrows, especially if there are any other evil directions operating at the same time. The native should avoid worry as much as possible, for he will be liable to become over-anxious, being prone to ponder and brood over his troubles. He will be somewhat discontented and gloomy, desponding and giving way to depression, and thus affecting his health, the circulation being slower than usual, which will upset the general health if he happens to take cold or get a chill in any way. It is a bad time for all engagements, and for dealing with other persons, especially elders or those who hold responsible posts. It is not a good time to commence anything fresh or to enter into any serious undertakings; in fact it is a time when affairs will tend to go wrong and when it will be the best course to cultivate all the hope and cheerfulness possible. This aspect sometimes causes deaths or sickness in the family circle.

☽ ⚹ ♄ A weak aspect which will not affect the native very seriously, though the influence of Saturn is never good so far as the Moon is concerned. It tends to bring a more serious and sober tone of mind, and will cause the native to look upon life and his general surroundings in a far graver and more steady mood than usual. It is not a good time for the health, as the system is never in very good order while Saturn aspects the Moon: the circulation should be kept in good order and the system toned up as much as possible. It is not a good time for financial affairs, or for taking up extra responsibility unless the native knows that he can carry it through without risk. If he is careful not to become too depressed or despondent he may do well with the steadying conditions it brings; but if he frets or pines it will only cause him to come under the worst side of the influence, so that it will retard his progress and delay his affairs and keep him back in many ways, personal and general.

☽ ☍ ♄ This is an evil position for the Moon, as it tends to brings about delays and disappointments, and hinders the native's progress in all directions. He will now be inclined to brood and despond and look upon the dark side of things. It is a critical period, and if the native is in any way run down his health will certainly suffer. Yet if he is wise he will not allow himself to become depressed or to give way to melancholia; for it is one of the most depressing lunar directions, and may affect the health, since the circulation will be poor, and the whole system liable to suffer in consequence of deficient vitality. It is a very trying time indeed, and unfavourable for financial affairs, while all matters of responsibility and importance will also cause anxiety. The native should not trust too much to others, and have as few dealings as possible with very old persons. This position sometimes causes a death to occur in the family circle, and rarely passes without causing sorrow or grief. It is in fact an ill time for all who have not sufficiently advanced to overcome the lowering tendency it has, whether upon the mind, health or disposition. The native should very carefully watch all he says or does while this aspect is operating, but a fearful or timid attitude should be avoided and a firm, resolute and positive condition of the will maintained in spite of all discouragement.

☽ P. ♅ This parallel will operate for some time, causing the native to have some very peculiar experiences, for it acts in strange ways, bringing about conditions that are quite out of the common. His magnetic conditions will now be readily affected by others, and he will form very unique attachments, the friendship or acquaintance of some one who will have a marked and somewhat romantic effect upon his life. This position sometimes produces sudden changes and unexpected travel, or even entirely new conditions are brought about by this lunar influence; for it generally causes worry and anxiety and denotes a period in which domestic affairs are upset, estrangements often being brought about and troubles between those with whom intimate relationship has previously been the result of personal magnetism or sudden friendship rather than real esteem or true love. It is not a good time for affairs in general, and sudden developments are sure to take place if other directions are evil. All kinds of changes and disadvantageous affairs result from this parallel and the native should therefore act with great care and do nothing impulsively or without due forethought.

☽ ☌ ♅ This direction will produce a sudden and probably entirely unforeseen change in the native's affairs, either physically or mentally. His magnetic conditions will now be such as to cause him to have peculiar experiences, and he is likely to form sudden attachments which will be more of a romantic and possibly illicit order than the orthodox or conventional attachments sanctioned by custom. The native should beware of doing anything rash or hasty during this time, for this position causes a tendency to unpremeditated and impulsive actions, and his disposition will undergo some change under this conjunction, causing him to feel more than usually acute, or perhaps irritable, inclined to be rather too sharp and quick or even sarcastic. This position will make him intuitive or impressionable, according to his stage of spiritual growth : to the advanced it brings the opportunity to change thought from the purely objective to the subjective or metaphysical, to become more original and inventive, and also to investigate occult subjects, especially inclining them to the study of astrology and kindred subjects. This direction brings all latent fate or karma to the fore ; but this is really good

In many ways, for whatever evil effects it may have, it is only to break up existing conditions that the native may build anew.

☽ ⊻ ♅   This is a very weak but somewhat good aspect, and may bring the native some good if his mental or magnetic conditions are such as to enable him to respond to this peculiar vibration. It will certainly cause some changes, either in mental or in physical conditions, and it will give him an opportunity to raise his consciousness to a higher stage of thought; hence action resulting from this aspect should not be impulsive, or hasty, but of a deliberately reformative and progressive nature. It is not a bad influence, and may bring new friends and some relationship with others th t will be useful to the native mentally. If any changes are desirabl   his will be a good time to set them in motion, and if he is on the ale to respond to the vibrations operating it may bring him some slight gain and advancement. He will find himself peculiarly attracted to the opposite sex, and the magnetism of others will affect him strangely : he should guard against yielding too readily to his feelings.

☽ ∠ ♅   This is not good, and it is likely to cause some worry and anxiety; for although a weak aspect it will tend to upset the native's magnetic conditions and disturb his mind, and bring changes, and probably removals, that will not be pleasant. It will be well for him to avoid changes as far as possible, for they cannot be conducive to his good. The mind will be somewhat sarcastic and irritable, and he will be inclined to act abruptly and far too quickly, without adequate forethought : hence he should set himself to act cautiously and discreetly while it operates. His relationships with others at this time, especially the opposite sex, will not be conducive to his happiness, for he will be magnetically attracted to others and peculiarly affected by them. If the other directions are evil this tends to cause all things to go wrong unexpectedly, and it will be necessary to exercise care, not only in financial affairs but also in the domestic relations. An erratic state of mind and an abrupt manner usually result from this lunar position, and very often fate is precipitated in quite an unexpected and peculiar manner by the native's own hasty conduct.

☽ ⁎ ♅   This is a very fortunate aspect in many ways, principally in elevating or raising the consciousness to a higher level. It brings into the life important and often sudden and unexpected changes which are beneficial in many ways. It will alter the native's magnetic currents, and the acute tension which it will bring will make him very intuitive and quick to perceive. He will form some remarkable friendships under this influence, or come into touch with some new thought, probably astrology or some kindred study, for this is the influence that stimulates the imagination, giving inspiration and inventive genius. It is a very good time for removals, and often brings changes for the better that will be beneficial and of good import for the future. It will act either directly or indirectly upon the mind, and the more he uses his intuitive faculties the more ingenious will the native become. Only the truly progressive type of person can rightly appreciate this aspect, and for the ordinary individual it brings nothing more than a good physical change; but to the awakened it means an advent of new thought, and fresh opportunities to expand and grow in refinement and originality.

☽ □ ♅   This is an evil aspect, threatening the native with sudden, unexpected, and adverse changes. He should as far as possible avoid removals or quick changes while it operates, for it will be the result of a mental attitude toward his surroundings and environment that will induce changes at the time, changes he is likely afterwards to regret. His mind will be wayward, abrupt, whimsical and fanciful, causing him to become somewhat eccentric and erratic. He will now meet with those who will affect him magnetically, and all relationships with the opposite sex at this period should be carefully guarded, for there is a liability to act indiscreetly and very impulsively, giving way to acts that will occasion remorse. This is an evil aspect for all domestic affairs, and any tendency to say more than he means or to speak harshly or sarcastically should be avoided by the native, for he will be prone to strange impulses and very liable to act without thinking. To those who are advancing it means reform, and the changing of old conditions for new, but with many obstacles to overcome in order to accomplish this new advance and take advantage of the opportunity for progress.

☽ △ ♅   This is a very good aspect, for it increases the native's magnetic currents and awakens vibrations in him that will enable him to respond to a higher state of consciousness than usual. He will be intuitive and very original under this influence, his mind inclining to the study of metaphysics and the investigation of occult subjects; it will, moreover, make him inventive and ingenious, and very responsive to all improvements and reforms for the good of others. He may now make important changes and removals, and seek to advance his interests in all directions. He will form new and very remarkable friendships and become magnetically attached to others, and may also gain very suddenly either by investment or speculation; for the unexpected generally happens under this influence, and it is nearly always in the direction of improvement and advancement that the change is made. It is a good time to travel, form fresh plans and join societies; in fact to the progressive individual it is a splendid aspect, while even to the lethargic it is favourable, quickening the nervous forces and rendering them alert and sprightly.

☽ ☐ ♅ This is not a good aspect, for it is very likely to cause the native to act rather too impulsively and to become irritable or abrupt, and to do acts that will either bring immediate remorse or cause him to repent later, owing to their consequences. He should be very careful of attachments or engagements made under this influence, not allowing himself to be hypnotised or magnetically affected by others, for he will now be very impressionable and easily influenced. It is not a good time to have removals or make changes; it is also an unfavourable period to form new acquaintanceships or friendships, for the native is liable to be mistaken and to entertain notions that will not be to his advantage in the future. It is an aspect that tends to upset all existing conditions, and for those who are not mentally balanced it is liable to cause them to go to extremes and to become far too changeable, not sufficiently reasonable, and more prone to act upon impulse and through personal bias than from any well-defined motives.

☽ ⚹ ♅ This is an aspect that may only affect the native indirectly or at a much later period, for the magnetic conditions it induces are often latent, and not brought into direct activity until the magnetism of another sets it in motion. It is not a very good time to form attachments, as the influence of another is likely to have a rather peculiar effect upon the native, causing him to act rather by impulse than with discretion. He should not make changes suddenly, nor allow himself to be moved from his purposes for insufficient reasons, but act with care, and watch his interests, keeping from erratic and fanciful notions. This influence may be made beneficial if used in the reformer's spirit, but not to destroy before there is the opportunity to build anew. The native will be inventive, or impressionable and constructive, or abrupt and foolhardy, according·to his " root of merit," and to the nature of the other directions operating at this time.   It will, in fact, be a good or evil aspect just as he may choose to make it.

☽ 8 ♅   To the majority at our present stage of evolution this is a very evil position, for it acts suddenly and very unexpectedly, chiefly because the vibrations acting through the magnetic conditions it induces are difficult to understand.   To the awakened it denotes a period in which reforms may be made in the life, and when existing habits and customs may be replaced by new and more improved methods.   It will cause the native to have some sudden changes, and it will bring into his life some separations or estrangements ; in fact it is a most critical period, for it means the breaking up of ties and the forming of strange and peculiar attachments and some remarkable undertakings or engagements. It is not a good time to travel or make important changes, and there is danger of accident as well as many a peculiar experience indicated.   The native should not allow himself to act abruptly, and should guard against eccentric and strange conduct.   This is a period when he is very likely to be misunderstood and to cause others to take sudden dislikes to him, so that he should be careful not to offend superiors and be circumspect in his dealings with friends and acquaintances.

☽ P. ♆   This is a weird and strange direction of which the true nature cannot be accurately known.   It may have no effect whatever upon the life, but if it does it will be to bring the native into the most strange and peculiar experiences, and will make this period quite unique in his life history.   He will have very remarkable dreams and some peculiar impressions, and will probably come into contact with persons who are quite out of the common, very likely such as have some peculiar affliction, either physical or mental.   He will have his sympathies drawn out in many and varied ways.   The planet Neptune is connected with hospitals, asylums and places of confinement, and he may therefore have some direct or indirect connection with these institutions about this time, and it will be well for him to avoid any conditions that would tend to deprive him of his liberty at this period, for confinement in some form is probable, the influence of the planet being invariably *hampering* and *restrictive* as regards physical things.   [See " Dreams," *Mod. Astro., Vol. III.* (New Series).]

☽ ☌ ♆   The conjunction of the Moon with the planet Neptune is rather a peculiar lunar direction which may act upon the native in many different ways.   It will probably bring him into contact with strange and peculiar persons, and cause him to suffer or gain through them according to the attitude of his mind at this time. He will have some rather remarkable and strange dreams which it would be well to tabulate for future consideration. Many weird and psychic impressions will come to him, for in some manner this conjunction will act upon his consciousness and bring some peculiar experiences. It is impossible to say exactly how this will affect the native, but he will probably find himself under influences that will either awaken the sub-conscious mind or give very new and original mental conditions. This is a good aspect under which to try thought transference or to study psychometry, the brain being now very receptive.

☽⚼♆ A very weak but at the same time a peculiar aspect. It will probably give the native some weird moments when he will receive impressions from other planes, or become peculiarly receptive to mental and psychic vibrations. This will be a good time to study telepathy or psychometry; but it is only those who are growing very responsive to new conditions who can take advantage of the aspect, weak as it is, so that if he feels no new impressions coming to him it will be a sign that the vibration is passing him by and that the time has not yet come for him to answer to its high rate of motion. To some it will mean new thought, or some new friend whose influence will be more psychic than physical. It is however an unimportant aspect at best, and it is difficult to understand its full influence. It is beneficial for the investigation of spiritualistic matters.

☽∠♆ The semi-square aspect of the Moon to the planet Neptune is a weak aspect which may not affect the native in any marked manner, but it will be well for him to be on his guard with respect to forming new friends and acquaintances while it operates. He should be prepared for deception, fraud and illusions, for his mind will be easily influenced by those who seek to take advantage of him. His dealings with the opposite sex should be only of the most select and approved order, and he should not undertake anything he does not fully understand, watching his interests in every direction, so that he may not be unwittingly imposed upon or deceived. His dreams will now be very strange and peculiar; in fact this influence will probably affect him chiefly when out of the body in sleep.

☽✶♆ The sextile aspect of the Moon to the planet Neptune is a somewhat strange aspect, indicating a change of consciousness and a

I

very receptive mental attitude while it lasts. It will bring the native into contact with unique and strange individuals who will in some manner be psychic or quite uncommon characters, and he will now have strange and remarkable dreams, probably symbolic—dreams which will convey some warning or message to him while in sleep out of the body. This will be a very good time for him to study the Astral Plane, and he would do well to read up the subject of dreams, dream-consciousness, and the astral plane. Thought-transference or psychometry may be attempted with advantage, should the nativity indicate any aptitude, or any study that is either occult or mystical; but it is rather a psychic than a mental influence, and inclines chiefly to music and poetry.

☽ □ ♆   The square aspect of the Moon to the planet Neptune is a very strange influence which warns the native to be very careful in all dealings with others. He will be liable to suffer from some deception under its influence, and should watch all his affairs carefully and minutely. It will bring some peculiar and possibly weird experiences, for this is usually the aspect under which ghosts or apparitions are seen though it does not follow, of course, that *everyone* under this direction, will see something of that kind. The native will have remarkable dreams and will have strange experiences when out of the body in sleep. He will be very impressionable, and perhaps mediumistic, and should not give way to fancy or to any notions that go against common sense or outrage reason, for it will be important to distinguish between the false and the true, the real and the unreal. It is a strange influence, not favourable by any means.

☽ △ ♆   The trine of the Moon to the planet Neptune is a very peculiar aspect. It will probably bring the native some entirely new experience of a psychic nature, for his mind will now be peculiarly sensitive, and it is even possible to open up some of the higher senses under this influence. He should very carefully note all dreams and psychic impressions, and this would be a good time for him to read Leadbeater's book on" Dreams " or the " Devachanic Plane," for it might help to put him *en rapport* with the conditions needed to awaken this latent influence, an influence which is rather connected with higher states of consciousness than the purely physical. If he will keep an open and unbiassed mind at this time he may come into touch with impressions that will help him to understand another part of his being, but he will have to live very purely to do so. To the ordinary person it will probably bring

about nothing more out of the common than some particularly enjoyable
excursion or picnic, in which the watery element will play an important
part. But even here there is a peculiar charm about all Neptunian
experiences, and the excursion or what not is likely to be long remembered.

☽ ⚼ ♆ This is an influence very uncertain in its operation, but it
tends to produce a morbid or hypochondriacal frame of mind. In those
whose nativities indicate a mentality constitutionally weak, and where
there is a decided affliction from Neptune, there are even likely to be
decided aberrations (though not of a violent character) under this
influence. To the everyday person little is likely to result save a series
of petty annoyances, unpleasant dealings with vulgar persons, etc. The
disintegrative character of the sesquiquadrate aspect blends with the
peculiarly elusive nature of the planet to produce a singularly unsatisfactory period. A slack time in business and many petty worries or
losses are probable. This is nevertheless an aspect that may be taken
advantage of for the reading of mystical and devotional books.

☽ ⚻ ♆ This is not a powerful aspect, but may make itself distinctly
felt by those who are susceptible to Neptune's influence, which may be
ascertained from a study of the nativity. The hampering and restrictive
influence of Neptune is peculiarly marked under this aspect, and some
more or less unimportant and temporary affection of the brain or eyesight
is likely to impair the native's executiveness at this period. The
sensuous element in the nature is likely to be awakened, and indulgence
of any kind—especially any experimentation with drugs—should be
rigidly discountenanced. For those who are highly devotional, and for
all who lead lives of exceptional purity, this aspect will bring a stage of
psychic consciousness or religious ecstasy.

☽ ☍ ♆ The opposition of the Moon to the planet Neptune is a very
uncertain position. It may bring the native into touch with very
undesirable persons, either when in the body or when out of it in sleep:
his dreams therefore will probably be very remarkable and not altogether
pleasant. He will be liable to come into contact with frauds and
shams, also to suffer from weird and uncommon fancies, and should in
particular keep himself free from the influence of those who do not live
pure and chaste lives. He will probably have some strange attachment
or will separate from others and suffer through estrangements, and the
breaking of ties. This influence may bring strange episodes, and not
pleasant happenings; but it is impossible to enumerate all the events

that have been known to happen under its influence, for it is always that which is uncommon and often absurd that comes to pass ; things which it is almost impossible to decide.   It is probable that in the majority of cases "nothing at all" may happen, such is the elusive nature of Neptune ! For it is only upon the more advanced of humanity that this planet's influence makes any marked impression.

CHAPTER XII.

MUTUAL ASPECTS.

MUTUAL ASPECTS are aspects formed between the planets themselves, apart from the luminaries. They denote events of the nature of the houses which the respective planets rule, also events in harmony with their own nature. Thus, Saturn when aspecting any other planet will limit that planet's influence, and cause time to be a consideration that must be taken into account; when afflicting, it will retard and delay events promised, and in all its actions will act as a restraining and retarding force. If afflicting Venus there will be disappointment, and probably sorrow, or depressed emotion. If afflicting Mars the passional nature will be affected, and more premeditation will be mixed with passional desires of any kind. If afflicting Jupiter it is unfortunate, depressing the social and moral faculties and generally bringing disfavour and discredit. Mars will act as the reverse of Saturn, causing impulse and a quickening of the out-going energies, giving less restraint and precipitating actions without the balancing power of thought.

In this connection the following paragraphs should be carefully studied and thought over :—

WHEN THE PLANET VENUS plays the most prominent part during the period for which the calculations have been made, to obtain the full advantage of this benefic planet's vibrations it is needful to know the nature of the vibrations of the good star angel Anael or Venus.

All grades of love, as manifested on this earth, are under the rule of Venus—from the lowest and most degraded form of sensual attraction to the highest attitude of pure love, in all its stages from sincere personal affection to universal sympathy. To come under the highest and what appears to be the most refined influence of this planet, it is necessary to purify the personal affections. For it is not the vibration of Venus that is altered, but *the medium through which it acts* that must be refined and purified; and when the selfishness of personal feeling is removed from mere sensational expression and transmuted to the higher emotions in which the *mind* acts as a guide, then there are no limits to the expression of this benefic influence. To those who can respond to them every aspect and every vibration of Venus act to raise and elevate the consciousness, all stages being grades of expression through the vehicle or "matter" in which the influence is clothed, and which is of every degree of coarseness or refinement.

It is the *same* vibration that guides the artist's brush or the musician's finger, that draws two persons together by mutual attraction; it is also that same vibration that raises their feelings from physical attraction to soul union. And to comprehend the possibilities of this wonderful force is to grow ever more loving and more wise until love becomes Wisdom and wisdom Love.

WHEN THE PLANET MARS plays an important part in the "directions" under consideration, there is denoted a period in which the native will be tried in the fire of animal heat, which the vibration of the fiery "God of War" expresses. Now there is no real *evil*, except as "thinking makes it so"; and if Mars seems to most of us the Great Tempter, it is only so because we have drawn into ourselves more of the vibrations of Mars than of any other planet.

In the period under discussion the native will be tried through the passions and the personal feelings; and according to his impulses and out-rushing tendencies so will he suffer. For by the strength of his martial or desire nature he will learn those experiences which the planet Mars has to teach. The steps of the pathway that lead to the castle of the "God of War" are many, from physical and muscular force to persistent energy and endurance, moral integrity and courage, and from animal passion, lust or wrath to righteous indignation or championship, and the strength of the wise Protector. Stage by stage those who climb the spiritual ladder of Mars come to the final realisation of motion and directive energy wisely and unselfishly applied.

When the influence operating calls the native forth from his centre —as it is sure to do at some time or other—let him see that his desires are not controlling him, but let him seek to control his desires, and hold in check the force that rushes downward, endeavouring to uplift it and to turn *force* into *motive*. Let him seek to transmute Desire, which is always attracted from without, to an inner Aspiration, striving to raise his consciousness above the attractions of the external world to aspire after the things of the spirit.

WHEN THE PLANET JUPITER plays a very prominent part in the " directions " that have been calculated, it is well to know something of this mighty and majestic power, known to the ancients as Zeus, the angel of power and beneficence.

Its influence is always most potent in the social world, or where sympathy and unity gather groups of persons, or even single individuals, together, blending them into union by love and harmony. The prosperity and success which this planet brings to those who come under its vibration is generally the result of an inner expansion, which enlarges the whole nature and brings an elevation or upraising of the mind beyond those limitations which in the past the vibrations of Saturn have imposed, thus paving the way for new realisations in better surroundings and a more congenial environment generally.

From personal feeling to individual sympathy, and from generosity to benevolence, also from love to compassion, the steps of the pathway of Jupiter lead to the Mercy-Seat, where Universal Love becomes the final goal of all those lessons in the school of life which the angels and devas of the Archangel Jupiter have to teach mankind.

WHEN THE PLANET SATURN has chief influence during the period for which the " directions " have been calculated, as this planet's influence is sometimes more favourable than otherwise* much may be learned by knowing the virtues of that cold planet and the message its vibrations are destined to bring. From economy of material, to conservation of energy; from caution, to meditation; from self-control, to patience and faith; these are the steps which lead to the gate of heaven, where St. Peter (the patron saint of Saturn) waits, holding the keys of the sacred door to admit those who have learned those lessons which this mighty angel has to teach all mankind sooner or later. The keynote of every vibration of Saturn sounds the oft-repeated command " Man, know thyself "; the good influences of Saturn should therefore be used for this purpose, and the native should strive to be steadfast and faithful to the trusts and responsibilities that will be placed upon him, endeavouring to serve others through the opportunities that he will have to guide and lead them. He should weigh his thoughts and control his actions through this good influence.

* According as the aspects thereto are benefic ($\triangle$ ¥) or adverse ($\square \overline{\wedge}$ ♂).

When this is an afflicting planet a sad and troublesome time is denoted. Still, Saturn is the Purifier, the chastening planet, so that there is some necessity for the affliction which the influences indicate. This period will be in some respects critical, and care will be required to keep the influences operating from becoming too severe. This can be done by endeavouring to understand the nature of the planet Saturn and all that it signifies. The virtues of Saturn are thrift, patience, industry, caution, perseverance and economy. By keeping these ideals before him and by trying when sorely afflicted by financial troubles or deaths and disappointments to realise the impermanence of the changing forms of this world, and also by endeavouring to perceive the effects these causes have upon his individuality, or *inner nature*, the native will catch a glimpse of the method by which character is moulded and destiny foreshadowed.

There may be sorrow, sickness and failures, but the author of this treatise *knows*—from personal experience—that, as the poet has said,

> " Men may rise on stepping stones
> Of their dead selves to higher things."

WHEN THE PLANETS URANUS OR NEPTUNE are prominent in the directions that have been calculated it will be well to refer to what has been said in the second and third chapters of *How to Judge a Nativity, Part II.*, which should be read through in their entirety in order to refresh the student's mind as to their inherent natures. For the hints regarding their influence that are given in the succeeding pages are necessarily brief and incomplete.

———

The remainder of this chapter will be devoted to the influences of the various Mutual Aspects of the planets, in a general sense, apart from the houses from which they are operating or the houses which they rule, which will of course produce appropriately modified effects in each individual case.

PRELIMINARY NOTE.

MUTUAL ASPECTS AND "MIXED" PRIMARY DIRECTIONS.

"Mixed" Primary Directions* are those coming under the heading of *Solar* and *Mutual* aspects. The Sun forming the major influences, which hold in latency the potent force, while waiting for lunar aspects of a similar nature to call them forth into physical activity.

It has been explained previously, either in this book or other works of this series, that in a general sense the planets *per se* govern the mentality of man—by which is not meant the intellectual faculties merely, but the purely *mental* development, as considered apart from the emotions and the senses. It will be readily understood, then, that the Mutual Aspects produce their immediate effect upon the mental plane direct, and do not necessarily result in actual *events* at once, since their influences are first gathered up into the Sun, which may be regarded as the synthesiser of planetary influence, and thence conveyed by conjunction or aspect to the Moon, (ruling the feelings and emotions), whence they are precipitated into the sense world of physical matter through the medium of the Ascendant of the Progressed Horoscope in its annual progress through the twelve signs (see *Appendix I.*). Consequently a given Mutual Aspect does not always produce visible effects the moment it becomes technically complete, since it has to wait for the process described to take place, though it is true that the latter may sometimes be "short-circuited," as it were—at least in the case of highly developed or very responsive people—by means of a direct aspect between the Moon and the planets concerned.

This explanation is necessary in view of the fact that so many students expect a mutual aspect to produce immediate effect directly it is formed.

Thus the aspects that the Sun forms to planets denote the possibilities of the future, according to the nature of the aspect and the planet aspected. But these "primary" influences extend over a period of several years, and only culminate when a lunar aspect coincides with them. In a similar way the "mutual" aspects, which are the aspects between planets, are even more dependent upon the lunar aspects then the solar, as they simply point to conditions forming, and to mental states preparatory to the period when the influence of the Sun and Moon is ripe to bring the mutual influences to fruition.

When there are no solar or mutual aspects in operation, the "directions" tend to become more or less unimportant.

[As in the case of the solar aspects (*q.v.*) the ensuing delineations are intended to apply to the *progressed* position of one planet in relation to the *radical* position of the other.]

* The term "primary," AS HERE USED, applies to the *Solar* aspects only. The uses of this term as ordinarily employed are given elsewhere.

MERCURY.

☿ P. ♀   This acts practically in a similar manner to the conjunction, but on the one hand it is longer in operation, extending over several years, and on the other it is more of the nature of an inclining than a compelling force—corresponding to environment rather than to character, to use a suitable simile.

☿ ☌ ♀   This is very good for the mind, making it bright and cheerful and likely to bring benefit in many ways, especially from a social and mental standpoint.   The native will benefit financially through this conjunction, more especially through the help of friends, or partners, or those who are associated with him in the domestic sphere: he will meet with mirthful friends, will incline to associate with others, and will come into contact with musical and artistic people.   Under this influence he may gain many social advantages, and the more he exerts himself socially and makes himself free and expressive, the more will he benefit and make this period successful.   It is not a powerful influence, and depends a great deal upon lunar aspects in force to bring the good it promises ; otherwise it may pass with only minor benefits.

☿ ⊻ ♀   This is a very weak and comparatively unimportant aspect. It is usually regarded as good on the whole, but it brings little to pass in any material sense and is chiefly of service to those of the artistic or poetic temperament, to whom it will bring a considerable degree of inspiration and mental upliftment.   To the highly devotional it will bring a period of spiritual enlightenment, accompanied, perhaps, with some grief as regards everyday concerns.   To the average man it is more likely to be a source of petty annoyance than delight.   The paragraph relating to the sextile aspect of Mercury and Venus may be read with advantage.

☿ ∠ ♀   This will tend to hinder the benefic influence of Venus from acting, and keep the mental vibrations of Mercury from working harmoniously.   During this period it will be well for the native to have as few dealings as possible with those who are not favourably disposed to him, and it is especially advisable to be careful in all correspondence, writings, or intercourse with others.   It is never a very powerful aspect and often passes without effect, but it is just as well to act discreetly at this time, especially if the lunar aspects are not good, for the worry and tendency to anxiety that any affliction to Mercury causes will act

against progress and make this period rather trying, and affairs will not
go particularly smoothly between the native and those to whom he may
be attached, or to whom he may be in any way bound by sympathy and
affection.   It is not a good: ime to sign papers or documents of any
kind, unless thoroughly experienced in such matters.

☿ ⚹ ♀   This will bring social advantages and enable the native to
express himself successfully in any direction he may wish, and will give
him the ability to use the opportunity it offers.   A great deal, however,
will depend upon the innate capacity to use either the artistic or mental
abilities.   He will probably gain financially, or in some manner in which
friends, or those in the domestic circle, are concerned.   He should
cultivate his mind under this aspect, and also do all in his power to
improve the social conditions.   It is a good time for travel, or for
pleasant changes, and it should bring pleasure and happiness to the
native, helping him to realise some of his hopes and wishes, bringing
attachments or beneficial engagements which will expand the feelings
and emotions, and enabling him to live in the higher part of his being.
It is a good influence for peace and good will.

☿ □ ♀   This aspect of course can only be formed between the
progressed ☿ and the radical ♀ ; or *vice versa*.   It is similar in its
nature to the semi-square, but somewhat more drastic, indicating a
forcible separation of the thinking principle (☿ p. □ ♀ r.) from habitual
feelings and conventional thoughts, domestic customs and hide-bound
observances of all kinds.   Similarly, the converse aspect (♀ p. □ ☿ r.)
will indicate that the feelings in their new expansiveness are at war with
fixed habits of thought, and artistic enlightenment is therefore likely to
result at the cost of some sacrifice to any pedantic tendencies there may
be in the native's disposition.

☿ △ ⚼ ⚻ ☍ ♀   These progressed aspects *cannot* be formed during
the normal span of earth life.

☿ P. ♂   This will accentuate all the mental faculties and render the
native acute, active, enterprising and ambitious.   This aspect will endure
for some time, and as a continuing influence it will be behind all the other
influences operating.   It is liable to cause too much activity, with a
tendency towards impulsiveness, and towards acting without counting
the cost.   Care should be taken with regard to writings, signing papers,
correspondence, all mental activity generally, and matters connected
with travel.   It is not a good time to be concerned with legal affairs, nor

to deal with solicitors or agents, nor with persons who are over active
mentally. The mind will tend to give some trouble, as the native will
be easily excited, and will meet with persons whose influence over him
will not be good. The nervous system will be liable to suffer, and any
tendency to neuralgia will be a sign that the general health is suffering
through this position, which affects the mind and nervous system
generally.

☿ ☌ ♂ This influence will accentuate the native's mental conditions, and cause him to be either very practical or dogmatic and
somewhat severe. He will be observant, shrewd and alert, but inclined
to over-estimate, and to be too expectant, with a tendency to commit acts
of indiscretion or to give way to impulsive conduct. He will meet with
very shrewd persons, and his life will be active and enterprising. He will
be very assertive and confident of his abilities, and well able to hold his
own under any circumstances. This conjunction is very good for making
the mind bright, cheerful and active, but it also denotes a period in which
care is necessary to avoid going to extremes, or giving way to strong
passional desires, and to avoid hasty speech and a tendency to be bitter
and sarcastic. The native is likely to become the victim of sharp
practice, or to suffer from fraud or by the actions of others, especially
where writing, correspondence, or literary work is concerned. This
conjunction excites and over-stimulates the whole nervous system ; it is
therefore necessary to act cautiously during this period : it is not a good
time either to travel, or to deal with literary persons.

☿ ⚹ ♂ This is a very weak influence, but it adds some force to the
mind, and stimulates the mental activities, causing the native to be
mentally more active and alert than usual. It will bring some slight
financial advantages, principally by exercising the mind in the direction
of improving general conditions. He will incline to be more assertive
and self-confident, and if impulse is avoided it will enable the native to
gain through enterprise and the help of agents or persons who can in
any way act for him. This aspect sometimes brings a small gain through
the death of others, or if there is no one from whom the native is likely to
benefit in this way, then gain or benefit through co-workers, partners, or
those with whom the life is in any way bound up.

☿ ∠ ♂ This is a weak but unfavourable aspect, giving a tendency
toward impulse and making the mind over active and inclined to become
hasty and too easily excited. The native must be very careful in speech,

also in writing and in all dealings with agents, solicitors, or those who would have any power to affect him adversely if over-expressive or in any manner indiscreet. He must guard against fraud in dealing with those whom he is not certain of, or fully acquainted with, for under this influence he is liable to financial loss, and also to suffer either through travel or through dealings with friends, relatives or those with whom he is intimately related. It is a period in which care is necessary, especially in speech or communicating thoughts to others in any way. The aspect does not last for a very long time, however, and it is very subject to lunar influences.

☿ ✳ ♂ This is a very favourable aspect for the mind ; it will make the native very keen, bright, sharp and active, and he will gain through all mental pursuits, through travel, writings, correspondence, and all matters wherein papers and literature are concerned. This is a good time for him to exert his mind and keep it well employed, for he will now perceive clearly and will in general be able to exercise his mental faculties to the best advantage. He may now profitably deal with agents, solicitors, clerks, or any persons who can act for or be of service to him in any way; friends and relatives also will now be well disposed towards him, and he may now confidently assert his personality and allow the self-assurance which this influence gives to act in the best manner, either to overcome adverse or to make the most of good lunar influences. It denotes a period in which much activity and mental force will be to the fore, and if the native knows how to use the influence wisely it will greatly benefit him and bring success to his wishes.

☿ □ ♂ This is an evil aspect, as it makes the mind too impulsive, inclined to act rashly and without due consideration regarding the outcome of those actions. The native will be liable to make errors in speech and say much more than he means, or than it is wise to say, and will be inclined to be unkind and cutting in his speech : he must, there-fore, be careful in all dealings with those intimately connected with him in the domestic sphere, and also with inferiors or those who can affect his honour and reputation.   This is an evil time to sign papers, to write or have much correspondence, or to deal with solicitors or agents ; the native should guard himself against fraud, and beware of being imposed upon by others.   In fact this is a time when the greatest care should be exercised, especially if there is a natural tendency to uncon-trolled speech or to act upon impulse. Removals should not be made if they can be avoided, for it is an unfortunate time for changes of any kind.

☿ △ ♂   This will sharpen the mentality and render the native eager to learn and to gain experience, active, energetic and industrious: very keen, shrewd and practical in all matters requiring mental ability. It is a splendid influence for the mind, and gives ability to put into practice any latent ideas.   Hence the native will become enterprising, aspiring, and speculative, and should meet with success in most of his activities as he will be able to observe accurately and quickly.   This is a capital influence for travel, writing, correspondence or literary undertakings of any kind, also for dealing with agents, solicitors, or those who act in a mediary capacity.   This influence is good for the nervous system, and also for the general health, as the mind is rendered bright and cheerful and keenly alive to the hopeful side of things.   When the lunar influences are good this aspect will make it a good period for general success and material welfare, as the mind will be eager to take advantage of opportunities and will see clearly how to act.

☿ ⧠ ♂   The native will have rather an anxious and trying time under this influence, his mind being restless and too active, prone to act from impulse and to over-estimate ; he will be somewhat snappish in speech and liable to say more than is wise or than he really means. He should act very discreetly while it operates and be generally careful in all dealings with others, especially as to what papers or documents are signed, undertake as little correspondence or writing as possible, and do all he can to restrain his impulses. It will be well for him to avoid travel and also to safeguard health, for under this aspect worry or anxiety will react upon the nervous system and cause him to suffer in health. It renders the native liable to fraud and deception, and he should be very careful with regard to all attachments, and all matters where the feelings are concerned, as he is liable to illusion in these matters.

☿ ⊼ ♂   This is quite a weak aspect, the two planets being 150° apart, and may not affect the native very seriously ; but still its influence is not favourable, for it tends to make the mind too acute at times and over active.   If he acts impulsively or rashly he will suffer, his health will be affected through exhaustion, and nervous strain will be upon him while this aspect operates.   If any other (especially lunar) influences are operating it will make this period not successful ; rather unfavourable, in fact, particularly if the native is one who is indiscreet in speech or who acts without thinking. In many cases this aspect affects the personal conditions and gives much more assertiveness, strengthening the mind by making it more positive and more forceful, but at best it is only a weak influence and depends a great deal upon the lunar aspects operating.

☿ 8 ♂ This is an adverse aspect, and one likely to bring the native much trouble and opposition. He will suffer through fraud and deception, and should act very discreetly in all dealings with others. His affections will also suffer more or less, and this will upset the mind and cause him to worry a great deal. During this period he should watch all papers that he signs, and deal cautiously with all correspondence, avoiding all that is not absolutely necessary; moreover it is not a good time to deal with agents, solicitors, or those who could affect him adversely. He may be the subject of scandal, libel, or ill-repute under this aspect; in fact may even be threatened with litigation or attacks upon his honour. He will be separated from friends or relatives, and will have serious quarrels or disputes with others while this influence operates. It is not a good time to travel or to commence any new undertakings, and it will be well for the native to guard against accidents or inflammatory tendencies when the Moon is adversely aspected, but if he can keep the mind in a calm and orderly state and avoid impulse his troubles will be greatly lessened.

☿ P. ♃ This is a very favourable influence, which will extend over a period of several years, being a kind of "background influence" operating favourably whenever the lunar or other influences are good. It will benefit the native in many ways, socially, financially, mentally, and at times spiritually; he will come into contact with helpful and well disposed persons, and they will be the means of inspiring him to greater efforts, and also of raising his mind to a much higher standard. His general health will benefit, his mind become more hopeful, cheerful and joyful, and all things will tend to improve and go better with him. His attachments will be successful and promising, with the possibility of forming permanent friendships and lasting ties. It will be a good time to travel and engage in literary work, to sign important papers, write and correspond—in fact do all things in which the mind may be well and successfully employed. A very favourable period and one that should be made the most of.

☿ ☌ ♃ A very favourable and fortunate position, which will bring good judgment, sound reason and intuition regarding all mental matters,

The native will see clearly, will become hopeful with regard to the future, philosophical, and very much inclined to higher thought, looking on the bright side of all things. He will probably travel under this aspect or will gain through travel and foreign affairs. He will benefit either through kindred or relatives or else through their affairs, either directly or indirectly. The general health and tone of the nervous system will be good and he will feel much more confident and capable of managing his affairs to advantage. This position will greatly strengthen the radical horoscope, and—when under good lunar influences—a very good period is before the native in which success and prosperity are to be looked for. It is good for all literary work and for the general expansion of the mind.

☿ ⚹ ♃ Is a weak good aspect and will benefit the native in some slight way, financially or socially. His mind and general mental conditions will improve, a philosophical tendency being denoted by this aspect; it is good for travel, friendship and general health. This aspect is rather too weak to operate of itself, but when others correspond, especially the lunar ones, its good effects will be felt. It is good for correspondence, writing, reading, and literary work generally. The native will probably form some new acquaintance under this influence, or a friendship which will ripen into a deeper attachment. It will make his mind more hopeful and free from anxiety, giving him an opportunity to expand and to learn more of the *inner* side of life. In quite a general sense it is a good aspect, but weak and not very pronounced in character.

☿ ∠ ♃ This is a weak aspect, somewhat unfavourable in its character but not sufficiently strong to affect the native very seriously, if he does not allow it to overcome his judgment. It will be well for him to watch expenditure and to avoid becoming security for others, also to sign no more papers than necessary: he will not gain through travel or any journeys he may undertake under this influence. The native should keep his mind free from doubt and suspicion; and he should note that there is a liability to make errors in judgment, as the mind will not be so clear as usual, being very prone to see things from a biassed or pre-judiced standpoint: for this influence gives a distorted and illusory condition of the mind, causing things to be seen out of due perspective, so to speak. There is a liability to suffer through deception, and inferiors will cause some trouble; indeed, it will be well for the native to act very discreetly with all persons not of the same social standing as himself.

☿ ✳ ♃ This is an excellent planetary position, for under its influence the mind will expand and become hopeful, bright, and intelligent. The native will be intuitive, will have excellent judgment, and will be able to arrange his affairs satisfactorily and successfully : he will gain through all affairs where writing or correspondence is required, and many financial benefits will come to him under this benefic aspect.   He will either have profitable journeys or travel for gain and pleasure, and will meet with those whose influence upon his life will be helpful and peaceful. He will become more than usually interested in philosophy, or will engage his mind upon higher thought subjects, to his permanent advantage. This aspect brings successful engagements and attachments that have a very lasting good effect; and when the lunar aspects are in sympathy it will cause the native to so deal with others as to make ties and friendships that will not easily be broken. It is a very good period for general concerns.

☿ □ ♃ This aspect will tend to made the native liable to grave errors of judgment, mistakes that will produce much worry and anxiety. He should guard against hypocrisy and deceit, and do all he can to protect himself against fraud and treachery.   It is by no means a good influence and if the native is not careful in regard to all papers or correspondence, etc., he is likely to get into trouble, either through writings or through speech.   He should act as discreetly as possible when dealing with others, for he is liable to legal troubles, litigation being easily brought about under this aspect.   He should be mindful of his promises, but should not place too much reliance upon the promises of others at this time.   Inferiors and those in a lower station of life will now be inimical to him and cause him anxiety, especially if he has been unwise in speech where they are concerned; for this influence often causes libel or scandal, in which one's good name is likely to be imperilled.

☿ △ ♃ This is a good and a powerful aspect, causing the mind to become intuitive, sound in judgment and full of common sense. The native will now expand in consciousness and see clearly a path before him, becoming more philosophical and of a truly religious frame of mind. He will in all probability gain by investment, speculation or commercial enterprise: he will also be inclined to travel, and will form ties and attachments of a permanent and very beneficial character. His nervous system will be in good order: dealings with inferiors will be profitable; and he can now engage agents to act for him who will manage

K

his affairs honestly and discreetly. He will have success through writing, correspondence, matters concerned with papers and legal transactions. If other influences are good he will now come under a series of very favourable and successful happenings and should in every way make the most of this period.

☿ □ ♃ This is an unfavourable aspect in many ways, chiefly, however, from a mental standpoint, the mind being very liable to prejudice, bias, and misconception at this time. It is not a good time to speculate or invest money, for there is a liability to losses and to incur heavy liabilities. The native should not become surety for another or lend money, as his financial affairs are liable to undergo a change for the worse under this aspect. He should avoid writing or correspondence, be careful and discreet in speech, and never say more than he means to stand by. It is not a good time to travel, to deal with agents or solicitors, or to take part in any legal transactions. If the other aspects and influences are not good at this time, the native is likely to suffer under this aspect, but more through the mental attitude than from any other cause.

☿ ⚹ ♃ This is a very weak aspect and may not have any appreciable effect ; but when other influences are favourable it will help them to bring out the benefits promised. It is slightly good for the mind and may benefit those who are associated with the native, or he may gain through them in some manner. It is slightly beneficial for health and gives some impetus to the nervous energy, favouring matters relating to travel, correspondence, servants and the general affairs of life, the mind acting more harmoniously and smoothly under its influence. If the lunar aspects are good it will tone up the mind and increase the mental faculties. To come under the good influence of this aspect it is necessary to read and study the best and highest literature that can be procured and thus cultivate the philosophical side of the nature, which this aspect is especially fitted to strengthen and benefit.

☿ ☍ ♃ This position is not favourable, for it impairs the judgment and causes the native to make errors and mistakes, either through speech or in writing and correspondence. This position will produce separations, also a liability to suffer through litigation or legal troubles. The native should not lend money or become surety for anyone, and great care will be necessary with regard to finance, for expenditure will tend to exceed receipts. In all attachments and dealings with others

where feeling is concerned he should act very discreetly, for he is liable
to offend others or be in some way separated from them, either through
misunderstanding or through conditions arising from outside matters
which will cause unpleasantness or trouble to arise.   This position is
highly important from an occult standpoint, for it means a conflict
between the higher and the lower mind, in which a struggle for mastery
will take place, bringing very peculiar realisations mentally.   When the
lunar aspects are not good this position of Mercury and Jupiter will
cause much trouble and anxiety. .

☿ P. ♄   This influence is not confined to one year in its operation
but usually occupies several years in working out its adverse effects.   It
slows down the mental activities, making the mind more solid and concentrative ; yet at the same time it tends to hinder and delay the native's
progress, though it keeps him from being too assertive or unduly liberal :
he will incline to be more industrious or plodding and patient than usual,
and somewhat supicious or mistrustful and apprehensive withal, though
keenly alive to his own interests in a quiet way.   This may be a good
influence when the other aspects are favourable, as it will steady and
solidify the mind, making the native careful and thoughtful and well able
to look after the advantages that the lunar aspects may promise ; but,
generally speaking, the period over which this influence operates will not
be good.

☿ ☌ ♄   This is not a good position, hindering the activities of
Mercury and retarding the mind from full expression.   It will make the
native very careful of his own interests, rather suspicious and apprehensive, and, when the mind is depressed, it will incline him to melancholia
and despondency.   It is not a favourable position for health, impeding
the circulation, chilling the blood and affecting the nervous system,
which may give rise to neuralgia or some congestion.   Under this
influence, however, the native will become more ambitious in his ideas
and will in all probability have some responsibility placed upon him, or
will engage in some difficult task where much tact and diplomacy are
required.   He will experience some mental disappointments and is likely
to suffer at the hands of persons older than himself, or those having some
power or authority over him.   He should not become too critical or fault
finding.

☿ ⊼ ♄   This is a very weak aspect but slightly beneficial, tending
to make the mind calm and balanced, and enabling the native to benefit

to some extent, either financially or through the energies of his mind : he will become graver in manner, and will tend to be more thoughtful and serious than usual. He will benefit slightly by this aspect, but it may pass without his being immediately conscious of the influence unless the lunar aspects are good, when it will help to make the time a more favourable one owing to his more concentrative mental condition. He will discharge his duties more faithfully and become more conscious of his actions while it operates. It may not perhaps be important in its effects, but it is more good than evil. Under this aspect elderly persons will benefit ; a far more temperate state of mind is engendered, and some steps may be taken to economise both time and money.

☿ ∠ ♄   Although weak, this is not a favourable aspect and denotes some financial losses and troubles, and difficulties through others, particularly elders, or those having authority : the mind should be kept free from worry and anxiety and not allowed to despond or become too depressed. The native will suffer some discredit and may lose friends or reputation under this influence : he should avoid taking cold, and should be careful to keep his circulation in good order and his system well nourished. It is not a good time for correspondence, to sign papers, or to deal with agents; theft and fraud moreover should be guarded against. The mind will become somewhat suspicious and inclined to look on the dark side of things ; and therefore the native should cultivate all the hope and cheerfulness he can and not give way to over-anxiety or apprehensiveness.

☿ ✶ ♄   This is a very good aspect for the mind, rendering the native steady, thoughtful, careful and prudent. He will seek to act with great discretion and order his affairs wisely and systematically. He will have more than usual responsibility put upon him, and may improve his position by the honour and credit that this aspect will bring thereby. His dealings with agents, elderly persons and those who are serious-minded or much concerned with commercial undertakings will be satisfactory, and all things will tend to go smoothly and well with him. This aspect makes one think well of the physical virtues of purity, chastity, and temperance; and the whole aspect of the mind is improved and made more sober and earnest. The native may take long journeys under this influence, or come into good relationship with kindred and those to whom he is intimately related. It is a good aspect for contracts and engagements,

☿ □ ♄　This is an evil influence, causing many delays and hindrances to progress.　It will cause the mind to be warped and suspicious, and the native will be inclined to fret, worry and look upon the black side of things while it operates.　It is an evil time to sign papers, or enter into any correspondence with others ; also to deal with elders, agents, solicitors, or those who have power to injure him in any way.　He will not agree with those related to him in the domestic sphere, and may suffer losses which will affect him mentally and cause grief and sorrow.　It is a period full of mental disappointments and worry.　The native should safeguard honour and reputation, and exercise care in all actions, but not become too desponding or low-spirited under this depressing influence.　There is a liability to scandal or slander and to suffer in credit or reputation, unless great prudence is exercised and care taken to keep all action above suspicion.

☿ △ ♄　This is a very good aspect and should benefit the native in many ways, as his mind will be very steady, sincere and honest.　He will undertake responsibilty and enter into the details of life with a serious and earnest endeavour to discharge all his duties faithfully and to the very best of his ability.　It is a good time for him to invest money or to so arrange affairs that future gain and benefit may result from the exercise of care and forethought, and will gain either through science, philosophy or the higher thought, and will derive benefit from any study or research-work in which he may be engaged.　This is a good time for important correspondence or for signing papers, also to see agents and solicitors and make all arrangements for permanent and future good.　If the lunar aspects are good while this mutual influence is operating it will be a splendid time when all will tend to go satisfactorily.

☿ ⚼ ♄　This is not a favourable influence and tends to make the native despond and give way to worrying and depressing conditions of the mind.　He will see things from a limited standpoint, and will not be as expansive or broad minded as he should be while this aspect lasts. It is not a good time to sign papers, write letters, correspond, or deal with others in any way personally.　Under its influence the native will be liable to fraud and deception, and should be very careful in all dealings with others : he should not speculate, or invest money, but act with great discretion while this aspect is in force ; neither should he travel nor deal with relatives, nor allow himself to be influenced by those who are not well disposed towards him.　It is a bad time for the mind

generally, and either some disappointment or an unfavourable attachment
will result from it.

☿ ⚹ ♄   An aspect which spoils the good influence of Mercury by
hindering and delaying thought and clear perception. The native will
however find his mind more steady and less impulsive than usual, though
he will be inclined to fret, or to give way to anxiety and worry under its
influence. His nervous system will not be so well ordered as usual, and
there will be some liability to take cold or to suffer from nervous prostra-
tion if the mind has any unusual care or worry during this period. In
many cases this influence (although a minor one) may be turned to good
account, there being some tendency to delay matters that would otherwise have been precipitated; the critical power of the mind is also
enhanced. Out of evil will then come good, if the right use is made of
the opportunity thus given to understand the circumstances and conditions
in which the native finds himself placed. Honour and friendships are
sometimes adversely affected by this aspect, but in any case it is a minor
one and comparatively unimportant.

☿ 8 ♄   This is by no means a favourable period. The native will
meet with deception, fraud and treachery, and his mind will be depressed
and given to despond and look upon the black side of things. Separation
and estrangement will result from this opposition, and he will find those
in whom he has placed his trust prove untrue to his interests. It is not
a good time to sign papers, to write or correspond, or to study or incline
the mind to serious thought. The native cannot be too careful in his
dealings with others, and he should especially avoid law or serious
disputes; for all affairs will tend to go wrong under this aspect, especially
if the lunar aspects are also adverse.

☿ P. ♅   This is an important position for these two mental rulers,
as it extends over a rather long period and during this time its influence
will be of potent effect. It will expand the native's mind and broaden
his intellect, causing him to become interested in the deeper side of
things and inclined to study metaphysical subjects, to investigate
astrology, for instance, and those subjects which are more related to the
higher mind and subjective world than the purely objective. He will
meet with strangers whose influence upon him will be peculiarly felt.
He will become more original and inventive, and whenever the lunar
aspects are favourable he will travel or make important changes, and
otherwise break up the old or existing conditions. He will now either

join some eclectic society, or make some very strange and romantic attachments. It is a good time to study science and medicine, engineering, etc., also to deal with all matters of an occult character.

☿ ☌ ♅ This will bring sudden and unexpected mental changes, and make the native acute, ingenious and original : there will be a tendency for him to become abrupt and nervously irritable. Quick changes in his attitude towards others are denoted and it is probable that his mind will undergo a complete alteration accompanied perhaps by an entire reversal of his previous opinions and beliefs. He will meet with strangers whose influence will impress him deeply. He will probably take sudden journeys or travel and make changes while this conjunction operates, and will suffer estrangements from relatives or those to whom he has been closely attached. If he avoids giving way to impulse the vibrations of this influence will benefit him, for his magnetic conditions will be highly accentuated, and he will be able to influence and impress others by his inventive ingenuity.

☿ ⊻ ♅ This, though slightly favourable in its nature, is but a weak aspect, so that it may not have much effect upon the life except to expand and broaden the native's mind and cause him to take a deeper interest in metaphysical subjects. He will probably gain unexpectedly some benefits from a monetary standpoint, or form some new and strange acquaintanceship which will be of a magnetic and attractive nature while it lasts, though liable to be as suddenly broken off as it was formed. This aspect gives some tendency to romance, or to form attachments that are of an independent and free nature, and in which the mind is more exercised than the feelings. The native will have some strange mental experiences while this aspect lasts, if the lunar aspects coincide ; but if not, the aspect is liable to pass without much effect, its operations being confined to the mental plane *per se* and not entering the normal consciousness.

☿ ∠ ♅ This is a weak aspect, but at the same time one that is not at all favourable, as it causes the mind to be wayward and at times irritable, and also gives a liability to meet trouble through those in any way connected through friendship or acquaintance. Some unexpected financial loss is probable under its influence, also difficulty in connection with travel, writings, correspondence and literary affairs ; but its chief effect is connected with the mind, which tends to be irritable and almost nervous in its expression. The native will probably speak unwisely of someone, and suffer disappointment or sorrow through his own attitude toward others.   He should not travel any more than is necessary under this influence and should keep as quiet and calm as he possibly can.

☿ ✶ ♅   This is a very good aspect, making the mind original, thoughtful and ingenious. The native may now find himself very inventive and fertile in construction, with original plans, good ideas, and the ability to put them into practice. He will form some romantic mental attachments, and come in contact with those who will attract him mentally ; while his own magnetic aura will be powerful, and able to affect others. This influence will give the power to hypnotise and impress others, also to turn the mind to the study of metaphysical and occult studies. The mind will expand and progress, with a desire to reform and improve existing methods, also to take a broader and more comprehensive view of life and its expression. This good aspect will bring success in travel and will enable the native to get on favourably with kindred and relatives ; it also favours the forming of attachments of a unique and uncommon character.

☿ □ ♅   This is an evil aspect ; one which threatens sudden and unexpected changes, also strange and peculiar episodes in connection with any attachment or friendship that may have been formed : the mind will not be peaceful or harmonious, and a cantankerous temper with a sarcastic turn of speech will be engendered. The native should exercise great care in speech, and should avoid signing papers or entering into any correspondence that is likely to bring discredit or dishonour. He will become interested in reform, and will tend to hold strong views ; but unless he can be temperate and avoid going to extremes there will be danger of his becoming too iconoclastic, and thus injuring the very cause he would espouse. He should act very cautiously in his dealings with others, and also with regard to those in the domestic sphere. The nervous energy will now be in a state of extreme tension. It is not a good time, in any sense of the word : women under this influence are liable to hysteria. *A dangerous aspect, calling for the exercise of great self-control.*

☿ △ ♅   This is a very good and powerful aspect, benefiting the native's mind and causing him to be deeply interested in all metaphysical and occult subjects. He will have sudden or unexpected benefits, and form some very unique and original attachment, which will assist him in many ways. He will gain in some quite unexpected way, by speculation or investments (more especially by business connected with transit, such as railways, etc.), if he puts his mind into the matter. This aspect is especially beneficial to those who enter into any study of astrology or kindred subjects, and also for literary work and for dealing directly with others where magnetic conditions are able to influence them.   The native will be very original in his thought and fond of reform, becoming interested in all movements connected with humanitarian principles and advanced thought. He should make the most of this very good influence and expand the mind to its fullest limit ; for when the lunar aspects are good there will be much success under this aspect.

☿ ☐ ♅ This is by no means a favourable aspect, for by it the mind is afflicted, and there is a danger of taking a distorted view of life and going to extremes, particularly with regard to matters of reform, so that exceptional conditions are generally the result of this aspect, which, acting upon the nervous system, tend to affect both health and mind. The native should be very careful in his dealings with strangers, and be prepared for disappointments and estrangements from friends and those to whom he is in any way attached, especially kindred and relatives. He should avoid travel or the making of any important changes, and should also be cautious with regard to his speech and correspondence, dealing very carefully with all papers he may be called upon to sign. This is an unfavourable aspect in many ways, and if the lunar aspects are adverse, he will find it a very trying period.

☿ ⚹ ♅ Although a weak aspect, this will cause the native some trouble and annoyance if he allows his mind to get into any imaginative or fanciful mood. It will make him inclined to go to extremes, and to take distorted views of things. This aspect may not act in any appreciable manner until a train of adverse lunar aspects is operating, when this mutual influence will affect the nervous system and react upon the mind. The native should endeavour to act discreetly and be careful in all his dealings with strangers, friends and acquaintances; he should not sign papers or enter into more correspondence than is necessary, and he should also watch his magnetic conditions closely. Travelling should be avoided while this aspect operates. In some cases the influence would be very good, but only where the mind is already very broad and expansive in outlook, when it would allow more expansion, and bring into play magnetic conditions that would incline the mind to the study of metaphysical and occult lines of thought.   This aspect is essentially regenerative in nature.

☿ 8 ♅   This is a very evil aspect, tending to make those who are not well balanced mentally inclined to take unreasonable or very extreme views.   The native will find himself liable to serious and persistent opposition, and will have opponents whose effect upon him will be decidedly hurtful.   He cannot be too careful at this period in whom he places his trust ; also in all his dealings with strangers or acquaintances, for some disappointment will come to him, and he may become the subject of charges or accusations which it will be difficult for him to refute.   There is a decided tendency towards eccentricity, and with this influence operating, he will, if he gives way to the mental exhilaration it brings, develop bohemian tendencies, or will incline to be strange and peculiar in manner, with some abruptness of speech and action, as a sequel to the mental attitude it brings.   In the lives of all to whom it occurs it is an extraordinary influence, bringing sudden and quite unexpected events into the life ; but to advanced characters it breaks up all conventionalities and loosens bonds that have grown irksome, giving rise to separations that seem to be fated or inevitable.   Many romantic and very strange episodes follow this aspect.

☿ P. ♆*   This, in common with all parallels, is rather an inclining than a determinative influence, and tends to act chiefly on the subjective planes.   Should the native be an imaginative writer, a poet or musician, his work at this period will be tinctured by that vein of semi-sensuous mysticism that characterises the works, among many others, of Poe, Maeterlinck, Wagner and Swinburne, or such humour as is found in the writings of Artemus Ward and Lewis Carroll—to mention two extremes. In less refined natures the position is likely to incline to " decadence," if the natal aspects to Neptune predispose thereto.

☿ ☌ ♆*   The influence of this position will depend very largely on the innate susceptibility to Neptunian influences, and whether or no it is likely to be of a favourable character.   Where little susceptibility exists, this influence is certain to prove almost negligeable, amounting to no more than a meeting with some singular or *outré* character or some

---

* The elusive character of Neptune's influence renders it extremely difficult to convey in words any idea of its nature.   The reader will do well to refer to the information given in *How to Judge a Nativity, Part II.* (pp. 10, 19, 42), as well as to the interpretation of the solar aspects to Neptune given on pp. 92, 93 of this book.

weird experience—perhaps a strange and vivid dream. But in very refined or artistic characters, there will be at this period a flow of inspirational or creative ability of a mental character, and of a very high order. This essential mental fecundity is almost certain to produce effects of some kind in all who come under this influence, but in the less evolved it is only likely to result in a disposition to scheme for the attainment of some desired object, either personal gain or the gratification of passion. However, in some form or other *scheming* (either in the good or in the bad sense of the word) is sure to be the outcome of this position of Mercury and Neptune.

☿ ⊻ ♆* This aspect has but a slight influence on the mind in most cases. To those who are highly mercurial, or who have Neptune prominent in the nativity, it is likely to bring moments of rare mental exaltation of a more or less ecstatic character, with poetical or musical inspirations at times. Unless the lunar aspects assist, however, these rapt conditions are hardly likely to take effect on the physical plane, and will consequently only be conveyed in the form of dreams, *some* of which at any rate are likely to be remembered. Where Mercury is *behind* Neptune in the Zodiac, there may be some inhibition of speech or the mental faculties for a short period in some cases.

☿ ∠ ♆* This is a weak aspéct, and will probably pass unnoticed in the majority of cases. It indicates a change of phase in the vibrations passing from these planets to the earth, and hence to those sensitive thereto it portends a harassing and distressing period, when things will go wrong in a most unaccountable way, and petty persecutions and restrictions will cause sorrow and annoyance. The mind will, as it were, oscillate between two courses, uncertain which to take.

☿ ✳ ♆* This is probably the best aspect between these two planets, and should the nativity indicate any such possibility, poetic, mystical, fanciful or humorous inventions will flow in upon the native's consciousness, and he may reap a lasting benefit from the exercise of any literary or artistic skill at this time. To others it will bring pleasant journeys, friendships, religious or mystical experiences, invariably connected in some strange way with the sea.

☿ □ ♆* This is a very unfortunate and in some ways a perilous aspect. The mind is obscured by vague and indeterminate fears, longings or aspirations ; so much so, that in some cases the moral sense may

* See previous footnote.

become quite perverted and the native achieve an unenviable notoriety through some evil deed. (This of course depends upon the indications shown in the nativity.) Otherwise, fraud and deception of some kind or disease or hypochondria will be likely to cause the sorrow and meditation which may lead to the expansion of consciousness this aspect is destined to give rise to.

☿ △ ♆* This is very similar in nature to the sextile (*q.v.*), but less definite in its operation. The mind is usually in a pleasant—and in some cases humorous—state, and all things signified by Mercury in the horoscope run well and smoothly. The trine aspect of Neptune is often the indicator of *pronounced* good fortune, but only, of course, in the absence of affliction at birth.

☿ ⌧ ♆* This is practically identical in nature with the semi-square (*q.v.*). It is, however, more likely than the latter to act upon the feelings rather than the mind, and some trouble of a more or less romantic nature, or other similar cause for secret grief, is probable.

☿ ⊼ ♆* This is somewhat similar in its nature to the semi-sextile, but is of a more critical and resolvent nature. A cloud will hang over the native's consciousness, of which no one, probably, will be aware save himself, and which no friend or helper can avail to lighten.

☿ ☍ ♆* This is, if not worse than the square, at least as evil. The native will find himself deserted by those whom he has trusted in, deceived in his speculations, and disappointed in his hopes. The exact nature of events will depend on the houses ruled by ☿ in the nativity, but in a general sense clerks, servants, messengers or agents will be the source of trouble.

VENUS.

♀ P. ♂ This parallel, in common with all parallel aspects, will last over a considerable period, and is not specially confined to one year for operation. It will expand the feelings from a personal and passional standpoint, and will cause the native to come into contact with, and to form attachments to, the opposite sex, suffering and experiencing pain or pleasure according to the attitude of the mind during the operation of this expressive and expansive vibration. It is not an evil

---

* See previous footnote.

aspect, and may be made good and beneficial if the native acts discreetly while it operates ; but if he is rash and imprudent he will find himself liable to suffer from excesses and from too much excitement, or through being too eager and intemperate in his desires.   Much will depend upon the lunar aspects, whether adverse or benefic—if the latter, all will go well, but if the former, then care must be exercised in all actions, taking thought always before yielding to impulses.

♀ ☌ ♂   This is a very impulsive and expressive position, and always produces either " love at first sight," or some very hasty decisions which affect the feelings and emotions. If the native can quell the desire for sensation—and keep from rash conduct—this influence will benefit him, as it will make him liberal and free, and bring success through his quick response to mirth and cheerfulness and his readiness to participate in any pleasure or gaiety that may come in his way. The inner meaning of this aspect is the conjunction of the Soul and the Senses, bringing a fuller and a more sensuous expression of either than would otherwise be the case ; so that much will depend upon which is the stronger force in the nativity, *soul* or *senses*. If both are evenly balanced then a full and liberal time is before the native ; if the soul is the stronger, then the senses will be raised to a higher level, and love will absorb them, but if the senses have the greater hold then there is a liability of the soul being made captive to sensuous or sensual feelings. The native will himself know best his own position in this matter, and so will be able to judge how the conjunction will act.

♀ ⊻ ♂   A weak good aspect of very little account in the ordinary sense, but vital to those who respond to every vibration. It will benefit the native by causing his nature to be more expressive, and may also help him financially by the social advantages which it brings. It some-times denotes unions or attachments that are well founded, the feelings responding to those who may at this time be attractive and who are passing through a similar vibration. It is good for the desire-nature, which is now helped to accomplish many of its hopes and wishes, for it makes all matters connected with the desires to run smoothly, adding as it does some of the passional element, which in the more cultured of mankind is expressed as motive power, strengthening the whole nature as regards the feelings and emotions and rendering all more inclined to be demonstrative and to give expression to their feelings, also to seek the society of others, more especially that of the opposite sex.

♀ ∠ ♂   This is an unfavourable aspect, although somewhat weak in its nature. It will cause some struggle to take place between the Soul and the Senses, and may possibly be the first faint quiver between the two, denoting that a struggle is about to begin—a struggle which may not have its ending for many lives to come, according to the native's attitude while this influence operates. If he gives way to his passions and to sensation he will increase the force of his desire nature, but if he uplifts his emotions he will realise that in his soul there is love free from sensation and that passion may be transmuted into a higher force which has more to do with individual love than personal affection or sensation. He will now experience certain temptations, and the feelings will be keenly alive. He will have danger of financial losses, also of separations and disappointments, all of which will bring the right kind of "realisation" in the end.

♀ ✳ ♂   This is a favourable aspect so far as harmony between the Soul and the Senses is concerned ; but a great deal will depend upon the native himself as to whether Mars or Venus becomes the stronger influence. If the former, he will now enter upon a liberal and rather free experience of sensation, wherein personal feeling and desire will play a prominent part; but if the Venus influence be the stronger, then his mind will become more artistic and the force of this aspect will give him great mental energy, and will raise his feelings into a higher expression in which the soul will express a purer and a fuller love, enabling him to form good attachments which will lead to a successful and fruitful union. He will now find the influence of another affecting his life and he will be linked in a friendship that will be binding in nature and very pleasant in its course. If the lunar aspects are similar in nature it denotes a very good period in which to distinguish between *soul* and *sense.*

♀ □ ♂   This is in many respects an evil aspect; for it denotes a conflict between the Soul and the Senses, in which either may gain according to the native's own attitude toward the circumstances in which he will be placed. If he falls under the influence of the afflicting planet Mars, he will act indiscreetly, and on impulse without forethought ; this will cause him to go to extremes of feeling, and the passional side of his nature will then be uppermost. He will be severely tempted just now and many events will occur to upset domestic affairs and to bring disappointment and maybe pain to the feelings. It is not a good time either financially or socially, and the greatest care will be required to avoid either disgrace and dishonour or some affliction which will cause him to regret and to repent of some of his actions. He cannot act too discreetly during this period, especially where the feelings and emotions are concerned.

♀ △ ♂   This is a benefic and successful aspect, although, in common with all aspects between Mars and Venus, it shows some danger of the passions overcoming the higher feelings. But it is nevertheless harmonious and peaceful in character and will bring fruitful attachments and satisfaction to the feelings and the emotional side of the nature. The native will make permanent ties or unions that will be successful and fortunate.   This aspect strengthens the love-nature and gives opportunities for the realisation of hopes and wishes; it brings financial gain, presents, social advantages and the society of those who will minister to his happiness and pleasure. It will bring joy into the native's life, according to his power to respond to its benefic vibration; but if he goes to extremes of feeling and allows sensation to overcome love, then he will suffer through any excess of emotion and thereby miss the opportunities that are placed in his way for the expansion of the higher feelings and emotions which belong to the vibrations of Venus. But if he chooses he may make this one of the most happy and successful times of his life.

♀ □ ♂   This is not a favourable or fortunate aspect, and denotes a period in which the feelings are liable to suffer. However, it is not a powerful aspect and therefore much of the evil it indicates may be overcome, especially if the native exercises his will to restrain the passional or sensational element which will be aroused in him by it. He should be very careful in all his dealings with others, and act as discreetly and as prudently as possible and do all in his power to prevent his feelings being misplaced. He should be prepared for disappointments and for troubles affecting his personal feelings. He will either have some financial losses or some social disadvantages under this influence; and if the lunar aspects are evil at this time it will be a rather trying period. Since much, however, will depend upon the feelings and the attractions exercised over him by others, he should see to it that he mixes only with those who are pure-minded.

♀ ⊼ ♂   This, although slight in its influence (being one of the minor aspects) is favourable, as it tends to quicken the emotional side of the nature and stimulate the feelings to greater activity than usual. If care is exercised in all dealings with the opposite sex this aspect is on the whole favourable, but if other—and especially the lunar—aspects are unfavourable then it will tend to involve the native in difficulties, in which a certain amount of impulse and lack of premeditation bring troubles arising from excess of feeling. As a stimulating and quickening influence the aspect is a good one, but care is needed to keep the emotional nature under control during the period in which it is operating.

♀ 8 ♂ This denotes that the native has come to a period in which a struggle is to take place between the Soul and the Senses, and much will depend upon his own internal attitude as to which will conquer in the conflict. He will meet with much opposition, and will suffer disappointments in his attachments and love-affairs. He will be torn between Will and Desire, and will find himself severely tried and tempted; and a very great deal will depend upon his actions while this influence lasts as to his future destiny. This aspect also denotes some financial losses, and social troubles and disadvantages. It is a very evil time to make engagements, to bind one's self to others, or to allow the feelings and emotions to be drawn out in any way toward sensation or passion. The native should act very discreetly and be careful in whom he puts his trust, especially when the lunar aspects are unfavourable. *On the whole this is a dangerous period.*

♀ P. ♃ This is a very favourable and fortunate position, though rather indefinite in its time of action, the influence being spread over a time that has only vague limits. Its influence is really only operative when other influences are favourable, more especially when the lunar aspects are in harmony with it. It denotes a good period generally, in which social affairs and monetary prospects improve, and circumstances gradually shape themselves towards a good ending; so that many events may occur that come under this influence which cannot be directly traced to it, since it may be the seed, so to speak, of events that are not manifest until later.

♀ ♂ ♃ This is a somewhat mild influence between these two benefic planets, and can only be fully appreciated by those who are making for harmony and seeking a higher mode of expression for their life. It brings peace, happiness, and success to those who are well disposed and living on the principle of "*Noblesse oblige*," for it is an influence that can be attracted only toward those who are able to respond to its very high vibration. It brings some financial gain and much social success when the lunar or other influences are good, but when there is no lunar link between this and the other influences it is very liable to act in an indirect manner, bringing benefits through others, who are thus the channel for the distribution of this benefic vibration. The higher he can raise the feelings and emotions the more will the native feel this influence of Venus and Jupiter.

♀ ⊻ ♃   This is quite a general and in many respects an unimportant aspect, but as it is good in its nature, it may be made to benefit the native when the lunar aspects are good, by bringing him some social advantages, agreeable company, pleasant travelling and friendships that will be helpful and favourable in the future. This aspect will only act with any force when the lunar aspects or other influences are good, for then the two benefics will have a greater force than when acting alone. To increase the value of this vibration it will be well for the native to act as calmly and peacefully as he can, so that the good influences can be felt. It will benefit him in some way financially, but only in a general and indirect sense. He will, if religiously inclined, have an access of purer and better thoughts, and he will feel more than usually sympathetic and tolerant under its influence.

♀ ∠ ♃   This is a weak mutual aspect and not likely to effect very much, but at the same time as it is adverse it will act as a hindering or delaying influence, especially if other aspects are also adverse. It will not be a good time for social affairs, or monetary prospects, expenditure tending to exceed receipts ; and there is also a liability to lose money through friends and their affairs. The native will not find travel or journeys so pleasant as anticipated, and he will find it inadvisable to form attachments that are in any way not in keeping with his ideal of friendship. It is generally speaking a minor influence and not likely to be productive of anything very definite or decisive, but the native should be warned against extravagance, excess, or dabbling in legal matters, there being a tendency to waste money under this aspect. If, however, the lunar aspects are good, then very little harm is to be expected.

♀ ✳ ♃   A very favourable and fortunate aspect ; one which will greatly benefit the mind, making it very intuitive and more than usually inclined to the philosophical, tending in fact to bring out the inner part of the nature. The native will have very pleasant dealings with kindred or relatives, and with those who will benefit him socially and also financially. He will be drawn towards pleasure, all things tending to go

L

evenly and smoothly with him while this harmonious influence is operating. It will act very beneficially in conjunction with other aspects, and when the lunar aspects are good its influence will be most powerful. This is a splendid aspect for travel, also for making binding and lasting attachments, and it often leads to unions that are highly satisfactory, and out of which many benefits are obtained, not only from a financial standpoint but also socially, tending to increase of honour.

♀ □ ♃ This is not a good influence, although being an aspect between two benefics its power for ill is slight ; it will, however, cause some financial losses, also losses through travel and through dealing with religious persons, while those who have influence in the social world will not be well disposed to the native at this time ; he should therefore take care not to come into conflict with superiors, nor with those who are in any way connected with the law. This is not a good aspect for domestic affairs, nor for any attachments that may be formed at this time, as it is likely to cause disappointment or some temporary loss and difficulty ; probably someone to whom the native is attached will go abroad, or will have some important engagements which will necessitate a separation while this influence is in operation. It is not on the whole a good influence for pleasure ; there is, in fact, usually a mixture of pleasure and sorrow combined under this square aspect ; but with care it will not affect the native seriously unless the lunar aspects are also evil.

♀ △ ♃ This will bring general gain, and many financial benefits, for all things tend to go well while this aspect operates. The native will experience many social advantages through this influence, will make lasting attachments, and will attach himself to others by a bond that will be not only permanent, but very helpful and profitable: he will gain by travel under this aspect and much pleasure will come into his life (especially if he is under good *lunar* aspects at this period). His affections and sympathies will expand, and he will feel generously and kindly disposed to all with whom he comes in contact. He should make the most of this period, for the more he expands and allows himself to enjoy life, the more will he benefit by its very good influence. This aspect sometimes brings others into the life who do all they can to help and assist to make it happy and prosperous. It is a good time for spiritual and higher thought meditations, for it tends to expand the sympathies and the religious sentiments.

♀ ⧉ ♃ A weak aspect. It will cause financial losses and some social difficulties, the native's general affairs not going so well under its influence.   He should not lend money or be surety for anyone, should also guard against extravagance or waste, studying thrift and economy as much as he can while this influence lasts.   It is not good for engagements, promises, or matters in which feeling and emotion are concerned, and the native will suffer disappointment, be liable to some deception, or find himself under obligations he cannot realise.   If the *lunar* aspects are adverse at this time it will not be a good period, but if good, then this aspect may pass without any serious effect, simply causing some slight monetary or social troubles.   It is not a good time to travel or visit friends and acquaintances, however.

♀ ⊼ ♃   This influence is somewhat indefinite in its effect, which operates chiefly on the emotions, in which a conflict is likely to take place between personal and religous devotion, to the consequent purification or degradation, as the case may be, of the inner nature.   A reflection of this inner struggle may show itself in the material world, in which case it will probably take the form of financial losses, in which most likely inherited or family property will be swallowed up in speculation. In any case, the effect upon the feelings may be considerable, but as both these planets are concerned with the higher part of the nature, ultimate benefit to the soul will be the result of the suffering undergone. Much will depend upon the houses ruled and the signs occupied ; in some cases this aspect will effect little beyond temporary family or domestic disagreements.

♀ 8 ♃   This is very liable to bring a separation between the native and some one to whom he is much attached : it is very unfavourable for social affairs, for travel, and for monetary affairs also.   He should avoid all waste, see that expenditure does not exceed receipts, and be sure not to lend money to anyone or become surety for another, as he is liable to be involved in heavy losses or in pecuniary embarrassments.   Money or love affairs are sure to go wrong under this influence if the other aspects operating are of an unfavourable nature (more especially the *lunar* aspects).   This is a period in which legal troubles are threatened, and much opposition may result, therefore great care is necessary to avoid grave risks, especially where money is concerned.   It is unfavourable for religious matters, and for dealing with ecclesiastics or with those who are proud and aristocratic.

♀ P. ♄   This is an affliction that will extend over several years, operating with a force more or less evil, according to the nature of other influences that may be in action; for when they also are evil the effects will be severe. It denotes financial difficulties, trouble with regard to possessions, sorrows, love disappointments, and also, if care is not exercised, loss of honour. The favourable side of this influence is to bring attachments to older persons, also to form ties or engagements that are binding and of long duration. This is the aspect that causes, when operating in the horoscopes of those who are single, long courtships with little or no prospect of marriage. In a general sense it gives economy and thrift, also a love of saving, but when carried to excess danger of hoarding wealth and becoming far too careful and parsimonious. It causes delays to progress, hindering the flow of affection that Venus gives, and it sometimes even completely chills affection, stopping the outflow of feeling altogether. The native should act discreetly while this influence operates.

♀ ☌ ♄ This is by no means a favourable conjunction, and tends to cause disappointment and loss of honour and credit. It is not good for financial affairs, nor for the affections. It sometimes indicates attachments to elderly persons or to those who are older than the native, and in its good effect causes faithfulness and very binding attachments. The thrifty and careful side of this aspect should be used for purposes of economy, or for securing a steady and permanent income by application to professional or business undertakings, but any tendency to over acquisitiveness or avarice should be vigorously contended against. It is not a good position for expansion of the feelings, and is apt to limit the affections and thus cause the native to be a slave to his emotions. It causes grief and tends to chasten the feelings by suffering and to purify by sorrow; to the undeveloped it is a dangerous position, more especially when the Moon is also afflicted.

♀ ⚺ ♄ This is a very weak aspect, but favourable enough in its nature to steady the influence of Venus and bring more faithfulness into the affections, so tending to bring attachments that are more binding and permanent. It brings some slight financial benefit, but much will depend upon the other influences operating. The native will gain in honour and reputation under its influence by taking upon himself any duty or responsibility where he can acquit himself favourably, and to the satisfaction of those who may in any way be concerned with his welfare. He should while this aspect lasts seek to form the friendship and acquaintance of those older than himself, for any attachments of this kind will be beneficial. If the lunar aspects are also good, this influence will be the more beneficial.

♀ ∠ ♄ This is not a good aspect, but is somewhat weak in its influence; it will bring some disappointment with regard to any attachment that may have been formed, and is adverse to the even or steady flow of the affections. It is not good for financial affairs, nor for dealings with persons older than the native; and he should now safeguard his honour and act as discreetly and prudently as he can, for the conditions in which he is likely to be placed are inimical to his material welfare. Social undertakings will not go well, nor will any dealings with elders, or persons in authority, for those holding responsible posts will not be well disposed towards him, and if the lunar aspects are also unfavourable, it will be an unfortunate period altogether. Great care will be needed in all the native's actions, especially actions undertaken in association with others, for he is more likely to suffer through than gain by friends and acquaintances, and should therefore guard against deception.

♀ ✳ ♄ This is a favourable influence and it will benefit the native in some way financially, or help him to add to his income, probably through his own industry or by some efforts on his part to improve his general conditions. He will form some very favourable and permanent attachments which will end in a successful and fruitful union; he should gain in honour or reputation while this influence operates, and should raise himself into a more responsible and important position in life. This aspect denotes a steady period, in which improvement is made and progress is of that honest type which is so beneficial to the growth of the individual character. When the lunar aspects are good, this will be a very good and prosperous period, in which the foundation may be laid of much future good.

♀ □ ♄ This is an evil influence for all matters concerned with the affections, and tends to bring a period in which very intense emotions will be experienced, causing grief, sorrow, and disappointment. The native will not only suffer through his feelings but will also have some financial losses. It is an evil time for all attachments or unions, also for domestic and social affairs. This influence sometimes affects the morals, and tends to make one careless and less self-controlled than usual. The native should do all he can to avoid deception and fraud, and should not trust others too much : for he is now liable to be imposed upon, and to suffer libel and dishonour or general ill-repute. If this affliction is supported by other influences it will be a very evil time, though if the lunar aspects are good it will not act so severely. But it is a trying time in any case, and care should be exercised in dealing with friends, superiors, elderly persons, creditors, and those who have any power to affect the financial affairs. Forethought and discretion should be the native's watchwords, but he should courageously determine not to give way to despondent or remorseful feelings.

♀ △ ♄   This is a very benefic aspect and tends to bring a very steady period for the feelings and emotions. The native will now have faithful attention from others and will incline to be chaste, thoughtful, sincere and thrifty, his moral character undergoing improvement while this influence operates. He will gain in some way financially, either through judicious and careful investment, or by the advice of friends or others whose interests are also in some way his own. This is a good time for the strengthening of the general health, for the study of hygiene, and for the enjoyment of social pleasures and entertainments of all kinds. It tends to the formation of lasting attachments, binding people together, cementing friendships already established and rendering them enduring. The native will find himself faithful to all ties, and moreover feeling a deeper devotional spirit than usual. It will bring him credit and honour and help him to establish his monetary affairs upon a sound basis; thus, under this mutual influence it would be well to make a settled provision for the future. If the lunar aspects are also good it will be a very good period.

♀ □ ♄   This is an unfavourable aspect, and under its influence unfavourable lunar aspects will either cause domestic affliction or some serious disappointment. It is an evil time to have dealings with elderly persons, to sign contracts, or to enter into any engagements where the feelings and emotions are concerned. The native should do all in his power to maintain control over his feelings under this aspect, should not allow himself to be influenced by others to his detriment, and should keep his own counsel and act as discreetly as possible: it is not a good time to pay visits to friends or to form new acquaintances. He is liable to suffer in various directions from dishonour, discredit, or scandal— whether deserved or not. He should live temperately during the period of this aspect, and study *thrift* and *economy*.

♀ ⚹ ♄   A very weak aspect, but sometimes decidedly harmful

when other directions or aspects are evil, especially lunar ones. It then denotes deaths in the family circle and losses in connection with domestic affairs: there is also some liability of taking poison or of being injuriously affected by drugs at this time, if care is not exercised. There are many troubles threatened by this aspect, and where attachments or friendships are affected by it there is always danger of disappointment and sorrow through the affections; therefore, deliberation is necessary in all matters connected with the emotional side of the nature. As this mutual influence is weak it may have no appreciable effect, but it will be well for the native to be prepared for the unfavourable conditions it produces. When the lunar aspects are of such a nature as to bring this aspect into operation, especial care is necessary.

♀ □ ♄ An evil position, likely to bring much trouble and anxiety while it operates. The native will have disappointments in all his attachments, and will suffer in consequence, his feelings and emotions being acutely tried whenever the lunar aspects correspond in being similarly unfavourable. This position denotes separations, and often bereavements and sorrowful partings; it also brings financial losses and monetary troubles. It is an evil time to deal with elderly persons, or those who have any serious claim upon the native; it also threatens him with scandal and a liability to be secretly attacked or to have his good name assailed. He should therefore act as discreetly as he can, for this position causes persons to become his enemies—whether deservedly or no—and to seek to injure him. If care is maintained he may avoid much of the evil of Saturn's affliction, for by a knowledge of its nature the causes that set the evil in motion may be minimised.

♀ P. ♅ This peculiar influence will last for some considerable time; for all parallels act over more than one year, often extending over a period of many years, since it is a gradual and not a sharply-defined or decisive aspect. Under its influence the native will undergo strange and somewhat remarkable experiences in connection with the feelings, forming attachments or connections that will not be in any sense of the word orthodox, but somewhat bohemian and free, tinged with romance, and having all the elements of independence and originality. It is a period therefore during which care should be exercised, as his motives and actions are very liable to be mistaken, and have wrong constructions placed upon them; this will be due to the magnetic vibrations playing upon the native, which will make him act from unpremeditated and spontaneous promptings of a somewhat impulsive character, rather than from deliberately reasoned motives.

♀ ☌ ♅   This is a peculiar and indeed remarkable position, which will tend to precipitate the feelings and so bring to a premature consummation or sudden termination any attachments formed under its influence. The native will form sudden ties, or will be peculiarly affected by others, whose magnetic influence will move him to actions that will have lasting effect upon his life. Sudden gains or sudden losses are likely under this influence, according to the nature of other mutual aspects operating, either good or ill. Of this conjunction it may be said that "the unexpected always happens," for under its influence nothing transpires just as one would expect; experience, however, shows that the affections and emotions are often stimulated to their highest pitch when the Uranian vibration thus affects the impressibility that Venus gives. The native will be more than usually idealistic and imaginative, also very susceptible to the influence of others, and will seek to act as independently and originally as his nature will permit: it may at least be said that he will certainly not be apathetic or callous under this influence.

♀ ⚹ ♅   This is a very weak aspect, but often has an effect of some importance as the result, since it tends to excite the feelings and emotions, rendering them unusually susceptible, and bringing an accession of sentiment into the nature, acting thus in various ways, more especially by prompting to impulsive acts where feeling is concerned. During the operation of this aspect, it will be well for the native to be guarded in the formation of fresh friendships, making only such acquaintances as are social rather than exclusively personal : for he will be idealistic and imaginative, and through his idealistic tendencies prone to give way to the mental impressions of another, and will thus be affected according to the conditions and circumstances in which he will be placed. It may bring some increased financial prospects or monetary gain, for its influence is beneficial in many ways, none of which can be very definitely indicated. A good time to travel, also to investigate subjective ideas, as the intuition will be active.

♀ ∠ ♅   Not a very strong, but at the same time not a good aspect, likely to affect the feelings if sensitive, and to bring sudden estrangement and disappointments into the life. It will bring some unexpected losses, and all the native's business affairs should be carefully

watched; for it is a time in which his financial prospects are most liable
to fluctuate. He should not cultivate chance acquaintances nor make
friendships with those of whose character he is not certain. It is by no
means a good period, but it will not have serious effects unless the lunar
aspects are very evil, in which case affairs are likely to go wrong
suddenly, or in some manner that could not very well be avoided. All
aspects between Venus and Uranus are peculiar in their nature, and
generally tend to bring about romantic and strange attachments in
which magnetic influence plays a prominent part.

♀ ✶ ♅   This is in many respects a very favourable aspect, but in
some cases the good that it brings may end unfavourably: it brings
strange attachments, in which the feelings and emotions are much moved
and affected. This will be a splendid time for social pleasures,
entertaining friends, and mixing with others generally. The native will
feel sociable and magnetically drawn towards others, more than usually
inclined to act freely and independently; for the feelings will be moved
rather by sentiment, and a tendency towards the idealistic, than by more
commonplace interests. He will find himself now strangely linked with
others, and liable to unexpected rushes of feeling, which will cause him
to act somewhat impulsively; and if he is not very discreet, or if he
allows others to take advantage of his susceptible conditions, he will
ultimately suffer. This is a good time for inventive ability to be
displayed; it also shows the prospect of some financial gain and many
unexpected advantages: in fact, should the lunar directions be good this
will be a very favourable period generally, more especially if the native
is capable of displaying any originality in his methods, and if he acts up
to the highest standards of his moral nature.

♀ ☐ ♅   This is an evil aspect, that will cause domestic troubles,
sudden estrangements, or very unfavourable family conditions. This
aspect often leads to notoriety, for it brings out any latent tendencies to
singularity or eccentricity, more especially in regard to the expression of
feeling. The native should therefore be careful to do nothing that will
be likely to arouse scandal or cause others to be hurt or offended by his
conduct; for his magnetic conditions will be such as to make him a little
erratic and inclined to act peculiarly where feeling is concerned, and it
may cause attachments or connections that will not be favourable
to his prospects, events arising out of them that will tend to injuriously
affect his honour or seriously thwart his hopes and wishes. He will

suffer some financial loss and also be affected by the action of others in some harmful manner. No removals or changes should be made while this influence operates. *A decidedly critical period.*

♀ △ ♅   A very favourable aspect and one likely to bring success, not only financially but also emotionally and socially. The native will have some sudden gain under this aspect, and should he speculate or invest money it will benefit him unexpectedly or bring him sudden profit. He will also find himself magnetically attracted to others, and forming fresh engagements and attachments which will influence his life in some very marked way: this is a good aspect for travel and making important changes. Friends will help and benefit him, and if he is in any way inclined to be imaginative or idealistic he will now have abundant opportunity to experience friendship of a romantic character, for he will be easily affected by mental attractions. This is a good aspect for all occult matters, and for studies of the metaphysical and higher thought type: it gives the ability to study astrology and kindred subjects. It is a good period in every way and should be made the most of.

♀ □ ♅   This is not a favourable aspect and warns the native to avoid all travel, changes and removals, for it threatens him with sudden and unexpected troubles. It is not a good time to enter into any engagements or to have attachments of a romantic character: imaginative mental conditions, in which either fancy or fascination plays an important part will be the result of this magnetic influence, which is in no way a good aspect for friendships of any kind. This is not a good time for legal affairs, nor for dealing either with solicitors or those who are engaged in any work where law is concerned. Financial affairs should be watched, for monetary losses are likely, and if the lunar aspects are now of an adverse nature it will not be a good time. The native should act as discreetly as he can, and should be guarded in all his dealings with others; especially those who have any influence over his feelings, as he will now be very impressionable.

♀ ⚹ ♅   An aspect that is very weak and may have little or no effect upon the life; if it does in any way affect the native it will be owing to the fact that other influences of a similar nature are operating, especially those shown by the Moon; for when the Moon aspects either Venus or Uranus it will set this aspect in motion. Its influence will be felt in the general health, as it will cause a tendency to nervous disorders; and some indications of those nervous troubles will be a tendency to become easily effected by others magnetically, to be over-impressionable, whimsical, and sentimental. The native will meet with those whose influence upon him will be more attractive than is ordinarily experienced. He should not lend money or allow himself to be over-indebted to others, for this is a period in which care will be needed not to fall too much under the influence of others.

♀ 8 ♆   This is an affliction which is far from good in its influence. It will bring separations and estrangements from those loved and cause sorrow and pain while it operates.   The native's feelings and emotions will be at a high tension and liable to be easily affected, and he should therefore be careful in all attachments to guard himself from sensation or becoming too susceptible to the influence of others; for the magnetic conditions will be such that his sensibility to the personal attractions of others or their plausibility of manner will put him very much at their mercy; it is an evil time for legal affairs and for all monetary matters, especially as regards speculation and investment. The native cannot be too careful in all Venus affairs while this influence operates : he will either make some sudden and unwise change, or display a general inclination to do things abruptly and suddenly : the unexpected is sure to happen under this peculiar mental aspect and he cannot be too careful in all his relationships with others.   It is a very critical period, especially for women.   *A dangerous time.*

♀ P. ♆ *   This is virtually equivalent to the conjunction (*q.v.*) but acts over a longer period, and is more general in its effects.

♀ ♂ ♆ *   This will bring some very remarkable attachments or engagements that will be unique and quite out of the common.   It sometimes produces platonic love-affairs, in which no thought of sex enters.   Upon those who are advanced or making attainments it has a very beautiful influence, acting in a manner that can only be understood by those who have passed through a similar experience.   It has in the majority of cases the effect of refining the love element, and raises the affections to a far higher level than the ordinary individual can understand.   If there is no response in consciousness to this vibration it will in all probability pass by, and not act for several lives to come, in which case the vibration merely acts upon the environment, bringing social and financial benefits, unusual popularity and adulation being often a marked characteristic of its influence in this way.

* See note on p. 154.

♀ ⊻ ♆* This is to a certain extent similar to the conjunction, but has less material effect, operating chiefly upon the inner consciousness. Inspirational moments and artistic or poetic intuitions are likely to result from this influence, but only the very refined and sensitive will be capable of responding to them. To the mystical and æsthetic it will bring true delight. Where the planets are in mutual affliction at birth secret sorrows, strange persecutions, hallucinations or obsessions are likely to result.

♀ ∠ ♆* This is somewhat allied in its nature to the square aspect (*q.v.*), but as the semi-square always indicates that the interplay of the planetary vibrations is undergoing a change of phase, this period will be more than usually harassing and indecisive. The influence is most likely to show out as a series of petty worries or some small scandal. It may affect the health, in which case functional derangements in obscure parts of the system are probable.

♀ * ♆* This is a most harmonious and beautiful influence, and, unless it is marred by some other contrary influence, betokens a period of pure joy. Some friendship or intercourse of a peculiarly sweet character, yet with something mysterious and secret about it, is indicated; and the events resulting from this influence are certain to be looked back upon with delight throughout the whole of the life. To the religious minded, a period of cloistered seclusion and happy musings; to the ambitious schemer, a period of marvellous prosperity; to the artist or poet, a period of unparalleled creative fecundity.

♀ □ ♆* This will bring very strange and peculiar attachments, and cause the feelings to be affected by magnetic conditions quite out of the ordinary. The native should avoid all persons who exercise any strange magnetic influence over him and keep away from all those who are not strictly honest and pure in all their dealings. He cannot act too discreetly while this influence is operating, for its effects upon him cannot be of the best, or in any way conducive to his future happiness. Only those whose desires are chaste and who live a very pure life can escape the baneful influence of this planet's afflictions, and it is sure to play a part in the native's history which will be long remembered; *or*, it will have no perceptible effect whatever. None can say precisely how it will act, for "extremes meet" when Neptune has any vibration to Venus, especially in all matters where feeling is concerned. In any case,

* See note on p. 154.

however, financial affairs should be very closely watched during this period.

♀ △ ♆ *   This, like the sextile, is also an aspect denoting a joyful period. Unless contradicted by adverse aspects between other planets, the native will experience a period of complete satisfaction, when the sweets of life will be tasted to the full, success pouring in upon him from all quarters—unsought for, as it were. Financial matters will prosper amazingly, and all will go " merrily as a marriage bell." This, like all good influences, may be used either for material or spiritual ends, and the effects which result from it will depend upon the inner desires of the native. There is a possibility of rare spiritual experiences in this aspect, ecstasy, illumination, and mystic vision.

♀ ⚼ ♆ *   To the majority, the effect of this aspect will be much the same as that described for the semi-square. To the progressive soul who aspires after the purification of the inner nature, however, it is likely to be a time of severe suffering, the feelings undergoing a complete depolarisation and regeneration. The native should watch his actions and his thoughts, and guard against self-deception. Weak-minded or very negative people are liable to hallucinations under this aspect.

♀ ⚺ ♆ *   To the average individual little or nothing is likely to arise from this aspect, but to the refined and æsthetic person it will bring some poetical but withal sorrowful experiences, leading to a refinement of the artistic sensibilities. To all will come some opportunity for gaining control over the emotions. In all aspects to Neptune, and especially the adverse ones, there is invariably a certain *tantalising* element—hopes aroused but unfulfilled, success promised in greater measure than is attained; and this will prove no exception to the rule.

♀ ☍ ♆ *   This position denotes the balancing of the ' objective ' and ' subjective ' feelings and emotions. In grasping at what appears to be the substance, the native will discover that substance and shadow are relative terms. He will attain the fruit he has desired only to find it turn to ashes in his mouth ; or he will be baulked of his success at the last moment. To those who live chiefly in their feelings, this aspect is productive of the keenest sorrow, secret though it may be. Only those who have experienced it can appreciate what it means. To the ordinary easy-going person, however, it is not formidable in its effects, and at worst will amount to no more than some experience of fraudulent

* See note on p. 154.

misrepresentation. The native should be constantly on his guard concerning all business matters during the time that this aspect operates.

MARS.

♂ P. ♃ In common with all parallels this influence is spread over a period that is longer than that for which ordinary aspects endure, therefore it is more or less at work behind all the other influences which may be operating at this time.   No influence of Mars to Jupiter is good, and this position will cause the native to be rather over-liberal and, unless very careful, wastefulness or extravagance, either on his own part or on that of his inferiors, will occasion loss.   Moreover while it lasts he should avoid litigation, or he may be involved in much expense or in some loss of honour.   If care is exercised in all affairs it may only operate as a stimulating influence where money is concerned, or as an excitant where enthusiasm is affected.   The native should not borrow or lend money under its influence; he should live as temperately as he can, and let it work as a motive power to raise his ambitions to a higher level. It is not a satisfactory period for religious matters nor for dealing with religious persons, but it will give great religious enthusiasm, where the nativity itself shows any such tendency.

♂ ☌ ♃ This position of Mars and Jupiter is not altogether good, but it can be usefully employed for the betterment of the native's personal conditions, if he can avoid over-much dignity or pride.   It will make him very liberal, not to say extravagant, and will be accompanied by some desire to " plunge," and if he is not careful over financial affairs there will be some danger—especially if he should become involved in litigation—of losing large sums of money.   He may either gain or lose suddenly under this influence, according to the nature of the other aspects in force at the time, more especially the *lunar* ones. To the weak or those who lack full self-consciousness it brings a tendency to frivolity and giddiness, but to the developing soul it gives a spirit of enterprise, a feeling of independence, and a great increase of energy. But it is a good position only for those who have both ability and *prudence*.

♂ ⚺ ♃ A very weak influence, one that may not affect the native in any appreciable measure.   He may turn it to some good account by looking after financial affairs; and by putting some of his Mars energy to the Jupiter side of the account, so to speak.

but they are usually small, and take the form of presents more often than otherwise. He will be wise to look after monetary matters, for he can gain in this way by giving attention to the improvement of his financial affairs.

♂ ∠ ♃ This is a weak aspect, but not a good one, for it shows a liability to lose money; and if the native has any tendency towards being lavish he may become too extravagant and give way to excess. He should watch his expenditure and check any waste that may be going on in his affairs. It is not a good aspect in many ways: sometimes it gives impure blood and inflammatory conditions, especially when the lunar aspects are evil; but this would be due to excess in diet or to not living temperately, and might therefore soon be remedied if proper attention were paid to the laws of hygiene. The native should neither lend nor borrow money while this aspect lasts, should avoid litigation, and become surety for none : nor should he either speculate or invest under this influence, but use great care in all his affairs.

♂ ✱ ♃ This is favourable in its nature, but as Mars is never very suitably combined with Jupiter it cannot give all the benefit that might be expected from it. It will have the effect of making the native very generous and liberal, and unless he is careful to avoid excess of any kind, perhaps extravagant also and inclined to go to extremes. It will make him enterprising and fearless, rather too inclined to take risks, especially where money is in question. It gives social advantages and brings associations into the life which have an expanding tendency, and in all enterprises or undertakings the native will not hesitate to push forward and use all his energies to increase and improve his conditions. To those who are devotionally inclined it gives an extra impetus to religious thought; for it is the aspect that often brings "conversion" or a great uplifting of the emotions, the feelings being very easily excited to enthusiasm. If impulsiveness is avoided, the influence will prompt to useful activity, but unless it is kept under a certain amount of restraint rash actions will ensue, ending unfavourably.

♂ ▢ ♃ This is a very evil aspect in many ways, but only active or evil in a particular sense when the nativity is not a very progressive one. The native is liable to some heavy financial losses, or to become extravagant in expenditure and too lavish in giving; for this aspect shows some sign of waste going on, either in the physical system or in the surroundings. He must avoid litigation, for any legal troubles are likely to involve him in heavy loss, since decisions will go against him. This aspect sometimes brings false imprisonment or confinement or other conditions tending to deprivation of liberty. It is not a good influence for social affairs, or for religious matters, as it inclines to over-enthusiasm and excess of feeling. It is never so evil as it appears, however, unless the lunar aspects are at the same time evil, in which case many troubles are threatened, especially troubles arising through extravagance or excess and a spirit of too great liberality. Lending money and long journeys should be avoided. *A critical period generally.*

♂ △ ♃ This benefic aspect is good for those who know how to speculate or invest money, since those who are judicious enough to act without impulse can make things very brisk and profitable under this enterprising influence. It is good for social affairs and for money making, but like other aspects of Mars to Jupiter it tends to excess and an over-estimation of opportunities. It will give the native enterprise and freedom enough to allow him to venture where others would hesitate and hold back; and, as " fortune always favours the brave," in accordance with his ability will success be assured where undertakings are of the adventurous type. This aspect promotes feeling to the highest side of the emotional nature, but there is always a danger of reaction in this direction, and hence it is only the very pure who can get the true spiritual benefit out of this aspect. It is the only aspect that (theoretically) promises a fortune through speculation; but the lunar aspects must coincide and the whole directions tend that way to make this an accomplished fact.

♂ ▢ ♃ It is not a good aspect by any means, threatening many troubles, financial, social and personal. It acts upon the health, by over-heating the blood and giving some blood disorders; upon the monetary affairs, by bringing losses, either through deliberate extravagance, by robbery, or from unavoidable expenses; and it affects the social conditions either by differences of opinion concerning religious matters, or through assuming more than can be well substantiated. It is not a good period for travel; changes and removals are best avoided, or postponed. If the lunar aspects are evil while this mutual aspect is in operation, it will be a trying and troublesome time; but if the lunar aspects are all good then its effects will be readily overcome.

♂ ⊼ ♃ This is by no means a strong influence, and may pass without causing any serious consequences, or even without affecting the native at all, unless the lunar aspects are evil, when it will add its tribute to make the period rather trying and troublesome. It sometimes denotes a death in the family or social circle, from which either gain or loss ensues according to the natal conditions. It is an aspect of the indifferent order, good when Jupiter is the stronger planet and evil when the influence of the planet Mars is the more pronounced; in the latter case it will cause blood disorders or ill-health through surfeit and excess of bile, etc. It acts upon the health, and affects those connected with the native according to the general testimony of the directions in force at the time.

♂ □ ♃   This is decidedly evil, and it will be necessary for the native to exercise extreme caution while it operates. He will have losses caused by separations or by dealing with his opponents in the wrong spirit, or perhaps by actual robbery: it threatens losses, either through extravagance and waste or by being too liberal and inclined to overdo things and go to extremes. He should not be too assertive under this aspect and should not allow himself to become pragmatical or too egotistical, or he will overstep recognised bounds. He should not allow himself to be carried away by feeling or to become too zealous, for all tendencies towards extremes will now be *dangerous*. This position marks a very critical stage in the career and may mean shipwreck, or indeed utter ruin, if there be a train of evil lunar aspects operating at the time ; and hence the native cannot be too careful in all his actions, at this period, studying to take a temperate and a just view of all questions he is called upon to decide. *Great care is needed at this time.*

♂ P. ♄   This, like all the parallel aspects, will last over a very long period, for Saturn is a slow moving planet, and Mars is not quick enough in motion to allow the influence to work off in one year. It is not a favourable aspect, for Mars represents heat and Saturn cold, and therefore unless these planets neutralise or balance each other, by "mutual disposition" or favourable aspect in the nativity, one of them will exercise the stronger influence, with all the evil of the other added. In common with all parallels this must depend upon the operation of the lunar aspects and their nature to awaken from latency its evils. When, therefore, the lunar directions are evil, it will cause the temper to be too readily affected, any tendency to give way to anger resulting in awakening the passional side of the nature, and by the very strong feeling it engenders giving an inclination either to go to deliberate extremes or to act very indiscreetly.

M

The period may be made good by allowing the strength of Mars to be blended with the tact of Saturn, this giving the finest form of diplomacy and persuasiveness.

♂ ☌ ♄   The conjunction of these two malefic planets marks a very important period of the life; for this sudden blending of heat and cold acts in many cases disastrously, much as though a bar of red-hot iron were plunged into cold water. To the undeveloped person this is a very serious conjunction, for it stirs up the animal side of the nature and causes all the passions and the vices n the character to be awakened into activity. The native should curb his desires and seek to act temperately in all things, doing all in his power to keep from being called out from his centre; or he will find it difficult to control his temper and may be moved to act rashly or impulsively and either say or do things he will bitterly regret later on. If the lunar directions are evil it will be by no means a good time, and according to the nature of the other directions so will be the effect of this aspect. This aspect may be likened to the blending of iron and carbon to form steel: if the proportions are not right, or the "conversion" is not properly done, only brittle and useless cast iron will result. It will affect the native according to his response to either Saturn or Mars; or to both, if he has not yet learned how to control himself. *It is a highly critical period.*

♂ ⚺ ♄   This is a weak aspect, but more favourable than otherwise. It will strengthen the will power and give more determination and purpose than would be the case without it. Much need not be expected to come from this influence unless the lunar aspects are very favourable, when it will strengthen the lunar influence by giving more stability and a more enterprising spirit. The native will incline to be more enterprising, ambitious and energetic than usual; for the force of Mars and the tact of Saturn combining will benefit him by giving both purpose and stability. In many cases this aspect has no appreciable effect, except to make desire and action blend more harmoniously; but by asserting himself the native will become firmer, and will find himself possessed of a stronger will to carry into practical expression the good lunar aspects operating.

♂ ∠ ♄   This is an evil aspect, but not at all powerful, and only operates to a marked extent by exciting the passions, causing an expression of energy which may be excessive if the nature is not well under control: when other directions, especially the lunar aspects, are evil, this is likely to act very adversely. The native should now exercise care, in order to avoid accidents, never acting rashly or impulsively, for there are elements of danger in this aspect, making the present period a very trying time for those who are ruled by impulse: many under its influence act imprudently, and often rush into danger without stopping to think before acting. It is only by taking care not to give way to the impulse that is produced by external attraction that the dangers of this influence can be avoided. To many it may have no other effect than that of increasing the activities, but those activities will be the result of desire and impulse more than careful thought. This mutual aspect rarely operates unless the luminaries are aspecting either Mars or Saturn.

♂ ✳ ♄ This is a favourable aspect between the two planets; but since they are malefic in their nature and the aspect is good, extremes are being blended thereby. It is very difficult to interpret the two natures of these influences blending, but to those who are seeking to harmonise the will and desire it gives force of character and much directive purpose. The native will be more than usually courageous and perhaps venturesome, but if competent, he will blend desire and action in such a way as to make him very decisive and capable, carrying through all plans to a successful and well-foreseen issue. He will be steady and clear-headed, with enough force and tact combined to enable him to accomplish a great deal. Much, however, will depend upon the lunar aspects; if they are very favourable this will be a splendid period, as it will give all the energy required and all the diplomacy necessary to bring affairs to a successful issue ; but if the lunar directions are not good, not much is to be expected, for while the ability and energy will be there, circumstances will militate against its successful employment.

♂ □ ♄ An evil aspect, which will act very much against the native's progress, causing him to be at the mercy of two very opposing forces, corresponding to heat and cold, force and inertia. He will be prone to give expression to outbursts of temper or exhibit very hasty and at times rash conduct, which will bring trouble ; indeed, if the other directions operating are very evil it may cause dishonour or disgrace, if not complete ruin, through his impulsive desires and wilful actions. There is no occasion on which this aspect may be said to operate favourably, for it is a war between two very powerful malefics and is likely to rend the native in its violence if the vibrations are more than he can control ; therefore more than usual care is necessary at this period to avoid quarrels, disputes, or any friction with others, especially if it is likely to deprive him of his liberty for any time. This is an excitable and turbulent aspect, and when not otherwise acting as a disturbing element gives over-enthusiastic and extreme tendencies. The more evil the lunar directions, the more evil this mutual aspect. *A very critical and trying period necessitating great caution and self-control.*

♂ △ ♄ This is a very powerful aspect between the two malefic planets. It will give a very strong will while it operates and inspire the native with enthusiasm, courage and enterprise in plenty. He will be able to add strength to tact, to work diplomatically, and to manage his affairs with both insight and skill and with sufficient steadiness of character to carry through his schemes successfully. It will give him authority, with enough dignity to hold firm and to act with bravery under the most trying circumstances. If the lunar aspects are good and the other directions favourable he will find this a splendid period for his ambitions, as it will cause him to be enterprising, though judiciously so, risking ventures that others would not undertake. He may make it a very good time for all his affairs, as he will be sufficiently assertive and very reliable, managing all duties so that they will bring him honour and respect. With some persons it will not act; only those whose " root of merit " is established can make full use of this vibration, which means the using of desire in the direction of emotion turned to purpose. According to the native's soul growth, so will this influence act for good.

♂ □ ♄ This is an evil aspect, somewhat similar in its nature to the semi-square (*q.v.*), but still more drastic in its operation. It is less likely than the square or opposition to show out in the everyday concerns of life, but will take effect chiefly in the inner mental or spiritual life of the native, who will go through a very trying period of doubt and uncertainty and mental instability. As in all semi-square and sesquiquadrate aspects, the vibrations of these planets are now going through a change of phase, as it were, and this is likely to lead to a complete breakdown, or rather reconstruction of the centre of thought and feeling. It may take effect on the health, which is sure to be affected more or less in any case, but, with advanced souls at any rate, it is most likely to manifest in a period of disbelief in all one's previous ideas—in short, a state of mind briefly summed up in the street arab's cynical question : " Wot's the good of anyfink ? Why, nuffink ! " The native should strive against this despondency and hesitancy, by bringing his will to bear in the enforced carrying out of previously-determined-on lines of conduct : the extent to which this can be done will prove an excellent test of the moral standard which has been reached.

♂ ⚹ ♄   This is perhaps the least harmful of the evil aspects between Mars and Saturn, for the Saturnine element serves as a suitable balancing or adjusting agent to the Mars force, and the feelings and mind will operate as mutual critics, the mind enquiring into the operation of the feelings and the latter serving as a corrective to the limiting and contracting tendencies of the former. It is necessary, however, to take care that the feelings are not allowed to fritter away the mind force in useless repinings, and that on the other hand the mind is not permitted to repress all natural strivings after new experience or emotions. The native will find this an excellent aspect for critical or analytical work, especially in all such technical subjects as chemistry, scientific agriculture, hygiene, etc., should he have any natural abilities in these directions. The senses will become the servants of the mind under this aspect, and will be sharpened in their discriminative power.

♂ ☍ ♄   This is an evil aspect, which will bring a liability to accidents and some very acute physical experiences. The native should act with great discretion and do nothing impulsively, for this aspect brings some very rash tendencies in which action will be guided by sudden and unpremeditated desire to do some deed of either great bravery, or perhaps foolhardiness, or even crime, which may have fatal results. He will find himself easily irritated and prone to give way to anger, and may commit some violent act if not sufficiently self-controlled to keep the desire nature well in hand. If the lunar aspects are evil at this time it will be a very bad period, especially if the other directions operating are also adverse. If the lunar directions are good, this mutual aspect will not act fully at this time, but will wait till other influences set it in motion. In any case it is an evil time, and much opposition is to be feared ; separation and marked estrangements are usually the chief features of this aspect. *A dangerous period, in which all possible self-control should be practised.*

♂ P. ♅   This parallel, which remains in force some years, is by no means a favourable influence, for it will bring an irritable and excitable tendency, and is a period when the native will be liable to accidents and violence. He should be very guarded in all dealings with strangers and should avoid quarrelling with anyone. The best side of this influence is to give energy and activity, with inventive, constructive and mechanical ability. The native will do wisely to avoid litigation or conflict with others, also to keep from being too abrupt in manner or too impulsive in action, and should restrain all tendency to rashness. He should act very discreetly in the presence of any magnetic attraction; for when the magnetism has passed off he will find that he was affected rather by outside influences than directed from within by his own will. He should avoid travel and removals.

♂ ☌ ♅ This is in many respects a remarkable influence, and it will make this period unique in the native's life history, for it will bring sudden and unexpected events and peculiar experiences which will commence in an unexpected and strange manner and end as abruptly. He will find himself in some way drawn towards the occult and the mystical side of things, and will have the courage to investigate phenomena or to study psychical subjects at first hand. This position at birth is generally found to accompany clairvoyance or seership of some kind, and hence is likely, as a progressed aspect, to be accompanied by a temporary manifestation of the same faculty, which in many cases is apt to be regarded as "hallucination." It is not a good time for taking journeys, for removals, or forming any new acquaintances. In fact it is a period when great care should be exercised, for the whole nervous system will be at extremely high tension while this conjunction lasts, which in some cases is a considerable period, and those who have friends coming under this influence should exercise the greatest patience and sympathy in their dealings with them. With the possible exception of the square and opposition between the same planets this is perhaps the most trying aspect that can be lived through.

♂ ⚹ ♅ This is a weak aspect, and one that is not likely to affect the native very much, but it is good in a measure and he may be able to take advantage of it. It will bring some opportunity to improve either himself or his conditions and surroundings. It will cause him to be energetic and enterprising, and may bring some temporary financial benefits. It will stimulate the native mentally, and it promises the advent of some friend or acquaintance whose influence will be helpful. He may take some journeys or removals under this influence, travelling being good, or any movement of an enterprising nature likely to become advantageous. A great deal of good may be extracted from this minor aspect if the lunar

directions are also good at this time. Those of a mechanical or inventive
turn of mind are likely to have some "happy thoughts" in connection
with inventions and mechanical appliances.

♂ ∠ ♅ This is not a good influence, but it is rather weak in its
nature, and therefore may be overcome if care is used. It is not a good
time for the native to dispute or contend with others, for he will find
himself somewhat irritable and inclined to go to extremes, since this
influence tends to awaken all the latent energy of the nature, resulting in
either rashness or a very dictatorial attitude. He should not travel any
more than is necessary, should avoid strangers, or be very careful in his
dealings with them, and should be on his guard against breaking ties or
suffering disappointments and estrangements. His magnetic conditions
will be at a very high tension, and whenever the lunar directions are
likewise evil it will be a very bad time for him, and he will need all his
self-control to pass through the ordeal satisfactorily.

♂ ✳ ♅ This is a very favourable aspect for all practical work
involving enterprise and original methods. It stimulates the inventive
ability, gives insight and quick perceptiveness, and increases energy and
general readiness of resource. It is excellent for journalistic enterprise,
for stock-jobbing and all concerns where incisiveness of action and
comprehensive judgment are required ; but no continuous success in such
matters is to be looked for unless these planets are favourably aspected at
birth or other indications of inherent capacity are present. The native
will make some accidental acquaintance which will prove greatly to his
advantage, and which will (if other aspects are also favourable) give him
the "lift" that he may have needed for a long time. The personal
magnetism is greatly increased, and commercial travellers and others
will find this aspect "spell business." It is beneficial for psychic
studies, mesmerism, etc.

♂ □ ♅ This is one of the most unfortunate aspects that can be
experienced, either causing the native to behave with insane rashness,
or overwhelming him with some great trouble from an entirely unexpected
quarter. In any case, the feelings will be subjected to the utmost stress,
and all the self-control the native can command will be required to
prevent some action which will lead to his utter ruin. Accidents by fire,
electrical installations or explosives are occasional concomitants of this
influence, and all unnecessary exposure to risk in such matters should be
avoided. The whole period will be one of extreme tension, and the

native should study to preserve as far as possible a calm and well-balanced attitude, by bringing into play his own divine will-power, striving to meet his misfortunes with fortitude and scorning to despair. *It is a very dangerous aspect, and can only be contended against by the power of the spirit.*

♂ △ ♅   This is a remarkably good influence, for it will stimulate the native to greater mental activity, and make him deeply interested in occult and psychical studies, mesmerism, etc. He will find his nervous aura highly charged, and there will be every opportunity to make the present period particularly active and enterprising. It is a good time to travel, to deal with strangers, friends and acquaintances, also to join societies or seek alliance with groups of persons ; further, it will add to the native's general attractiveness, and in addition make him one whose society will be beneficial to others. He will find this influence help him to become inventive and constructive, his mental tendencies being original and advanced, and if the lunar aspects are good it will be a good period ; he will be capable of making much headway, advancing himself by his own inherent ability, which will now be called forth from latency. This mutual influence sometimes brings forth the powers of genius.

♂ ⊔ ♅   This, although an evil, is a comparatively weak aspect, and is more likely to result in a very unsettled time with a host of petty worries, fruitless enterprises and abortive efforts, than in any disaster of great moment. The nervous system is sure to be in a highly irritable condition, and the magnetism of the native will be repellent, resulting in many annoying disagreements and "scenes." He should endeavour to preserve a just and equitable frame of mind, and guard against being led by his feelings, which will be more than usually deceitful guides at this time. He is likely to meet with some trickery or underhand dealing, and should look well to all his affairs and guard against being imposed on by subordinates. It is his own impulses, however, that he has most to fear from, and should either Mars or Uranus be afflicted at birth, especially the latter, this is likely to be a memorable time in his life history.

♂ ⋆ ♅   This is a somewhat indeterminate aspect, neither good nor evil. It will provide a fund of energy, however, which may be turned either to improvement of character or to betterment of conditions according to the native's choice and desires. It is a splendid aspect for those who are studying physical regeneration, and in any case will ·ncrease the flow of magnetism, serving doctors, mesmerists and magnetic healers well, and spurring the ambition of those who naturally are somewhat indolent. The native will feel himself impelled to the study of some subject which he has previously looked upon as recondite, and his previous theories and beliefs will undergo a marked transformation. This is an excellent aspect under which to make any important journey regarding business affairs of serious moment.

♂ 8 ♆ It is difficult to say whether this or the square is the most disastrous aspect between these two planets; probably this is the more far-reaching in its consequences. The native will undergo a complete break-up of existing conditions, involving the taking up of an entirely new environment, either moral, mental or physical, probably all three. A disastrous termination to any love affair or any affection of a matrimonial nature that may have been recently entered into is certain, and some acute suffering either as the result of accident, violence or extreme passion or grief is highly probable. This is a most trying period, and the native should summon all his philosophy and all his fortitude to go through with it courageously, bringing his will to bear upon the ideal of *maintaining his own centre;* for all the forces now acting on him will seek to draw him from it. *A period of extreme tension, requiring the utmost self-control.*

. [The following paragraphs are from the same pen as those on pp. 92, 93.]

♂ P. ♆ * This, in its general scope, is somewhat similar to the conjunction, but in common with all parallels lasts over a longer period, remaining in force for some years. It will act in a manner which may be best apprehended by studying what is said below regarding the other aspects: by synthesising these, and supposing the combined influences to be maintained in a state of suspension, as it were, ready to manifest at any favourable opportunity during the period in which the aspect remains in force, the student will have a good idea of the nature of this parallel and its influence in the progressed horoscope. All parallels, it should be remembered, act as *inclining* rather than as *determining* factors.

♂ ☌ ♆ * The effect of this position will depend entirely on the stage reached by the soul in its spiritual evolution. A stupendous fund of

---

* The elusive character of Neptune's influence renders it extremely difficult to convey in words any idea of its nature. The reader will do well to refer to the information given in *How to Judge a Nativity, Part II.* (pp. 10, 19, 42), as well as to the interpretation of the solar aspects to Neptune given on pp. 92, 93, of this book.

energy, a wealth of creative fecundity—poetical, literary, speculatory or merely animal, according to the temperament indicated by the nativity and the zodiacal sign in which the conjunction takes place—will be poured into the nature, and undreamt of possibilities, both of desire and of capacity, will make themselves manifest. Should this take place in a favourable nativity, and from suitable houses, something very like genius may be looked for in the direction of artistic or literary creative work. There is always, however, a danger that the *Kâmic* or sensual animal nature may obtrude itself to the detriment of the spiritual influence, though this will be the less likely where fiery or airy signs are in question. *To the undeveloped this, or indeed any aspect between Mars and Neptune, is a dangerous position.*

♂ ⚹ ♇ * A curious psychological state will be experienced by the native at this time. Strange and unfamiliar emotions will force themselves upon him, and new and perhaps questionable tastes will show themselves. The hidden characteristics of the nature will be more or less dragged up to the surface and exposed. Much, however, will depend upon the houses ruled and the signs occupied by these planets as to the probable way in which this influence will work out in real life, though there is always a great probability of some morbid tendencies being displayed. Those inclined to intemperance will find this a very troublesome period. It may be remarked here that all aspects of ♂ to the occult planets ♅ and ♇ appear to produce effects, (in the case of the more highly evolved souls, that is to say), through the medium of *other people*, the evil current working through someone associated with the native rather than through himself and his own actions, as it were; so that instead of himself committing a violent or dishonourable deed he is made the victim of some such outrage himself. The philosophical or esoteric student will perceive the reason of this.

♂ ∠ ♇ * The native is likely to become involved in some disreputable transactions, or mixed up in discreditable company, either blamelessly or otherwise. A very harassing state of mind and feeling will be experienced, an unsatisfactory and discontinuous flow of plans, and a magnetic state that proves antagonistic to others and consequently subjects him to more or less ill-favour. (If the aspect between these planets in the nativity is harmonious, however, this will be very much modified, and little harm will result.) Disagreeable conditions in his daily environment will beset

* See footnote on previous page.

him, and he should at this time take precautions to see that he does not
suffer from defective drains, adulterated food, or other enemies to sound
health.

♂ ✳ ♆* This is a thoroughly favourable position and one that
promises (other things being equal) a very agreeable and prosperous
period. The positive personal magnetism of the native will not only
prove beneficial in all business and social relationships, but will tend
to promote a cheerful and humorous outlook on life which will minimise
its troubles and magnify its joys. A special feature of this period is
likely to be excursions, picnics, or other similar social gatherings of a
more or less "bohemian" character. The health will be good and the
spirits buoyant. There is usually also a religious tendency to be noted
about this influence, inclining the native to religious enthusiasm of an
emotional kind.

♂ ☐ ♆* This is a decidedly dangerous aspect, more especially in
the case of those in whose nativities the influence of either planet is strong.
A host of turbulent desires will descend upon the native, and he will
become the subject of sudden and unaccountable attractions and dislikes
—probably the former. Should there be any latent tendency to
sensuality or eroticism in the nature, this influence will bring it out, and
if the native is wise he will see to it that all impulses of affection,
religious emotion, etc., are subjected to a very close analysis of the
reason, and that no temporary enthusiasms are permitted to hurry him
into actions or declarations that he will be afterwards disposed to repent.
This aspect rarely or never passes without marking its presence by
violence of some kind, either physical or emotional, which will either be
expressed by the native himself, or suffered at the hands of others. (See
remarks under ♂ ⚹ ♆.)

♂ △ ♆* This aspect is very favourable in its influence, being in
many respects similar to the sextile, but operating rather on the feelings
and internal centres of the nature, than through the mind and brain. It
is good for travel and adventure, also for all hazardous enterprises,
speculations and investments, emigration and similar prospects where an
entirely new field has to be entered on,—though other aspects must of
course be taken into consideration also. An access of bodily vigour will
assist in these plans, and abundant ideas and schemes will present themselves to the mind. There is only one disadvantage attending this and

* See footnote on page 185.

similar good aspects of Mars to Neptune, and that is that the personality is apt to get somewhat the upper hand, to the disadvantage of the higher or more impersonal part of the nature; and there is consequently some tendency to essay more than can be carried out satisfactorily, or with perfect honesty to all concerned.

♂ ⚼ ♆* In common with all semi-square and sesquiquadrate aspects this marks a change of phase in the vibrations interchanged between these planets, and this change of phase is likely to be attended with unpleasant results. Fitful surges of emotion, unorganised plans, vague tendencies to jealousy, and various other combinations of disturbed mentality with distraught feelings, will prove a decided hindrance to progress at this time. Care should be taken to keep free from all doubtful alliances or questionable schemes during the operation of this aspect; and the health, moreover, should be looked after, care being taken to see that the dwelling is free from defective drains, escapes of gas, or other obscure sources of ill-health, blood-poisoning, etc.

♂ ⚻ ♆* To those who are sensitive to the Neptunian influence this brings an opportunity for the purification and exaltation of the desire nature, which by the experiences now undergone tends to be lifted from things earthly to things spiritual, the first lessons of renunciation thus being learned. There is likely to be grievous friction between the desire nature and the moral sense, and a wearing struggle will be the result in the case of sensitive and highly strung persons. In those of a more ordinary stamp, little is likely to result save an apparently purposeless episode or adventure. Those of a passionate or sensual temperament will be in danger of being so stirred up as to commit some indiscreet act, and should therefore do all they can to guard themselves from intemperate thoughts or desires.

♂ ☍ ♆* This is a very trying and, to impulsive people, a somewhat dangerous influence: with all it is likely to mark a memorable period. The whole of the desire nature will be in arms, as it were, against a sea of troubles, and unless the faith of the native is well grounded, he is likely to give way to despair, or to commit some rash act which will only prove to add to his sufferings. Only through a firm reliance on his spiritual birthright can the native hope to come unscathed through this ordeal, which may be compared to that passage through the "underworld" of which we read so often in the ancient myths. Women under

* See footnote on page 185.

this influence should take care not to place themselves in any situation where advantage might be taken of their defenceless condition. It is perhaps a fit place here to add that no one can hope to escape the effects of the occult planets ♅ and ♆ by a mere reliance on precautions or defences of a purely physical kind, since both these planets are concerned with the spiritual nature, and therefore only spiritual remedies can prevail against them.

The remaining planets, JUPITER, SATURN, URANUS and NEPTUNE, are so slow in their motion that by progression they can seldom or never form any aspects to planets in the radical horoscope that were not "within orbs" at birth. Hence it is unnecessary to take up space with any delineation of the nature of such aspects, which will all be found duly set out in their proper places in *How to Judge a Nativity, Part II.*

CONCLUDING NOTE TO THIS SECTION.

We have now dealt with all the aspects formed by the Sun, Moon and Planets, but, as stated at the foot of page 136, these aspects are described in a general sense only, and quite apart from the houses through which they are operating; for it is obvious that had the details of each aspect operating through each one of the twelve houses been delineated it would have required much more space than could be spared, in fact a volume ten times the size of the present book would hardly have sufficed. But any student who is familiar with the instruction given in *How to Judge a Nativity* will know how to fit the various aspects to the different houses.

For instance, the lord of the first house in affliction with the ruler of the seventh, would cause disharmony between the native and his partner; in affliction with the lord of the fourth, trouble in the home, removals of an unfavourable nature, and trouble in connection with parents, or those more or less directly connected with the domestic sphere; in affliction with the lord of the tenth, troubles in connection with employment and profession, or some discredit, slights upon the honour, etc.; in affliction with the ruler of the eleventh, trouble through friends and acquaintances; afflicting the lord of the third, disputes and troubles through relatives, etc.; and so on, in accordance with the rulers of the various houses: while on the other hand, the benefic aspects of the lord of the first to the various houses would bring pleasure and joy from similar sources, according to the strength of the aspect. The same rule may be applied to the ruler of each house in succession; the lord of the second affecting all monetary affairs, so that the ruler of the second in affliction with the lord of the fifth would denote loss through speculation and investment; in affliction with the lord of the eleventh, loss and trouble through friends, acquaintances, etc., etc. These houses are to be understood as those of the radical horoscope of course: similar interpretations may be made in relation to the houses of the progressed horoscope also, but it must be remembered that these will relate only to that environment, and those qualities of mind and character, that the native has achieved for himself by his own power of adaptation; and since few, comparatively speaking, possess such a degree of adaptability, the interpretation from the radical houses will be of most service as a rule.

All these considerations will depend entirely upon the student's judgment, and there can be no fixed or hard-and-fast rules by which any judgment can be made absolute, but it is again necessary to emphasise the fact that above all considerations the radical positions and aspects must be first carefully studied before any judgment is given with regard to their progressed positions; for a powerful square at birth can only be slightly modified by a trine aspect in the progressed horoscope, while a powerful trine at birth cannot be overborne by any severe aspects in affliction with that trine. In fact, the nature and character of the native should be carefully studied before considering him a mere puppet of directions—which, after all, are always more or less transitory, whereas the radical influences are practically permanent. So that they should be thought of as modifying or accentuating the radical influences only when they are more or less of a like nature.

It should also be borne in mind that Mutual Aspects remain in force for several years, but are never wholly complete till the Moon forms some aspect thereto, and then only *fully* when the solar influences are of a similar nature.

A personal illustration may serve to make the meaning of the above quite clear.

The author was born with Jupiter in the ninth degree of Leo and the Sun in the fifteenth degree of the same sign, as will be seen by reference to the map of his nativity, therefore the Sun was within six degrees of a conjunction, an especially powerful solar influence, for at the same time the Moon was in trine to both Sun and Jupiter,

However, it was not until his thirtieth year, in 1890, when the progressed Jupiter arrived at the place of the radical Sun, that the effect of the radical Asc. ☌ ♄ was removed and a period of prosperity commenced, for in that year the "Astrologer's Magazine" (now *Modern Astrology*) was commenced, and all other pursuits were put on one side, in order to take up the study of Astrology as a life work. Thenceforward all other progressed positions, no matter how severe or evil, must be moderated by this benefic progress of Jupiter over the Sun, trine Moon; for to considerably accentuate this benefic influence, Jupiter at the same time by progression reaches the parallel of the Sun at birth, a position which will remain in force for a great many years.

It will also be noticed that Venus is in square aspect to the Moon at birth, but that in the forty-eighth year Venus comes to the trine aspect of that luminary and passes over the Sun's place. Now noting the houses governed by these planets at birth, it is not difficult to interpret the nature of the influences that will be operating in the future; but it will suffice to say that by this favourable progress of the two benefic planets Jupiter and Venus,—the "Greater Fortune" and the "Lesser Fortune"—all aspects of an adverse nature will be considerably mitigated, and it will thus be seen how nativities may in some cases be improved by the progression of the planets, or how, in others, where the malefics pass to affliction with the luminaries at birth, a period of adversity will set in.

Just a few hints may be added as to the best way of utilising the descriptions that have been given in this section.

Having made out a tabulation of the aspects of *Progressed* to *Radical* planets, as described in Chapter VII., the student should carefully read through the delineations here given of their nature, and he should endeavour to epitomise the whole of each delineation in one or two pithy sentences. He should then embody the whole of these in a short report or *précis*, which he should place on one side until he has executed a similar condensation of the aspects which the *Progressed* planets form among themselves.

The next thing to do is to compare these two reports and carefully balance the various testimonies, always remembering that the aspects of progressed planets to radical ones (*p*. to *r*.) tend to work out in terms of the Nativity, relating to family matters, inherited social conditions, etc., etc.; whereas the aspects occurring among the progressed planets themselves (*p.* to *p.*) tend to express themselves in terms of the Progressed Horoscope, affecting the native and his environment in relation to the modifications of character and circumstances that he himself has effected through the operation of his own thought and will. (This has been stated before, it is true, but it is well to remind the student of it here.)

Having done this, it only remains to weigh up these two more or less independent series of influences, and to estimate their probable effect as a whole. The final judgment should then be committed to writing, and the three papers preserved and afterwards studied together, in connection with the actual events that take place during the year, at any suitable time—say the next birthday.

At a first attempt, this will certainly be found rather a formidable task, (though by no means an uninteresting one, in any sense of the word). But it will have the effect of developing the judgment in a very remarkable manner, and it will encourage systematic and definite habits of thought, the value of which cannot be over-estimated. Moreover, every time that the task is repeated it will be found more simple and less tedious, until in the end the student will be able to sit down and write out a prognostication for the ensuing year without any reference to the book at all.

The student is recommended to avoid, for the present, all consideration of "transits," for until he has acquired a fair power of judgment by the method just described, he is only likely to fall into error thereby, and, by according undue importance to their influence, (as many beginners do), lose sight of the fact that *all* "transits" are subsidiary in their effects to the "directions" operating at the time, just as the latter are in all cases inferior in power to the "radical" influences—a fact which cannot be too often insisted on, as it is only too frequently overlooked.

Section C.

CHAPTER XIII.

Transits.

The favourable and adverse periods of each person's life may be approximately known by giving a little attention to the "*transits*" of the superior planets, Jupiter, Saturn, Mars and Uranus; *i.s.*, the dates on which these planets cross the various sensitive points in the nativity. This method of forecasting can be adopted by all who know the symbols of the planets and who possess an ordinary ephemeris. The period of Saturn is thirty years, of Jupiter twelve years, of Mars about two years, and of Uranus eighty-four years, this being the time in each case that the planet takes to complete the circle of the zodiac.

The transit of Saturn through a nativity produces contraction, and that of Jupiter expansion, these planets being opposite in their vibrations the one solidifying and the other expanding.

The transit of Mars quickens and that of Uranus hastens, these planets tending to press forward all things, Mars ripening matters quickly and Uranus tending to precipitate things prematurely, as it were —somewhat in the same way that electricity ' forces ' the growth of plants.

Any prognostications based upon "transits" without having regard to the current directions then in force (as shown in the progressed horoscope) can necessarily be only vague and general in their scope and are chiefly introduced here on account of the ease with which they may be ascertained by those who shrink from calculations. They are in great favour with those who incline towards what may be termed rough-and-ready methods. While "transits" form an easy means of supplementing and to some extent defining the events shown by ' directions,' it should be remembered that their effects are *always*

N

subsidiary to those of the ' directions' in force at the time. We will take the four planets in order, commencing with Saturn.

SATURN

♄   passing through the *First House* of the horoscope will produce depressing influences in any nativity where desponding tendencies are shewn to exist in the native's mind and character. In a nativity of the progressive order, it will bring responsibilities, and a patient and careful frame of mind, producing caution, reserve and tactfulness.

♄   passing through the *Second House* will produce a diminishing income, loss of finance and monetary anxieties to those whose horoscopes denote financial troubles ; to the progressive individual, economy, carefulness regarding expenditure, and *prudence* in giving to others, tempering mercy or benevolence with justice.

♄   passing through the *Third House* denotes hindrance and delays in travel, disappointments and difficulties through relatives. To the progressive type this will bring gravity of mind, thoughtfulness and an inclination to engage in profound and deep studies, or perhaps a desire to investigate occult and mystical subjects.

♄   passing through the *Fourth House* will bring domestic troubles, bereavements, unfavourable changes, and hallucinations, etc. To the more highly evolved individual a desire for rest, and more attention to the needs of his household, preparation for the closing years of life, and the making secure of benefits to family and heirs after the close of the earthly career.

♄   passing through the *Fifth House* will cause disappointments, the breaking of attachments, loss of children, ill success in speculation, troubles over investments ; but to the enlightened it will bring chastity, prudence in affection, careful examination of all investments and the avoidance of hazardous enterprises, and more care and thought with regard to the welfare of the young.

♄   passing through the *Sixth House* will depress the vital conditions, cause sickness and liability to take chills, and also to have trouble with inferiors. Those who have not a weak Saturn at birth it will incline to carefulness regarding diet, a cautious preparation against change of climate and temperature, and prudence in all dealings with servants, aunts, uncles and elderly relatives.

ʰ̩ passing through the *Seventh House* will cause domestic sadness, grave misunderstandings, separations and grief; but to those who are not affected by transitory changes, and who do not succumb to passing moods, it will strengthen conjugal ties, give faithful adherence to contracts and vows, and bind closer the ties that unite and cement true unions.

ʰ̩ passing through the *Eighth House* will bring deaths; and troubles through partners, or legacies. To the awakened individual, however, it will bring some connection with occult societies, reconciliation to change of consciousness, and thoughts concerning the soul's condition after death.

ʰ̩ passing through the *Ninth House* will bring legal troubles, disputes with partners, relatives, and unfavourable voyages; to progressive natures, calm and deliberate thought regarding metaphysics, an inquiry into philosophy and a devout mind, prone to meditate and think deeply.

ʰ̩ transiting the M.C. and passing through the *Tenth House* will bring failure, scandal, trouble with superiors and loss of honour and credit. To the cultured and refined it will cause prudence in speech and conduct, the undertaking of great responsibilities, and a strict scrutiny of moral conduct.

ʰ̩ passing through the *Eleventh House* will bring false friends, deception and frustration to hopes and wishes; in the thoughtful it will produce a respect for elders and a scientific turn of mind, it will also bring care in choice of acquaintances and a true appreciation of friendship.

ʰ̩ passing through the *Twelfth House* will produce sorrows, enmities, confinements, and sad experiences generally; to the mystic, strange realisations, careful reflections, a patient review of the past and an in-turning of the mind in search of latent possibilities.

All persons will feel the transit of Saturn through the various houses of the nativity according to their capacity to respond to his dark and searching influence. Those who ridicule this idea as contrary to their own experience are either wholly immersed in the senses, or have the "milk-and-water" nature, and are therefore indifferent to any but Martial vibrations.

Those who have not controlled the senses will feel the adverse side of Saturn's transits, but those who are not fettered and handicapped by the lower mind and senses will have an opportunity of solidifying and concentrating the special indications pertaining to each house.

When Saturn transits the places of the luminaries or passes to an adverse aspect thereto, it denotes a critical period; if in square, opposition or conjunction with the place of the Sun or Moon at birth, it denotes a period of depression, ill-health and loss, depending as to its precise nature upon the houses and the signs occupied by both; but the transit will have less effect if merely traversing the houses and not affecting either of the luminaries.

The most important transits of Saturn are when this planet is passing through one of the angles, for then critical periods are reached. When in the first house or Eastern Angle the health is affected, the whole body being susceptible to cold and chill, and if the "directions" are adverse decided ill-health is denoted. When passing through the mid-heaven or Southern Angle business affairs are affected, the native's credit is not so good, and grave risks are run, all matters of a responsible nature having reached a critical stage. While passing through the Western Angle oppositions and obstacles are met with of a trying and difficult nature. The transit of the planet Saturn through the fourth house or Northern Angle is felt more when occurring toward the close of a life than at the beginning, but it nearly always upsets domestic affairs, and causes trouble in the home life.

The work of Saturn is solidifying, concreting and tending to make the affairs of life more stable and secure; and hence if the native is not ready for these conditions it disturbs and unsettles the mind, causing resentment at the conditions which it imposes. Saturn tends to produce permanent moods of consciousness, and produces settled habits which become firmly built into the character. This transit consequently is often the beginning of conditions that finally become permanent.

JUPITER.

The transit of Jupiter is a blessing of a more or less definite character. It brings fortune of minor or major importance according to the power of the native to respond and the conditions imposed by the nativity under which he is born. The transits of Jupiter bring opportunities for improvement and progress in all departments of life, but mainly social and spiritual. In some cases social advancement takes place when Jupiter sets in motion a benefic direction, in other cases a spiritual upliftment is experienced by those who are given to prayer and aspiration; in all it tends to expand and increase the emotional side of the nature.

♃ passing through the *First House* brings good health, renewed vigour, increased vitality, much cheerfulness, hope and joyousness. It often brings advancement, and social advantages and opportunity to make the most of personal abilities.

♃ passing through the *Second House* rarely fails to increase financial prospects, or to bring some opportunity to make money, and if the nativity is a good one for financial success, it increases the income and adds considerably to possessions.

♃ passing through the *Third House* improves the mind, gives favourable journeys and establishes a good understanding with relatives and neighbours. It is good for correspondence, travel, and all literary work or mental pursuits.

♃ passing through the *Fourth House* is good for domestic affairs and home life and for the termination of any important matter that has been in hand awaiting settlement.

♃ passing through the *Fifth House* brings opportunity to speculate to invest, or otherwise increase income through enterprise. It brings some pleasure, increase of consciousness, and favours love-affairs, courtships and attachments.

♃ passing through the *Sixth House* benefits health and is good for work and industry, bringing gain or success through inferiors, agents, servants, etc. It also favours all ceremonies, forms of respect and accepted customs. It is good for relationships between aunts and uncles and distant relatives.

♃ passing through the *Seventh House* is good for marriage, partnerships, and unions of all kinds. It binds persons together, causing unity, amity and satisfactory ties. It is favourable for lawsuits, when undertaken with pure motives, and brings favours from those who are lovers of justice.

♃ passing through the *Eighth House* brings legacies, or gain through partners and co-workers. It is good for all occult or psychic investigation, and favours dreams and the psychic or sub-conscious side of the nature. To the dying it brings a peaceful death and to those who are receptive enough some religious experiences.

♃ passing through the *Ninth House* is favourable for the mind, bringing aspiration, clear thinking, intuitions and philosophic thoughts. It is good for all foreign affairs, and all benefits or emoluments coming from abroad, and sometimes produces travel and long sea voyages if the directions are also favourable.

♃ passing through the *Tenth House* is good for honour and reputation, and if the nativity and the directions indicate it, fame and good report follow this transit. It strengthens credit and often brings much good fortune.

♃ passing through the *Eleventh House* is good for friendships, favours and unions. It brings a peaceful and happy state of mind and some internal spiritual realisations.

♃ passing through the *Twelfth House* brings indirect success through foes or enemies, and often good following on bad or unfavourable conditions. It is good for occultism, romance, secret adventures and unpopular enterprises.

An unfortunate nativity is often improved by the transits of Jupiter, but without the power on the part of the native to *respond* to the transits of this planet it will avail very little. For Jupiter acts more upon the interior planes than the exterior, and by working through the consciousness from within prompts to success and fortune, rather than actually producing good fortune from outside, therefore the most intuitive and the most highly cultured will gain most by its transits. Experience has proved that in this case fortune favours fortune and verifies the statement that " to him who hath shall be given."

Jupiter transiting either of the luminaries is always a promising period, bringing opportunities that come at no other time. It takes Jupiter one year to pass through each sign of the zodiac and as it occupies fully one month in passing over the radical place of the Sun or Moon, it brings out all the influence received by the luminaries from the other planets ; and if either are in aspect to Jupiter at birth, the benefic nature of Jupiter is then seen to most advantage. The secret of its influence lies in expansion and fulness of expression.

MARS.

The transits of the planet Mars are quick and soon over, they tend to precipitate matters and rarely give any choice of action, being hot and somewhat impulsive, rapid, and expansive—not temperate, as in the case of Jupiter.

This rapid expansion produces impulsive and unpremeditated action, and seems to act as an explodent, so to speak—mild or violent according to temperament—for the thought force that has been generated in the past: therefore much depends upon the nature of the native's past thoughts as to how the transits of Mars will act. In an undeveloped Ego, where impulse and feeling sway the mind, the transits of Mars will find a convenient field for operation, but in a developed Ego the thought-control normally exercised will tend to counteract the explosive nature of this planet, and the transits of Mars will consequently avail but little, and in some cases have no appreciable effect upon the life other than by supplying an extra fund of working energy. The passage of Mars through the houses is of less importance than that of either Saturn or Jupiter, but seems to have more effect when passing over the luminaries.

♂ passing through the *First House* arouses the temper, and stimulates the desire towards action and impulse.

♂ passing through the *Second House* tends to impulsive expenditure, extravagance and some waste. It promotes both acquisitiveness and inquisitiveness.

♂ passing through the *Third House* is not good for travel, giving liability to accidents. It makes the mind turbulent and hasty.

♂ passing through the *Fourth House* is not good for changes of residence or removals.

♂ passing through the *Fifth House* inclines to prodigality, violent demonstration of feeling and the awakening of the passions.

♂ passing through the *Sixth House* affects health through overwork and brings trouble through inferiors.

♂ passing through the *Seventh House* is not good for marriage, attachments, lawsuits, or partnerships. It tends to promote quarrels and leads to much opposition.

♂ passing through the *Eighth House*, unimportant.

♂ passing through the *Ninth House*, enthusiastic and rash speech.

♂ passing through the *Tenth House*, scandal, loss of credit and ill-repute.

♂ passing through the *Eleventh House*, trouble through friends or acquaintances.

♂ passing through the *Twelfth House*, liability to false accusations and trouble from enemies and ill-wishers.

Mars has very little effect in any other houses but the angles, or when passing over the luminaries. It then gives a liability to accidents and impulsive actions, feverish tendencies and general excitability. If the directions denote ill-health, inflammatory complaints and sudden relapses are caused by a transit of Mars over the points of direction. If accidents are denoted the transit of Mars over the luminaries indicates serious results, although not necessarily fatal.

URANUS.

This planet has been left to the last because it is quite separate in its mode of action from the foregoing "normal" planets; it has chief influence on the most advanced of humanity. Uranus takes eighty-four years to complete the circle and is therefore about seven years going through each sign, and a similar period in passing through each house. Its influence is that of the "Awakener," and it is slow but sure in effecting the changes it is destined to produce in the life while transiting each house. To many the change is quite imperceptible, and when accomplished it is often not attributed to this planet's vibration but set down to other causes. It acts directly upon the mental side of consciousness, indirectly only upon the feelings and emotions, and very faintly if at all upon the physical body. In one sense Uranus may be considered the purifier or the cleanser, and as such is the disorganiser, breaking up all that which has been made permanent by Saturn, destroying or regenerating old conditions and introducing important changes and improvements.

As the great "Regenerator" he tries every soul who is aspiring to rise above the senses, and he may be said to be the greatest enemy of the feelings when they are made too personal or purely selfish. Although it may appear somewhat of a paradox, these are the very types who feel his influence most of all. The principal regenerative power of Uranus is felt in connection with sex, and in such matters the vibration of Uranus is peculiar and difficult to fully comprehend; but we find the chief influence concerned with the "magnetism," Uranus acting directly upon the magnetic aura, and in this respect we can see why Uranus has little or no effect upon undeveloped Egos, for their magnetic aura is insufficiently charged to receive its vibrations.

♅ passing through the *First House* or ascendant brings sudden and unexpected changes of environment, a chequered career, and many strange experiences. It causes nervous troubles, neuralgia and peculiar ailments.

♅ passing through the *Second House*, financial changes, good or ill according to the nativity, often producing reverses of fortune.

♅ passing through the *Third House*, much travel, changes in the mind, an inclination towards the occult, and inventive tendencies. It awakens the mind to interior or subjective thought.

♅ passing through the *Fourth House*, changes in the home life, sudden and unexpected endings to general affairs.

♅ passing through the *Fifth House* is often inimical to love affairs and causes strange realisations on questions of sex.

♅ passing through the *Sixth House*, the health is affected by psychic conditions and impure magnetism.

♅ passing through the *Seventh House*, separations, divorce, etc.; in some cases platonic unions are formed at this time.

♅ passing through the *Eighth House*, occult and psychic experiences.

♅ passing through the *Ninth House*, psychic experiences, desires for reform and travel, awakening of the Higher Mind.

♅ passing through the *Tenth House*, changes of profession, loss of credit, or sudden reversals of fortune.

♅ passing through the *Eleventh House*, strange friendships, peculiar inner longings.

♅ passing through the *Twelfth House*, strange experiences, danger of false imprisonment.

SUN, VENUS AND MERCURY.

The Sun's passage over the important planetary positions in the nativity stirs into activity any principal features that they indicate. This is often shown in ordinary life, where a certain day of the year becomes well-known as some person's "unlucky day." (See *Modern Astrology*, *Vol. I.* (New Series), p. 355). The Sun passing through the twelve houses stimulates into activity the planets occupying those houses.

Venus and Mercury have very slight influence as transiting planets and are rarely, if ever, noticed. If either is the ruling planet, however, the fortune and temperament will be found to vary somewhat with the course of the planet, its motion, rapid, slow, or retrograde, and aspects—

afflictions or otherwise—reflecting themselves in the career or temporary welfare of the native. This is especially the case when the temperament is highly sensitive.

THE GENERAL EFFECT OF TRANSITS.

Too much stress should not be placed upon the influence of transits, for it should ever be remembered that they are necessarily ephemeral in their nature and can therefore only bring into activity the natal influences operating at birth. Thus, if Saturn is an afflicting planet at birth the good transits of Saturn will not mitigate or in any way lessen the evil natal effects, but Jupiter's transits will assist to raise the hopes of the native. In a similar manner the adverse transits will depress and hinder the good vibrations of Jupiter or the other planets. It may be taken as a safe rule that when an evil direction is operating an adverse transit will accentuate it. The most potent and noticeable transits are the following :—

When the Moon by "direction" is forming a square or opposition to Saturn, a transit of Saturn over the place of the Progressed Moon will bring out all the evil of the lunar directions. In the same way a benefic aspect of the Moon to Jupiter will be doubly benefic when Jupiter by transit is passing over the Moon's progressed place.

One of the most certain and direct transits is that of Saturn "hunting the Moon," as it is termed, that is, when Saturn is in transit over the Moon's progressed place. Since the progressed Moon takes twenty-eight and Saturn thirty years to complete the circle, this will often last for many years and in some cases for a lifetime. The most unfortunate aspect in a nativity is the affliction of the Moon by Saturn, either by square or opposition, and when the aspect is very close and the progressive Moon is moving slowly, or at the same rate as Saturn, the transit of Saturn goes on for the best part of the life. For the Moon by progressive motion moves through one sign of the zodiac in two years and a half and Saturn's motion by transit is at the same rate, therefore, unless the Moon is moving fast and moving out of the sphere of influence of Saturn, a double affliction is kept up for the best part of the life. This, of course, can only be the case where the Moon is in conjunction, square or opposition with Saturn at birth.

A very careful study of transits is necessary to obtain the best results or take full advantage of their influence. When the planets are grouped together in one sign transits have most effect, especially when there is a satellitium of planets in an angle.

The declinations of the transiting planets should always be carefully noted, for they are very powerful and from their slow formation are operative for a much longer period than the ordinary aspects.

CONCLUSION.

It is intended from time to time in the pages of *Modern Astrology* to deal with examples, illustrating the method of directing adopted in practice by the author. But it would be to the student's advantage, before proceeding to examine these examples, to form his own judgment as to the best way of applying the various methods mentioned in the present work. Too much stress cannot be laid upon the fact that the *radix* or Horoscope of Birth contains the germ of the whole life : it is the root of the tree, so to speak. Everything depends upon the *character* and *temperament* of the native as to how he will act under any given series of directions. To become a competent judge of the fruit of the tree, as indicated by the directions, the student will require to possess a certain amount of belief in the New Psychology ; for it will often happen that influences are maturing under certain aspects which cannot eventuate without the opportunity for their true expression.

The most reliable and the most simple method of directing is to take the nativity as a fixture and move the *planets* according to their position each complete day after birth (which is equivalent to one year), and then to see what aspects they form to the radical positions, always keeping an eye, however, on the root character as indicated in the nativity.

I will take my own case as an example of what I mean. The map has been given on the page facing Chapter I., and in my remarks on p. 190 I alluded to the fact that Saturn is upon the ascendant, an unfortunate position, hindering the personality and retarding progress, but that when 30 days (years) after birth Jupiter came to the conjunction of the radical Sun, and almost simultaneously to the trine of the radical Moon ($\mathrm{2\!\!\!\!/}$ p. d $\odot$ r., $\triangle$ D r.), it relieved the radical conjunction of Saturn with the ascendant and liberated a great deal of benefic influence which brought a period of rising fortune.

But it was the radical position of Saturn which gave the perseverance and caution necessary to enable the expansive Jupiter to act temperately and steadily, thus making a practical application of the good influences, and enabling a permanent position to be built up from the year 1890 onwards, since when the benefit promised by Jupiter's favourable position to the luminaries has gone on steadily increasing.

A few words may be added on the *time* element in relation to events marked in "directions." All positions and aspects denote the nature of events likely to happen, *sooner or later*, the actual time usually depending upon opportunity, impulse, and also, to some extent, the "directions" operating in the nativities of others closely affecting the native's life— the latter an important consideration that is generally overlooked.

Where it appears advisable to know the best time to anticipate favourable directions, or use means to modify and if possible avert the worst effects of unfavourable ones, a "horary figure" may be taken for a definite question upon the subjects involved ; or, a suitable time may be *Elected** when the ephemeral influences are favourable for the more satisfactory working of the directions under consideration—suppose, for instance, that an interview was necessary with some person whom the current directions indicated as likely to be hostile to the native, if the most suitable time were chosen, it would be far more easy to come to an amicable arrangement.

Never should the student allow himself to look upon events as fixed and irrevocable at a certain definite time. The time in many cases is not determinable, prayer in some instances having the power to modify evil directions and accentuate the favourable influences, while in others a strong and determined will, aided by knowledge and foresight, can alter the course of events indicated as *probable* by the nativity and the directions.

[At this point the student is advised to proceed to the Appendices at the end of the book, and to carefully consider what is therein said before going on to the difficult subject treated of in the next section.]

---

* An "Election" is the choosing of a favourable time for the performance or commencement of any important undertaking. Thus, the laying of the foundation stone of the Royal Observatory at Greenwich was made the subject of an "Election" by the then Astronomer Royal, Flamstead, and its history since has justified his choice. But great skill and much experience are needed to choose the most appropriate moment for any given work.

Section D.

PRELIMINARY EDITORIAL NOTE.

In introducing this section, which consists of a treatise on the Art of Directing, simplified and condensed from a series of articles expressly written for *Modern Astrology* by Mr. HEINRICH DÄATH, (who has himself supervised this arrangement), the Editor feels it desirable to add a few prefatory remarks for the benefit of those readers who have studied the foregoing pages, but have not as yet attempted to grapple with the system known as Primary Directions. The natural basis of this system is discussed in Appendices II. and VII.

At the outset, the student should be reminded that the number of 'arcs of direction' (measuring to various periods of the life) owing to the number of possible aspects between the various planetary bodies, and between the latter and the angles of the figure, is very considerable. Moreover, from the variety of methods, "direct," "converse," "rapt," etc., all of which may be, and are, legitimately employed in these calculations, this number becomes enormously increased, so that it is possible if sufficient ingenuity is brought to bear on the matter to discover arcs of direction, *of some kind or other*, for every month of the native's life. This need occasion no surprise, for it is certain that events of some kind, whether significant or otherwise, are constantly happening.

But it is necessary, for the reason just stated, to be very cautious before jumping to conclusions as to the relationship between any given arc and any given event, even although they synchronise as regards time. And this is particularly the case when the methods now to be treated of are employed for the purpose of "rectifying" a doubtful time of birth. Nevertheless, there is no warrant for casting aside as useless all, or any, of these processes of calculation and measurement, merely because they produce what may at first seem a bewildering array of possible influences.

What is necessary, however—although unfortunately too often overlooked, even by those who make this a life-long study—is, to pay a rigid regard to: (1) the primal attributes of the planet concerned; (2) the quality and nature of the aspect; and (3) the mode of formation of the latter, and what it implies in its relation to the circle of day, month, or year;—whether it is more, or less, ephemeral in its essential nature than another which may produce an arc measuring to about the same period of life, for instance. These are the chief considerations, and they should be constantly borne in mind, whatever the calculation that is in progress. For it is clearly quite useless to know accurately at what time a given influence will be in force, unless one has at the same time a well-defined idea of the nature of such influence.*

To these recommendations may be added one more, namely, the point which has been so insisted on in all the previous chapters, that the Horoscope of Birth is the " Radix " whence all Directions come forth, and that nothing can come to fruition that is not in accordance therewith. The student should not therefore expect "great good fortune" from the direction " M.C. ☌ ♃," if that planet is heavily afflicted in the nativity, nor on the other hand grievous misfortune from " Asc. ☌ ♂ " if Mars is well placed and essentially dignified or in good aspect to the Sun in the nativity.

With these preliminary injunctions well kept in view the reader may be encouraged to proceed, with a full assurance that he will find his time and labour well spent. No astrologer worthy of the name has ever ignored the methods now to be unfolded, and no one is justified in belittling their worth till he has made himself practically acquainted with them. More than this, no astrologer can form just and accurate notions of the value of the various aspects till he has studied their formation in detail, and has grasped the essential differences subsisting between the Right and the Oblique Sphere. And no one is entitled to look down on "mere mechanical methods" till he has transcended those methods, which can only be done by mastering, and not by merely omitting them.

For the rest, to the earnest student "difficulties" will ever prove a stimulus, not a hindrance.

NOTE.—For such calculations as are here required *Raphael's Ephemeris* (or any other good Ephemeris giving the *latitudes* and *declinations* as well as the *longitudes* of the planets) will be needed. Better still is the *Nautical Almanack (Eyre and Spottisswoode*, 2/6), for in it the Right Ascensions of the planets are given, which saves their calculation ; but some years of this publication are out of print. *Chambers' Mathematical Tables* will also be required.

The student will hardly need to be told that he must select an accurately timed (or properly rectified) nativity to work with.

---

* Some suggestions on this head will be found in an article on " Rectification " in MODERN ASTROLOGY, Vol. II. (New Series).

The Art and Practice of Directing.

An *Aperçu* by

HEINRICH DĀATH.

INTRODUCTION.

DIRECTING, or the art of computing angular distances between planets, arising through motion in longitude and by the diurnal movement of the earth subsequent to birth, is by far the most difficult and involved portion of the science of astrology, not only as relates to the time element but also to the nature of the event produced by the aspect itself. That the physical factor is not concerned so much as the psychical one, even in the production of many events which appear solely to proceed from the rational plane, is almost beyond dispute. The root of all lies in the fact that every element has its archæus or spiritual principle. It is through the astral soul that planetary influence functions. This is the repository of stellar forces. The rational soul is a part of the Divine or intelligible world-principle. As the astral soul regulates the body, so the rational soul dominates the whole man.

Yet consistent and inviolable methods are requisite in any case, and to what extent astrology can offer these must be judged by actual results. However, there is nothing empirical in any process appertaining to the casting of the theme of nativity, the tabulation of planetary aspects, and the computing of others which must inevitably form within a certain period ensuing. They are matters which belong to the realm of practical astronomy, and are certainties in the light of modern knowledge. It is premised that before the astrologer can step in, the required calculation must be truly performed in order to deduce the period of operation of certain magnetic or other forces; for if errors be made here it cannot be expected that the stars should substantiate conclusions based upon them. We pre-suppose likewise in this treatise that the student who intends to apply himself to the solution of problems associated with primary directing has already a practical acquaintance with the processes involved in casting the horoscope and estimating the radix.

CHAPTER I.

Of Aspects and their Nature.

"An aspect is an angle formed on the earth by the luminous rays of two planets; efficacious in stimulating sublunary nature."—KEPLER.

ALL radical aspects are ordinate,* and intrinsically able to form a regular-sided figure which may be inscribed in a circle, the angles of the said figure touching, each one, the circumference of such circle.

The word aspect comes from the Latin *aspectus*, from *aspicio*, I look on. The reference is to the astrological manner of supposing, truly enough indeed, that planets posited at certain distances of longitude *look upon* each other, or receive and distribute each other's special influence more readily and powerfully, than when situated at distances apart, the joining line of which to their centres, considering them as geometrical points having no objective existence, does not form the side of an equilateral circumscribable figure.

The geometrical nature of aspects is best illustrated by the performance of the problems in geometry which have reference to the construction of regular-sided figures within a circle.

The circle, great or small, is always considered as being composed of 360 degrees, this being the approximate number the sun travels in a year through the great circle of the zodiac, corresponding to the 365 days which the civil year contains. "A year for a day and a day for a year," likewise also a degree for a day and so a day for a year.

It must be understood at the outset that each aspect is an angle of a certain number of degrees depending upon the varying planetary situations in the zodiac. The particular reasons of the general credit or discredit of a planet's ray we have not now to consider, or where such ray has its origin, whether in the planet's natural or aural atmosphere, whether from the bulk itself or from any other cause. We know that a

* This, of course, does not apply to *derivative* aspects, such as the ⬚ and ⤬, which are formed by portions of two radical ones,

certain force *does* exist and is able to distribute its power through millions of miles of void, but to the question how it is generated and in what manner conserved science as yet gives no definite reply.

Claudius Ptolemy says that aspects made from like signs, *i.e.*, masculine or feminine (positive or negative) agree, and transmit favourable influences, while those made from signs of an opposite nature disagree, and are the occasion of discord. This theory being untenable in the case of the opposition, which is always made from like signs, it becomes necessary to look upon the supposition with some amount of suspicion, notwithstanding the esteem in which its promulgator is held, for we know the opposition to be almost an unmitigated evil.

We may take the zodiac as representing a vast ethereal sea, as did the Egyptians, who have symbolically typified the sun's passage through the signs as a ship passing over the bended body of a woman whose robe is studded with stars, while beneath reclines another figure, the little *Horus*, the earth. In the crypt of an ancient church at Piacenza there is a mosaic pavement before the altar, upon which water is symbolically represented by waving lines in the Egyptian manner with fishes swimming therein, and plaques containing the zodiacal signs, the whole representing the zodiac as a great ethereal θάλασσα encompassing the earth.

In this zodiac move the sun and planets, the former never removing its track from the central line or ecliptic, but the latter occasionally temporarily leaving it, and by that means producing *latitude*, north or south, as the case may be. The sun, never quitting the ecliptic, is said to have no latitude.

I may here remark, though it is not of great importance in considering aspects primarily, that the signs of the zodiac and the constellations of the same name must on no account be considered as one and the same thing. Ages ago the constellations occupied the signs now bearing their names, but by the precession of the equinoxes, the case is now altered.*

And this brings us to a question frequently put to the astrologer, *viz.*,

* A full treatment of this subject does not come within the province of this treatise, but any good astronomical work will supply the deficiency. Briefly ♈ changes its place backwards 50″ in arc yearly, and the plane of the equator crosses the ecliptic 20sec. sooner in time, so that the equinoctial point retrogrades a degree in 72 years. This makes a difference also in the longitude and latitude of the stars, necessitating revision in celestial globes, atlases, etc., every 72 years. The first point of the *sign* Aries is now in the *constellation* Pisces.

Readers interested in this matter should refer to "Precession," "Pisces or Aquarius?" in Index to MODERN ASTROLOGY, Vols. XIV. (Old Series), I., II. (New Series).

O

if the constellations no longer occupy the signs bearing these names, how comes it that the same qualities are attributed to the signs now as in former ages, there being not the slightest deviation practically from the powers ascribed to them in those times ? The reason is that an occult property belongs to each thirty-degree section into which the zodiac is apportioned, a property quite inherent, unchangeable, and in no wise dependent upon the groups of fixed stars which bear the same names as the signs in question.

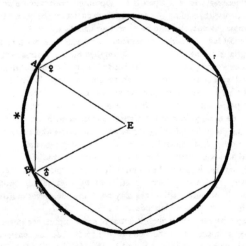

FIG. I.

If it can once be understood that actually the zodiac is a vast sea of wonderfully mobile ether impressed universally with specific virtues and using the planets more or less as mediums between it and things mundane, the difficulty will have vanished. But to continue. Aspects themselves are not straight lines, as the figure here given will illustrate. (Fig. I.) Here a regular hexagon is inscribed in a circle, illustrating the aspect known as a *sextile*, or an angular arc of sixty degrees, which is one-sixth of the whole circle of 360°, so that the true aspect is the measure of the intercepted arc between two angle points, as A B, the incidence of the rays being at E—the earth, where the power would manifest. Planets being posited in such wise that the arc lying between will equally divide the great circle into six parts, are said to be in sextile aspect to each other. And so with the other distances.

It now becomes evident at once, if we look into the matter, that we may form three distinct series of progressions or affinitive aspects, *viz.*—

α   An *even* series, the number of degrees being divisible by 6.
β   An *even* series   „   „   „   „   5.
γ   An *odd* series   „   „   „   „   5.

The following are the respective aspects :—

α   18°, 24°, 36°, 72°, 108°, 144°, 150°.
β   30°,   60°,   120°,   150°.
γ   45°,   90°,   135°,   150°.

The first two series are good, the latter evil,* while the Quincunx,† 150°, appears common to the three groups. There are some alien and irreconcilable elements in the division on this plan, I admit, but it serves in a general sense.

The aspects comprised in the series denominated α are little used, mainly because they are comparatively modern additions to the list, their influence, therefore, not being fully understood. They appear to act on the psychical plane, and have little to do with our ordinary everyday life. For this reason they are only transitorily and tentatively appreciated and appertain chiefly to the occult.

The two other series act in all cases more or less powerfully on the material plane—our loves, our hates, passions, worldly prosperity and good fortune, or the contrary. The β series comprises those aspects indicative and productive of the pleasures, and the γ series those of the indignities and pains of mundane existence. They are the worldly rewards and punishments the ego has aforetime earned, and are not to be regarded merely as the result of accidental positions of the heavenly bodies at the birth, or rather rebirth, of the ego. Properly the conception is one of indications, the horoscope being a species of passport

---

* The parallel of declination, here omitted, must be understood in a similar sense as the conjunction, *i.e.*, good with good planets, evil or mixed otherwise.

† As to the Quincunx, Browne regarded it as a figure of peculiar excellence, a universal menstruum, containing everything of use or pleasure, " though therein," he says, " we meet not with right angles, yet every rhombus containing four angles equal unto two right, it virtually contains two right in every one." He likewise gives a relation of things circumscribed by the number, observing that *five* was the ancient conjugal or wedding number, " the ancient numerists made out the conjugal number by two and three, the first parity and imparity, the active and passive digits, the material and formal principles in generative societies."

accurately *visé*, or a signboard in which the past may be read by a due appreciation of the merits and demerits intended for the present. The whole question of aspects may be studied in the light of the Qabalah.

It may be noticed, however, that the β series is built on the triangle, while the γ series is founded on the square, and inasmuch as the Pythagoreans maintained that in the first of the five regular solids, *viz.*, the tetrahedron, or pyramid, the tetractys is to be found—for that a point answers to unity, a line to the number two, a superficies to three, and solidity to four—we may conceive something of the bonds in which the two last of our series hold each other,* while remaining free enough to operate in seemingly opposite directions, or rather, by opposite methods. The Pythagoreans further maintained that the judicative power is fourfold, and consists in mind, science, opinion, and sense; or in physics, metaphysics, ethics, and theology. In fact, the number four was made a universal measure, and the idea was asserted that the *tetrad* typified God himself. For the number four contains the decad—the finite interval of number—as before the ten is completed the sum of the first four presents all the virtue of the ultimate decad; thus $1+2+3+4=10$.

Four is the arithmetical mid-point between 1, the unit (God), and 7, which is called the Virgin, inasmuch as it produces no number between itself and 10; 8 is the reflection of 4, and $1+2+3+4+5+6+7+8=36$, the number of decanates of the zodiacal circle, also representing the letters of the tetragrammaton and the numbers of the Sephiroth.

Though of course the position of greatest intensity in an aspect is at its exact formation, such formations being rarely found in the horoscope, it yet behoves us to consider the ratios of the gradually lessening or increasing activity of the force from or up to a certain known point. For there are no blanks in the zodiac, nor in the circle of aspects, but only an appearance thereof, to be satisfactorily explained on rational grounds. Everything is continuous, there is no hitch, no flaw, but undeviating progression along lines fixed and immoveable. Apart from this, there inheres a particular nature to each several aspect. We are used to lumping trines, sextiles and quintiles together and denominating

---

* For instance, the number 3 expresses the triangle in the ternary nature of its sides and angles. Looked upon as dissociated units, they are triple, but together they constitute a unit—the synthesis of the whole, angles and sides, forming the containing figure. This is what is known as completing the Trinity by the Quaternary. The angles of a triangle, it may be remarked also, are equal to two right angles.

them *good* ; and semi-squares, squares and oppositions, and stigmatising them as *evil*. When we do this, however, we wilfully ignore the fact that each has a special character and influence of its own, which can be shown to be substantially the case.*

The general efficacy of each and every aspect arises from its harmonical proportion, and bears equally on the laws of light, colour, and harmony, as on those of astral science, and moreover, every agent acting by itself does so only according to its own peculiar form and virtue. It will thus be understood that aspects are not active forces, but passive mediums, which, being formed, enable the influences proceeding from the heavenly bodies to function. They unlock, as it were, the sluice-gates through which the forces rush, just as at the moment of birth only that ego with which the stars are in sympathy can attach itself to the clay.

---

* A useful hint on this point is given in *What is a Horoscope and How is it Cast*, p. 42, also in *The Horoscope in Detail*, p. 9, where the analogy between the various aspects and the houses of the horoscope is pointed out. Thus, let the slower planet be regarded as corresponding to the ' ascendant,' and the quicker as corresponding to the ' house-cusp '; then the □ is a 4th house or 10th house influence, the △ a 5th house or 9th house influence—and so on with the others : the ∠ and ⊔ corresponding to *half way through a house* are hence more or less anomalous in their nature.—EDITOR.

CHAPTER II.

PRIMARY DIRECTING. SECTION i., DIRECTIONS *in mundo*. SECTION ii.,
DIRECTIONS *in zodiaco*.

SECTION I.

" WHAT are you muttering to yourself, Menippus, talking about the stars
and pretending to measure distances? As I walk behind you I hear of
nothing but suns and moons, parasanges, stations, and I know not what."

ICARO-MENIPPUS.

DIRECTIONS proper are of two kinds—Mundane and Zodiacal;
primary directions, strictly speaking, belong entirely to the former and so-
called secondary ones to the latter, *i.e.*, one is made according to the
circle of the zodiac and the other according to that of the world, or in
respect to the mundane distances of houses and angles.

(1) Primary arcs are constituted by the *diurnal* motion of the earth
immediately preceding and following the birth; and it must be conceived
from the commencement of the study that the planets' places at the
moment of drawing breath only are dealt with, they having all the efficacy
impressed upon them of the heavenly bodies which have moved away.
So that it will be comprehended that the Primary Directions for a
lifetime are formed within a very few hours after birth by the diurnal
motion of a planet or planets, either bodily or by aspect, to: (*a*) the
angles; (*b*) to other planets; (*c*) to its own or another planet's original
place.

These are considered the most powerful agents in the production of
events, but their calculation entails patience and a certain share of
mathematical ability, two things not always at the disposal of the
ordinary student.

(2) The other or secondary system, primarily intended as an aid to
the foregoing, is purely zodiacal, and was much in favour with the
Hermetists and Arabians, hence it frequently goes by those names. It

is based on the daily motion of the sun, moon, and planets subsequent and antecedent to birth, possesses undoubted power, and appears to be the method which finds most favour in the eyes of the modern astrologer; perhaps this is scarcely to be wondered at seeing the rapidity at which the age lives. This method is, in fact, that of the "progressed horoscope," to which the previous sections of this work have been devoted.

Certainly it cannot be boasted that either of these two methods of calculating for future events is perfect. Far indeed from it, and there lies the trouble. The whole subject is the most alluring and withal the most provoking in the field of astrological research.

At the outset we are confronted with a grave matter—a crucial point in very truth—upon which a great deal must radically depend, i.e., the division of the circle of the world into proper mundane houses. To do this there are some wonderfully various methods, the majority of which have some rational basis hard to be overlooked, and all of which have at one time or another been experimented upon and adopted with more or less success. Memory will easily recall the systems of Alcabitius, Julius Firmicus, Cardan, Campanus, Ptolemy, Schoner, Porphyrius, Regiomontanus, etc. Even these are not all, but they are sufficient to show that a great diversity of opinion must exist, and inculcate the necessity for accuracy in this particular.*

The method of setting out the twelve cusps of the mundane houses almost universally followed by present-day Western astrologers, is according to the method advocated by Ptolemy and followed by Placidus, viz., by oblique ascension, so for the present the others may be dismissed, for they constitute a separate enquiry which the exigencies of time and space now prevent.

In directing it is quite possible that a number of methods may exist, it is equally probable that they may lead to the same end, but it certainly becomes impossible when they do not define similar arcs in similar times, and this is what inevitably occurs when one enquires into the subject.

The object aimed at in directing, is to ascertain the value of the arc intercepted between the degree held at birth by a planet and the degree at which, when it arrives, it will form an aspect of a particular number of degrees with another planet, or the bodily conjunction itself, always bear-

* Cf. Chapter IV. of this section. See also The Construction of the Celestial Theme in MODERN ASTROLOGY, Vols. I. and II. (New Series).

ing in mind that the so-called *body* is circumstantially one point only—that being the point of a radical position at a certain moment, and that moment the one in which the child inspires its first breath.   Now if there is any intrinsic virtue in an aspect, it evidently resides in its constitution of a definite number of degrees, antecedent and subsequent to the formation of which, power must increase in a certain definite ratio.   It follows then, and this view is perfectly tenable, that the events produced by the completion of a directional arc are the outcome of longer or shorter lengths of time, the inception being the approach of the aspect.   If we grant this we shall find no difficulty in understanding the reason for such an event as death happening in some cases before an arc is completed. For directly the significator and promittor are within orbs the exertion of force must begin to be appreciated, according to the radical weakness or otherwise exhibited in the geniture, so that either in a person of advanced age, or in one whose vital forces are radically low, having been so induced by previous affliction, it is consistent to expect that the spark of life may not be able to suffer the full strenuousness of the perfect aspect before the demise occurs.

In Primary Directions proper, we have both mundane and zodiacal arcs, so called, although in reality they are all mundane or formed by the diurnal revolution of the earth on its own axis, as will be shown later. The distinction consists in this, that whereas the former are measured in the world independent of the zodiac and have to do with the angles, cusps and houses of any figure and are taken with latitude, the latter appear to be measured by zodiacal degrees only, the latitude of the promittor not being taken.   Closer distinctions will be observed during the progress of this treatise.

THE TRIGONOMETRICAL FUNCTIONS OF AN ANGLE OR ARC.

Since in operating the formulæ concerned in the calculation of what we term Primary Arcs, we must proceed by trigonometrical means, and therefore employ the logarithms of certain lines related to the radius of a circle, it will facilitate the understanding if some explanations are first submitted.   The mathematical ability actually requisite is really trifling and an average intellect will be able to solve all problems related to directional arcs solely by close attention to the formulæ presented, without any special technical knowledge whatever.

Trigonometry means literally the measuring of triangles (τριγωνος' *triangle* ; μετρον, *measure*) and is founded on the mutual proportion subsisting between the sides and angles of a triangle. This proportion is known by finding the proportion which the radius of a circle has to certain lines called trigonometrical functions, *viz., sines, tangents,* etc. The reader is therefore requested to observe the following definitions, which convey the most important conceptions applicative to the subject in hand.

The *circumference* of a circle, large or small, is always reckoned to consist of 360 degrees.

Angles are measured by such degrees.

A *right angle* is one of 90 degrees—the astrological quadrate aspect.

The *complement of an angle* is its defect from a right angle. Thus, $90° - 35° = 55°$, which is the complement of 35°.

The *supplement of an angle* is its defect from two right angles. Thus $180° - 35° = 145°$, which is the supplement of 35°.

An *arc* is any portion of the circumference of a circle.

A *quadrant* is the fourth part of a circle, or the arc subtending a right angle.

The *sine of an arc* is a straight line drawn from one extremity of the arc perpendicular to the diameter passing through the other extremity of it. Therefore, the sine of 90 degrees is the greatest possible. The sine of an arc is equal to the sine of its supplement.*

The *tangent of an arc* is a straight line "touching" the circle at one extremity of the arc and meeting the "produced" diameter that passes through the other extremity. The tangent of the eighth part of the circumference is equal to the radius.

The *secant of an arc* is the straight line drawn from the centre to the furthest extremity of the tangent of that arc.

The *cosine and cotangent* are the sine and tangent of the complement of an arc.†

The *sine*	of an angle	$=\begin{cases}(a)\text{ the } cosine\\(b)\text{ the } sine\end{cases}$	of its *complement.* „ *supplement.*
The *cosine*	„ „	$=\begin{cases}(a)\text{ the } sine\\(b)\text{ the } cosine\end{cases}$	„ *complement.* „ *supplement.*
The *tangent*	„ „	$=\begin{cases}(a)\text{ the } cotangent\\(b)\text{ the } tangent\end{cases}$	„ *complement.* „ *supplement.*
The *cotangen*	„ „	$=\begin{cases}(a)\text{ the } tangent\\(b)\text{ the } cotangent\end{cases}$	„ *complement.* „ *supplement.*

The tangents, cotangents, secants and cosecants can be determined from the sines and cosines. For, if A be any angle,

---

* *Supplement of an arc, i.e.,* the difference between that arc and 180°.

† *Complement of an arc, i.e.,* the difference between that arc and 90°.

$$tan\ A = \frac{sin\ A}{cos\ A} \qquad\qquad cot\ A = \frac{cos\ A}{sin\ A}$$

$$sec\ A = \frac{1}{cos\ A} \qquad\qquad cosec\ A = \frac{1}{sin\ A}$$

$$sin^2\ A + cos^2 = 1 \qquad\qquad sin\ 30° = \tfrac{1}{2}$$
$$sec^2\ A - tan^2 = 1 \qquad\qquad sin\ 60° = \tfrac{1}{2} \times \sqrt{3}$$
$$cosec^2\ A - cot^2 = 1 \qquad\qquad sin\ 45° = \tfrac{1}{2} \times \sqrt{2}$$

The *sines*, *tangents* and *secants* of angles from 45° to 90° are the same respectively as the *co-sines*, *co-tangents* and *co-secants* of angles from 45° to 0° since

$$sin\ A = cos\ (90° - A)$$
$$tan\ A = cot\ (90° - A)$$
$$sec\ A = cosec\ (90° - A)$$

$$\qquad\qquad °\quad ' \qquad\qquad °\quad ' \qquad\qquad °\quad '$$

Thus, $cos\ 60\ 42 = sin\ (90 - 60\ 42) = sin\ 29\ 18$
$\quad\ \ sin\ 60\ 42 = cos\ (90 - 60\ 42) = cos\ 29\ 18$
$\quad\ \ tan\ 60\ 42 = cot\ (90 - 60\ 42) = cot\ 29\ 18$
$\quad\ \ sec\ 60\ 42 = cosec\ (90 - 60\ 42) = cosec\ 29\ 18$

There is a conventional mode of thought adopted for convenience by mathematicians and geometers, whereby any angle or arc is supposed to be traced out by a line, which becomes the radius of the ensuing circle, revolving about a point in a direction contrary to that of the hands of a clock (called " counter-clockwise "), and starting from the horizontal position. In completing the circle thus traced out, the angle or arc increases from 0° through 90°, 180° and 270° to 360°, thereby passing through four quadrants, known respectively as the first, second, third and fourth. Lines above or to the right of the central point are considered as *positive* in value, those below or to the left as *negative*. The radius is *always positive*. Thus, in figure 2 CB, CH, FB, GH, DE, CG are positive, CA is negative. Hence the values of the sine (say) of an angle will oscillate from positive to negative and back again, as that angle increases from 0° to 360°, as the reader may easily verify for himself if he follows out the process with the aid of paper and pencil, drawing diagram for himself.

The sequence of algebraic signs in the four quadrants is

$$\text{for } sine \quad\text{ and } cosecant \left(+ + - -\right)$$
$$\text{for } cosine \quad\text{ and } secant \left(+ - - +\right)$$
$$\text{for } tangent \text{ and } cotangent \left(+ - + -\right)$$

sin and *cosec*
cos and *sec* } are reciprocals and have the same conventional sign.
tan and *cotan*

While the arc increases from 0° to a quadrant, the *sine* increases from *zero* to *radius* (its greatest value), and the *cosine* diminishes from *radius* to *zero*. While the arc increases to a semi-circle, the *sine* diminishes to *zero*, and the *cosine* (whose sign is now negative), increases in magnitude till it equals *—radius*.

As the arc increases to three quadrants, the *sine* is negative and its magnitude increases from *zero* to —*radius*, while the (negative) value of the *cosine* diminishes from —*radius* to *zero*. From three quadrants to four the *sine* (still negative) diminishes its negative value till it becomes *zero*, while the *cosine* (now become positive) increases from *zero* to +*radius* as at first.

The *tangent*, while the arc increases from 0° to 90°, increases from *zero* so as to become greater than any assigned quantity; (when the arc =90° or 270°, in fact, there is really no tangent, as the lines by whose intersection the tangent is defined do not meet). Then, until the arc = 180° the *tangent* is negative, and diminishes from a value indefinitely great to *zero*; then for the third and fourth quadrants the values are the same as for the first and second respectively.

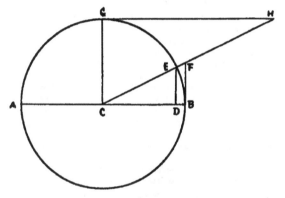

FIG. 2.

AB=*Diameter*   GH=*Cotangent*
CE=*Radius*   CF=*Secant*
ED=*Sine*   CH=*Cosecant*
CD=*Cosine*   ECG=*Complement* } of the *angle*
BF=*Tangent*   ECA=*Supplement* } BCE
BE=the *arc* to which these lines belong
BCE=the *angle made at the circle of reference*, or the *equivalent angle*

IMPORTANT NOTE.—It should be borne in mind that the *sine, cosine*, etc., of the above, are the lines mentioned *in respect of their relation to the radius of the circle.* Hence they are *ratios, rather than quantities.*

Thus *sin* ∠ ECB=$\frac{ED}{CE}$; *cosine* ∠ ECB=$\frac{CD}{CE}$; and *tan* ∠ ECB=$\frac{BF}{CB}$. Again, *cotan* ∠ ECB =$\frac{CD}{ED}=\frac{GH}{GC}$; *sec* ∠ ECB=$\frac{CF}{CB}=\frac{CF}{CE}$ ∠ ECB=$\frac{CE}{ED}=\frac{CH}{CG}$; CB, CE, CG, being all radii.

The *sine, tangent*, etc., of an arc which is the measure of any given angle bears the same proportion to the *sine, tangent*, etc., of any other arc which is the measure of the same angle, as the radius of the first arc bears to the radius of the second. (See "Important Note" on previous page.)

Sines and *cosines* of arcs and the *tangents* of arcs less than 45°, being less than 1 (the unit of linear measure being the radius), have their logarithms negative.* The working of these would be inconvenient, and to overcome this, the logarithms of the tables are made greater by 10 than the real logarithms of the numbers.

For example, using *l.* for the true log. and *L.* for the table log.,

$$tan\ A = \frac{sin\ A}{cos\ A}$$

therefore, *l. tan* A=*l. sin* A—*l. cos* A,
"   L. *tan* A—10=L. *sin* A—10 —(L. *cos* A—10) ;
        or L. *tan* A=L. *sin* A—L. *cos* A+10.

On the basis of a knowledge of the *sine*, trigonometrical tables have been constructed, such that either (1) their numbers express in terms of the radius the proportional length of the sines, cosines, tangents, secants, etc., of all possible arcs in a circumference, in which case they are called "Tables of Natural Sines, etc."; or (2) their numbers express the logarithms of these natural sines, etc., and then they are "Tables of Logarithmic Sines, etc." Thus a table of the values of *sines* may be readily transformed into a table of the values of *cosines*. Likewise, since the *tangent* A=*sin* A÷*cos* A, the log. of the *tangent* of an angle may be obtained by subtracting the log. of the *cosine* from that of the *sine*, while the log. of the *cotangent* is obtainable by the subtraction of the log. of the *sine* from the log. of the *cosine*.

The radius is the sine of 90°.   In other words, *sin* 90°=1 ; *l. sin* 90°=0, or *L. sin* 90°=10·0.

The *arithmetical complement* is found by subtracting the logarithm from the radius. (The logarithm of the radius in the ordinary tables is 10·0.)

A *Right Sphere* is that in which the equator cuts the horizon at right angles, or that in which the poles are in the horizon and the equator is in the zenith. Such is the position of the sphere with regard to those who live directly under the equator. The consequences are they have no latitude nor elevation of the pole. In a Right Sphere the horizon is a meridian circle, and if the sphere be supposed to revolve, all the meridians successively become horizons.   In an *Oblique Sphere* the horizon cuts all the meridians obliquely (*e.g.*, the celestial sphere as seen at London).

The *Right Ascension* (R.A.) of a star or planet is that degree and minute of the equinoctial,† counted from the beginning of Aries, which comes to the zenith meridian with that star. The reason of thus referring it to the meridian is because the latter is always at right angles to the equinoctial, whereas the

---

* The meaning and use of Logarithms will be found fully explained in Chapter IX. of *Astrology or All, Part II*.
    † In other words the *Celestial Equator*.

horizon is only so in a right or direct sphere. Right Descension is opposed to Right Ascension; it is, in short, the opposite degree of the equinoctial (R.D.).

Oblique Ascension (O.A.) is the arc of the equator intercepted between the first point of Aries and that part of the equator which in an oblique sphere rises with the star concerned. Oblique Descension is opposed to Oblique Ascension (O.D.).

Ascensional Difference (A.D.) is the difference between the Right and the Oblique Ascensions of the same point.

The *Equator* or *Equinoctial* is the intersection of the plane of the earth's equator with the celestial sphere. It lies midway between the two poles and hence is distant 90° from each.

The *Ecliptic* is that great circle of the sphere which is the apparent path of the Sun. The *ecliptic obliquity* (O.E. or E.O.) is the angle made between the equator and the ecliptic. It is therefore equal to the Sun's maximum declination or greatest distance from equator.

The *Poles of the Ecliptic* are two points 90° distant from the ecliptic.

Longitude differs from *Right Ascension* in being reckoned along the *ecliptic* instead of the *equator*.

Latitude is the angular distance of a star north or south of the ecliptic, measured on the star's circle of latitude.

Declination is the angular distance north or south of the celestial equator.

The *Meridian Distance* (M.D.) of a star or planet is its distance measured in R.A. from the zenith.

The *Semi-arc* (S.A.) of a star or planet is half the arc formed above the earth (*diurnal*), or below (*nocturnal*), by its motion from rising to setting, or from setting to rising.

The *Horizontal Arc* (H.A.) of a star or planet is its distance from the nearest horizon, eastern or western as the case may be. It is, of course, the difference etween the semi-arc and the meridian distance, or briefly: S.A.—M.D.=H.A.

Promittor is a name given to the planet chiefly concerned in the production of some event.

Prorogator is synonymous with *Apheta* and *Hyleg*—the giver of life. The Sun, Moon and Ascendant are the vital points.

In constructing the *Speculum* (that is, a table as appended to Map 1 showing the elements required of each planet), the longitude, latitude and declination will be found from the ephemeris. When, as in some old ephemerides, the latter is not given, it may be calculated thus:—

Add *log. tan obliq. eclipt.* to *log. sin. long. of star* from *nearest equinox*, and call the result *tan ∠* A. If the latitude and longitude be of the same name † subtract star's latitude

---

* *I.e.*, star or planet or given point of the celestial sphere.

† Both north or both south, that is: by "south" longitude is meant between ♎ and ♈; by "north," between ♈ and ♎.

EXAMPLE MAP: No 1.

Natus 7hrs. 52min. 12sec.p. m., G.M.T. (rectified time),   April 23rd, 1869; Lat. 52°28'N., Long. 0°7'W.

R.A.M.C. 149°50'.

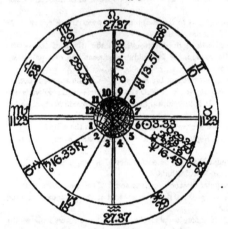

R.A.I.C. 329°50'.

SPECULUM.

	Lat.	Dec.	R.A.	M.D.	S.A.	H.A.
	° '	° '	° '	° '	° '	° '
☉	0 0	12 44N	31 23	61 32	72 54	11 22
☽	3 38N	3 23N	181 23	31 33	94 25	62 52
☿	0 46S	9 24N	25 28	55 38	77 33	11 55
♀	1 7S	10 16N	27 47	57 57	76 22	18 25
♂	2 19N	17 9N	142 45	7 5	113 41	106 36
♃	1 18	10 6N	27 3	57 13	76 35	19 22
♄	1 44N	21 3S	255 34	74 16	120 5	45 49
♅	0 25N	23 9N	105 5	44 45	56 11	11 26
♆*	1 35S	5 9N	16 5	46 15	83 16	37 1

NOTE.—In compiling a speculum for practical use it is a good plan to add beneath the M.D., S.A. and H.A. the respective "proportional logarithms" (see note on p. 230).   For the sake of clearness they are omitted here, however.

---

* The long., lat. and dec. of ♆ here, and also in map No. 2, are as given in the Ephemeris for the 1st of the month.   No material error is introduced, as the motion of ♆ is so slow.

from 90°, otherwise add. Take difference between result and angle A. Call it angle B. Then say "As *cos ∠ A* is to *cos ∠ B* so is *cos obliq. eclip.* to *sin star's declination*." If latitude and longitude be of same name (both north or south) the declination will be the same.

EXAMPLE.—*What is the declination of* ☽ *in Map* 1 ?

Log tan Obliquity Eclipt. (23°27')		9·637 2646
„ *sin* Long. ☽, 179°55' (0°5')		7·162 6960
„ *tan* ∠ A	0°2'	6·799 9606

Then	90° 0'	
minus Lat.	3 38	
equals	86 22	
minus ∠ A	0 2	
equals ∠ B	86 20	

Log. Cos ∠ A (arith. comp.)		10·000 0000
„ *Cos* ∠ B		8·805 8523
„ *Cos* Obliq. Eclip.		9·962 5624
„ *Sin* Declin. ☽	3°N23'	8·768 4147

The *Right Ascension* of the various planets may either be obtained by the help of tables specially constructed for that purpose, or computed in the following way.

Say, As *cos star's declination* is to *cos longitudinal distance*, so is *cos latitude* to *cos R.A.*

EXAMPLE 1.—*Required the R.A. of* ☽ *in Map* 1.

Log. Cos Dec. ☽	3°23'	(ar. comp.)	0·000 7576
„ *Cos* Long. ☽ (— 0°5' *from* ♎)			9·999 9995
„ *Cos* Lat. ☽	3°38'		9·999 1262
„ *Cos* R.A.	1°20' (*from* ♎)		9·999 8833
Half Circle 180 0			

R.A. ☽   181 20   (Note that here the ☽'s R.A. *exceeds* the R.A. of her ecliptic longitude ♍ 29°55'.)

EXAMPLE 2.—*Required R.A. of* ☉ *in Map* 1.

log. Cos Dec. ☉,	12°44'	(*ar. comp.*)	0·010 8144
„ *Cos* Long.	33°38'*		9·920 4360
„ *Cos* R.A. ☉,	31°23		9·931 2504

Let us now proceed to the examination of Map 1.

---

* The Sun, of course, has no latitude.

The M.D. is found by subtracting a star's R.A. from the R.A. of the M.C. or I.C. (*Imum Coeli* or Nadir ; cusp of fourth house).

Thus in the nativity above I would find the M.D. of Mars. As it is above the earth the result will be its distance from the cusp of tenth house. I proceed as follows:

		°	′
R.A.M.C.		149	50
R.A. ♂		142	45
M.D. ♂		7	5

which is also the arc of Mars to the mundane conjunction of mid-heaven. Take another case, *viz.*, to find Neptune's M.D.; this will be its distance from fourth house, that planet being under the earth and nearest thereto. This time we must add the circle to Neptune's R.A. before making the subtraction, because computation must always be made in the order of the signs:—

		°	′
R.A. ♆		16	5
	Circle	360	0
		376	5
R.A. I.C.		329	50
M.D. ♆		46	15

The Semi-Arcs are generally found by adding the log. tan. latitude of birth-place to log. tan. declination of star, the result being the log. *cosine* of semi-arc. Now if the latitude of birthplace and declination are both of same name, *i.e.*, *both* north or *both* south, the result is the *semi-nocturnal arc*, and if the diurnal is required it must be subtracted from 180°. If, however, the declination of star and latitude of birthplace (observe, not star) differ in name—one being *south* and the other *north*, the result will be the *semi-diurnal arc*. The opposite arc is always the supplement necessary to form the half circle (180°); therefore when an arc of either name is obtained, to find the other, be it nocturnal or diurnal, subtraction must be made from 180°.

EXAMPLE.—*What is the semi-diurnal arc of the Sun in Map 1 ?*

Lat. of birthplace	52°28′N.	*log. tan.*	10·114 4965
Declination of ☉	12°44′N.	„ „	9·354 0530
Cosine of Semi-nocturnal arc 72°54′		„ *cos.*	9·468 5495

As, however, the declination is of the same name as the latitude (which latter will always be north in our hemisphere) the result is not what we seek, it being the semi-*nocturnal* arc. Therefore we perform subtraction thus:—

	°	′
Half Circle	180	0
Semi-nocturnal arc ☉	72	54
Semi-diurnal arc ☉	107	6

There are other methods, but they need not here be detailed, one being quite sufficient when the ends arrived at are identical.

The speculum being completed, the nativity stands in a position for directing in real earnest, and to do this with pleasure some systematic attention must be given to the order in which aspects are progressively formed from the earliest period of the native's infancy to the latter period of his old age. This, however, need not be rigidly enforced, for a collection of the arcs in proper sequence may be made after all computation is finished.

The best way is to commence with the various directions to the angles *in mundo* in as near the natural formative procession as possible, and follow these with the mundane directions amongst the planets themselves, not forgetting the Rapt Parallels. Then the zodiacal aspects to angles may be taken and the mutual configurations of the planets. A very few problems will suffice to enable any fairly intelligent person to bring up these various orders—the pith of the primary system—with ease, profit and pleasure; for the directing of cusps of houses, the part of fortune, fixed stars, *caput* and *cauda draconis* may be best ignored. If the student wishes to investigate these and other points of astrological doctrine he should first be able to perform the problems necessary in the computation of the directions mentioned above.

I shall now bring forward some examples of mundane and zodiacal directing, so that the student may form some idea of the practical processes concerned, and the theoretical reasons for them, and thus be enabled to follow subsequent remarks with a clearer understanding.

Within the limits of this essay there is obviously not sufficient room to extenuate greatly the various problems. Even if there were, there are so many different methods of working, that an account of them all would fill more than one fat quarto.

P

OBSERVE : For those in which the M.C. is concerned we employ right ascension. Those to the ascendant are worked by semi-arc of the body moved.

By attending to the following method, all directions to the angles *in mundo* completed in an ordinary lifetime may be computed easily in something less than half an hour by one who has his Mercury or Moon aspected by Mars. For it must be noted that after the M.D.'s are obtained in the speculum you also have the conjunctions and oppositions to the mid-heaven, as well as the mundane squares to the ascendant ; because when a planet is on cusp of either tenth or fourth, it is in exact square to one on cusp of first (supposing there to be a planetary body there) *in mundo*. These being obtained, the several aspects to M.C. and ascendant may be derived therefrom by aliquot portions of the various semi-arcs.

In doing so we commence with those to the M.C., premising that when on the completion of the aspect the planet is above the earth, the *semi-diurnal* arc is used, but when below, the *semi-nocturnal* arc must be worked with. *N.B.—This point should be particularly noted.*

For instance, in the foregoing nativity, when the Moon arrives at cusp of eleventh it forms a semi-sextile to M.C. and a sextile to ascendant : so that by one computation you have two directions, both of which are calculated with the *diurnal* arc. When Saturn reaches cusp of second house a trine to M.C. is completed, but the planet being sub-terrene, necessitates the employment of its *nocturnal* arc.

In the speculum the semi-arcs are for the radical positions of the planets, *i.e.*, in all cases where the planet is below the earth the arc in the column is its nocturnal one ; and if above, its diurnal. By the rule previously given either arc required is easily found.

I shall give now a table of complementary arcs to the M.C. and ascendant *in mundo*, which will show at a glance what synonymous aspect is formed to the ascendant, if any, when a star is directed to an aspect of the M.C. or *vice-versâ.*

TABLE OF ARCS TO THE M.C.

AND THEIR COMPLEMENTARY RELATIONSHIP TO THE ASCENDANT.

M.C.		*Formed above the Earth.*		Ascendant.
☌	The body.	Complementary arc forms		☐
⚹	One house or ⅓ s.a.	,,	,, ,,	⚹ or △
∠	One house and a half or ½ s.a.	,,	,, ,,	∠ ,, ⧠

| ✱ | Two houses or ⅔ s.a. | Complementary arc forms | ⊻ or ⌅ |
| ☐ | Three houses or whole s.a. | „ „ „ | ☌ „ 8 |

M.C.   *Formed below the Earth.*   *Ascendant.*

△	Four houses or 1⅓ s.a.	Complementary arc forms	⊻ or ⌅
⬓	Four houses and a half or 1½ s.a.	„	„ „	∠ „ ⬓
⌅	Five houses or 1⅔ s.a.	„	„ „	✱ „ △
8	Six houses or whole arc	„	„ „	☐

The remaining aspects are independent or of minor importance.

As an illustration I shall direct the M.C. and ascendant to the above aspects of Mars in Map. I.

	°	′			
M.D. ♂ (or M.C. ☌ ♂)	7	5	also	☐	ascendant.
⅓ Semi-diurnal Arc	37	54			
M.C. ⊻ ♂ (= diff.)	30	49	„	△	„
+ ⅓ s.d. a.	18	57			
M.C. ∠ ♂	49	46	„	⬓	„
+ ⅓ s.d. a.	18	57			
M.C. ✱ ♂	68	43	„		„
+ ⅔ sd. a.	37	54			
M.C. ☐ ♂	106	37	„	8	„
+ ⅓ S. Nocturnal Arc	22	6			
M.C. △ ♂	128	43	„	⌅	„
+ ⅓ s.n. a.	11	3			
M.C. ⬓ ♂	139	46	„		„
+ ⅓ s.n. a.	11	3			
M.C. ⌅ ♂	150	49	„	△	„
+ ⅓ s.n. a.	22	6			
M.C. 8 ♂	172	55	„	☐	„

It will be seen that the proportional parts of the semi-arcs have been employed according to the table inserted previously, and in like manner any other desired aspect can be computed by taking the aliquot part in accordance therewith. The whole semi-arc lies between cusp of tenth and cusp of seventh so far as the Mars aspects in the above calculations are concerned, and ⅓ of this will be equivalent to one mundane house, ⅔ to two houses, and ⅙ to half a house, so that the reason for the above mode of calculation becomes apparent at once.

From the M.C. to cusp of ninth is ⅓ of semi-arc, measuring 37°54′, consequently if ♂ were exactly at the zenith this would be the arc of direction of M.C. ⊻♂ or ascendant △♂. But allowance must be made for the number of degrees ♂ is deflected from tenth, which amount of course must be taken from 37°54' to find the true measure, as shown in the previous working. Note particularly what happens after the double line. The square of ♂ and M.C., or what is the same thing, the opposition of ♂ and ascendant, has been formed, and consequently to proceed in the order of the lengthening of the aspects it becomes necessary that the planet move below the earth in order to form the succeeding ones.

From that moment the *nocturnal* arc is used, continuing in all else as before. Of course, before the square has formed to M.C. in this case, the native would probably long have succumbed ; but that fact does not invalidate the object for which I have given the calculation, that is, to show how one aspect can be obtained from a foregoing one in unbroken continuity.

The whole arc stretches from tenth house to fourth, and should consist of 180 degrees, neither more nor less, therefore the opposition of ♂ to M.C. should equal 180° minus its distance from cusp of tenth. In other words, ♂'s M.D. plus the arc of direction (♂ M.C.) should both sum to 180°. Let us see :

	°	'
Arc of direction M.C. ♂ ♂	172	55
M.D. ♂	7	5
The half circle or whole arc	180	0

We thus prove the correctness both of the method and the working, and all the aspects may be tested in the same manner.

All the aspects of ♂, it is needless to remark, were formed after birth by mundane motion, or that motion which the planet would appear to have if regarded for a few hours, as we would the Sun or Moon—its rising, culmination and setting, which happen daily, irrespective of its position in the zodiac.

It is seen, then, that the conjunction of M.C. and ♂ occurred shortly before birth, and if we take the M.D. 7°5' as the directional arc, it must be so understood, for Mars will not travel back to the M.C., the daily motion of the earth never varying its direction of rotation. On this account, because such aspect as the conjunction of ♂ and M.C. could not be formed after birth, many practitioners disallow the effects, and reprehend the calculations of such arcs. Experience will show the student what he may expect, and by this alone must he decide.

Aspects to the ascendant may be similarly calculated, recollecting that, in doing so, many will probably have been already included by complement when computing those to the M.C. Note also that the direction of a planet to the mundane square with the ascendant, is always equal to that planet's meridian distance, either above or below the earth; the opposition, as likewise the conjunction of the ascendant, is of course a square to the M.C. Such positions will soon become familiar, and I should advise much practice in bringing arcs to the angles *in mundo* before extending the purview further, so as to obtain a thorough comprehension of the process, and the reasons for same. When the student has made progress here, and feels ground under him, he may proceed to the computation of the mundane directions to the luminaries.

DIRECT AND CONVERSE DIRECTIONS.

These are based upon certain relative distances from angles and cusps of houses, and depend for their constitution and dissolution on the diurnal motion of the earth. A *direct* direction is one in which the Sun or Moon is supposed to stand still, mundanely of course, so that to it other planetary bodies exert completed rays, formed successively by their apparent motion from east to west. Thus it will be seen that the zodiac is not requisitioned. For instance, in the exemplary horoscope (p. 222) the Sun being supposed to stand in its relative position to the western cusp, or rather, the Sun's mundane place being understood to retain the radical solar power,—(for the body of the Sun itself moves on in continuity),—Saturn rising in diurnal conformity will form an opposition in the twelfth house, at an equivalent distance from the eastern angle; so that the problem resolves itself: *first*, into a question of knowing the radical distance of Sun from cusp of seventh: *second*, of determining the distance Saturn must travel in order to arrive at the same distance on the other side of ascendant. And this will be the arc of direction—not to the real Sun, which has moved away, but to a former *locus*, in which it happened to be posited at a critical moment, and that moment the birth. At this highly psychic time, it is understood that the specific irradiations of a heavenly body become, like the image focussed upon a photographic negative, as it were, fixed and efficacious.

EXAMPLE 1.—*Required the arc of* ⊙ 8 ♄ *in mundo by direct direction.*
(Map I.)

As semi-arc ⊙	72°54′	*prop. log.**	9·607 46 (*a.c.*)
Is to distance of ⊙ from 7th cusp,	11°22′	,, ,,	1·199 64
So is semi-diurnal arc of ♄	120° 5′	,, ,, †	0·477 72
To secondary distance of ♄	9°21′		1·284 82

Then, Distance of ♄ from cusp of 1st (= H.A.)   45° 49′
    Plus secondary distance of ♄   9 21

    Gives arc of direction, ⊙ 8 ♄ d.d. *mundo*   55 10

Notes :—All these directions must be worked by logarithms, remembering that in performing the golden rule of three by their aid the
first term must be the *arithmetical complement*, to be obtained by
subtracting the proportional logarithm from an integer that is a multiple
of ten. The *tens* are then cast out in the answer, as in the above
example.

(2) The distance of Sun from seventh is determined by taking the
difference between its S.A. and M.D., that of Saturn from ascendant by
similar means. As, however, the latter planet forms the opposition *above*
the earth, its semi-*diurnal* arc must be taken, and this applies in all cases
where the directed planet crosses the horizon from below. Had the
positions of Sun and Saturn been changed about in the radix, the Sun
being above cusp of first, and Saturn say on cusp of eighth, to complete
the oppositional aspect Saturn would have descended into sixth, and then,
instead of working with its radical semi-diurnal arc, necessity would
have required its nocturnal arc. This point cannot be too well regarded.

(3) One word more—the primary and secondary distance of Saturn
have been added together to obtain the directional arc, according to this
rule, the bearings of which will be seen immediately. If secondary

---

* These " proportional logarithms " are found in *Chambers' Mathematical Tables*,
which will be found a quite indispensable requisite for all work of this kind. They are
there given as " Ternary Proportional Logarithms," and run from 0°0′0″ to 3°0′0″. In
using them for our present purpose call the *degrees*, as there given, 60 degrees ; the
minutes, degrees ; and similarly the *seconds*, minutes. Thus, in the present example the
semi-arc ⊙ according to the Speculum is 72°54′, which, translated as explained in the last
sentence, is equivalent to 1°12′54″. The " ternary proportional logarithm " of this
amount is found in the table to be 0·39254 (the 0 being *understood*, and not given in
the table). The "arithmetical complement" (*a.c.*) of this is its difference from
10·00000, namely 9·60746, as shown in the example, and is most quickly written down
by subtracting each digit, from left to right, from 9—the last digit being taken from
10. This may be found puzzling at first but in practice it is easy enough.
    [These *proportional logarithms* should not be confused with the *logarithms of sines*,
tangents, etc., used elsewhere. In this present work the latter have seven figures, the
former five.]

† The S.A. in the speculum is of course the semi-nocturnal arc.

distance of planet be on the side of cusp whence primary was taken when aspect was complete, subtract primary and secondary distances; otherwise *add*.

EXAMPLE 2.—*Direct the Moon by direct motion* in mundo *to a square of Sun.*

As semi-arc ☉	72°54′	*prop. log.*	9·607 46 (*a.c.*)
Is to distance of ☉ from 7th cusp, 11°22′	„ „	1·199 64
So is semi-arc of ☽	94°25′	„ „	280 22
To secondary dist. of ☽	14°43′		1·087 32

Secondary dist. of ☽	14° 43′
Dist. of ☽ from cusp of 10th	31 33
Arc of direction, ☽☐☉ d.d. *mundo*	46 16

Note :—In this case the Moon moves forward through the tenth house, crosses the cusp, and partially travels through the ninth before reaching the point where it forms the square aspect, and therefore primary and secondary distances being taken from opposite sides of the cusp, the two distances are added together.

The process, it is hoped, being quite clear, CONVERSE DIRECTIONS may be introduced.*

In these the luminary itself is moved forward until the required aspect is formed with the place of the promittor, and this will necessitate a slightly different method of working, the formula being :—As *semi-arc of fixed planet* IS TO *its distance from nearest cusp*, SO IS *semi-arc of body directed* TO *second distance of ditto.*

EXAMPLE 1.—*Direct* ☉ *by converse motion* in mundo *to a conjunction of* ♆.

As semi-nocturnal arc ♆	83°16′	*prop. log.*	9·665 20 (*a.c.*)
Is to dist. of ♆ from 6th cusp,	9°15′	„ „	1·289 13
So is semi-arc of ☉	72°54′	„ „	392 54
To secondary dist. of ☉	8° 6′	„ „	1·346 87

To form the conjunction the Sun will have to pass cusp of sixth, from which its primary distance is (s.a. ☉72°54′; H.A. ☉11°22′; ½ of 72°54′−11°22′=) 12°56′; therefore, as stated in the foregoing problem, the sum of primary and secondary distances is to be taken for the directional arc, thus :

Primary dist. of ☉ from 6th cusp	12° 56′
Secondary dist. of ☉	8 6
Arc of direction, ☉ ☌ ♆ *conv. in mundo*	21 2

---

* The student should be careful not to confuse the term " converse " as here employed, with its use in a quite different sense in Appendix I. and elsewhere.—EDITOR.

Notes :—(1) To find the distance of Sun or any other body from the sixth when below the earth, take two-thirds of its semi-arc from its M.D.

(2) In this direction the Sun arrives at the place of Neptune by the diurnal motion of the earth in the same manner as in the direct direction Saturn was shown to do to the opposition of the Sun, and as it crosses the cusp of house whence primary distance was taken, primary and secondary are added together.

EXAMPLE 2.—*Direct* ☉ *to a square of* ♄ *in mundo, conversely.*

			prop. log.	
As semi-arc ♄	120° 5'		9·824 21	(a.c.)
Is to dist. of ♄ from 2nd cusp, 5°47'		" "	1·493 09	
So is semi-arc of ☉	72°54'	" "	392 54	
To secondary dist. of ☉	3°31'		1·709 84	

Primary dist. of ☉ from cusp of 5th	37° 14'
Secondary dist. of ☉	3 31
Arc of direction, ☉ □ ♄ *conv. mundo*	33 43

Notes :—(1) In this instance the Sun has to be brought to a distance within cusp of fifth proportionate to Saturn's distance inside cusp of second. To find Saturn's distance from the second cusp, take two-thirds of semi-arc from its M.D. The distance of the Sun from fifth is found by taking one-third its semi-arc from its M.D. Then as the aspect is completed on the same side of the cusp from which primary distance is taken, the secondary distance is *subtracted* therefrom to obtain the directional arc.

(2) I shall now give an example in order to illustrate the method of obtaining one arc from another without having recourse to separate computations, such as those just exhibited. Instead of having to perform five problems to obtain the arcs of direction of ☉ ⚹, ⚼, ✳, □ and △ to the ☽, we are able by the use of aliquot parts of the several semi-arcs to bring them all up in a much shorter time and more compact form. At this point I may refer the reader back to the beginning of this chapter, where an identical use of these is made in computing directions to the ascendant and M.D. As an example, and for the clearer comprehension of the matter, I will direct ☉ to above aspects of ☽ by direct direction.

As semi-arc ☉	72°54'	*prop. log.*	9·607 46 (a.c.)
Is to distance of ☉ from 7th cusp, 11°22'		" "	1·199 64
So is semi-arc of ☽	94°25'	" "	280 22
To secondary dist. of ☽	14°43'		1·087 32

(3) To form the trine the Moon crossed the cusp of eleventh, from which its primary distance is 0°5'; therefore to find arc for △ ⊙, we must add primary and secondary distance. When the trine is obtained, before the square can be formed, one whole house or ⅓ of semi-arc must be travelled, therefore while the aspects will decrease in length owing to the positions of the two planets concerned, the arc of measurement will increase. The Semi-Arc to use in these proportional parts is that of *the body which is moved*—in this case the Moon.

Secondary dist. ☽	14° 43'	
Primary dist. 11th	5	
	14 48	⊙ △ ☽ d.d. *mundo.*
+ ⅓ ☽'s semi-arc	31 28	
	46 16	⊙ □ ☽ „
+ ⅓ „ „	31 28	
	77 44	⊙ * ☽ „
+⅓ of ⅓ or ⅑ s.a.	15 44	
	93 28	⊙ ∠ ☽ „
+⅓ of ⅓ or ⅑ s.a.	15 44	
	109 12	⊙ ⊼ ☽ „

(4) The reasons for the use of these aliquot parts of the various semi-arcs have been already explained, so that it will be sufficient to remind the reader that, in calculating, he must use the proper arc. Converse directions may be obtained in exactly the same way. It is highly important to recollect that the semi-arc used is that of the body directed. Otherwise, there are no great difficulties to be overcome.

Taking the directional part of a nativity in systematic order, we come next to consider Mundane Parallels, direct and converse, and then, finally, Rapt Parallels.

MUNDANE PARALLELS.

Mundane Parallels are those equal distances formed in the world from the upper and lower meridians, in contradistinction to those formed in the zodiac by being equally posited from the equator. Thus a star on cusp of twelfth, and another on cusp of eighth, represent equivalent distances from the M.C., so far as the world is concerned, as likewise from the nadir, of course, they being removed from the former point by the space of two houses, or two-thirds of the semi-diurnal arc; and they are therefore understood to be in mundane parallel. In like manner other distances; it matters not whether formed from the upper or lower heaven, in the same hemisphere or different, so long as the relative distances are the same; remembering, however, that if a star has to pass the horizon to complete the aspect, the complementary (*diurnal* or *nocturnal*) arc must be used. They are simple in calculation, and one or two problems will suffice to exhibit the method of working them.

First to Direct directly. The formula is: AS *semi-arc of Sun or Moon* IS TO *its* M. D., SO IS *semi-arc of planet moved* TO *its second distance*; from which to find the arc, the primary distance from M.C. or I.C. (nadir) must be subtracted.

EXAMPLE 1.—*Direct* ☽ *to the parallel of* ♂, *d.d.* mundo.

As semi-arc ☽	94°25′	*prop. log.*	9·719 78	(*a.c.*)
Is to M.D. ☽,	31°33′	,, ,,	756 27	
So is S.A. ♂	113°41′	,, ,,	199 58	
To secondary dist. of ♂, 37°59′			675 63	
Secondary dist. of ♂			37° 59′	
Primary dist. from M.C.			7 5	
Arc of direction, ☽ par. ♂ d.d. *mundo*			30 54	

Notes :—(1) In this case ♂ must be moved on until it arrives beyond cusp of ninth, where the aspect is completed: so that the problem is to find, *first*, the distance ♂ must have from tenth to be the balance in mundane power, or distance, of the Moon's radical M.D.; *secondly*, to determine the intercepted arc between this, which we shall call the secondary distance, and the radical or primary position of Mars, *i.e.*, its M.D. The difference gives the arc of direction.

Converse directions have a slightly different formula, but only apparently so, for in these converse directions the luminary's semi-arc occupies the third term of proportion. In other words, the third term is the semi-arc of the moved or directed planet, be they converse or direct directions.

EXAMPLE 2.—*Direct* ☉ *to the parallel of* ♄, *converse, in* mundo.

As semi-arc ♄	120° 5′	*prop. log.*	9·824 21	(*a.c.*)
Is to M.D. ♄	74°16′	,, ,,	384 48	
So is S.A. ☉	72°54′	,, ,,	392 54	
To secondary dist. of ☉, 45° 5′			601 23	
Primary dist. of ☉ from *nadir*			61° 32′	
Secondary dist. of ☉			45 5	
Arc of direction, ☉ par. ♄ *conv. mundo*			16 27	

Notes :—(1) This being a "converse" direction, the luminary is moved on until it stands in the same relation to the *Imum cœli*, from which the calculation is made (it being formed below the earth), as ♄ radically posited does. Computation, of course, may be made from the upper meridian with the same results, but there would be no gain in doing this, and only a more cumbrous method of working.

(2) When a parallel will also be the conjunction or opposition of the bodies it need not be calculated, for the arc will be the same as the aforesaid aspect, presumed already to have been obtained.

Rapt Parallels.

In these the radical places of the planèts are not taken into account with reference to the completed aspect, as in the parallels before dealt with ; for the places are supposed to be carried on by the "rapt" motion of the earth* (or, according to the ancient astrologers, by what they termed the *primum mobile*), in such wise that when a certain number of degrees of right ascension has passed over the meridian, the two planets will arrive, should they be agreeably posited at birth to justify the event within the ordinary lifetime, at equal distances from the meridian angles.

Rapt Parallels entirely differ from the foregoing Mundane Parallels, inasmuch as while in these latter the planet directed to remains immovable in the horary circle of position, the *directed* planet bearing eventually a relationship thereto, in the former, *i.e.*, "rapt" parallels, the places of *both* are carried forward, and thenceforth in computation bear no direct relation to the radical *loci*.

General rule : Add together S.A.'s of planets for first term, and take the differences of R.A.'s for third term, while for the second term use the S.A. of directed planet, which will always be the one approaching zenith or nadir when aspect is complete : the result is the secondary distance of directed body. For the Arc of Direction, the difference between this and its primary distance must be found.

Example 1.—*Direct* ☽ *to the Rapt Parallel of* ♂ .

Semi-arc	☽	94° 25'		R.A.	☽	181° 23'
" "	♂	113 41		R.A.	♂	142 45
		2) 208 6				2) 38 38
½ sum		104 3		½ diff.		19 19

* Lat. *raptus*, carried away.

As ½ sum of semi-arcs	104° 3′	*prop. log.*	9·761 97 (*a.c.*)
Is to ½ ☽'s S.A.	47 12	" "	581 33
So is ½ diff. of R.A.'s	19 19	" "	969 34
To ½ secondary dist. ☽	8 46 × 2		1·312 64
Secondary dist. ☽	17 32		
Primary dist. of ☽			31° 33′
Secondary dist. of ☽			17 32
Arc of direction, ☽ to Rapt Parallel ♂			14 1

Notes.—(1) As this problem generally provides bulky numbers, it is better, as well for correctness as for ease, to work with ½ or even less of the amounts,—remembering however to increase the proportional part of secondary distance, when obtained, by so many aliquot parts as have been worked with.

(2) In some instances the two bodies will be located in opposite hemispheres, and in such case the *opposite* place of the one which will be receding from the M.C. or I.C. on formation must be taken, for in these directions the arcs must be of the same denomination. This procedure will only necessitate 180° being added to (or subtracted from) its right ascension, the semi-arc remaining as before.

EXAMPLE 2.—*Direct* ☉ *to the Rapt Parallel of* ♄.

Semi-arc ☉	72° 54′	R.A. ☉+360°	391° 23′
" " ♄	120 5	R.A. ♄	255 34
	2) 192 59		2) 135 49
½ sum	96 30	½ diff.	67 54

As ½ sum of semi-arcs	96° 30′	*prop. log.*	9·729 25 (*a.c.*)
Is to ½ ☉'s S.A.	36 27	" "	693 58
So is ½ diff. R.A.'s	67 54	" "	423 40
To ½ secondary dist. ☉	25 39 × 2		846 23
Whole secondary dist.	51 18		
Primary dist. of ☉			61° 32′
Secondary dist. of ☉			51 18
Arc of direction, ☉ to Rapt Parallel ♄			10 14

With these Rapt Parallels I conclude the practical portion of Mundane Direction; the problems given being quite sufficient to exhibit the method of bringing up all the principal arcs of that nature in whatever nativity. Those difficulties which may appear at first sight will lessen under a little application; and the more of the latter there is, the quicker and more certain will be the results obtained.

SECTION II.

DIRECTIONS *in zodiaco*.

We come now to an entirely new set of arcs, denominated zodiacal, since instead of being formed by the mundane motion of the earth, they are *apparently* constituted by the proper motion of the various bodies through the belt of space in which they move: in reality, however, it is not so, as the student will soon see for himself. They are of several kinds, *viz.* :—M.C. and Ascendant (direct and converse); planets to ascending and culminating degrees, and to Sun and Moon (direct and converse); etc., etc.

As in the mundane group, we shall find it best to commence by bringing up all arcs to the M.C. and ascendant and then to follow them up among the various planetary bodies. And in doing so the student must observe that he cannot proceed with an assumption of extracting one arc from another previously obtained. Each arc will have its separate problem, which must be worked out *in toto*, for he cannot here use the proportional parts of the semi-arcs. Yet although doubtless zodiacal directing will present greater initial difficulties than mundane, these will not be found insuperable by any means.

THE MID-HEAVEN (*direct and converse*).

Commencing as we did in the former section, we require to direct a planet to an aspect of the M.C. The matter is a very simple one: the difference between the R.A. of the M.C. and that of the place of aspect (taken without latitude) is the required arc.

In considering *Direct Zodiacal Directions*, whether the planet is on the eastern or western side of the M.C., on the mid-heaven itself the degrees must advance in regular conformity. For instance, take the M.C. to ☌ ♅. Here when the twenty-seventh degree of Cancer (or, to be more correct, ♋ 26°38′) arrives on the M.C. the conjunction is formed; but had ♅ been on the other side of cusp it could not have been so,—except by *converse* motion.

EXAMPLE MAP: No. 2.

NATA 3*hrs.*, 51*min.* 42*sec.*, *a.m.*, G. M. T., *October* 27*th*, 1870; *Lat.* 52°28′N., *Long.* 0°7′W.*

R.A.M.C. 93°7′.

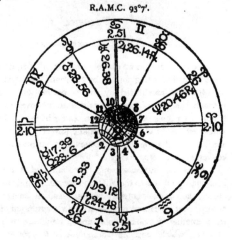

R.A.I.C. 273°7′.

SPECULUM.

	Lat.	Dec.	R.A.	M.D.	S.A.	H.A.
	° ′	° ′	° ′	° ′	° ′	° ′
☉	0 0	12 44S	211 17	61 50	107 6	45 16
☽	2 45N	18 57S	247 56	25 11	116 33	91 22
☿	2 4N	5 3S	197 2	76 5	96 36	20 31
♀	1 19N	7 43S	201 50	71 17	100 11	28 54
♂	1 33N	13 19N	151 37	58 30	107 31	49 1
♃	0 33S	22 50N	85 53	7 14	143 14	116 0
♄	0 56N	22 26S	264 18	8 49	122 30	113 41
♅	0 29N	21 20N	118 45	25 38	120 33	94 55
♆†	1 43S	6 31N	19 51	73 16	98 33	25 17

* This diagram was originally printed with M.C. ♋2°45′ and Asc. ♎2°13′, which figures are used in the calculations that follow.

† See Map 1, footnote.

EXAMPLE 1.— *Direct M.C. to ☌ ♅ d.d. zod.*

The conjunction falls in ♋26°38', the right ascension of which, *without latitude*, is 118°39'. Thus, according to the rule before stated, we find

R.A. of place of ☌, ♋26°38'	118°	39'
R.A. M.C.	93	7
Arc of direction, M.C. ☌ ♅ d.d. zod.	25	32

Notes :—(1) *Direct* motion in zodiacal arcs implies that which follows in the order of the signs, while *converse* motion is zodiacal retrogression.

(2) In the case above, the twenty-seventh degree of Cancer actually arrives in the M.C. by direct *mundane* motion ; for it is foolish to suppose that the M.C. proceeds backwards degree by degree until it reaches the radical place of Uranus : yet every portion of the intercepted arc between such planet and the M.C. must have travelled over the latter before the former operates its conjunction.

The next example will be sufficient in this department.

EXAMPLE 2.—*Required the arc of M.C. to the square aspect of Neptune d.d. zod.*

The square falls in ♋20°46', the R.A. of which is 112°26'.

R.A. of place of aspect, ♋20°46'	112°	26'
R.A. M.C.	93	7
Arc of direction, M.C. □ ♆ d.d. zod.	19	19

Notes :—(1) Here, instead of applying to the bodily impact from a position east of the tenth house cusp, it completes an arc of 90° by mundane recession therefrom. When the twenty-first degree of Cancer arrives on the M.C. 19°19' will have been passed over, or, in other words, that is the measure of R.A. requisite to complete the square aspect approaching at birth.

(2) Parallels may be computed in dentical fashion by taking the R.A. of the nearest point of the zodiac which possesses the same declination as the planet concerned in the direction, and working exactly as before.

Converse Zodiacal Directions are the reverse of the forgoing, they being formed by an apparent retrograde motion in the zodiac, or, considering all arcs without distinction as being formed by the diurnal motion—as, in point of fact, they actually *are*—then by the opposite of this, *i.e.*, by such a revolution of the earth as would necessarily present us with the Sun rising in the west and setting in the east. For instance, Jupiter in Map No. 3 has passed the meridian, and as in these directions it is the

M.C. itself and not the planet which is supposed to be the directed point, consequently it must move to the planet. In reality it does no such thing.

The practical procedure is exactly as before (direct directions), *i.e.*, the difference between the R.A.'s of the two places gives the arc, with the exception of course that the R.A.M.C. will always form the *minuend* and the R.A. of the place of aspect the *subtrahend*, instead of the contrary, as in direct motion.

EXAMPLE 2.—*Required the arc of M.C.* ♂ ♃ *by converse motion in zodiac.*
The conjunction falls in ♊ 26°14′, the R.A. of which is 85°53′.

R.A. M.C.	93°	7′
R.A. ♊ 26°14′	85	53
Arc of direction, M.C. ♂ ♃ conv. zod.	7	14

EXAMPLE 2.—*What is the arc of M.C.* ✳ ♆ *conv. zod. ?*
The sextile falls in ♊ 20°46′, the R.A. of which is 79°55′.

R.A. M.C.	93°	7′
R.A. ♊ 20°46′	79	55
Arc of direction, M.C. ✳ ♆ conv. zod.	13	12

Notes—(1) The lessening R.A. by the retrograde motion will naturally increase the arc because it represents degrees that have passed the meridian at more or less remote times *previous to birth*. In short, these converse directions are " pre-natal," as a moment's consideration will show, and the above illustrations ought to make this clear. If in the latter example the student supposes ♊ 20°46′ to possess the M.C., then the place of Neptune will be in sextile thereto.

THE ASCENDANT (*direct and converse*).

Zodiacal directions to the ascendant will take longer to compute than those to the M.C., the procedure being more involved, and offering greater opportunities for errors to creep in. They are all calculated by *oblique* ascension (in contradistinction to the meridian ones, in which we invariably apply *right* ascension), the arc being the difference between the O.A. of the aspect and the O.A. of the ascendant.

The latter is found by adding 90° to the R.A. of the M.C., and the method of obtaining the former is shown below.

EXAMPLE 1.—*Required the arc of ascendant to* ☌ ♀ *by direct direction in zodiac.*

The conjunction falls in ♎23°6', the R.A. of which is 201°22' and the declination 8°59'S. The ascensional difference being that between the oblique and right ascensions it will be found by adding the log. *tangent* of the latitude of birthplace to the log. *tangent* of the declination of aspect, the result being the log. *sine* of ascensional difference:

Latitude of place of birth 52°28'	log. tan.	10·114 4965
Declin. 8°59'	„ „	9·198 8941
Ascens. diff. 11°53'	„ sine	9·313 3906

This added to the R.A. of place of aspect will give the corresponding oblique ascension. Note that when the dec. is N., the A.D. must be *subtracted*; when S., as in the present instance, *added*: that is, for places in the Northern Hemisphere, such as the example we are considering. In the Southern Hemisphere, as has been explained before, this rule must be reversed.

R.A. of ♎26°6'	201° 22'
Ascens. diff.	11 53
Oblique ascens. of ☌	213 15

We have now the element primarily sought, for by the simple process of subtraction between this and the oblique ascension of ascendant the desired arc comes to light thus:

Oblique ascens. of ☌	213° 15'
Oblique ascens. Ascendt. (R.A. M.C.+90°)	183 7
Arc of direction, Ascendt. ☌ ♀ *d.d. zod.*	30 8

The next example is worked out below, so that the process can be seen at a glance.

EXAMPLE 2.—*It is required to direct the Ascendant to an* ☍ *of* ♅ *by direct motion in the zodiac.*

The opposition falls in ♎20°46', the R.A. of which is 199°12' and the declination 8°6'S.

Lat. of birthplace	log. tan.	10·114 4965
Declin. 8°6'	„ „	9·153 2692
Ascens. diff. 10°40'	„ sine	9·267 7657
R.A. of ♎20°46'		199° 12'
Ascens. diff. (*add*, declin. being South)		10 40
Oblique ascension of ☍		209 52
Oblique ascension of ☍		209 52
Oblique ascension of Ascendant		183 7
Arc of direction, Ascendt. ☍ ♅ *d.d. zod.*		26 45

♎

Notes—(1) Particular attention should be paid to the quality of the declination, *i.e.*, whether north or south, so that it may be known whether the A.D. and the R.A. must be added or subtracted. A "slip" is easily made here, and occasions in most cases an inequality in results.

Converse directions exhibit no fresh difficulty. They are made in the backward order of signs as those to the M.C. were, but are calculated just as were the direct ones,—with the exception of a transposition of *minuend* and *subtrahend* in the concluding process between the two oblique ascensions, that of the ascendant forming the *minuend* as being the greatest number.

EXAMPLE 1.—*Required the arc of Ascendant to the zodiacal parallel of Neptune by converse motion.*

The parallel falls in ♍13°26′, where the declination is 6°31′N. and the R.A. 164°44′. Then:

Lat. birthplace	*log. tan.*	10·114 4965
Declin. 6°31′	" "	9·057 7813
Ascens. diff. 8°33′	" *sine*	9·172 2778
R.A. ♍13°26′		164° 44′
Ascens. diff.		8 33
Oblique ascension of parallel		156 11
Oblique ascension of Ascendant		183 7
the difference between which gives Arc of direction. Asc. par. dec. ♆ *conv. zod.*		26 56

EXAMPLE 2.—*Ascendt. to ☐ ♄, conv. zod.*

The square aspect falls in ♍24°48′, where the declination is 2°5′N., and the R.A. 175°16′.

Lat. of birthplace	*log. tan.*	10·114 4965
Declin. 2°5′	" "	8·560 8276
Ascens. diff. 2°43′	" *sine*	8·675 3241
R.A. of aspect		175° 16′
Ascens. diff.		2 43
Oblique ascension of aspect		172 33
Oblique ascension of Ascendant		183 7
the difference between which gives Arc of direction, Asc. ☐ ♄ *conv. zod.*		10 34

DIRECT DIRECTIONS OF SUN AND MOON.

We are now prepared to enter upon the computation of directions to the luminaries, and a reference at this stage to that portion of this chapter which dealt with the equivalent mundane series will not be amiss. (*See p.* 229.)

The terms *direct* and *converse* had there quite a different meaning, and it is no doubt owing to the confusion which this double import of terms occasions, that students fail in their earlier attempts to grapple with the theory or practice of Primary Directing.

It is well constantly to bear in mind that Direct Motion *in the zodiac* is in the natural order of the signs from ♈ to ♉, etc., while *mundane* Direct Motion is that diurnal movement which results in an apparent track made by a heavenly body from east to west.

In this latter form, however, the Luminaries must be considered as *fixed*; otherwise, arcs are said to be "converse."

Direct zodiacal arcs of the Sun and Moon are more akin, in one sense, to "secondary" directions proper, and frequently in the case of the inferior planets they agree with them very closely as to time.

Upon examining Map 2 (*see page* 238) we find Uranus in ♋26°38′, and the Sun in ♍3°33′. It is evident that before the trine aspect can be formed the luminary must traverse a certain number of intervening degrees between its radical position and ♍26°38′, and so if we wish to find when such an aspect will operate, the process must be arranged accordingly, *i.e.*, so that the result may furnish such degrees.

Therefore the general rule is : (1) to find the place of aspect, its declination, R.A., M.D. and semi-arc; (2) to work by logarithmic proportion the formula : AS *S.A. of Sun or Moon* IS TO *M.D. of the same*, so IS *S.A. of aspect to second distance of aspect*; (3) to take the sum or difference of primary and secondary distance, and this will give the required arc.

N.B.—If either luminary crosses the upper or lower meridian to form the aspect, then the two distances must be *added* together; otherwise, *subtract*.

EXAMPLE 1.—*To direct* ⊙ *to* △ *of* ♅ *by direct motion in zodiac.*

The trine aspect falls in ♍26°38′, the declination of which point is 19°26′S., the R.A. 234°18′, the semi-arc 117°21′, and the M.D. 38°49′.

As semi-arc ☉,	107°6'	prop. log.	9·774 52 (a.c.)
Is to M.D. ☉,	61°50'	" "	464 05
So is semi-arc of aspect,	117°21'		185 79
To secondary dist. of aspect,	67°45'		424 36
Secondary dist. of aspect			67° 45'
M.D., or primary dist. of aspect			38 49
Arc of direction, ☉ △ ♅ d.d. zod.			28 56

Notes.—(1) Primary and secondary distances must be taken from the same angle. The luminary not having to cross the I.C. to form the requisite aspect the two distances are subtracted.

(2) Remember also that, in working proportion by the aid of logarithms, the first term must be the *arith. comp.*, ascertained as previously shown by subtracting the prop. log. from an integer.

EXAMPLE 2.—*Direct* ☉ *to* ♂ ☽ *d.d. zod.*

This aspect falls in ♐ 9°12', the declination of which point is 21°50', the R.A. 247°30', and the S.A. 121°26'

As semi-arc ☉	107° 6'	prop. log.	9·774 52 (a.c.)
Is to M.D. ☽	25°11'	" "	464 05
So is semi-arc of aspect	121°26'	" "	170 93
To secondary dist. of aspect, 70°6'			409 50
Secondary dist. of aspect			70° 6'
Primary dist. of aspect			25 37
Arc of direction, ☉ ♂ ☽ d.d. zod.			44 29

In directing the Moon, the process followed is exactly similar, and as an illustration of lunar directing *sine latitudine* we will take this :

EXAMPLE 3.—*Direct* ☽ *to the square of* ♆ *by d.d. in zodiac.*

The square aspect falls in ♑ 20°46', the declination of this point being 21°42', the R.A. 292°27', the S.A. 121°12', and the M.D. 19°20'.

As semi-arc ☽	116°33'	prop. log.	9·811 24 (a.c.)
Is to M.D. ☽	25°11'	" "	854 16
So is semi-arc of aspect	121°12'	" "	171 77
To secondary dist. of aspect, 26°11'			837 17
Secondary dist. of aspect			26° 11'
Primary dist. of aspect			19 20
Arc of direction, ☽ □ ♆ d.d. zod.			45 31

Notes.—(1) In this case the moon has crossed the lower meridian to form the square, consequently the two distances have been added together to arrive at the resulting arc. In all other respects the procedure has not differed from the previous examples.

(2) Zodiacal parallels of declination between the luminaries and the planets, and aspects to the ascending or culminating degree of a geniture may be computed in like fashion.

One example of the latter may be useful.

EXAMPLE 4.—*Direct* ☽ *to a square of ascending degree d.d. zod.*

The aspect falls in ♑ 2°13′, the declination of which point is 23°27′, the R.A. 272°24′, S.A. 124°23′, M.D. 0°43′.

		prop. log.	
As semi-arc ☽	116°33′	9·811 24 (*a.c.*)
Is to M.D. ☽	25°11′	„ „ 854 16
So is semi-arc of aspect	124°23′	„ „ 160 51
To secondary dist. of aspect, 26°52′		825 91
Secondary dist. of aspect		26° 52′
M.D. of aspect		0 43
Arc of direction, ☽ □ ascending deg. *d.d. zod.*		26 9

N.B.—In tabulating any such directions, be careful to use the term "ascending degree" and not "ascendant," since in this connection the terms have different meanings, as a little thought will show. The Ascendant is a point in mundane square to the M.C.; the Ascending Degree is the point of the Ecliptic (Zodiac) which has that relationship at the moment of birth. But we are here concerned with it as a zodiacal point pure and simple, without regard to its mundane significance at birth.

In the case of the Moon, nearly all the old authors advise taking into account the latitude of the place of aspect.* To the elements necessary to be extracted from the place of an aspect, as tabulated at the head of the previous example, he will of course add the latitude, which moreover must be taken into account when determining the R.A. of the point.

With these few illustrations there should be no difficulty in calculating similar ones in any other part of the horoscope, if the student will study them well and be sure of each step he takes.

* See Chapter III., p. 251, however, where the advisability of this is discussed.

CONVERSE DIRECTIONS OF SUN AND MOON.

These are made backwards in the zodiac, and to all intents and purposes are "pre-natal." I find them so little operative by themselves as to be scarcely worth the trouble entailed in their calculation. As, however, they find favour in some quarters I shall present a few problems.

The process is a reversed one to that of direct directing. We get the same elements in the first instance, but the formula for the rule-of-three to be performed is :—AS *S.A. of aspect* IS TO *M.D. of aspect*, so is *S.A. Sun (or Moon)* TO *the secondary distance of Sun (or Moon)*. Then subtract (or add), as before, the two distances of whichever luminary happens to be involved.

EXAMPLE 1.—*Direct ☉ to ☌ ♀ by converse motion in zodiac.*

The conjunction falls in ♎23° 6', the declination of which is 8°59', the R.A. 201°22', the semi-arc 101°53', and the M.D. 71°45'.

As semi-arc aspect	*prop. log.*	9·752 83 (*a.c.*)
Is to M.D. aspect	" "	399 45
So is semi-arc of ☉	" "	225 48
To secondary dist. of ☉, 75°26'		377 76
Secondary dist. of ☉		75° 26'
M.D. ☉		61 50
Arc of direction, ☉ ☌ ♀ *conv. zod.*		13 36

EXAMPLE 2.—*Direct ☉ to ✶ ☽ conv. zod.*

The ✶ falls in ♎9°12', the declination of which is 3°39', the R.A. 188°28', the semi-arc 94°46', and the M.D. 84°39'.

As semi-arc aspect	*prop. log.*	9·721 38 (*a.c.*)
Is to M.D. aspect	" "	327 65
So is semi-arc of ☉	" "	225 48
To secondary dist. of ☉, 95°40'		274 51
Secondary dist. of ☉		95° 40'
M.D. ☉		61 50
Arc of direction, ☉ ✶ ☽ *conv. zod.*		33 50

Lunar converse directions follow the same rule, as also do converse arcs of planets to degree on ascendant or M.C.

EXAMPLE 3.—*Direct ☽ to ☐ of ♂ conv. zod.*

The square aspect falls in ♏28°56', the declination being 19°56', the R.A. 236°41', the S.A. 118°10', and the M.D. 36°26'.

	prop. log.	
As semi-arc aspect		9·817 22 (*a.c.*)
Is to M.D. aspect	,, ,,	693 77
So is semi-arc of ☽	,, ,,	188 76
To Secondary dist of ☽, 35°56′		699 75
Secondary dist. of ☽		35° 56′
M.D. ☽		25 11
Arc of direction, ☽ □ ♂ *conv. zod.*		10 45

EXAMPLE 4.—*Direct Uranus to a square of the ascending degree by converse motion in the zodiac.*

The □ falls in ♋2°13′, the declination of which is 23°27′, the R.A. 92°25′, the S.A. 124°23′, and the M.D. 0°42′.

	prop. log.	
As semi-arc aspect		9·839 49 (*a.c.*)
Is to M.D. aspect	,, ,,	2·410 17
So is semi-arc ♅	,, ,,	174 11
To secondary dist. of ♅, 0°41′		2·423 77
Secondary dist. of ♅		0 41
M.D. ♅		25° 38′
Arc of direction, Asc. □ ♅ *conv. zod.*		26 19

There is one point which needs emphasising, and that is, to be sure to take the proper semi-arc of the directed planet, for there may be a change from nocturnal to diurnal in computing an aspect, by reason of the passage of a body to a position above the horizon, or the change may be the other way about, from a point in elevation to a station *sub-horoscopic*, intimating also one from the diurnal to the nocturnal semi-arc.

CHAPTER III.

NOTES ON SOME THEORETICAL POINTS.

MUNDANE *versus* ZODIACAL DIRECTIONS.

IT will have been seen from the foregoing chapter that because zodiacal and mundane directions are made in two different circles, and by two different motions, the luminaries meet all bodies that have latitude twice. For, in the first case, by motion forwards through the ecliptic all stars' rays are encountered in that pathway without latitude; whereas in the latter, the significator is supposed to remain fixed in its hour circle meeting rays by the diurnal motion of the earth.

According to Ptolemy, the prorogator ought never to be directed except to the west angle, " for," as Wilson says,* " according to the actinobolia, the prorogatory place is that point of the horary circle in which the prorogator is found at the moment of birth, which always retains the same relative position to the meridian and equator. It is consequently immovable and exposed to the bodies or rays of promittors, whether good or evil, as they arrive by mundane converse motion."

This is the reason that the latter form of directing is so powerful, and should obtain attentive consideration ; but it must be borne in mind that the mundane circle is referred to, and *not* the zodiacal one; for in the latter, as reiterated before, direct motion, or motion *in consequentia*† in the zodiacal series is the most powerful, that *in antecedentia*‡ being decidedly weak.

Ptolemy describes both mundane and zodiacal aspects, although the invention of the former is generally imputed to Placidus, as, for instance,

---

* *Tetrabiblos*, by James Wilson. Preface, page v.
† According to signs ♈ to ♉, etc.; the actinobolium of Ptolemy.
‡ Retrogression, converse motion, ♉ to ♈, etc.

in Lib. III., cap. xiv., where he describes the method of bringing up the following to the preceding places, or, in other words, a converse or direct mundane direction, the places being the fixed ones of the horary circle. And Wilson, in an appended note, even goes so far as to state his opinion that there is no zodiacal direction in the whole quadripartite, and that the system of application and separation is entirely mundane; with which I am in great measure inclined to concur.

In Lib. III., cap. xii., other proof occurs, for it is stated that the ascendant and eleventh house are in sextile, the ascendant and M.C. in quartile, the ascendant and ninth house in trine, and the ascendant and western angle in opposition. And in the *Syntaxis Megistis*, known to the Arabians as Al Magest, a work treating wholly of astronomy, it appears quite evident that Ptolemy was acquainted with and taught aspects in the world as well as in the zodiac. He speaks, too, in the *Tetrabiblos*, of a sextile of the Sun and Venus, from which also it may be inferred that a mundane aspect is intended.

From these and various other passages scattered throughout his works, it is, I think, conclusively shown that both systems were understood; and as Placidus himself admits this, it appears futile for aspects *in munde* to be relegated solely in the first instance to the disciple.

In respect to mundane and rapt parallels, however, Ptolemy does not seem to be very much enlightened, and perhaps Placidus may justly claim the honour of introducing them at any rate.

By mundane motion each temporal house obtains its value solely from a proportional part of a star's semi-arc, which must always be a third, either nocturnal or diurnal, as has been shown before; and as in spherical trigonometry* every section of a sphere made by a plane is a circle, it follows that these mundane houses are constituted by a series of great circles† above planes which cut the sphere of the heavens and form the boundaries of the several houses. It is well thoroughly to understand this and other things connected with the sphere, as such

---

* Let ABCD be a sphere, of which the centre is O; AFCG the curve in which a plane cutting the sphere intersects its surface; OE a perpendicular from O upon the cutting plane. Join E with F, any point in AFCG, and join FO. Then since OE is perpendicular to the cutting plane, it is perpendicular to EF, a line in that plane. ∴ E F = √ (O F² – O E²) const. Now E is a fixed point in the cutting plane and F is any point in the curve AFC. Therefore AFC is a circle whose centre is E and radius E F.

† *I.e.*, those which pass through the centre of the sphere, in contradistinction to those which do not, and which are denominated *small circles*.

knowledge will advance one greatly in the study of primary directing, and a course of trigonometry is easily obtainable and to be desired.

Mundane motion being caused by the diurnal rotation of the earth from West to East, which is completed in the twenty-four hours and is responsible for the alternating effects of day and night, it follows that *it is uniform*, so that when one direction is given others are easily deduced therefrom by a proper use of the aliquot parts of the semi-arc. Whereas in zodiacal motion *pure and simple* the appulse may be interrupted by retrogression,* stationary attitude, or slow motion; or may be quickened by the adoption of a higher rate of progress than the mean. So that, taking these things amongst others† into consideration, zodiacal arcs obtained in the usual manner appear artificial as contrasted with the natural and regular motion which is responsible for the mundane ones; and the only conclusion one can arrive at is that ALL primary arcs are *mundane*, and determined solely by the rotation of the earth.

This appears also to be the decision of Mr. Pearce, and some few years ago he cited in a letter to the since defunct *Fate and Fortune* several instances, and further commented on the matter in his own paper *Urania*.

"In 1860,"‡ he writes, "when computing my own nativity, in which the Sun was above the eastern horizon and Mercury was just below it, I found that in directing the Sun to conjunction with Mercury in the zodiac I had to take the diurnal semi-arc of the place of Mercury; and this led me to conclude that all directions are formed by the rotation of the earth, and that those termed zodiacal for the purpose of classification are really mundane."

So that in point of fact instead of Sun descending into the first house, as it would by zodiacal motion, to form the conjunction, Mercury itself rose above the eastern horizon to the place of the luminary.

It appears from this then—merely a representative and not an isolated fact—that the only pure zodiacal directions are those formed by "secondary motion" after birth, and that practically all primary arcs are mundane, inasmuch as when computing direct directions *in zodiaco* it is

* Both in the number of degrees passed over and in the time occupied by the motion in zodiac the eastward direct motion always exceeds the retrograde. The excess is smallest in the case of the remoter planets, *viz.*, from 3° to 10°; in the case of the nearer ones, as Mars and Venus, it is from 16° to 18°.

† In such cases, too, where a planet is directed zodiacally, for it is evident that in the nativity (No. 2) for example ♄ could never by its own direct zodiacal motion form a sextile with the radical place of the Sun during the native's life-time.

‡ *Fate and Fortune*, August, 1890, p. 61.

not in reality the luminary which is directed but the place of the aspect.

Therefore, when directing the Moon, the latter should be taken without latitude and not otherwise, as is generally advised, and as laid down in the *Text Book*—to which doctrine, however, I believe the author of that work himself no longer subscribes.

It is stated by Placidus in the 6oth segment *et seq.* of his *Elementary Philosophy* that angles cannot be conversely directed, that they only receive rays in the world, but not parallels or rays in the zodiac; and that the other significators by a direct motion receive the rays and parallels both in the zodiac and in the world; but by a converse motion the rays only and parallels in the world, and by no means in the zodiac. Ptolemy himself denied the efficacy of zodiacal directions to angles, but Wilson disagrees.

When Simmonite* was directing the nativity of the Queen he brought Mercury, Mars and the similar positions to the cusp of the ascendant and added a note in explanation of this procedure, which he supposed would be objected to by some professors. He remaked that he found such positions to have a very powerful effect and therefore he unhesitatingly adopted them.

PRE-NATAL DIRECTIONS.

As a matter of fact, converse directions to angles are formed before birth; that is, they are pre-natal. If, as Mr. H. S. Green has shown, Pre-natal Secondary Directions† are powerful factors in producing events, it will not be unwise to look upon Primary Pre-natal ones in this light; and indeed, their effects fully warrant it.

PARALLELS.

There is one point to be regarded in computing parallels, and that is, that their effects generally precede their formation, owing, as Placidus thinks, to the magnitude of the luminaries by which their bodies are affected before they are completed centre to centre. This may or may not be the case, but it is a matter which is more or less attributable to aspects which are *not* parallels. For greater accuracy a small equation might be used if it were thought worth while, but it need not concern us here in taking a broad view of the subject.

* See his *Arcana of Astral Philosophy.*

† [NOTE.—These are practically the *a, b, c,* figures described in Appendix I.—ED]

INFANT MORTALITY AND DIRECTIONS

In children who do not survive infancy it is very usual to find no source of manifestation in Secondary Directions, although many times such a configuration will occur; but by far the most satisfactory and luminous in these cases of infantile mortality are undoubtedly Primary Arcs.

We hear of children being " killed by position." It will be well to enquire what the term " killed by position " means. Simply it is this, a child may at its nativity have a conjunction of Saturn and the Sun; it does not follow however that we take this to mean that both heavenly bodies hold the same degree and minute in the same sign of the zodiac, for they may merely be in that orb, say four degrees apart, so that by taking a degree for a year, roughly, the aspect would not be complete until about four years of age, before which time however, other things concurring and conducing thereto, the child might die, there being no perspicuous operative direction complete at the time. It is easily seen that this, the anaretic arc, is nothing more nor less than a gradual planetary appulse from partial to complete, or, as it is technically termed, ' platic' to ' partile' conjunction; the said arc being the distance the two bodies stand originally from each other, which equated should point out the period of death, although it is possible that the child may be born with such a low vitality that before the full power of the major arc is completely exerted by a close conjunction, death may ensue—yet even then, not, I am disposed to think, without *some* minor direction being formed.

But in the majority of cases it will be found that these early arcs act very closely to time, frequently receiving the most startling fulfilment, such as would incline one to believe in a fate as rigid, cruel and uncompromising as ever was meted out by the triune Parcæ.

THE HYLEG

No mention has yet been made of the *Hyleg*, or life-giver, which makes a point of considerable distinction between certain contending schools of natal astrology, but an impartial glance may be taken at the subject as there seems to arise a fitting opportunity here.

In early works upon Astrology the determination of the hyleg consequent upon an evident confusion and ignorance on the part of the writers, appears an almost inextricable point, it being mixed up with the Part of Fortune, the Ascendant, dispositors, etc. Later the matter has undergone some amount of purging, but even now there is so strong a savour of artificiality connected with it that a great number of students ignore and a still larger number look askance upon the rules bequeathed by predecessors for the selection of the 'apheta' or giver of life, and prefer to follow the hermetic views in relation thereto. I do not for one moment question that the *Pars Fortuna* may contain more verity and reason for its existence than are recognised at the present hour, but for myself I draw the line when it comes to its selection or constitution as hyleg.

The ordinary method used to distinguish this latter now is as follows :—

The Sun, Moon, and Ascendant *only* can be hyleg, and under the following conditions. (1) The luminary must occupy one of the hylegiacal or prorogatory places; these are the whole of the first, tenth, seventh and ninth houses, and the half of the eleventh nearest the mid-heaven : in each case an orb of five degrees is taken into the reckoning, (computed by oblique ascension); so that the first house limits would be from five degrees above the cusp of ascendant to twenty-five below, and the western angle from five degrees *below* to twenty-five *above*. The remaining houses, other than those previously mentioned, can never be occupied by the hyleg. Then the luminary which possesses any part of these divisions of the horoscope is accounted the true prorogator, and as such is directed. (2) If both luminaries are discovered in hylegiacal places either the Sun is chosen or the luminary aphetically strongest by accident. (3) If neither luminary hold such position then the office falls upon the ascendant.

Now as, according to Ptolemy, the ascendant cannot meet aspects in the zodiac, and as Placidus further states that even mundane aspects (not parallels) can only be received by *direct* motion, it frequently happens that under such restrictions few directions can be formed by the ascendant, and if it chanced to be hyleg an ordinary lifetime might not provide affliction sufficient to cause or account for death. Unfortunately, these tabooed conditions do take effect, and it is senseless to ignore them.

Experience shows that there is much verity in the *apheta* chosen according to the foregoing rules, although the system does not appeal greatly to one's reason; yet on the other hand it is useless attempting to deny that it is not so trustworthy as generally advertised. I have

nativities in which their owners have died without the hyleg being
afflicted in any way, and Ebn Shemaya also cites an example.*

THE SUN THE TRUE SOURCE OF ALL LIFE.

Solar energy, will, vital force, I take to be emanations from the
photosphere of the Sun, and life, from the lowliest to the most complex,
to proceed thence and thence alone. It signifies nothing in respect to the
sex in which it happens to reside, for the real life-principle is not sexed.
In feminine horoscopes the Moon has, of course, an influence in excess
of its dominion in male genitures, because of the rule it bears over
functional matters; but this does not justify us in considering it as
apheta.

It requires small power of comprehension to grasp the idea that if
life proceeds from the solar orb and from it alone, it must be literally and
naturally " giver of life."

---

* *The Star*, p. 207, 1839 edition.

CHAPTER IV.

PARALLAXIS et distantia stellarum fixarum, non potest certa et evidenti observatione humanitus.—RICCIOLI.

THE parallax of a heavenly body is the angle between the directions of two lines drawn to it, the one from the observer, the other from the centre of the earth. Reference to the diagrams will make all perfectly clear and plain.

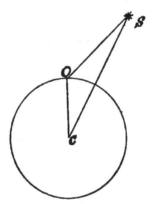

FIG. II.

In this, S is some star, O is the observer, and C the centre of the earth. Then the angle O S C is the parallax for the observer at O.

It is self-evident that the larger the body from which another is viewed, and the nearer the body under inspection, the greater will be the parallactic angle O S C; and the smaller the globe from which another is viewed, and the farther the distance of the orb in question, the more minute and inappreciable will it be. It likewise follows that it will be at its maximum when a star is on the horizon, and absolutely nil when in mid-heaven. From this it is seen that different mundane positions will cause differences in the amount of parallax, which would necessitate varying factors in the calculation of any heavenly body, unless some definite point were decided upon to which all others may be referred. Such *is* the case, for astronomical positions are calculated to the *centre* of earth.

If the child at birth is supposed to be the centre (O) of all extra-mundane.force, and aspects are calculated, notwithstanding, to the centre of our sphere, (C), a discrepancy must arise, and this discrepancy calls for consideration, amendment, and an equation.

This will introduce also the division of the mundane circle into houses, to do which it is very necessary to know from which point they must take their rise, from the observer's superficial and tentative position, or from the mathematical centre of the globe.

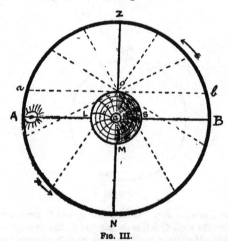

Fig. III.

We shall be told at once that man is, for all purposes, the focus of planetary influence in regard to the horoscope, and this, whether he be situated at the poles, at the equator, or elsewhere; and as he cannot dispose himself centrically he need not trouble about such centre, which is evidently not for him.

There are, then, two horizons, the plane of one passing through the eye of the observer, and called the *sensible*, and the plane of the other passing through the centre of the earth parallel to the sensible plane, and called the *rational* horizon.

Now, as the diameter of the earth is roughly about 8,000 miles, it follows that these two planes cut the sky at a distance of 4,000 miles apart, and are extended illimitably into space. They are parallel to each other, and parallel lines and planes, however far they are extended, never meet; but we are told that "on the infinitely distant surface of the celestial sphere, the two traces sensibly coalesce into one single great circle, which is the horizon as first defined. In strictness, therefore, while we can distinguish between the two horizontal *planes* we get but one *horizon circle* in the sky."*

We know that theoretically this cannot be right although practically it may be partially so,—even entirely so in some instances, perhaps.

For all ordinary practical purposes the earth may be considered as a mere point in space, since though all influence is exerted to the central point, the fractional differences introduced by the observer's superficial position are too small to cause serious error.

The appended diagram (Fig. 3) is intended to exhibit, at a glance, the two different positions of the mundane circle into houses. I have not made the house-division from the centre, except the four cardinal points, in order to eliminate as much as possible the element of confusion created by a multitude of lines.

The dotted lines exemplify the twelve houses divided from the point of an observer at O, his horizon being a, b, and his zenith and nadir respectively Z and N.

O is an observer, *a b* is the sensible horizon, A B the rational one, and the earth is rotating in its usual manner in the direction indicated by the arrows, at, or about, the time of her equinox. At L it is noon; at O, 90° west longitude, it is understood to be 6 a.m.; at M, 90° east longitude, it is 6 p.m.; and at S, 180° west or east, it is midnight, while 45° west it is 9 a.m. Before the observer at O can catch sight of the orb, it must—disregarding refraction for the moment—rise above his horizon *a b*—but it does not do this really, as we know. What happens is, that the observer's horizon becomes deflected or extended in the direction of O A, although the sun *appears* to be just elevating itself above the point *a;* so that a small discrepancy ensues, not, of course, as regards the opposite

* *Vide* Young's *General Astronomy.*

R

point but those involved in the quadrature, because it cannot be exactly
6 a.m. at O when it is mid-day at L. Yet the very minute amount of
disagreement is far too small to cause much difference in effects, so far
as the astrologer is concerned, the sun itself having had no deducible
parallax for a long time by usual methods. Various observers have since
given their results: thus Newcomb, in 1867, gave it as 8"·85; Leverrier a
little earlier, as 8"·86, while others make 8"·78. The first, I believe, is
the standard used in American, English and French year books and
Ephemerides; but it has been stated latterly that the most correct
appears to be 8"·8+0"·03, and still again 8"·80.

It must be remembered that the horizon A B, the rational one as
regards O, is not the horizon at all for a person at L, but his zenith; Z N
becomes the rational horizon, and, of course, a parallel plane to this
through the observer at L, the sensible horizon.

If we assume the astronomical coincidence of the two horizons at
vast distances, there is no need to trouble over the problem at all, as I
stated previously. But it appears very plain that if we admit that
planetary influx, as we understand it, comes like light* in straight lines
to the earth, and supposing there to be some star at Z, 90° distant from
the sun at A, the square aspect will be formed at G, and at G only, not
at O. But as we see, the earth is relatively so small a quantity in
relation to the enormous stretches of space across which light and
influence come, that it is probably little else than a point at the apex
of a triangle—no more; certainly this is so in relation to the majority
of the fixed stars, which are too remote to exhibit any sensible parallax.
It is only when we enter the planetary region that parallax becomes
evident; the mean parallax of the moon for instance, is as much as 57"2',
while the horizontal parallax of Mars is only about 24"·64.

The points of observance in this matter of commutation are, (1) that
it increases the right and oblique ascension, and diminishes the equivalent descensions; (2) that it diminishes nothern declination and latitude
in the eastern part, increases them in the western; (3) increases the

---

* Light, when it reaches the earth's atmosphere, becomes bent out of its true
course, or, as we say, *refracted;* but this is only a visual matter, however. There is no
reason to suppose that the *influence* emanating from a heavenly body is disturbed by
such a factor. Ptolemy was the first to announce that a ray of light, proceeding from
a star to the earth, underwent a change of direction in passing through the atmosphere.
See the Μεγάλη Σύνταξις. Tycho Brahe also investigated the subject and he
constructed the first tables. Those, however, now in most general use are those of
Bessel.

southern ditto in the eastern and diminishes it in the western part; and (4) that it diminishes the longitude in the western, and increases it in the eastern part. So that its effects are just opposite to those of refraction.

For the sake of perspicacity I shall here give one example of calculating parallax,* for some altitude above the horizon in a given latitude, bearing in mind what has been stated respecting parallax being greatest at the horizon, and at its minimum at the mid-heaven,—where it only affects the declination.

EXAMPLE.—*Required the Moon's parallax when its declination is 20°20′N. in latitude for a place 52°28′N., the horizontal parallax being at the time 56′.*

First find the altitude of the equator, which will be the complementary number, and so form with latitude 90 degrees. Thus:

Quadrant or ¼ circle	90°	0′
Latitude of place	52	28
Altitude of Equator	37	32

As the Moon is in *north* declination, it will be above that circle, so that the declination must be added to its height for the altitude of the Moon.

Moon's declination north	20°	20′
Altitude of Equator	37	32
Altitude of Moon	57	52

Now add the log. *sine* of the horizontal parallax of the Moon, and the log. *cosine* of the Moon's altitude together. The sum will be the log. *sine* of the parallax corresponding to that altitude.

Horizontal parallax, ☽ 56′	log. sine	8·211 8949
Altitude, ☽ 57°52′	log. cosine	9·725 8229
Required parallax 30′		7·937 7178

The other elements must be calculated similarly.

Parallax will of course make some slight difference in computation if we suppose each man to be the centre of planetary influx, but whether it will ever become important enough for serious notice appears problematical. The method of taking the moment of birth will have to be a far more accurate one than it now is.

* For an explanation of the principles of measurement, see Guillemin's *Le Soleil*.

CHAPTER V.

ON THE EQUATION OF THE ARC OF DIRECTION

WHEN the arc of direction has been obtained, there still remains food for consideration in the equation and timing thereof. For as it stands it is in degrees and minutes of arc, and these must represent an equivalent in time. The question to be decided is, *what* equivalent ? The four principal methods of equation in use are those advocated by :—

1. Ptolemy.
2. Valentine Naibod.
3. Placidus de Titus.
4. Simmonite.

1. THE PTOLEMAIC METHOD

Ptolemy himself does not advance any methods of equation, strictly speaking, such as the remaining three. "There is but one rule to be observed," he says.* " by such as would calculate agreeably to nature, namely, to ascertain in what number of equatorial degrees the succeeding place (whether it be the body or aspect of a planet) will arrive at the preceding place in the geniture, and as these degrees pass the horizon as well as the meridian, all distances must be calculated according to the various positions of the planets in question with respect to those angles, and every degree signifies a year."

This has the merit of extreme simplicity but nevertheless does not always prove correct, although if the birth-time is doubtful or known to be inexact, it provides probably the best scheme that can be adopted. On the whole it is by far the easiest, and in his period of probation the student will naturally take kindly to it. It consists in allowing one year of life for every degree of arc, and for minor periods in like proportion ; *i.e.,* five minutes of arc (one-twelfth of the whole degree) would be

---

* *Tetrabiblos, Lib. III., Cap. xiv.*

equivalent to a month of actual time, and so on, as the following arcs of space and time show :

Arc of Direction.		Conversion to Time.		
°	′	yrs.	mths.	wks.
20	15	20	3	0
19	45	19	9	0
53	3½	53	0	2
60	55	60	11	0
4	33	4	6	2
80	59	80	11	3

2. NAIBOD'S METHOD

The method of Naibod is to convert the arc into time by allowing the mean daily motion of the Sun to represent one year of life, and a minute to equal six days four hours. And so we get a table known as Naibod's, by reference to which any arc may be easily converted into the equivalent time of operation.

To use it, we enter the degrees of the table with the level *degrees* of the arc, and opposite we get a period of time in years and days which we set down ; with the remaining minutes of arc (if any) entrance is to be made in the *minute* column, where a further period is given, this however being in days and hours, which must be added to the other to obtain the true time.

EXAMPLE.—*Required to turn 20°15′ of arc into time*

	years.	days.	hours.
20 degrees give	20	106	0
15 minutes give		92	16
Whole arc of 20°15′ gives	20	198	16

The hours can be conveniently neglected.

This is, so far as my experience shows, one of the most satisfactory ways of equating, and the one which gives the closest results when the Ptolemaic measure fails to approach in an inconsistent degree.

In arranging the arcs after computation, I generally turn them into time by both methods, unless I am convinced by a knowledge of events that one of them bears an advantage over the other; the native can then see, by repetition of observance, which period gives the more accurate time of planetary action.

NAIBOD'S TABLE OF THE MEASURE OF TIME.

Measure of Time for Degrees.   *Measure of Time for Minutes.*

°	Yrs.	Days.	°	Yrs.	Days.	'	Days.	Hrs.	'	Days.	Hrs.
1	1	5	31	31	166	1	6	4	31	191	11
2	2	10	32	32	171	2	12	8	32	197	16
3	3	16	33	33	177	3	18	13	33	203	20
4	4	21	34	34	181	4	24	17	34	209	0
5	5	26	35	35	186	5	30	21	35	216	4
6	6	32	36	36	192	6	37	1	36	222	9
7	7	37	37	37	197	7	43	6	37	228	13
8	8	43	38	38	202	8	49	10	38	234	17
9	9	48	39	39	208	9	55	14	39	240	21
10	10	53	40	40	213	10	61	18	40	247	2
11	11	59	41	41	218	11	68	23	41	253	6
12	12	64	42	42	224	12	74	3	42	259	10
13	13	69	43	43	229	13	80	7	43	265	14
14	14	74	44	44	234	14	86	11	44	271	18
15	15	80	45	45	240	15	92	16	45	277	23
16	16	85	46	46	245	16	98	20	46	284	3
17	17	90	47	47	250	17	105	0	47	290	7
18	18	96	48	48	256	18	111	4	48	296	11
19	19	101	49	49	261	19	117	9	49	302	16
20	20	106	50	50	266	20	123	13	50	308	20
21	21	112	51	51	272	21	129	17	51	315	0
22	22	117	52	52	277	22	135	21	52	321	4
23	23	122	53	53	282	23	142	1	53	327	9
24	24	128	54	54	288	24	148	6	54	333	13
25	25	133	55	55	293	25	154	10	55	339	17
26	26	138	56	56	298	26	160	14	56	345	21
27	27	144	57	57	304	27	166	18	57	352	2
28	28	149	58	58	309	28	172	23	58	358	6
29	29	154	59	59	314	29	179	3	59	364	10
30	30	160	60	60	320	30	185	7	60	370	14

3. THE METHOD OF PLACIDUS.

The next method I shall draw attention to is that of Placidus. This consists in adding the Sun's R.A. at birth to the arc of direction, the sum being the R.A. of that point in the zodiac, which, when the Sun reaches it, will complete the direction. The *time* must be ascertained by allowing a year for each day he takes in arriving at such point, and the minor periods in proportion. So that after adding the two R.A.'s together, inspection must be made of the Ephemeris* in order to find the day and

---

* The *Nautical Almanack*, which gives the R.A. of the Sun for each day, is more convenient than the Ephemeris for this purpose.

hour after birth in which the Sun acquires that R.A.; *i.e.*, we must determine the longitude agreeing to the R.A. in question, and from the day and hour when the Sun reaches that longitude take the day and hour of birth. The difference is a certain number of days and hours after birth, which is to be turned into years and months in the ordinary way by allowing a day for each year.

EXAMPLE.—*Required to equate the arc of* ⊙ ♂ ♀ *13°36′ conv. zod.* (Map No. 2)

Right ascension of Sun at birth	211° 17′
Arc of direction, ⊙ ♂ ♀ *conv. zod.*	13 36
R.A. of Sun on completion of aspect	224 53

Now 224°53′ of R.A. is equal to ♏17°22′ of longitude which the Sun reaches on the 9th of November at 10hrs. 48min. afternoon.

Proceeding, we set down the number of days in the previous month, October being that in which the birth occurred :

	Days.	*Hrs.*	*Min.*
Number of days in October	31	0	0
Time of ⊙'s arrival at ♏17°22′, November	9	10	48
	40	10	48
Time of birth	26	15	50
Difference	13	18	58

To time this, we allow a year for each day and for every two hours one month; so that in the above case the direction of ⊙ ♂ ♀ would operate at 13 years 9 months 2 weeks.

4. SIMMONITE'S METHOD.

There is one other method I shall include here which, theoretically regarded, appears very rational but in practice is scarcely so satisfactory. I refer to the method outlined by Simmonite in the *Arcana*.

This requires a table to be made, for each geniture, of the Sun's motion after birth, *i.e.*, his proper daily motion and not the mean. In doing this we commence with the day of birth, setting down of course 0°0′ of R.A. and add to this the motion in R.A. for the following day. I shall exhibit the table—or rather a portion of it—which would be a necessary appendage to Map 2, taking it just so far as will suffice to equate the arc of ⊙ ♂ ♀ *conv. zod.* for comparative purposes.

Table of ☉'s motion in R.A. as from the noon of each day:

Year.	Arc.		Year.	Arc.	
	°	′		°	′
0	0	0	8	7	53
1	0	59	9	8	52
2	1	58	10	9	51
3	2	57	11	10	51
4	3	57	12	11	50
5	4	56	13	12	49
6	5	55	14	13	48
7	6	54			

Another table must be constructed for the minutes of arc, dating from the natal month and allowing five minutes for each successive one. Thus:

Arc.	27th of each Month.	Arc.
′	Month.	′
0	October	60
5	November	55
10	December	50
15	January	45
20	February	40
25	March	35
30	April	30
35	May	25
40	June	20
45	July	15
50	August	10
55	September	5
60	October	0

The utility of these tables now becomes apparent. The arc of ☉ to conjunction of ♀ before mentioned is 13°36′. To turn this into time we look down the second column of the first table, and find that the nearest expression to this is the last of the series, viz., 13°48′, and this is 22′ in excess, but it is equivalent to fourteen years of the native's life. We want to know then what deduction must be made for the 22′, and this we shall easily do by a reference to table No. 2.

Carrying the eye up the right-hand column (because the period will fall *before* the fourteenth birthday) we see that the 22′ fall in June, so that the complete arc would measure to thirteen years seven and a half months.

Instituting a comparison of this one directional arc, originally expressed in degrees and minutes, we shall be in a position to judge—not the superiority of either method over the other, from a single arc chosen at random, but to how great an extent they are synchronous in

the present instance.   No striking variations occur in the time exhibited
by the various processes tabulated below, it is true,

Arc of Direction, ☉ ☌ ♀ *conv. zod.* 13°36'.

Equated Ptolemaically		13°36' measures to 13yrs., 7½mths.				
"	by Naibod's mean measure	"	"	" 13 "	9¼	"
"	by Placidus' method	"	"	" 13 "	9¼	"
"	by Simmonite's	"	"	" 13 "	7¼	"

but practically there are two periods pointed out, and the balance of
favour cannot be expressed other than by direct observance of the actual
time of planetary influx, *minus* any well-authenticated series of events
as they are concerned with the calendar.

Another method of equation will be found described and illustrated
in appendix III.

———————

CHAPTER VI.

SECONDARY DIRECTIONS.

" I HAVE appointed thee each day for a year."—*Ezekiel*, iv. 6.

THE nomenclature of these aspects has of late years become very confused, and by way of clearing the ground I will briefly enumerate the various terms as employed customarily.

(1) As remarked in a former chapter, Primary Directions, properly so-called, are the aspects produced by the diurnal rotation of the earth, and are therefore *mundane* in constitution.

(2) In contradistinction to these, Secondary Directions are formed by the proper motion of the various planets, Sun and Moon, through the *zodiac*, each day's increase in longitude measuring exactly one year in time.

(3) But here an anomaly has crept in, by the too great attachment to one system. I refer to the denomination of *zodiacal* aspects, formed by proper motion after birth, in which are concerned the Sun, (progressive or radical), as " Primary " ; and those formed by the Moon, (progressive), as " Secondary."

(4) Raphael in his *Guide* distinguishes differently again. "In the first place," he says, "the directions termed 'secondary' are called by me 'primary.'" Later he remarks: "For distinction I call those directions which are made to the planets in the radix *primary*, and those made among the planets by secondary motion I call *local*."

Those in the habit of relying entirely upon the Arabian and Persian method, *i.e.*, secondary aspects as described in (2), are responsible for the confusion thereby instituted. For the sake of greater perspicuity it would be desirable to have set terms of art for these latter, terms of pointed applicability and significance, so that mistakes in the future may not arise by such an interchanging of appellations. Therefore, I append the scheme I shall use in the present treatise.

I. PRIMARY.

(a) *Primary Directions, i.e.*, those formed within a few hours after birth by mundane motion and computed by right and oblique ascension, the semi-arcs of planets, etc.; the result being an arc of direction expressed in degrees and minutes, to be reduced to time and equated by some particular method. (Chapter II.)

II. SECONDARY.

(b) *Secondary solar* directions formed by a planet's proper motion in longitude after birth to radical Sun; or by progressive motion of Sun to radical or progressed planetary places; or by Sun or planets, progressive, to M.C. and ascendant radical.*

(c) *Secondary fixed* (or *radical*) *Lunar, i.e.*, similar aspects to the Moon's place in Radix.

(d) *Progressive Lunar*—those formed from day to day by the Moon's increasing longitude: *i.e.*, with the Sun and planets, (radical or progressed); its own place at birth; M.C. and ascendant, whether radical or progressed.

Classes (c) (d) are generally included under one head in the secondary method of directing, and it may be asked why I have separated them, having regard to the increased power of the Moon when the radical place is directed to. If power in this respect were the sole reason of the arrangement, such might not have been the case, for there is an enormous difference between the Moon R. and the same P.; but a secondary radical Lunar direction is quite different intrinsically to a secondary Solar, and on this account I have thought it best to separate them.

When we come to enquire into the matter through the medium of works relative to astral science, we find secondary directions almost

---

* With this class are evidently to be included the mutual aspects formed by progressive planets to one another, *i.e.*, *Interplanetary* or *Mutual Directions*: see ASTRO-LOGICAL MANUALS, No. V., p. 19. What are there termed *Basic Directions* would include both classes (b) and (c) above.

The student will hardly need to be reminded that what are here described under the general term "Secondary Directions" are nothing more nor less than the aspects occurring in the Progressed Horoscope, to which Sections A. and B. of this work have been devoted. Indeed, this portion of the chapter might almost have been omitted, but that it furnishes an additional example of the method of calculation, and moreover exhibits an instance of the employment of the *radical* house cusps in connection with the *progressed* planetary positions—a practice largely adopted by many, though it does not commend itself to the author of this book, since it leaves out of account the influence of the Progressed Ascendant.—EDITOR.

universally condemned, or commented upon in the most lax and invidious fashion, as though their power were not even so great as that of simple transits, and, easy as their calculation is, not worth the small amount of labour entailed !

But upon pursuing our investigations further, we discover the strange and almost inexplicable fact that the system is in continual use, either solely or conjointly with certain others. We need not go far to seek the cause of this counter-procedure, if we consider briefly the plain facts of the case.

Let us see. Primary arcs themselves it is evident must inevitably require in their computation, more time, attention and accuracy from the student than any other method of determining periods of planetary activity. Unless the time of birth is known very correctly, directions are thrown months, perhaps years, out.

In secondary directions, on the contrary, there is a minimum of labour and sufficient return at least to more than compensate for its exertion ; the time need not be so correctly taken, although of course this is desirable ; the workings of the scheme are succinct, easily comprehended, and continually under view, which to meaner capacities are things to be thankful for. Added to these there are the conveniences arising from the ability to get out a year's influences *in toto* without having to calculate periods not required or encroach upon former or later arcs ; and in primary directing—unless the student is well acquainted with its internal economy by long use—this is a matter containing an element of confusion.

It is not always requisite to compute more than perhaps a year, though indeed when once the horoscope is cast a glance down the columns of the ephemeris will reveal to a trained eye the broad outline of the whole life, with very little trouble and very great accuracy. The important parts of the career are taken in mentally with ease, and with such perspicacity that, in the present condition of the science, to take a crutch like this from under the invalid's arm, is surely nothing short of cruelty !

But even apart from these considerations we must remark its highly symbolical aspect and its ability to point out the critical periods of life, those depending on certain positions of the radical or progressive Moon.

Summing up all advantages and disadvantages it will be admitted that while we know it is not wise to neglect other methods in the present state of our knowledge, there is yet so much to be said for these maligned

" secondaries" that (bearing in mind their ease of computation, moreover) they are convincing, important and valuable.

We will now turn to the practical working of the system and plunge *in medias res.*

HOW CALCULATED.

Secondary directions, as before remarked, are those formed by the progressive motion in the zodiac of the Sun, Moon and planets, antecedent and subsequent to birth. The motion taken into account is the *actual daily* and not the *mean zodiacal* motion. Thus it is demonstrated at once that regularity of motion not being a factor, calculation must be made for each day after the nativity and for every planetary body concerned.

The first step may be made with the help of a map containing radical and progressed places ;* but as the student advances he will prefer a map simply containing the progressed planets, and ultimately he will come to find maps a hindrance rather than a help, the tabulated positions being quite sufficient.

The motto I have chosen for the heading of this chapter hints at their archaic derivation, and points out exactly the method to be followed in taking these secondaries, as well as the structural basis upon which they rest, *viz.*, that each day after birth shall be equivalent to one year of life, measuring from the time such birth occurred on one day to the same on the next.

Thus, suppose a person born July 4th at 3 p.m. in any year, then from 3 p.m. July 23rd to 3 p.m. July 24th would represent the *twentieth* year of life† and for everything relative to that year such date would have to be dealt with. It is easy to remember that so many days after and inclusive of birth, so many *years* after ditto ; or in other words, the number of days after and inclusive of birth will be the number of years of life.

Owing, however, to somewhat vague statements in regard to this particular made now and again by writers upon the subject, there has arisen a doubt in the minds of some as to what is exactly meant.

---

* Using two different inks, say black for radical place and red for progressed, or simply marking radical planets with an R and progressed with a P.

† *I.e.*, from the completion of the nineteenth to the commencement of the twenty-first year ; in fact from the nineteenth to the twentieth birthday. [See Chapter VII., Section A., p. 34.]

Therefore, let me give one word of warning to those younger students for whom I write, and apprise them that when a number of days are mentioned as bearing affinity with an identical number of years, it is intended they should be counted from the inception of life; the natal day being the natural representative of the first year of life, and the day after the second, and so on. This measure it is apparent is a natural one and exhibits plainly, logically, and practically, the intimacy between the formation and dissolution of aspects and the rise and fall of the native's power, the increase or loss of wealth, etc., or the instillation of the germs of disease, leading through serious illness to convalescence or death as the case may be.

Cataclysmic effects are seen to be the outcome of longer periods than their action on the material plane warrants one in believing. But the inference is just and a thorough study of the subject confirms better than any words the continual growth of aspects, the slowly unfolding gates, or unlocked sluices, through which planetary influence can function ; cause and effect ramifying and interlacing, like the roots of a monster tree—not badly represented by the Scandinavian Yggdrasil, with the serpent Nithöggr gnawing at the bottom and the eagle perched atop, while the nimble squirrel runs up and down sowing strife between the two.

In these directions the Moon of course by her quicker motion will play an important part, calling forces into action and distributing the karmic rewards faithfully and unerringly, and hence it is to her aspects and positions that we must pay most regard. The other planets will not move so quickly, and in the case of Jupiter, Saturn, and those beyond their orbits, the positions will not vary much for days at a time, leaving however their impress on *years*.

I shall now commence the working out of the secondary directions in Map No. 2 for the year 1897. As it is more convenient to take the civil year than the natal year the tabulations will date from January and close with December.

In ordinary cases, if the planets are calculated to the hour of birth upon that day representing the year required, the positions will be found nearly enough correct, as the small motion, if divided by twelve to give monthly values would not be appreciable for practical purposes. Yet when the motion in longitude of Mercury, Venus and Mars does exceed the usual amount, or when the birth occurs in the first part of the civil year, the half-yearly position may be noted down. In the latter case it is almost imperative.*

As our directions are required for 1897 and the native was born in 1870, they will be for the twenty-seventh year of life, represented by November 22nd, which, natally speaking, commences at 3hrs. 50min. a.m., and extends to the same time on the day following. But as we are calculating for the civil year there are two months of time left between the commencement of one and the commencement of the other, and though this will not affect the major planets and only minutely the minor, it will produce a difference of some degrees in the *Moon's* position.

Therefore to find the place of the latter for the first day of January, 1897, we proceed as follows.†

	Years.	Mths.	Days.
Set down the year for which directions are required	1897	1	0
Take therefrom year, month and day of birth	1870	10	27
	26	2	4

As the years will equal days, and other time proportionately, we can call the years days at once, and if we multiply the months by two, we shall obtain hours, and multiplying the days by four, the result is equivalent minutes. Thus the above period is reduced to 26 days 4hrs. 16mins.

	Days.	Hrs.	Mins.
To this	26	4	16
add day, hour and minute of birth	26	15	50
which gives time of direction	52	20	6
As the birth occurs in the preceding month, subtract the number of days in same	31	0	0
	21	20	6

This brings us to the time for which the Moon's position is to be calculated agreeably to January 1st.

Referring to the ephemeris we see that the Moon travelled between

---

* Computation however may be made mentally.

† The commencement of the year is properly put thus, 1897y. 0m. 0d. ; but the reason for the plan adopted will be seen when we reflect that from October 27th to end of year there are four days and two months still to run. Perhaps a better way still would be to express it thus : 1896y. 12m. 31d.

noon on the 21st and noon on the 22nd, from ♏6°50′ to ♏22°5′ a distance of 15°15′ of longitude.   Proceeding by the aid of proportional logarithms.*

15°15′	*prop. log.*	·1969
3hr. 54min. (complement of 20hr. 6min.)	„ „	·7891
2°29′	„ „	·9860

Then long. on 22nd, noon		♏22° 5′
Less motion in 3hrs. 54min.		2 29
Moon's longitudinal place of direction, for Jan. 1st, 1897		♏19 36

We can now see for ourselves that the increase of longitude being so great, averaging a degree per month (or what is the same thing, a like quantity every two hours), some provision will have to be made for this motion, and it appears at once to be obtained by dividing the daily increase of longitude by twelve. This will give the motion for each *two hours*, and therefore will be equivalent to *one month*, for as the day measures the year, the twelfth part of either must bear a direct relationship ; so that what happens in the ephemeris in two hours will take one

EXAMPLE.—*Required the time of direction for twenty-seventh year of native, Map 2.*

The R.A.M.C. at birth is 93°7′, which is equivalent to 6hrs. 12min., 28secs., bringing us to the time of birth.

Referring now to the 22nd of November, which commences the twenty-seventh year, we find

	Hr.	Min.	Sec.
Sidereal time, noon, 22/11/'70	16	5	5
Taking therefrom the sidereal time at birth	6	12	28
Gives the required time of direction before noon	9	52	37

That is, the planets' places must be calculated to 2h. 7m. 23s. a.m., instead of 3h. 50.m a.m.

---

* These are the Diurnal Proportional Logarithms, given in *Chambers's Mathematical Tables* and also at the end of *Astrology for All, Part II.* They should not be confounded with the Ternary Proportional Logarithms used hitherto in this section.

† As will be seen, I have not referred to the method of calculation by sidereal time, this being a fixed factor, and unlike the mean time we have been concerning ourselves with here. This is merely because I thought it advisable that the student, for whom I mainly wrote, should be acquainted primarily with the ordinary method handed down to us, and also because I find myself to a certain extent unjustified in introducing a procedure which, notwithstanding its apparently rational basis, does not give proportionately accurate results. By it we take the sidereal time of M.C. at birth and on any following day for which directions are required, we find the equivalent mean time and calculate the planets to that time, the signs, etc., remaining as before, of course. This will result in the mean time being some four minutes earlier for each year required.

month to mature, when set in motion by the actual individual life-wave which when the due time arrives will reach it. Hence we divide the Moon's daily motion by twelve to obtain the monthly motion; a further division of the latter by four results in weeks, and may sometimes advantageously be made. The table below will exhibit this at a glance.

We can then fill in our secondary map. This map of course will contain the progressed places of the planets calculated to time of birth* on the subsequent day already noted, making an exception in the case of the Moon for reasons already explained. The skeleton of the map, *i.e.*, the signs and houses, will remain for our present purpose precisely the same as in the radical map. [Herein lies the distinction between this method and that of the Progressed Horoscope described in Chapter VI., Section A.—EDITOR.]

Directional place of ☽ Jan. 1st, 1897		♏ 19° 36'	
Monthly motion, (yearly ditto, 15°15'÷12)		1 16	
Weekly motion (1°16'÷4)=19'		*February*	20 52
			1 16
		March	22 8
Jan. 1st. ☽ *in*	♏ 19° 36'		1 16
	19	*April*	23 24
2nd week	19 55		1 16
	19	*May*	24 40
3rd week	20 14		1 16
	19	*June*	25 56
4th week	20 33		1 16
	19	*July*	27 12
Feb. 1st	20 52		1 16
	19	*August*	28 28
2nd week	21 11		1 16
	19	*September*	29 44
3rd week	21 30		1 16
	19	*October*	♐ 1 0
4th week	21 49		1 16
etc., etc.		*November*	2 16
			1 16
		December	3 32

☽'s position 1st of each month.

PROGRESSIVE MAP FOR 1897.

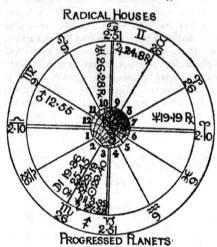

DECLINATIONS.

☉	20° 6's	♃	22° 47'N
☿	20 28 s	♄	22 32s
♀	18 37 s	♅	21 23N
♂	8 29 N	♇	6 3N
	☽ 12°49' s to 17°20' s		

N.B.—The Moon's place in the map is given twice, i being for the beginning and ii for the end of the year.

Before we continue further, it will be advisable to examine the various forms which come under the heading of Secondary Directions, considering them in the order of their importance.

First, then, we distinguish the

Secondary Solar.

1. Radical Sun and Progressive Planets.
2. Progressive Sun and Radical Planets.
3. Progressive Sun and Progressive Planets.
4. Radical M.C. and Progressive Planets.
5. Radical Asc. and Progressive Planets.

Next—

Secondary Radical Lunar.

1. Radical Moon and Progressive Planets.

And lastly—

Lunar Progressive.

1. Progressive Moon and Radical Planets.
2. Progressive Moon and Progressive Planets.
3. Radical M.C. and Progressive Moon.
4. Radical Asc. and Progressive Moon.

The solar group is the most important, for as the Sun is the source of all manifested life as we know it, it was natural for the ancient Hermetists to bestow thereon primary consideration. This must never be forgotten when judging the effects of the lunar ones, for these merely bring into play the emanations resulting from positions and conditions of the progressed or radical Sun, and depend to a great extent upon such major conditions for the constitutional direction in which they will function.

We have now a certain basis to work upon, inasmuch as from the elements calculated the progressive map may be drawn; and with the aid of the table showing the Moon's place at the beginning of each month, and the knowledge of the various groups of astral forces, we may further compute the aspects for the year decided upon, and finally deduce what measure of joy and pain, advance or recession, will be the legitimate fruit thereof. Some plain rules here follow :—

To direct the Sun (Prog. and Rad.).

(1) Take the Sun in radix first, and see what aspects are formed with it by the planets which have moved on since birth.* (2) Next take the actual position of the Sun on the day required (this is the progressed Sun) and see what aspects it forms with planets in the radix —in other words, with those as situated at time of birth. (3) Then ascertain what aspects occur between the progressive Sun and progressive planets. (4) Look again, and see if the motion of the Sun has brought it in aspect either to the M.C. or Ascendant. Do the same for the

---

* Attach r. to a radical planet and p. to a progressed one. Remember this throughout, so that no confusion may occur. It is better to use small letters than capitals, as is sometimes done, so as to avoid confusion with P. meaning *parallel of declination* and ℞ meaning *retrograde.*

remaining planetary bodies. Mundane aspects to M.C. and Ascendant
may be easily noted and sometimes profitably, for when the solar orb, or
any other body whatever, reaches the cusp of twelfth, a mundane sextile
to the M.C. will be formed as before shown, and the same if the cusp of
eighth is the point of position. It is merely requisite to take note of the
various cusps and refer to table given in an earlier chapter.

Secondary Directions to the Radical Moon

are, of course, made to that luminary. They are of great power, and
are ascertained in the same way, just as though the radical lunar were
the radical solar orb.

Lunar Secondaries.

In these, by a continually increasing longitude the Moon forms
aspects, as before tabulated, with radical and progressive planetary
places and with the angles. These will need the closest attention, in so
far as calculation is concerned.

In the whole of these various orders the *parallel of declination* must
upon no account be forgotten. It may occur as an aspect between
either radical or progressive places, or both.

As we have seen before, the Sun as being the source of all power is
well regarded as the mainstay of the system, and as it moves on the
average only 59' per day, an aspect may begin to exert force before the
partile condition obtains and may remain in a like state, *i.e.*, in the
ability to actively function as a solar direction, some time after the
actual completion of the number of degrees which exactly comprise it.
Upon this account directions in which the Sun and planets are concerned
—(but not progressive Moon)—will remain in action over comparatively
extensive periods of time, gradually of course increasing or decreasing in
power, while in the interim every lunar direction of a similar constitution
will arouse the latent power which resides therein.*

Thus it is not absolutely necessary to compute such positions, a
mere inspection of the ephemeris being sufficient to show the *year* in
which they are completely formed, and this will be the year of most
intense manifestation. It is desirable, however, in some cases to
calculate to more minute periods of time, and by so doing the student
will discover he has frequently to experience the pleasurable sensation

* This was discussed at length in Section B.

of being not the equivocal amount of two months behind or before the date of activity, but sometimes little more than a day.*

In looking through a whole series of years, or even broadly at the whole life, these solar positions are the groundwork, and it is astonishing with what precision, in a few moments after receiving birth data, one is able to approximate to actual fact in giving a brief outline of mundane matters as they have affected the individual. It is plain, then, that to get out this group of directions is a remarkably easy task, relatively, and in approaching the matter of secondary influences it is the first duty. For convenience, too, when considering this portion, we may include aspects to the Moon *radix*.

And now, before venturing further, and in order to render everything plain and straight-sailing to the youngest student in astral dynamics, we will make a tabulation of solar and fixed lunar directions from Map No. 2, comprised between, and inclusive of, the ages of twenty and thirty.

Counting the days from, and inclusive of, birth in the ephemeris for that year, we find that the natal twentieth year of life representatively commenced on November 15th and the thirtieth terminated November 25th.

SECONDARY SOLAR DIRECTIONS.

Ephemeris.	Year.	Direction.
Nov. 15	20	♂ p. □ ☽ r.
" 16	21	
" 17	22	☉ p. P. ☽ r.
" 18	23	
" 19	24	☉ p. △ ♅ r.; ☿ p. P. ☽ r.; ☉ p. ⚹ Asc. (*mundo*).
" 20	25	
" 21	26	☉ p. □ ♂ r.
" 22	27	☉ p. ☌ ☿ p.; ♀ p. △ ♅ r.
" 23	28	♀ p. P. ☽ r.
" 24	29	☉ p. ⚹ Asc. (*zod.*); ☿ p. ⚹ Asc. (*zod.*)
" 25	30	☉ p. ⚼ ☉ r.

As will be noted, the signs and houses these aspects fall in are not inserted. This is merely for the sake of clearness, so that no element of confusion may creep in while developing methods.

By this time the student will have obtained some notion both of what is required of him, and how practically to proceed in his exertions. Having arranged the solar forces that will operate in a year, a certain number of years, or a whole life period, to his satisfaction it will be high

---

* An example of the readiest means of making such calculation is given in Appendix V., in connection with which Appendix VI. should also be read ; see also *Astrology for All*, Part II., p. 63—EDITOR.

time to consider the remaining lunar ones. So far as the present elucidation goes, they are required for the twenty-seventh year alone, for which we have made certain computations previously.

Upon reference to the table of the Moon's motion, and comparing its various positions month by month, first with radical places, second with progressed ditto, we shall acquire a series of aspects that will occur at shorter intervals of time than those we have before dealt with, the time elapsing between two such, varying from a few days to a few weeks or months. These act only for a short period about their formation, and their dissolution quickly follows.

From January 1st to February 1st, the Moon travels the intervening degrees between ♏19°36′ and ♏20°52′. The only perfect aspect formed from a point included in such degrees of longitude is a Quincunx (150°) to the radical Neptune in 7th. In April a Quincunx is likewise formed to the progressed Jupiter, but nothing of importance occurs until the beginning of June, when a conjunction with the progressed Venus is completed, immediately followed by a trine of the radical Uranus.

And so we continue, noting the monthly advance of the Moon and comparing it with radical and progressive planetary places, marking the points where aspects are formed in terms of the civil year, until we obtain the list which the latter in question yields.

Both the signs and houses the bodies happen to be in when the aspect is formed, must be remarked and set down in the list, as well as some indication whether the direction is made to a radical or to a progressive place.

I think there is no need for further elaboration on this point, the operations being so extremely simple that they cannot fail to be comprehended and adopted after a little attention and study. I shall now, however, collect the whole of the various aspects under their proper headings, exhibiting at one view the stellar causes of certain events that would (and did) occur during the year 1897. The Roman figures indicate the houses from or in which the aspects fell.

SECONDARY DIRECTIONS FOR 1897.

From the Horoscope of a Female born October 27th, 1870, 3hr. 52min. a.m., G.M.T.

Solar.

☉ p. □ ♂ r. ♏-♌, XI.-III. (formed year previous but influence remaining).
☉ p. ☌ ☿ p. ♐　III.

Fixed Lunar.

☽ r. P. ♀ p. ♐-♏　III. (not completed till following year).

Lunar Progressive.

January	☽ ⚻	♆ r.	♏-♈	II.-VII.
April	☽ ⚻	♃ p.	♏-♊	II.-IX.
May	☽ ☌	♀ p.	♏	III.
	☽ Bq.	♆ r.	♏-♈	III.-VII.
	☽ Q.	♂ p.	♏-♍	III.-XII.
June	☽ △	♅ r.	♏-♋	III.-X.
August	☽ □	♂ r.	♏-♌	III.-XI.
	☽ ☌	☿ p.	♐	III.
September	☽ ☌	☉ p.	♐	III.
November	☽ ∠	☿ r.	♎-♐	III.-I.
	☽ ⚹	Asc.	♐	III.

We have now the framework upon which to build our judgment. We have the deep-rooted causes which will produce effects according to the nature and qualities of the factors we deal with. We have, in point of fact, logically to eventuate a series of passive positions on the plane of activity; and it is probably in this requirement that the majority of students fail to produce anything save food for further thought.

Obviously, extended observations on such particulars are out of the question in this place.* But to put the matter as succinctly as possible so that none may be left entirely in the dark, we can enunciate some general rules and considerations to be kept in the mind's eye when giving judgment of Secondary Directions.

Think of the solar positions as dividing the life into great periods and the lunar ones as filling in the smaller affairs of life. Thus during the travail of a Sun square Saturn there is no reason why, under suitable lunar directions, *some* pleasure and good health may not be experienced. The real state of the case can best be seen by looking backwards through the life to some earlier period when the depressing influence of Saturn was in action.

For several years round the completion of this aspect, remembrance will be vivid enough of the sorrowful experiences of the occasion, which appeared as though a heavy cloud had enwrapped the whole life fortunes. But at the time there would have been bright intervals when the clouds were temporarily dispersed by lunar positions; yet these being in their nature so slight and fugitive and, withal, enchained in a degree to the more powerful solar, are forgotten after they have served their

* Moreover, the reader who has carefully studied the foregoing Sections of this book will be now in a far better position to form a correct judgment than those students for whom this treatise was originally written.—EDITOR.

purpose; and the mists of succeeding years almost totally dissever them from association with the greater influence of the solar action.

Again, in judging a position we know that, by an occult sympathy, the various planets bear some relation to the zodiacal signs, and through these to the mundane houses, and so we get a series of highly important phases for consideration, which must claim our full regard before we can attempt to give a true judgment. They are :—

(1) The intrinsic nature of the planets concerned.

(2) Their modification by position in radix (sign and house).

(3) Their modification by aspect in radix.

(4) The signs from which direction is formed.

(5) The houses from which direction is formed (both r. and p.).

(6) The nature of the aspect itself.

(7) The whole collated with the indication of the radix.

The solar conditions will point out the quality and trend of the main influence, to which all lunar positions must be subjugated. It is idle to expect any lasting benefits from the latter, however promising in themselves, under evil solar aspects. When, too, no solar ones are formed in a particular year, we must refer to the year before or ensuing for the reigning influence, and should none be formed then we must find the nearest within an orb of five degrees, and take this into our reasoning, though of course the further from completion the aspect is, the less will be the force exerted, and the freer for unrestrained action will the lunar be left.

It must be borne in mind also that the heavenly bodies, when directions are formed, continually act according to their inherent natures, and the square aspect results in undesirable effects, simply because it is the principle of unbalanced force, and where this is, *there* is evil.

Again, each change of sign by the various bodies will incorporate a new influence, and the Moon, of course, as collector, transmits this to the individual. The Moon itself, by its frequent sign-change in its passage round the zodiac, will have to be carefully considered and compared with indications in the radix, for if the geniture exhibits stomach troubles, they will be felt most intensely when the progressive Moon is in cardinal signs; if heart troubles, then when she is in fixed signs, and so on.

Besides the zodiacal sign, the mundane houses are to be considered, for the location of the lunar orb in each and every one will bring to the fore, advantageously or disadvantageously as things happen to stand and as the radix imports, the powers ascribed to such house.

These secondary directions do not always act, even when there seems no cause to prevent them. The reason will be generally disclosed by reference to the primary forces in operation at that time. But, speaking broadly, it will be found in more than the average number of times that primary and secondary will agree in pointing out *the same event at the same time*, thereby adding a great utility to the secondary. Of course, there are, as I said before, exceptions; but nevertheless, that this should be so in a majority of cases is in itself an extremely significant fac .

As an illustration of how both series balance each other, take the exemplary nativity, No. 2. During September the arc of ☉ P . dec. ☽ *zod. d. d.* came up. In October the secondary lunar of ☽ ☌ ☉ p. Again in my own nativity by primary direction there was completed in June, 1897, the arc of ☉ ☌ ☿ *conv. mund.* The secondary solar for the year was ☉ ☌ ☿ (there being no relation as regards either the method or actual point of formation of the two similar forces), and in the June the secondary lunar were ☽ ✶ ♄ r., ☽ △ ♀ p., ☽ Bq. ☿ p., ☽ Bq. ☉ p., and a transit of Jupiter over my radical Mercury near the cusp of my ascendant in the sign Virgo. But there were no coincident positions with the ☽ □ ♄ *conv. mund.*, which eventuated in October.

Enough has been detailed on this head to awaken the student's reasoning powers and suggest channels for his activity, but there remain one or two other points which claim a few words before closing this section of my subject.

(1) The first is, that those years which are climacterical, *viz.*, those in which are formed the □, ☍ or ☌ of the progressed Moon to its radical place, are to be particularly noted, for if evil directions ultimate then, they are particularly dangerous, therefore it is best to tabulate such years and take them into account when executing a judgment.

(2) It is wise to note also that the directional motion of the Moon is very like that of Saturn by transit, and that it happens at times that the latter will be upon the directional place of the former, or in square or opposition thereto. Such positions will remain in close conformation, frequently for long periods, the two dogging each other's footsteps as it were by their allied rate of progress, bringing in their train consequent effects hard to overcome.

For instance, in the nativity No. 2, during October, 1897, the directed Moon catches up with Saturn *in transitu*, and remains pretty close till the conclusion of the year, when Saturn gets a pull, (but not a great one), and about May and June, 1898, by retrogression encounters the luminary again ; and so on, until the Moon gradually clears completely out of orb. It gives some bitter experiences while it lasts.

Another case : *female, born October 23rd, 1866.*   About the same time as above (to whom she is related) the progressed Sun conjoined with Saturn by transit,* and from the August onwards the progressed Moon was in opposition thereto, and a peculiarly unfortunate period set in for the life and interests of the family.   The temperament of the native became acerbid, and easily provoked into sarcastic rejoinders,—in fact the change was marked enough to be noticed.   Ill-health was also experienced.   Three members of the family came to grief by serious illness and accident, and there was scarcely anything but trouble during the whole of the period.

(3) Finally, it should not be overlooked that the Moon's change of sign (by direction) will tinge the mind with fresh colour; but *always* in accordance with the luminary's particular radical expression, which must never once be lost sight of.

----

* Or rather, technically, by ingress.

CHAPTER VII.

Minor Forms: Cyclic and Profectional Directing.

WE have now disposed of the more important and recognised aids to our peeps into futurity, but there are still left a number of minor operations which are of more or less doubtful utility, and which cannot be detailed at this time.

A method of Hindu directing has been already exemplified in a former volume,* and although I intended including an outline myself in this survey, yet the disparity of various factors between Eastern and Western methods causes me to doubt whether any good purpose would be served by a more extensive consideration of the peculiar systems of the Hindus, than that which I have alluded to. For until there is a more reasonable amalgamation of the two in essentials and preliminaries, it is idle to expect the average student to give much of his attention to the directional portion.

CYCLIC DIRECTIONS.

Let us turn now then to what is known as cyclic directing or directing by planetary periods. It has been found that each planet possesses a distinct period of its own, one not directly related to its actual motion: therefore, given the particular lengths of these periods as they concern each individual planet, the actual place of the latter attained by period at any stated epoch can be easily discovered by proportion, the motion being uniform throughout. Then we may see what aspects are formed to the places of the heavenly bodies, and consequently judge what influence is operating. The following is the usually given table:

* See *Dictionary of Astrology, Vol. I.*

TABLE OF CELESTIAL PERIODS.

Period.	Motion per year.	Motion per month.
☉ 19 years*	19°	1°35'
☽ 4 „†	90	7 30
☿ 10 „	36	3 0
♀ 8 „	45	3 45
♂ 15 „	24	2 0
♃ 12 „	30	2 30
♄ 30 „	12	1 0
♅ 84 „	7	0 35

This table, it must be confessed, is not very well attested in some of its parts, and many who use the system take nineteen years as the period of Mars. But be they right or wrong, the method of computing the places for any time required is simple enough. The major aspects alone need be dealt with.

For instance, if we desire Saturn directed to the conjunction of the Radical Moon in Map No. 2, we find that they are 15°38' apart, Saturn being zodiacally in advance of the Moon; then as the Saturnian period is thirty years, and, at the rate of 12° per year, 15°38' will be equivalent to 1 year, 3 months, 20 days, and this subtracted from the whole period, as Saturn has passed the place of aspect, gives 28 years, 8 months, 10 days, at which time Saturn, by cyclic direction, will be over the Moon's radical position. Seven and a half years after that, a square aspect would be formed, and another similar division of time would result in the opposition, and the half period of fifteen years added to this would bring about the second conjunction at 58 years, 8 months, 10 days. Other positions may be similarly calculated.

As will be seen in the following chapter, the use of these periods seems to consist in providing a broad and extensive basis rather than in denoting particular passing events. Simmonite avowed he would rather pay more attention to transits than periods; and I am inclined to endorse his opinion, until a wider investigation has yielded us a sounder and surer knowledge.

* This is the ἐννεακαιδεκαετηρίς or Metonic Cycle discovered during the eighty-seventh olympiad (432 B.C.), and which brings the solar and lunar periods to a point of relative incidence. It was a knowledge of this law that rendered the ancients able to predict eclipses, etc., with certainty

† The Greeks had a cycle of four years, τετραετηρίς, or as it was originally called, πενταετηρίς.

PROFECTIONAL DIRECTIONS.

There is a method of directing laid down in the last chapter of Ptolemy's *Tetrabiblos*, which is much akin to the Hindu system, in that each planet is brought to rule a certain term or period of life in succession, from which is derived another under sub-rule, a still lower descent being made to a circle beneath this. I refer to profectional directing. Briefly we proceed as follows.

Number the years from birth to the one for which the profectional directions are desired to be taken, and for every year add one sign to the *sign containing the Hyleg* at birth. The lord of the sign so deduced is the chronocrator for that year. Note that the computation is made from the degree of the sign holding the hyleg, therefore the term may include portions of two signs. Thus if it be required to find the annual chronocrator for the twenty-seventh year (Map 2), reference is made to the hylegiacal place, which is here the ascendant, and from $2°\Omega 13'$ to $2°\text{m}13'$ would be the ruling period for the first year, and from $2°\text{m}13'$ to $2° \text{♐} 13'$ that for the ensuing year, so that for the twenty-seventh year a progression through the various signs of the zodiac would have been completed twice before arrival was made again at the point required, *viz.*, $2° \text{♐} 13'$ to $2°\text{♑}13'$, the lords of which signs are the actual chronocrators for the year.

Having determined this point, the monthly profection may be acquired therefrom in this manner:—Allow twenty-eight days for the month,* and for every month after natal month add one sign, counting from the sign of the year.†

EXAMPLE : *Required, the ruling sign and planet for August 27th to September 27th, 1897 (Map 2).*

Counting from the annual sign, the first month of the natal year, *viz.*, October 27th to November 27th, has for chronocrator the identical sign governing the whole year, and proceeding with the enumeration we arrive at the month required, where we find roughly‡ $2°\Omega13'$ to $2°\text{m}13'$

---

* The true synodical period (the embolismic of Ptolemy) which appears to regulate this method is not 28 days, but 29 days, 12 hrs., 44 min., 2·684 sec. (29·5305887 days).

† They would probably be more correctly taken if from actual birth—but they serve.

‡ In reality a little more (the Arabian system allowed 30° for each year and month).

has dominion, Venus and in a minor way Mars being the implicated planets.

To the days may be also apportioned their respective rulers,* if desired, by allowing a sign for every two days and eight hours after birth, still keeping to the month of twenty-eight days, and counting (as Wilson thinks) from the day of the month on which the birth occurred.

Thus ignoring the days, we get *first*, the annual period bearing rule over the entire year; *secondly*, the monthly ones, having a sub-dominion over each month, thus:

Annual Period (27th year) ruled by 2° ♐ 13' to 2° ♑ 13', ♃ and ♄, monthly sub-periods (13 Embolismic Lunations).

E.L.	Days.	Horoscope.	Monthly sign and rulers.
1	0— 28	Oct. 27th—Nov. 23rd	2° ♐ 13'—2° ♑ 13'
2	28— 56	Nov. 23rd—Dec. 21st	2 ♑ 13 —2 ♒ 13
3	56— 84	Dec. 21st —Jan. 18th	2 ♒ 13—2 ♓ 13
4	84—112	etc.	etc.

E.L.	Days.		Days.		Days.
5	112—140	8	196—224	11	280—308
6	140—168	9	224—252	12	308—336
7	168—196	10	252—280	13	336—364

The method of giving judgment is similar to the Hindu, and is arrived at by a judicious combination in the first place of the several elements as they stand. The annual sign and its rulers will exhibit the general influence for the year, and the monthly places the equivalent monthly influences.

Notice, however, is to be paid to the representation of these places in the radix, both as regards sign and planet and their position by this progressed motion in regard to the ascendant, M.C., etc.; *also what planets, if any, are at the time of profection passing by transit through such signs ruling the year or month.* The principal use would appear to be, as stated of cyclic directions, in supplying media for primaries and secondaries to function in, and in this respect I can conceive an influence more than in any other way.

Of course, further division of the yearly sign itself can be made into solar months by dividing the 30° by 12, and so obtaining a measure of 2°30' for that time, and it follows, too, that this monthly period can be proportionately divided to ascertain daily minutes of passage, but this is scarcely practicable when we are so much at sea with the larger

* This of course has mostly to do with the fixed rulers, such as the Sun over Sunday, Saturn Saturday, Mercury Wednesday, etc.

influences and periods. That these cyclic progressions and returns, combinations and loci, have a value, seems pretty evident, and Raphael has somewhere said that he is inclined to discredit the usual forms of directing in favour of them, believing that everything runs in cycles. There is no doubt an element of truth in this, but we cannot honestly subscribe to much at the present hour. We must continue groping a little longer.

SOLAR REVOLUTIONS.

Another method of prevoyance is that of the Solar Revolution, which strictly is made from a map erected for the time the Sun reaches the exact degree and minute of longitude in the sign it possessed at birth. Upon this basis Simmonite has laboriously reared a complicated structure which to explain here, even partially, would exhaust many pages and most likely the reader's patience as well, so that an account and an explanation must be deferred to a future occasion ; and as it is not properly a method of directing, it may very well be omitted.

Methods are so numerous that it is well-nigh a hopeless task for one student to become thoroughly conversant with all. Far better would be the result if, while by no means neglecting to become acquainted with any and every matter appertaining to the art of directing, some one department were to be chosen by each worker, to be intended for special investigation, and the results, however small and apparently insignificant at the time, accurately tabulated.

In an *aperçu* like the present, it is totally impossible to enter deeply into every topic, when each one might have been in itself the subject of an inquiry quite as extended as the whole essay.

For my own part, I consider that the computation and combination of Primary and Secondary directions, with a due appreciation of *transits*, *ingresses* and *lunations*, to be, for all ordinary interests and purposes, the best method of procedure. It will be objected, doubtless, by some, that the first-named do not act commensurately with the time they occupy in calculating, but this is only partially true, the personal bias having a great deal to do with it. Even so, however, it is no excuse for neglect, and as our investigations deepen, little by little we shall see for ourselves the former objection removing farther and farther away, and our own ignorance becoming slowly but surely a thing of the past.

If a hasty or general survey of a subject's life be required, then secondaries provide a ready and excellent means. But when we come to consider what a *life* means, I think it will be admitted that to map out, year after year, possibilities and events, change and circumstance, advance and recession, intention and contingence, will be a more enormous task than the ordinary astrologer countenances; so that he might well feel justified in proceeding on the assumption that grave matters and lengthy operations need an equivalent consideration when attempting to ascertain them by means of astrological laws.

In the next chapter I shall outline what I consider an appropriate method of co-ordination of the several series implicated, including only those mentioned previously, which I think will be found to cover the most ground reasonably to nature and satisfactorily to *human* nature.

CHAPTER VIII.

THE CO-ORDINATION, INTERDEPENDENCE AND POWER OF THE SEVERAL
FORMS OF DIRECTING, WITH THE USE OF SUCH AUXILIARIES
AS TRANSITS, ETC.

" FORTASSE non omnia eveniunt quæ predicta sunt. Ne ægria quidem qui
a non omnes convalescunt, idcirco ars nulla medicina est."—*De Natura Deorum.*
CICERO.

IF we look over the subject carefully, it will be found that we can con-
struct a scale of the various processes involved in affecting man's welfare,
and approximately obtain a very fair idea of their relative intensity, their
scope, interdependence and order. Collecting the more universal ones
together, they may be arranged somewhat as follows in a gradually
ascending series. The correlation is probably not exact because we can
only in a general way at present—and clumsily at that—recognise fully
the interdependence and ramification of all systems, and the peculiar
sympathy of certain methods with others.

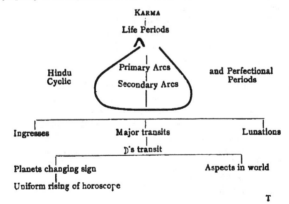

KARMA

Life Periods

Hindu   Primary Arcs   and Perfectional
Cyclic   Secondary Arcs   Periods

Ingresses   Major transits   Lunations

☽'s transit

Planets changing sign   Aspects in world

Uniform rising of horoscope

T

Such a tabular view I am well aware is, and must be, incomplete, so that I have not descended to details. It is almost impossible to include all the orders through which planetary influence communicates itself to us, and certainly so to fit them in their proper niches. Roughly, however, for our present purpose the tabular view will be sufficient, and we see at once that it forms a gradually ascending scale, whose component parts deal more hardly with us the higher we ascend, "Leading through nature up to nature's God." Or we may think of it as a ladder which all have to climb, the height not being proportionately lower for the nervous ones, but equally formed for both them and their more self-possessed brethren.

Immediately below Karma we find the Life Periods common to all men, *vis.:*

(1) The first four years of life ruled by the Moon before the rational mind is exerted, a period characterised by rapid growth and imperfection of parts. (0—4.)

(2) The period from four years of age to ten years immediately following, under Mercury, in which the rational and intellectual is shadowed forth and intelligence begins to be displayed. (5—14.)

(3) The next eight years, over which Venus dominates, and during which the seminal motion commences, resulting in eagerness, desire and rashness. (15—22.)

(4) The Sun's period of nineteen years during which, if ever, ambition, honours and authority are aimed at. (23—41.)

(5) Mars follows with fifteen years and brings the true age of manhood, with the incidental anxieties, difficulties and austerity. (42—56.)

(6) A period of twelve years under the dominion of Jupiter. Maturity with reflection, prudence, and all the vivid results of experience. Ease, honour and quiet. (57—68.)

(7) From here onwards to the end of life comes under Saturn. The animal spirits evaporate or become obstructed, and the mind, appetites and enjoyments become dull or entirely fail. (69—100.)

These things are so well-known* as the concomitants of the natural trend of life, that astrologically they are forgotten, but the possibilities

---

* Aptly illustrated by Shakespeare ("As you like it," Act ii., Sc. 7) in lines which have become part and parcel of the universal inheritance. So too Lucretius iii. 446 (*et seq.*) provides a fitting parallel in the following words :

    Præterea, gigne pariter cum corpore, et una
    Crescere sentimus, pariterque senescere mentem,
    Nam velut infirmo pueri teneroque vagantur,

of each and every age are required to be taken into consideration when judging the effects of directions.

When dealing with the Primaries it is best to tabulate them under the headings of ***nomen***, ***arcus***, ***mensura***, and ***eventus directionis***, as will be seen by the following specimen.

PRIMARIES (*from Map* 2).

Nomen Directionis.	*Arcus Direc.*	*Men. D. Naibodi.*	*Eventus Direc.*
☽ △ ♂ *d.d. zod.*	22°36′		
☉ ∥ ☿ (rapt. par.)	22 39	23rd birthday.	(In this column
Asc. ✱ ♂ *mund.*	22 40		insert the events
☉ ✱ ♂ *conv. mund.*	22 41		anticipated as the
☉ P. ♆ *con. zod.*	22 47	23 years 2 mths.	probable result
M.C. ∠ ♅ *con. zod.*	23 2	23 „ 5 „	of the several
M.C. ∠ ♆ *mund.*	24 0	24 „ 2 „	directions).
M.C. ☍ ☽ *mund.*	25 11	25 „ 7 „	
M.C. □ ♆ *zod. d.*	25 17	25 „ 8 „	
M.C. ☌ ♅ *zod. d.*	25 32		
M.C. ☍ ☽ *zod. conv.*	25 37	26th birthday.	
M.C. ☌ ♅ *mund.*	25 38		

Whether it is best to omit all mention of actual sources from which judgment is drawn, when executing such for the benefit of persons not astrologers and the matter not intended to see the light of day in print, is a point to be decided individually. Personally I see no reason to admit the least extent of tabulation or reference to originating influences for *causa latet* even though *res est notissima*; and in the majority of cases it will be found to depreciate rather than add value to the remarks when continual reference is made to signs, houses, arcs, etc., and the text plentifully bestrewed with symbols. Any astrological explanation to one who has no acquaintance with even the rudiments of the science, and who perhaps never intends to trouble about them, would not only be useless but unwise. To him of course who is endeavouring to grope his way in the study, I can conceive that in the initial stages of such attempt the purely astrological references would be suggestive and instructive if coming from a conscientious elucidator.

Returning from our digression it may be mentioned in passing, that the column for the event may be conveniently omitted when a horoscope is under treatment by various methods; for the results of these latter will require combining, as the unity of the whole will not be obtained by discoursing on each separate arc, aspect and transit, without having recourse to a consideration of the entire trend of planetary influence at any one period.

Let us first collect the parts of the various series together into a tabular statement, which will present such an appearance as here follows:

Directions for the Year 1897.

From the nativity of a female born October 27th, 1870, at 3hrs. 52mins. a.m., G.M.T.

Primaries.

Nomen Directionis.			*Arcus Direc.*	*Mensura D. Naibodi.*
⊙	∠ ♂	*conv. zod.*	25°47′	26 years 2 mths.
Asc.	✶ ⊙	*d.d. mund.*	26 8	} 26 „ 6 „
Asc.	∠ ♂	*conv. zod.*	26 8	
☽	□ ascend. deg.	*d.d. zod.*	26 10	26 „ 7 „
♅	□ ascend. deg.	*conv. zod.*	26 19	26 „ 9 „
⊙	P. ☽	*d.d. zod.*	26 24	26 „ 10 „
Asc.	☍ ♆	*d.d. zod.*	26 45	} 27 „ 1 „
M.C.	⚼ ♀	*d.d. zod.*	26 48	
Asc.	P. ♆	*conv. zod.*	26 56	27 „ 6 „

Secondaries.

Solar.

⊙ p. □ ♂ r.	♏-♌	III.-XI.	(in process of transition)
⊙ p. ☌ ☿ p.	♐	III.	(complete)

Radical Lunar.

☽ r. P. ♀ p.	♐-♏	III.	(in process of formation)

Progressive Lunar.

Jan.	☽ ⚻ ♆ r.	♏-♈	II.-VII.
April	☽ ⚻ ♃ p.	♏-♊	II.-IX.
May	☽ ☌ ♀ p.	♏	III.
	☽ Q. ♂ p.	♏-♍	III.-XII.
June	☽ △ ♅ r., p.	♏-♋	III.-X.
	☽ Bq. ♆ r., p.	♏-♈	III.-VII.
Aug.	☽ □ ♂ r.	♏-♌	III.-XI.
Sept.	☽ ☌ ☿ p.	♐	III.
Oct.	☽ ☌ ⊙ p.	♐	III.
	☽ ✶ Asc.	♐-♎	III.-I.
Nov.	☽ ∠ ☿ r.	♐-♎	III.-I.

Major Transits.

Jan.	♄ □ ♂	♃ □ ☽		*July*	♃ □ ☽	♂ □ ☽		
Feb.	♅ □ ♂			*Aug.*	♂ □ ♄	Asc. ☌ ♂		
Mar.	♂ ☌ ♃	♅ □ ♂	♃ ✶ ⊙	*Sept.*	♄ □ ♂			
April	♅ □ ♂	♄ □ ♂	♂ □ ☿	*Oct.*	♃ □ ♄	♃ □ ♃	♅ □ ♂	♂ ☌ ⊙
May	♂ ☌ ♅			*Nov.*	♃ over ascendant			
June	♃ ✶ ⊙	♄ △ ♅	♅ △ ♅	*Dec.*	♂ ☌ ☽	♄ approaching ☌ ☽		

*Ditto Ingresses.**

Jan.	♄ ☌ ⊙		*Aug.*	♃ ☌ ♂		
Feb.	♅ ☌ ⊙		*Sept.*	♃ □ ♃	♂ ∠ ⊙	
May	☿ ☍ ♀		*Oct.*	♃ □ ♄	♃ ✶ ⊙	
June	♄ △ ♅	♅ △ ♅	*Nov.*	♄ ☌ ☽	♂ ☌ ☽	♃ ✶ ☽
July	♂ □ ⊙	♂ ☌ ♂	*Dec.*	♅ approaching ☌ ☽		

Ditto Lunations.

March, April, June, July, August, October.

* "Ingresses" are the passages over the *progressive* places of planets in contra distinction to those over the *radical* positions, denominated "Transits."

We have now a fairly complete outline of the operative influences for the year, and one which will be adjudged sufficiently expanded to ensure a satisfactory explanation on a purely astrological basis of the events of the year. It remains only for the various factors to be skilfully blended and translated into plain and pointed language, and the task of the astral philosopher is complete. The length, the extent, the applicability and truth of the delineation depend obviously enough on the powers of the operator—powers which time alone and an intense, unwearied, conscientious study will obtain for him.

The transits, ingresses and lunations will bring all into play, and I should advise a particular attention to the former, as apart from directions they will indicate much to a true student. The latter will never allow a day to pass without ascertaining those in force for the twenty-four hours in advance, as well in his horoscope as in the world.

Those who look upon them as only acting when they happen to occur round the birthday must have small powers of observation, or such a ridiculous theory could never be supported. Let each examine for himself until it becomes clear in his own mind that transits are continually acting, and though occasionally they appear to produce nothing, a passage of ♃ bringing no benefits and one of ♄ no evil, the cause is not far to seek, and will be found in the strength and constitution of the direction at the time.

I could adduce many instances of judgment drawn solely from a series of transits, and what is more, with unimpeachable attestation, but I am of opinion that what has been previously remarked will be sufficient for my purpose—that of inducing students not to overlook them.

In writing the delineation, attention should be first paid to the general nature of the whole year deduced from a consideration of the primary arcs and solar secondaries. *Endeavour to realise what the great karmic law of nature has intended the ego should learn, suffer, or energise, at this one time. Try to understand what is the lesson to be learnt, the trial to be overcome, or the wisdom to be indrawn. They are there if we will read them.*

Thus on reference to the tabulation we find in this instance that worry, ill-health and intellectual advancement are the dominating characteristics for 1897.

The solar secondary of ☉ ☌ ☿ will throw open the intellectual channels as wide as the nature is fitted to allow, and there will result much dealing in books and association with literary persons and things.

This is intensified in September, when ☽ ☌ ☿ is formed. Mystical affairs are certain to be to the fore, and abundant opportunity is provided for the perceptive faculties to develop. It is pretty safe to assert that if this chance is lost the gates will be closed so far as this present incarnation is concerned. The opportunities the year affords will never arise again.

After thoroughly unravelling the major influences which affect the native more or less throughout the entire year, consideration may then be made of the minor aspects, reducing these to the heading of months, and noticing when there is any particular concatenation of major and minor influences, because then the resultant effects will be more serious, or beneficial, as the case may be. Directions also of planets which concur with similar life or planetary periods, will act powerfully by sympathy during such times, or the opposed planet by antipathy. Thus during Mars' period directions of that planet would act with full force by reason of its sympathetic accord, as well as those of Venus by antipathetic discord.

Finally, recourse may be had to the transits, etc., which, supposing all our calculations have been correctly made from correct data, will frequently appoint the exact day of planetary action, its incipience or its culmination.

There will be faults, assuredly, for neither directing nor the director is infallible, but that is no more argument that the art is false, as Cicero remarks in the note at the head of this chapter, than that medicine is so because patients die under the doctors' hands.

A last word. The *Radix* is ever the key to the whole matter. Let not the student anticipate the worst from "evil" directions arising out of a fortunate nativity, nor, on the other hand, the most favourable results from "good" directions from an afflicted geniture.

FINIS.

APPENDIX I.

THE PROGRESSED HOROSCOPE IN DETAIL.

To those who wish to study in detail the directions predisposing to a certain event—to find out, as far as possible, WHY the circumstances were exactly as they were and happened exactly when they did—the following little exposition of the general theory of The Progressed Horoscope And Its Offshoots will be of interest. It is taken from a paper which appeared in *Modern Astrology* in June, 1903 (Vol. XIV., p. 229), to which article those may refer who wish to see a practical exemplification of the method suggested. The whole idea is but the logical outcome of the principles previously enunciated.

The writer says, (referring to the death of native at 23y. 5m. 13½d.) :—

" I am here concerned chiefly with the question of *terminus vitæ*. This I propose to consider with reference to the ' progressed horoscope.'*

" The theory of ' progression ' I conceive to be, broadly speaking, as follows :— The three prime cycles (or circles) of *Day, Month,* and *Year,* are mutually sympathetic, *i.e.,* the influences dominant in the one are reflected in the events prominent in the others; thus, (A) the first *day* is a picture in miniature of the first year of life, (B) the first *month* (synodic month, 29·53059 days), is similarly a picture, in greater detail, of this first year, (C) the *year* itself filling in all the outlines; similarly, succeeding days and months picture succeeding years.

" The entire influences, therefore, going to produce the events of any one day of life are shown by

▽ : The Horoscope of Birth, the root out of which all events must grow, its influence extending throughout the life : *projected forward in any given year into*

A : The Progressed Horoscope for the year (a map erected for exact birth-time on equivalent day after birth)——1 *day* = 1 year : *particularised in*

B : The Progressed Lunar Horoscope (map for as many months after birth as subject is years old)——1 *month* = 1 year : *and actualised in*

C : The Diurnal Horoscope——1 *year* = 1 year†. The absolute *point of time* when any influence shall attain its maximum effect being indicated by the rotation of the latter figure.

" Thus we have *four* figures, giving us the influences as projected upon the native in the order of their intensity; first the generalised, then the particularised. The mode of operation of these influences may be illustrated by the following diagram, where the braces may be regarded as *lenses,* so to speak :—

---

* [*Nata :* 3h. 3m. 33s. p.m., local mean time (*rectified time*) 17/12/1878. Lat. 32°14'N., 1°28'E. ; *obiit,* 1/6/'02, about 0 to 3 a.m.]

† The "diurnal horoscope" is treated of in *Directions and Directing,* p. 58 ; " converse directions," to which reference is made below, are also discussed (under the term ' pre-natal directions ') on p. 60.—EDITOR.

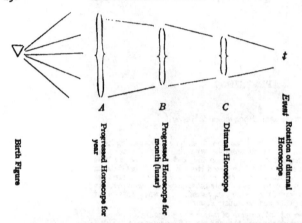

"Here we have a series of Three Horoscopes, *A*, *B*, *C*, which, taking certain generalised influences, focus them in a progressive manner, so determining the culmination of any given influence upon some one specific day. They may be compared to the wheels and dial of a clock:—it is the weight which maintains the motion; this is regulated in its action by wheels, corresponding to (*A*) hour-hand, (*B*) minute-hand, and lastly (*C*) second-hand; both hour and minute-hand may have passed the XII., yet not until the seconds-mechanism is in relation thereto does the midnight hour strike.

"It should here be borne in mind that, given a set of figures in this way, *no one of them stands still*—though they move at different rates. Thus, a figure for the 23rd day after birth represents the 23rd year of life, starting from the birth-day of that year; yet this same figure accomplishes one complete rotation—*plus one degree* (which gives the 'progressed M.C.')—during the said year. There-fore, say we desire to know the effective (major and minor) influences operating at the age of 23y. 5m. 13½d. (23·45156 years), we must *also* consider the corre-spondingly revolved figures—which I will call *A'*, *B'*, *C'*—in addition to the key-figures *A*, *B*, *C*; just as we must consider the progressed horoscope as well as the nativity in ordinary matters.*

"It will be seen, then, that the estimation of the total influences in action at any given time is a somewhat more complicated task than might have been supposed; but if the *relative* importance of the various figures concerned is well kept in view, no confusion need arise.

"Having, I trust, clearly established my working principles so far, I want' before commenting in any way on figures *A'*, *B'*, and *C'*, to turn aside for a moment, not without due grounds, to consider the question of the so-called "converse directions." For a careful discussion of this subject I must refer the reader to Mr. Green's admirable *Theoretical Astrology*, to which book I am

---

* NOTE. The figure termed *A'* is identical with what is called by some writers the "lunar equivalent"- a very inappropriate term, it seems to me.

indebted for a clear grasp of the principles underlying "directions." Briefly put, the proposition may be thus stated:—any given influence impressed upon any zodiacal point at any given time (say ♂ ☌ ♄ 22° ♊) may be considered to be *carried forward by the motion of the earth* and to reach M.C., Asc., etc., after the lapse of certain definite periods of time, when the influence of the planetary position will make itself felt as though actually active at that time. Thus twenty-three days, months or years *after* birth the influences of the same periods *before* birth will then have arrived at the ascendant, M.C., etc. Obviously, therefore, we have as many *converse* as *direct* progressed figures, 'solar,' 'lunar,' and 'mundane.'

"In the case under discussion we have, then, these periods: 23·45156 days' months and years respectively, *forwards* and *backwards*; yielding in all six figures, which I will tabulate symbolically as follows:—

BALANCE SHEET.

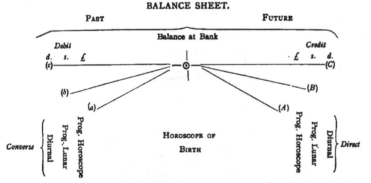

"This arrangement will I think make it quite clear what relative importance I attach to the various figures. It will also convey an idea which is strongly impressed upon me, *i.e.*, that converse directions pourtray past kárma chiefly, [in other words, the effect of actions committed under the various opportunities of the past, in previous lives] while the forward directions indicate the opportunities of the future [in this present life].

"The data required for above figures—which I regret that lack of space prevents me giving in their entirety—are as follows (Birmingham table of houses will do, or even London):—

Age 23·00 years[*]:—

A. 22-13-8.	*B.* 19-22-9.	*C.* 7-31-4.
a. 19-12-6.	*b.* 16-19-39.	*c.* 9-54-30.

Age 23·45156 years:—

A'. 10/1/'78: 9-3-5.	*B'.* 9/11/'80: 7-5-47.	[†]*C.* 31/5/'02: 7-31-4.
a'. 24/11/'78: 8-22-29.	*b'.* 24/1/'79: 10/19/48.	*c.* 6/7/'55: 9-54-30.

[*] 22-13-8: 9-3-5: etc., means the R.A.M.C. or *Sidereal Time* (in *hrs.*, *mins.* and *secs.*), on the dates in question, for which the maps should be erected.

[†] *C'* and *c'*, of course, would have been obtained—if we are to follow the analogy —by respectively adding and subtracting *the time after* 2h. 58m. 52s. *p.m.* that death (in this case a violent one) occurred, were this known.

"It is perhaps well to refer to a variant of (B', b'), the lunar progressed horoscope, that suggests itself.

Age at death=23·45156 years. (A', a')
            =290·067 months (synodic). (BB', bb')
            =8565 days. (C', c')

"If we call *each* of these periods days, we obtain (A', a', C', c'), and a new figure I will call (BB', bb'); our series then being constructed on the principle that each *mundane* rotation = a *solar*, a *lunar*, and a *mundane* revolution respectively. These maps are

$(BB') = 3/10/'79.$ 17·25·30. $(bb') = 2/3/'78.$ 21·21·4.

"Which of these is the correct lunar figure I am unable to determine. It will be seen that in the given instance *each* is remarkably significant of a sudden and violent end.

"In calculating these figures *mean* periods and *sidereal* time have been used.

"I feel certain that any student who will take the trouble to study these maps will be more than repaid for his labour in the clearer grasp he will gain of the nature of directions in general.

"(*I find it convenient to draw the maps on square post-cards; the houses and signs in* black, *and the planets in* red *for A' B' C, and* green *for a' b' c*.)"

We have quoted just so much of the article referred to as will suffice to make clear the procedure to be adopted. The student is recommended to take what he considers to be the most significant event that has occurred in his own life, and to tabulate the directions predisposing thereto, in the manner described—setting out his maps thus,

$$a'\ a \qquad A\ A'$$
$$b'\ b\ \triangledown\ B\ B'$$
$$c'\ c \qquad C\ C'$$

with the nativity in the centre—and to weigh in his mind the relative gravity of each map in relation to the event concerned. It may seem a very tedious matter to calculate such a number of maps, but it is surely better for him to spend this amount of work over *one* event, and get to the bottom of it, than to fritter away the same energy over a dozen or more different occurrences. At any rate, by this course he will learn, in a way he could not otherwise, how an event which may seem to result from a certain aspect, will be found on further investigation to be far more clearly indicated by another aspect, resulting from a different method of "direction."

He will thus be prevented from taking a short-sighted view of the subject, and he will find the breadth of outlook gained, which will be of great value to him in his later studies, more than compensate for the trouble involved

APPENDIX II.

THERE is one point which deserves attention, and that bears on the question of "primary" directions—which it is perhaps just as well that every student should understand, at least in principle if not in practice.

In normal cases, the fœtus is nine months in gestation, during which time the Sun completes three-quarters of his annual journey. For only three months of that particular cycle does the child see the light of day ; the previous nine are spent in the darkness of the womb. This gives us the proportion 1 to 3, and it suggests that the visible life upon earth is only a quarter of that particular cycle in the greater life of the Ego of which it is a section.

Now, if this is so, we see that the ninety years which form the normal complement of human life will correspond (a) to the three months or *quarter-year* succeeding birth, (*i.e.*, the ' progressed' or ' progressive' horoscope) and (b) to the six hours or *quarter-day* succeeding the moment of birth, (' primary' directions). The first of these analogies will be seen to hold good as regards the Progressed Horoscope, from what has been already said concerning the latter ; the second, on the other hand, affords a reasonable explanation of the principle underlying the so-called "primary" directions, which latter have undeniably established a claim to consideration through practical instances, but are yet (in our opinion) mistakenly conceived of when regarded as the *only* possible accurate means of foretelling the future.

The question now arises :—" If these methods are both true in some way as analogy suggests they should be, how are we to regard them : and, in the case of a ' good' direction in one coinciding with a ' bad' direction in another, to which are we to accord precedence ? " The answer to this appears to be that since the horoscope of birth is the prime factor involved, so that good directions therefrom can only be interpreted in terms thereof,—a consideration too often lost sight of by many students—in the same way, the quarter-rotation of the globe succeeding birth must be regarded as holding precedence over the Progressed Horoscope.

In other words, the six-hours-after-birth directions—(' primary')—may be regarded as determining, in conjunction with the birth figure, those conditions of life which constitute our *fate*, that portion of our " karma" which does not depend upon any actions of our own in our present life but is the heritage, good or bad, of our past lives ; that which we cannot escape by any circumspection on our own part. As examples may be instanced inherited or unexpected sources of revenue, death of parents, misfortunes brought upon us through national disaster, etc. ; in a word, our *fixed fate*, corresponding in a sense to the effects of Uranus, the planet typical of the inevitable and the unforeseen. It represents what may be termed the hereditary constitution of the soul—*The Form, and its limits of expansion*.

The " progressed horoscope," on the other hand, may be taken as representing the possibilities of individual growth within the limits of the form thus marked out : it indicates those trials and conflicts which are brought against us in order to test our strength, and by struggling with which we may develop and expand these resources we already possess ; and also, of course, those joys and benefits of which we may accept just so much as we can profitably use; corresponding to the planets Saturn and Jupiter. It represents, in fact, what may be paralleled as physical exercise, rest and nourishment: in brief, *The Life and its inflow.* No doubt this distinction will be found also to apply to the " converse " directions alluded to in Appendix I., if the suggestion there made as to the essential distinction between direct and converse directions is carefully borne in mind.

With these considerations we may leave the subject for the present. In another portion of this work will be found a treatise on the method of computing ' primary ' directions, and it need hardly be said that any delineations based on the " progressed horoscope " will be capable of application in an analagous way to the directions calculated according to this method—due allowance, however, being made for the fundamental difference hinted at above.

A Simple Way of Calculating Primary Directions.

A word in conclusion as to a brief and easy way of computing (approxi-mately) the most important ' primary ' directions for any year. Set up the houses of the horoscope just as you would for the progressed horoscope, but do not insert the planets' places: then refer the positions in the birth horoscope to this new map. Note particularly the *angles* of the new figure: any aspect therefrom to a radical planet is of importance, but by far the most important ' direction ' is the arrival at any angle of the radical position of a planet, for the influence of that planet will then reach its culminating or lowest point (M.C. or I.C.), or will thenceforward fade, disappear (Descdt.), or, on the other hand, increase (Ascdt.), according to the angle concerned.* Thus, suppose at birth M.C. is ♉ 15,° while ♅ is ♊ 11°: in the 26th year of life, when the M.C. has progressed to ♊ 11° the influence of ♅ in its *physical* aspect (calamities) will then reach its maximum, and the greatest crash will fall upon the native— that is, a sudden event, good or bad according to the nature of and the aspects to ♅ in the birth horoscope—will then happen. In this way the most striking years of life (in its external aspect at any rate) can be seen, by mere inspection, from a Table of Houses for the birth-place.

It should, however, be remembered that this method is only *approximate* in any case, and is at best incomplete, so that those who value accuracy should study carefully that part of this book which is devoted to the mathematical method of directing. (Section D.)

---

* This subject is treated of to some extent in Chapter VIII. of *Astrology for All, Part II.* (p. 47).

APPENDIX III.

THE SO-CALLED SECONDARY DIRECTION. A NEW METHOD.

THE following method of computing "secondary" directions (almost identical with what are termed "primary" directions by some writers) appeared in the December, 1904, issue of *Modern Astrology*, and is of sufficient interest and importance to be included here.   The writer, Mr. C. C. Massey, says :—

The presentation of the late Queen's horoscope in your October number induces me to send you the following correction in computing the secondary direction (considered primary by Placidus), which solves the problem of bringing ♃ exactly to the meridian as the direction for accession to the throne.

The method laid down in all the books, and always followed, is to allow a *day* for a *year*, and proportionally for additional months and weeks.   There is thus, without apparent reason, a departure from the Ptolemaic measure of time in the primary direction, which assigns *a degree of longitude* for a *year*, and so proportionally.

My suggestion is :—
(1) To apply this measure to the direction now called secondary, by addition to the Sun's longitude at birth, and

(2) To consider the "day = year" as determined, not by clock time, but by an *equivalent*—not an equal—distance of the Sun from the meridian.
By way of illustration, and also for verification, as far as one instance can avail, let me take the direction for Queen Victoria's accession, as follows :

Neglecting seconds, the direction, $18°4'$, is from the Sun at birth, Gemini $2°7'$ to Gemini $20°11'$, with R.A. $79°19'$, Decl. $23°6'$, Asc. Diff. $32°26'$ There is a slight error in your diagram of $12'$ in the R.A. of meridian, because you (with Mr. Pearce in his "Science of the Stars") have taken the time of birth given as local time, whereas it is presumably clock or Greenwich (mean) time.   A proportional deduction must therefore be made for the meridian at Kensington Palace, 51secs. less than Greenwich. This gives ♒$2°12'$ on that meridian, with R.A. $304°28'$, and M.D. of Sun $115°33'$. Now to find the meridian at direction, bring the longitude of ☉ then to the M.D. equivalent, by proportion of semi-arcs, to that of ☉ at birth.   Thus :—
Semi-arc of rad. ☉, $118°13'$ IS TO *Meridian Distance of* ☉ *then*, $115°33'$, AS *semi-arc o* ☉ *at direction*, $122°26'$ IS TO *Meridian Distance at direction*, $119°40'$.

By logarithms a°c. 9·81741
·19250
·16737

·17728 = $119°40'$)

The Meridian is therefore R.A. of ☉ $79°19'$ ($439°19'$) *minus* $119°40'$ = $319°39'$, the R.A. of ♃ at birth being $319°37'$.—a direction obtained without any rectification of the birth-time given, and, I submit, by an entirely rational procedure.

I have tried this method with success in other cases, but I do not pretend that the result is always satisfactory.   For what method of directing can that be claimed? But I hope that you or your expert readers will give it a trial.

Postscript.—To the foregoing, I will add another mode of directing, by which the same result is obtained for the same event, in the same nativity.   But a word of explanation or justification is necessary.

No one will object to the above simple direction of ⊙ in the zodiac, because it merely substitutes the exact proportional advance of ⊙ (or the equivalent of longitude to time observed in the primary zodiacal direction) for the diurnal advance, which does not keep that proportion. But I have now to propose a bolder innovation. I do not see why any planet should not be similarly directed, regardless of its actual rate of motion. In the one case, as in the other, we have done with the "day = year" of the old secondary direction. Every degree of the zodiac represents the Sun at that point, and whatever the rate of a planet's revolution, for the purpose of directing we may equate its distance from any other zodiacal point on the degree = year principle.

It is, in short, the Sun's proportional time that determines the period represented in Astrology by zodiacal distances.

By this method of directing I do not conceive the planet as moving out of his place at birth at all, but I feign the Sun advancing from that place to the directional point and then proceed as follows, (in the case of the late Queen's accession):

The longitude of ♃ is ≈16°57′, to which I add 18°4′ for the age at accession, bringing the longitude to ✕5°1′, with R.A. 336°52′, Decl. 9°40½′, Asc. Diff. 12°23′, semi-arc diurnal 77°37′. I now bring this longitude, ✕5°1′, to the meridian distance corresponding to that of ♃ at birth, which is 15°9′.

This correspondence is obtained, of course, by proportion of the semi-arcs, thus:

Semi-Arc of ♃ at birth   68°18′
Is to M.D. of ♃ at birth   15°19′
As Semi-Arc of the directional longitude (✕5°1′)   77°37′
Is to M.D. of ✕5°1′   17°14′•
Which is M.D. of ✕5°1′ east of Meridian
Therefore,
R.A. of ✕5°1′, 336°32′ − M.D. 17°14′ = R.A. of Meridian   319°38′.
R.A. of ♃ at birth   319°37′.

Thus by the direction of the Sun from the place of ♃, that planet is brought exactly to the Meridian, as also by the direction of the Sun from his own place, in both cases the *directional longitude* being brought to the *mundane position of the longitudes from which the direction is reckoned*—latitude being, of course, observed in the case of ♃ or any planetary body.

The suggestion here made opens up the field for a very interesting discussion. The real question at issue is much deeper than would at first sight appear, namely, "granted that a solar longitudinal motion of 1° is equivalent to a year, why should it be so, seeing that the ⊙ does not move exactly 1° during either a day or any integral fraction of a year?"

But in its practical aspect the method merely calls for *testing*, and we hope all students of 'directions' will make trial of the method on any nativity of unimpeachable accuracy.

———————

Or by logarithms, a.c. 9·57915 + 7·07438 + ·36532 = 1·01885 = 17°14′.

APPENDIX IV.

Summary of Measures of Time.

THE thoughtful reader who has carefully considered the new method advanced by Mr. C. C. Massey in Appendix III. will perceive that there is a somewhat formidable array of rival measures of time now before the astrological world. Perhaps it will conduce to a clearer understanding of the matter if a short summary of these is given.

(*A*) One degree measures one year. There are two possible varieties of this, in addition to the special modifications mentioned in the *Art and Practice of Directing*.

> (1) In this, the degree is taken as Right Ascension. This is the measure given by Ptolemy.

> (2) In this, the degree is taken as longitude. This is Mr. C. C. Massey's suggestion.

(*B*) One day measures a year. There are several theoretically possible varieties of this; but it will probably be sufficient to mention the following :—

> (3) The day is assumed to be a mean day. This is the method usually followed.

> (4) The day is assumed to be a true solar day. This means that the progressed horoscope is calculated for the *apparent* time of birth and not for the mean time. An explanation of this method is given in the astrological manual entitled *Directions and Directing*.

> (5) The day is assumed to be what may be called, for the sake of convenience, a mundane day; *i.e.*, it ends with the Sun's return to the exact mundane position from which it started. The progressed horoscope is calculated for the time when the Sun's meridian distance is in the same proportion to its semi-arc as at birth. An illustration of this method also is given in *Directions and Directing*.

A student familiar with the mathematics of the subject might really employ any one of these as the measure in either of the two systems of directing, the application varying according to whether it was applied to the progression of the meridian or to that of the Sun. When applied to the progression of the meridian by the axial rotation of the earth, the system is called Primary; when applied to the progression of the Sun in the zodiac by the orbital revolution of the earth, the system is called Secondary.

APPENDIX V.

HOW TO CALCULATE THE ACTUAL DAY ON WHICH A GIVEN ASPECT FALLS DUE.

It often happens that one wishes to know the actual *day* on which a given progressed aspect falls due, and it has therefore appeared desirable to give an illustration of how this may be done, in the simplest way, and with the least amount of calculation.

Let us take the Progressed Horoscope of the Editor, given on p. 37, for illustration, and we will calculate the first lunar aspect, ☽ p. ☐ ☿ r. which falls due somewhere in October, 1906. We have chosen a lunar aspect, because, although the method of calculation is precisely similar in the case of mutual or solar aspects, it is rarely that any good purpose is served by calculating them to the day, since, as has been previously explained (p. 68), it is the *lunar* aspects chiefly that are concerned with actual events. We proceed in much the same way as described for the calculation of the time of a New Moon on p. 63 of *Astrology for All, Part II.*—(which book, by the way, the reader will do well to acquire, if he does not already possess it, as it is a perfect treasury of knowledge on just those points students are likely to be in doubt about) ; using preferably an ephemeris for the year of birth, as it is more convenient than the " Condensed Ephemeris," where several calculations of this kind are required. We first find the Moon's daily motion :—

☽ 's place, noon	22/9/'60	♑	5°	54'
☽ 's place, noon	21/9/'60	♐	22	58
☽ 's motion per day			12	56
☿ 's position at birth		♌	20°	11'
☐ aspect			135	0
Zodiacal degree in ☐ to ☿ r.		♑	5	11
☽ 's place, noon, 21/9/'60		♐	22	58
Distance to be traversed			12	13

That is, we have to find how long it takes the Moon to travel 12°13' at the rate of 12°56' a day. We make use of Diurnal Proportional Logarithms,* as explained on p. 62 of *Astrology for All, Part II.* :—

Diurnal proportional logarithm	12°13'			2933
"	"	"	12°56'	2685
Difference, giving time required, 22h. 40m.				0248

---

* An abbreviated table of these is printed on last page of many copies of *Raphael's Ephemeris;* the fuller table given in the work referred to is still more convenient. The above example would have to be calculated backwards from noon 22/9/'60 if the former be employed, because 16°59' (or 16h. 59m.) is its limit.

which, it must be remembered, is mean solar time after noon 21/11/'60 (that is, 10.40 a.m., 22/11/'60), and therefore represents, roughly, *22h. 44m.* of sidereal time. Now since a day measures to a year, and we have found that *noon* measures to November 9th in any year (see pp. 35-37) we can easily find the day to which this measures, thus:—

			Y.	M.	D.
Noon, 21/9/'60	measures to		1905	11	9
22 hours	is equivalent to			11	0
40 minutes	,,	,,			10
I.e., 10.40 a.m., 22/9/'60	,,	,,	1906	10	19

or in other words, October 19th, 1906.

There is, however, a still easier and quicker way of finding the day required, which may as well be given here, as it greatly simplifies matters when a lot of dates have to be calculated; moreover it is more accurate than the above, in which the disparity of the months—some of which have thirty and some thirty-one days—is not taken into account.

This method, when once properly understood, is exceedingly simple. The native whose directions we are studying was born at London on August 7th, at 5.49 a.m., when the R.A.M.C. or Sidereal Time was:—

	h.	m.	s.
R.A.M.C. or Sidereal Time at actual moment of birth	2	52	54
,, ,, ,, ,, at Greenwich noon on day of birth	9	4	55
Difference, in sidereal *h. m. s.*	6	12	1
R.A.M.C. or Sidereal Time at Greenwich noon on day of birth	9	4	55
Sum,* gives S.T. noon on a certain day of the year	15	16	56

The day, then, that has this S.T. at noon, or the nearest thereto, as recorded in the Ephemeris, is the day of the year to which *noon* on the day of birth measures. This day, in the year 1906, is November 10th, and not the 9th, as we calculated approximately on p. 35, and hence the map on p. 37 is really calculated for the latter date—not that the discrepancy makes any material difference, of course.

Now we can at once see the application of this method to the determination of the date on which ☽p. ☿ ♃r. falls due.

	h.	m.	s.
Noon 21/9/'60 measures to a day in 1905 having a noon S.T. of	15	16	56
Add time elapsed 22h. 44m. (in sidereal *h. m. s.*)	22	44	0
	38	0	56
(Less circle of 24 hours)	24	0	0
I.e., 10.40 a.m. 22/9/'60 measures to a day in 1906 having noon S.T. =	14	0	56

On reference to an Ephemeris for 1906 we find this date to be the 22nd of October, and *not* the 19th as we had previously supposed.

---

* NOTE.—Had the Greenwich time of birth been 6-12-1 *after*, instead of *before* noon, the Difference would have been subtracted therefrom: *e.g.*, suppose R.A.M.C. birth 15-16-56; then R.A.M.C. noon 9-4-55, Difference, 6-12-1; subtract this from 9-4-55, giving 2-52-54, which would be R.A.M.C. at noon on day required, namely, May 6, 1906.

A little practice with this method will make it quicker, as well as more accurate, than the former, and in actual use the correction between mean and sidereal time may be omitted, since at most it can only make a difference of one day.

A further illustration may be given by way of making matters quite clear. We will determine the day on which) p. ⚹ ♀ p. falls due :—

♀ 's place, noon, 23/9/'60		♌	14°	36'
♀ 's ,, ,, 22/9/'60			13	40
♀ 's daily motion			o	56
) 's ,, ,, (♑18°28' — ♑5°54')			12	34
) 's acceleration, or rate at which she gains on ♀			11	38
Place of the ⚹ aspect to ♀ at noon	22/9/'60	♑	13°	40'
) 's position at noon, same date	22/9/'60	♑	5	54
Distance between) and ♀ 's ⚹ at noon	22/9/'60		7	46

We have, therefore, to find how long it will take the Moon to catch up to this ⚹ aspect; or in other words, how long it will take to traverse 7°46' at the rate of 11°38' in 24 hours. We use, as before, D.P. Logs. :—

Diurnal proportional logarithm 7° 46'	4900
,, ,, ,, 11 38	3145
Difference, giving time required, 16ʰ. 1ᵐ.	1755

This is the time after noon of the 22nd September : now we know that, in this native's horoscope,

	h.	m.	s.
Noon corresponds to a day of the year having a noon S.T. of	15	16	56
Add mean time elapsed	16	1	0
Correction to sidereal time		2	40
	31	20	36
(Less circle of 24 hours)	24	0	0
S.T. at noon on day required	7	20	36

and this day we find to be the 13th of July, the year of course being 1907.

Any other example can be worked in a similar manner, and the only thing the beginner needs to remember, in order to avoid confusion, is that we are here concerned with Greenwich time throughout, *never* local time, and with the R.A.M.C. of the radical and not with that of the progressed horoscope.

In the case of natives born elsewhere than in London it is important to remember that it is the difference between the actual R.A.M.C. of birth and the R.A.M.C. at Greenwich Noon on that day which is to be taken, and not merely the time before or after noon at the place of birth. A moment's reflection will show why.

APPENDIX VI.

The Progressed Birthday.

On p. 36 a passing reference was made to " The Progressed Birthday." This term deserves a fuller explanation, the more so inasmuch as the calculation of progressed aspects to the exact day of fulfilment is very possibly affected by it.

Briefly stated, the Progressed Birthday is as many days in advance of the ordinary " birthday " as the native is years old. But in order to explain how the term has arisen, and why the Progressed Birthday should be of importance, it is best to have recourse to an illustration. For the sake of clearness we will take the simplest possible case.

Suppose a person to be born on April 13th, 1906, precisely at noon, at Greenwich. The Sun will be found to be exactly on the meridian—in other words, the ⊙ is ☌ M.C.—in ♈ 22°38'. In a year's time the progressed Sun will be ♈ 23°37', and yet the native's " birthday " will be celebrated at noon on April 13th, when the M.C. is ♈ 22°38' and the progressed Sun consequently one whole degree away from it !

The discrepancy here is very slight, and to argue about the matter may seem like " quibbling." But it is otherwise when the native has attained to thirty years or so, and is, perhaps, living far more in his progressed than in his radical horoscope—which is especially likely in the case of highly strung and sensitive people. If the ' progressed ' horoscope, then, really is his horoscope rather than the ' radical,' it is quite clear that the Sun has not made a complete circuit of the Zodiac, so far as he is concerned, until it has reached the place of the progressed Sun, ♉ 22°, on the 13th May, which will accordingly be his Progressed Birthday when he has reached his thirtieth year.

In short, some able astrologers have contended that the Progressed Birthday is the true birthday anniversary, and that the true measure in ' directing ' is not " a year for a day," but " *a year and a day* for a day."

It seems very likely that no hard and fast rule can be laid down as to the general truth of this contention, and that just as there are some people who seem to live a whole life-time in one portion of the radical horoscope, scarcely being affected at all by directions, (*see* Introduction, p. ix), and others who are ready to respond to and take advantage of every new influence as it is shed upon them, so for some the Progressed Birthday may have no significance, while for others it almost entirely overrides the " birthday " ordinarily observed.

However this may be, there is one point which should not be lost sight of, and that is, that if the principle alluded to has any foundation in nature, directions measured from the ordinary birthday will (or *may*) be incorrect as to time.

For instance, to revert to the case we have imagined, we find that the Moon meets the sextile of Jupiter at noon on the 29th of May, 1906. When may this be expected to take effect ? In the year 1952, that is certain; but will it be upon the " radical birthday," April 13th, or on the " progressed birthday," May 29th ?

Only experience can decide. But in any case the calculation need be no difficulty. All the student need do is to calculate the time the progressed aspect becomes due, as just described in Appendix V., and note it in his pocket-book, making at the same time a similar entry on a date as many days ahead of this as he is years old at the time. Nothing could be simpler than this, and the student can thus establish the point for himself.

Some observations made recently incline the writer to favour the influence of the Progressed Birthday in the manner described, and he would be grateful if students would communicate the results of their researches in this direction to the pages of *Modern Astrology*.

APPENDIX VII.

The Unity of All Systems of Directing.

One of the first things that strikes a beginner is the multitude of "systems" and "methods" of direction, and he is tempted to think that if there are so many they will probably all be wrong, since they cannot all be right. Yet the advocate of each system claims that the one he follows gives results more reliable, according to his experience, than any other!

It is quite clear, however, that the tests of two people with regard to any system of directions will not be of equal value, even though the investigators be of equal integrity and ability. For one will look for his results in one direction, for financial losses, say, while the other looks for death, perhaps, or personal suffering;—this is only given as a crude illustration of the difference in mental bias between the two experimenters, (which difference of outlook will inevitably have its effect upon all results coming under their notice, nevertheless), and it is not, of course, intended to be taken too literally.

Nevertheless, the mere fact that careful individual investigators swear by many different systems, is strong presumptive evidence of a good measure of truth in each; and it immediately suggests itself to the mind that this common measure of truth is a fundamental principle, the operation of which through different media (so to speak) is observed and recorded by different witnesses.

Let us examine into the question and see if this one fundamental principle can be discerned.

We will first take the system of *Primary Directions*, so called, in which the angular distance by oblique ascension between two bodies is measured, and equated at the rate of $1° = 1$ year. No reason is as a rule advanced for this procedure, beyond that it was the practice of Ptolemy or Placidus or some other ancient authority, who may have had excellent reasons for his practice without, however, stating them. One degree of oblique ascension is one degree of the equator, and is the mean increment of the Sun (or the meridian) in Right Ascension *per day*.* If, therefore, the cuspal points of the "progressed horoscope" be considered in relation to the radical places of the planets, as suggested in Appendix II., we shall thus have what is virtually Primary Directing : except (1) that the measure of time will vary—very slightly; (2) that in the case of planets having latitude, they would not arrive at the angles or cusps of houses precisely as shown; and (3) that this process, while identical in principle, would not be so convenient in practice, since we should have no means of ascertaining thereby when one planet had arrived at the same distance by O.A. beyond a cusp that another was at birth, and thus formed with it the various mundane aspects (✳, □, ☍, mundane parallel, rapt parallel, etc.). Otherwise, however, these two processes are identical.

This holds equally true whether the directions are 'direct' or 'converse'; it is only a question of regarding the place of the first or the second planet as fixed and the place of the other as moving towards the ☍, ☌ or aspect thereof.

---

* To be quite precise, the actual mean increment is $\dfrac{360°}{365.26} = 59'8''\cdot325$

Similarly also, of course, for parallels in mundo, rapt parallels, etc. Thus we see that the Progressed Horoscope, taken in relation to the *radical* position of the planets, affords identical results—so far as it is capable of furnishing them at all—with the system of Primary Directing.

Secondary Directions have been defined in "The Art and Practice of Directing" as consisting of : (*a*) Secondary Solar directions formed by proper motion in longitude (zodiac) after birth by planets radical and progressive to Sun *ditto*, or by Sun or planets progressive to M.C. or Asc. radical, (*b*) Secondary Fixed Lunar, *i.e.*, aspects of above to the Moon's place in radix, (*c*) Lunar Progressive, *i.e.*, those formed from day to day by the progressive Moon's increasing longitude, either with the Sun or planets radical or progressive, its own place at birth, M.C. and Asc. radical, etc.

These, it will be seen, can all be classified under positions occurring in the Progressed Horoscope.

There are thus but two things left unaccounted for, the "progressed Ascendant" and the "progressed M.C." These seem to be the peculiar property of the Progressed Horoscope, as explained in Chapter V., and since they are found to be of undoubted efficacy it would appear to indicate that the latter method not only *includes* the Primary and Secondary Directional Systems within itself (if properly studied), but also *adds* a new factor of vital interest.

Thus it has been shown that amid apparent diversity there is yet a unity · of principle, *viz.*, that the circle of the *day* after birth reflects itself in the *year* of subsequent life, starting from the birth-moment and the birth-day respectively, as shown in Appendix II.—in which the rational basis of the conception, that the first six hours after birth impress their influences on the subsequent history, at the rate of a year for each four minutes, was explained, and which therefore need not be reproduced here.

There remains but one further consideration. Granted as above that the planetary movements per day after birth reflect themselves in due perspective on succeeding years, why should the conception be limited to the "year" defined by the orbit of our own planet merely ?

The period of Saturn's revolution is approximately 30 years. Let us suppose then that a mundane direction of $D \delta \xi$, say, occurs about two minutes after birth. This is (1) at the rate of 4m.=a year, (Primary Direction), equivalent to about *6 months* after birth ; (2) at the rate of 4m. = 30 years (one year of Saturn), *15 years* or so ; (3) at the rate of 4m. = 1° of precession,* *36 years*, or thereabouts.

From such a series of directions one would expect a parallel series of events, acting, of course, on different planes of environment as it were. As a matter of fact, in the illustration given that is precisely what happened. In the nativity† of a male well known to the present writer, the Moon is applying to the conjunction of Mercury, the joint ruler of 1st and 5th. (1) The events of the first six months have not been communicated, but it is known that a removal ($\delta \xi$) took place shortly after birth. (2) At 15 years native went abroad (the δ was in 9th) and met a youth to whom he became warmly attached. (3) At about 30 years he underwent a radical change of thought, was thrown into an entirely new mental environment and declares himself to have felt, as it were, illuminated in comparison with his past beliefs (9th house). At the same period, he became deeply attached (ξ ruler of 5th) to a lady somewhat his senior, in whose case‡ a similarly close mundane application of the ruler to the ascendant measured by the same process to the same event.

_____

* Equivalent to one "day " of the Sun's movement in the great year of precession, 26,000 years, *viz.*, 72 years per degree.

† Rectified by pre-natal epoch and substantiated in other ways as far as possible.

‡ Nativity also rectified and tested as above.

This is given merely as an illustration of what is meant, and is by no means advanced as a proof, of course; yet the widening sweep of the successive influences as regards the native is clearly to be traced, so far as he is known to the writer. The year abroad at 15 was a personal and domestic emancipation, the change of thought at 30 an intellectual one; the attachment likewise in the one case was personal, in the other individual, and doubtless other parallels could be noted were all the circumstances known.

By way of conclusion and in order to co-ordinate the various systems in use, they may be tabulated, in accordance with the above idea, as follows:—

ORDINARY "DIRECTIONS."

"Primary"   one day = the (so-called) "life-cycle" of 360 years
"Secondary"   ,,   ,, = the seasonal cycle of   1 year

THE PROGRESSED HOROSCOPE AND ITS OFFSHOOTS.

(Nomenclature as in Appendix I.)

Progressed Horoscope*	(A)	one day	= 1 year
Lunar Equivalent	(A')	,, ,, $+ \ 0 \cdot x$ day	= 1 ,, $+ \ 0 \cdot x$ year
Progressed Lunar	(B or B')	,, month	= 1 ,,
,, ,,	(BB or BB')	,, day	= 1 month
Diurnal Horoscope	(C or C')	,, year	= 1 year

In addition to these there may be considered the various exceptional or "fancy" methods of directing, such as:—

1 day (or, degree)	= 1 period of	Jupiter	=	12 years
1 ,, ,, ,,	= 1 ,, ,,	Saturn	=	30 ,,
1 ,, ,, ,,	= 1 ,, ,,	Uranus	=	84 ,,
1 ,, ,, ,,	= 1 ,, ,,	Neptune	=	164 ,,
1 ,, ,, ,,	= 1° of precession		=	72 ,,

The question which presents itself most forcibly to the mind on reviewing these many methods is—"which is the most important one?"

The answer appears to be that "Primary" and "Secondary" Directions, in conjunction with the Progressed Horoscope, have by far the most direct and immediate influence on ordinary concerns, the "Primary" apparently having chief relation to those events which can in no sense be considered dependent on the native's own actions,—in a word, his "karma"; while the Progressed Horoscope, on the other hand, seems to chiefly indicate the unfolding of the character and of the opportunities for its development.

In connection with this latter, many cases are found in which an unprogressive soul sticks in the rut of the radical horoscope, as it were, whilst a more progressive individual with a less favourable nativity responds at once to every new aspect or degree on the ascendant, with all the readiness and adaptability of those capable people who seize and utilise every opportunity for advancement.

The gist of the whole matter is, then, that each and every system of directing is founded on the universal correspondences of Nature, and that did we but know precisely the various "planes of operation, so to speak, of each system, every event on every plane could be read off on its appropriate plane and at its due time.

In the adjudgment of the "nature" of the effects—or rather the nature of the *influences* operating, for the *effects* depend largely on the native himself—

---

* Virtually equivalent to, and *almost* identical with, "Secondary" Directions.

resulting from directions lies a wide field for the employment of those higher
mental faculties which must be brought to bear in judging a nativity; a field as
wide at least, if not even wider, and needing a mind both even and well-balanced,
capable of both analytical and synthetic processes of thought.

"All are but parts of one stupendous whole, Whose body Nature is, and
God the soul."——"Ye suffer from yourselves."——"Each man's life the outcome
of his former living is."——"Ye are not bound, the soul of things is sweet." Let
these be the keynotes of our thinking in these matters.

For this life on earth is but a *part*—and not a disjunct part, save only in
appearance—of a wider life which embraces all planes of being; even as the
Solar System is itself A Whole, although we study the planets and note their
special characteristics separately.

IMPORTANT NOTICE.

As stated in the note at the end of Preface, it was originally intended to publish THE PROGRESSED HOROSCOPE in two volumes, the second dealing chiefly with examples and further hints on the blending of the aspects and their significance in the various houses. Experience has proved, however, that a work complete in one volume is more satisfactory, so far as the general student is concerned, than the same work spread over two, and therefore the whole of the matter was carefully condensed into the present volume without sacrificing any of the more essential parts, although the examples and illustrations had to be omitted.

In order to supply these valuable examples they will be given from month to month in the pages of—

Modern Astrology

ONE SHILLING MONTHLY.   **ANNUAL SUBSCRIPTION 10/6**

the first series, dealing with the Horoscopes of Sir Richard and Lady Burton, appearing during the year 1906, Volume III. of the New Series.

(Over)

ii

Every student of Astrology should endeavour to support this, the *only* Astrologer's Magazine in existence at the present time. Modern Astrology has appeared regularly each month for the past fifteen years: its contributors are Modern Astrologers who, while respecting the value of the old school in its day, are in sympathy with the spirit of the age and have realised that the old interpretation of Astrology is imperfect, and unsuited to our present stage of evolution, an entire revision of the old rules being necessary in order to keep pace with the development of Humanity, *which is not to-day just what it was a thousand years ago.*

The high opinion in which Modern Astrology is held by students may be readily conceived when it is stated that at the beginning of 1904 it was found advisable to commence an entirely New Series, many of the volumes issued up to that time having run out of print. Indeed, although precautions were taken to lay aside a good stock of copies of the First Volume of the New Series, at the time of writing there are indications that it will not be long before that volume also becomes scarce.

The Annual Subscription is only 10s. 6d. post free to any part of the world, the Magazine thus costing, when allowance is made for postage, only *ninepence per copy.* Some of the numbers contain Free Horoscope forms, and others offer various advantages to its readers in the shape of special coupons, etc. Each copy is replete with interesting and instructive matter, and no student can expect to keep abreast of the astrological thought of his time unless he is a regular reader and careful critic of its pages.

Every reader of this book, at least, should become a subscriber, not only as a duty to the science, but also that he may be in touch with the minds of those astrologers who are devoting their best efforts to the purification and re-establishment of the true principles of this ancient science.

The publication of Modern Astrology has for its main object the desire " through planetary symbology to explain the one universal spirit in its varied manifestations."

Should any reader of this advertisement desire it, a Specimen Copy will gladly be sent on receipt of twopence for postage. Address, *Magazine Department*, 9, Lyncroft Gardens, W. Hampstead, N.W.

The
Astrologer's
Annual

For 1906.

Edited by ALAN LEO.

THE articles and stories in this Annual have been specially written and arranged with a view to interest, instruct, amuse and please everybody, whether those having but a passing interest in Astrology or Star Lore, or those who are themselves actively engaged in a study of its mysteries; and it therefore forms an admirable medium for introducing the subject of Astrology to one's friends.

All dry technicalities and abstruse matters have been eliminated, and each writer has set himself to address his audience in a clear and simple manner, with the object of rendering Astrology as attractive as it is important. The following is a list of contents :—

EDITOR'S FOREWORD: Competition and Prizes. RISING STARS: by the Editor. THE HOROSCOPE IN THE HAND: by Bessie Leo. THE CIRCLE OF THE ZODIAC: by Frank J. Merry. NATIONAL ASTROLOGY: by the Editor of *Modern Astrology*. " FOR THE BENEFIT OF OTHERS," an Astrological Story: by Philippa Forest. A SIMPLE WAY OF READING HOROSCOPES. FACTS FROM AN ASTROLOGER'S NOTE-BOOK. ASTROLOGY AND ASTROLOGERS: by Heinrich Däath. WHAT IS AN OCCULTIST, AND WHAT IS THE RELATIONSHIP OF OCCULTISM TO ASTROLOGY? FATE AND FORTUNE AS REVEALED BY THE DAY AND MONTH OF BIRTH. THE WEATHER FOR EVERY DAY DURING THE YEAR 1906. Also TWO PRESENTATION PHOTO BLOCKS.

It is safe to say that no one, however "unlearned," can take up THE ASTROLOGER'S ANNUAL without finding both pleasure and profit in its perusal; while no student, however profound, need consider the statements made unworthy of his attention— the article on " The Circle of the Zodiac" being particularly instructive.

Price 1s.; post free 1s. 2d. *(In America, 30c.)*

From "Modern Astrology" Office, 9, Lyncroft Gardens, W. Hampstead, N.W.

iv

THE ASTROLOGER'S BAEDEKER.

Astrology for All.
PART II. *(Calculations and Ephemeris).*

THIS is designed to supplement Part I., described elsewhere, which deals exhaustively with all that may be treated of when the day of birth only is known but not the time. It is in fact a compendium of information concerning the correct "casting of a horoscope," and forms a necessary sequel to the former book in which only the general features of any nativity could be considered.

The thoughtful reader who has perused Part I. will naturally be desirous of going thoroughly into all the details connected with the calculation of a horoscope, so that he can investigate the statements there made and satisfy himself of their truth by making a test of the claims put forward through a practical examination into either his own nativity or that of a friend well known to him. If he is a careful man he will desire that this examination shall be self-conducted, and that he shall have to take nothing "on authority," so that in the end he can come to a decided conclusion about the matter—a conclusion that he can feel is a just and a warrantable one, based upon his own independent investigation. To serve such the present volume is especially fitted, since there are rules given whereby a horoscope may be calculated from the *Nautical Almanac* alone.

There are many others however, besides the enquirer, to whom this book is indispensable. For those who are already keen and eager students it offers a compilation of useful practical information concerning the technique of astrological calculations which is invaluable—a glance at the *Table of Contents* will show this—while on the other hand to those who are as yet in the early stages it is a *sine quâ non.*

Following upon the elementary instructions in the second of the shilling "manuals," there is given complete information regarding the calculation of maps of the heavens for any part of the habitable globe, with clear and simple yet precise explanations of the astronomical terms likely to be met with in any works the student may wish to consult.

In addition there is given a concise yet sufficiently comprehensive EPHEMERIS of the planetary positions during the last fifty-five years to enable the student to determine their celestial longitude to within two minutes of its true value.

The book is therefore an indispensable requisite for all who intend to make any serious study of the subject. And even for those who are indisposed to enter into intricacies of calculation, to have *an Ephemeris for fifty-five years* in so small a bulk, and at so low a price, is no slight boon.

Table of Contents: SECTION A. CHAPTERS—I. The Ephemeris and the information it supplies—II. Sidereal Time; what it is, and how it differs from clock time—III. Local time as a factor in the horoscope—IV. The Houses of the Horoscope—V. A few definitions—VI. Standards of time in different parts of the world—VII. A simple method of erecting a horoscope for any place in any latitude, without Tables of Houses—VIII. Rectification—IX. Logarithms—X. The trigonometrical method—XI. How to compute the places of Uranus and Neptune for any date.—SECTION B. The Condensed Ephemeris and how to use it, with simple rules and examples. Table of ascendants for all latitudes from 1° to 60°. Sundry tables useful for reference.

PRICE 7s. 6d. POST FREE: (in America $2.00)
FROM THE OFFICE OF "MODERN ASTROLOGY," 9, LYNCROFT GARDENS, WEST HAMPSTEAD, N.W.

(Each part is complete in itself.)

☞ The Compiler of *Raphael's Ephemeris* writes, under date of October 8th, 1905:—"I was extremely obliged by your lending me *Astrology for All, Part II.* Do you know, I think so much of the book that I must purchase a copy. I consider it on the whole—looking to the important subject it deals with, the lucid treatment of the same, the general get up and very moderate price—I consider it, I say, almost perfection." Could higher praise, or from a higher authority, be wished for?

THE ASTROLOGER'S "BRITANNICA."

How to Judge a Nativity.

PART I.   PART II.

(Each part is complete in itself.)

THE first two books of this series, elsewhere described, are designed to familiarise the reader with the groundwork of astrologic thought, and to enable him to correctly and intelligently erect a horoscope for any time and place. The present two volumes are intended to carry the student one stage further, so that being supplied with his horoscope he may be enabled to *judge* it, the most essential part of the process—and the most difficult. For there are many who can correctly "cast a horoscope," but few who can "judge a nativity." It is here then that the student chiefly needs both guidance and help, more particularly assistance in attaining solidarity of thought in connection with his judgment ; for a vague and invertebrate conclusion is of little value to anyone.

This need *How to Judge a Nativity* aims to supply, being especially designed for the beginner while yet conveniently arranged as a work of constant reference for the student. PART I. deals comprehensively yet tersely with each detail of the ordinary "reading" of the horoscope—character, temperament, health, finance, abilities, marriage, children, length of life, etc.—all considered from the ordinary everyday point of view and exclusively practical in method of treatment. PART II. on the other hand goes more fully into detail with regard to the nature of the planets, and treats of their relation to the inner Man. The whole work forms not only a useful guide but a valuable work of reference to all who are interested in Natal Astrology.

PART I. *Table of Contents.* CHAPTERS—I. The geometry of Astrology—II. The divisions of space; the signs of the zodiac—III. The planets—IV. The aspects—V. The three centres. Rising signs—VI. The ascendant—VII. The ruling planet—VIII. Health and the hyleg—IX. The second house and money—X. The third house—XI. The fourth house—XII. The fifth house—XIII. The sixth house—XIV. The seventh house: marriage, etc.—XV. The eighth house: death—XVI. The ninth house: philosophy—XVII. The mid-heaven or tenth house—XVIII. The eleventh house: friends—XIX. The twelfth house. Conclusion.

PART II. CHAPTERS—I. The esoteric basis of Astrology—II. The planetary kaleido-scope—III. ♆ Neptune (*Poseidon*)—IV. ♅ Uranus, the mystery planet—V. The physical planets and their mutual relationships (*with diagram*)—VI. ♄ Saturn: Chronos: Time—VII. ♃ Jupiter: Zeus: Being—VIII. ♂ Mars, god of strength—IX. ♀ Venus, goddess of love—X. ☿ Mercury: Hermes—XI. ☉ The Sun—XII. ☽ The Moon. Conclusion.

Price, each part, 7s. 6d., post free, or the two bound together in one volume or the two sent separately for 10s. 6d., 11/- post free.

☞ Of permanent value as works of constant reference.

A COMPLETE COURSE OF ASTROLOGY IN FOUR BOOKS

I. **ASTROLOGY FOR ALL,** part I. (without calculations), price 7/6 post free.
II. **ASTROLOGY FOR ALL,** part II. (calculations and ephemeris), price 7/6 post free.
III. **HOW TO JUDGE A NATIVITY,** parts I. and II. (together 10/6), each part 7/6 post free.
IV. **THE PROGRESSED HOROSCOPE, 10/6** complete; 11/- post free

(*This last volume completes the course of "exoteric" Astrology. Future volumes will deal with the esoteric nature of the planets and their aspects, the inner meaning of the Zodiac, etc.*)

A Remarkable Offer.

An Astrological Library for
FIVE SHILLINGS!

A complete set of SIX One Shilling Manuals, containing all the instruction necessary to judge any person's character, and forecast his or her future prospects, will be sent post free to any address for the small sum of Five Shillings.

Send P.O. 5/- (or P.O.O. $1.30) for:—*The Rationale of Astrology; Everybody's Astrology; What is a Horoscope and How is it Cast?; The Horoscope in Detail; Directions and Directing; Theoretical Astrology.*

These Manuals are written in a simple and clear manner, avoiding technicalities and explaining every necessary step in the simplest way possible. They form an admirable introduction to the science.

SPECIAL NOTICE.—Parcels of not less than six copies of "**The Rationale of Astrology**" supplied for propaganda purposes at *cost price*, on application to The Editor of MODERN ASTROLOGY, 9, Lyncroft Gardens, West Hampstead, London, N.W.

BUY HALF A DOZEN COPIES AND GIVE THEM AWAY TO YOUR FRIENDS. BUT READ IT YOURSELF FIRST.

IMPORTANT NOTICE.

OWING to the unexpected sale of certain issues of MODERN ASTROLOGY during the past year, several numbers ran out of print, and we have only been successful in purchasing a few of these numbers in order that complete volumes might be bound ; therefore the price of Vol. II. (new series), 1905, containing the twelve monthly issues, will, until further notice, be 15s. post free in Great Britain, or $4.00 post free to America.

Those desiring to purchase copies of this volume should do so without delay in order that they may not be disappointed.

On and after January 1st, 1906, the price of Vol. I. (new series) will be 15/- also,

Rays of Truth

By BESSIE LEO.

THE books dealing with Astrology hitherto advertised have dealt chiefly with the scientific and technical aspects of this study, or at most with its bearing on character delineation.

In *Rays of Truth*, however, the reader is introduced to its sublimer meanings; in a word, he is brought face to face with The Religious Aspect of Astrology.

The series of essays and short articles here presented in book form have severally appeared from time to time in the pages of MODERN ASTROLOGY, and are now re-issued in response to a general desire, many of them being out of print. The subjects dealt with are treated in a simple and reverent manner, and range from "The Value of Astrology in the Training of Children" to "The Shuttle of Destiny," separate chapters being devoted to:—*Astrology as a Guide in Life—Marriage—The Science of the Soul—Self-Development—At-one-ment—Fate and Free-Will*—and various other problems and ideals having an important bearing on our personal, social and religious life.

To those who delight in the contemplation of the Wisdom of the Heart this book is sure to be welcome, and being well printed on good paper, and tastefully bound, it forms

AN ACCEPTABLE GIFT-BOOK FOR ALL SEASONS.

PRICE 3s. 6d., POST FREE ($1.00.)
From the Office of "Modern Astrology,"
9, Lyncroft Gardens, West Hampstead, N.W.

☞ *Extract from a letter to the Author, received* 30/11/'05, *and too long for quotation in full*:—"Permit me to most gratefully thank you for your Astrological Essays entitled 'RAYS OF TRUTH,' a work I feel most distinctly helpful. . Written *from the heart*, and full of earnest purpose, it cannot fail to accomplish its mission—the purification of the life—where truly read. . . I have long seen it advertised, and only wish I had obtained it earlier. . . Astrology, imperfectly understood, has met with sternest denunciation, yet I trust this work will lead many minds to pause and deeply consider ere they condemn. . . I must say that 'RAYS OF TRUTH' simply possesses me, stirring heart and soul beyond expression. It is really the most inspiring work I ever read, and I must send it off on a round of visits, though most reluctant to part with it."

CPSIA information can be obtained
at www.ICGtesting.com
Printed in the USA
BVHW091536180621
609900BV00003B/317